ALL ARE INVOLVED

THE ART OF MARTIN CARTER

ALL ARE INVOLVED

THE ART OF MARTIN CARTER

EDITED BY STEWART BROWN

PEEPAL TREE

First published in Great Britain in 2000
New Edition 2020
Peepal Tree Press Ltd
17 King's Avenue
Leeds LS6 1QS
England

ISBN 9781900715263

Supported using public funding by
ARTS COUNCIL
ENGLAND

CONTENTS

Recollections by Martin Carter's Contemporaries

Martin Carter's Impact and Influence Upon Younger Writers

Obituaries

INTRODUCTION: 'WHAT I HAVE BEEN TRYING TO DO SO FAR IS TO PROVOKE YOU...'[1]

Who comes walking in the dark night time?
Whose boot of steel tramps down the slender grass?
It is the man of death, my love, the strange invader
watching you sleep and aiming at your dream.
('This is the Dark Time My Love')

The Guyanese poet Martin Carter, who died in December 1997, was without question one of the major poets of the English language in our time.

In the Caribbean Carter is regarded as one of the great poets who have chronicled the journey from colonialism to independence, alongside such figures as Aimé Césaire, Derek Walcott, Nicholás Guillén and Kamau Brathwaite. That his work is hardly known outside of the Caribbean is in part because of his early reputation as a political poet: he was imprisoned by the British colonial authorities in the early 1950s for his part in the 'subversive' actions of the first democratically elected, nonracial and idealistically socialist government in the Caribbean. His poems of that period were published by the London socialist press Lawrence & Wishart as *Poems of Resistance from British Guiana* in 1954. While a few of those early poems – 'University of Hunger', 'This is the Dark Time My Love', 'I Come from the Nigger Yard' and 'On the Fourth Night of a Hunger Strike' – have become classics of socialist literature, translated into several Eastern European and Asian languages, and are among the foundation stones of Caribbean poetry, his work has hardly been acknowledged in more general accounts of poetry in English. It was too easy for a casual critic or anthologist to settle for a version of Carter as the anti-colonial radical who swore to use his shirt 'as a banner for the revolution' and who consequently wrote 'plain bad verse' – as one commentator asserted – putting his cause before the necessary craft of making poetry. Such a view of Carter could not have been sustained by anyone even halfway seriously examining his work, even if they were restricted to the early pieces collected in *Poems of Resistance*. The linguistic cunning and rhythmical measure underpinning a poem like 'University of Hunger', for example, contribute as much to its mesmeric power *as poem*, as do the ideas that drive it and the imagery that so haunts anyone who reads it:

is they who rose early in the morning
watching the moon die in the dawn.
is they who heard the shell blow and the iron clang.
is they who had no voice in the emptiness
in the unbelievable
in the shadowless.
O long is the march of men and long is the life
and wide is the span.

Indeed, looking at his work overall it is hard to think of a contemporary poet who showed more concern for craft, who thought more about the intricacies of the relationship between art and politics, who measured his utterance with greater care than Carter. As he put it in his poem 'Words', written in 1957,

> These poet words, nuggets out of corruption
> or jewels dug from dung or speech from flesh

Like many poets across the world writing in the teeth of political oppression and cultural disintegration Carter knew the real value of words, knew that they might be both weapon and the means of spiritual survival: 'the bread that lasts', as Derek Walcott put it. But Carter also had a profound belief in the power of poetry to work at all sorts of levels and in all sorts of circumstances. Those famous poems-of-resistance – smuggled out of prison to be read aloud at political rallies, at trade union strike meetings, recited by crowds at popular demonstrations of dissent against colonial oppression – those poems acknowledged that particular context in their language and their form. Carter wrote them with a simplicity and directness that is not at all typical of his poetry as a whole; and while they remain crafted literary artefacts, they were liberated from the constraints of the library or the elite literary soiree – as he knew they would be – by their appropriation as orature, as a public poetry-of-resistance. In 1992 Carter came to the UK to take part in an Arts Council sponsored reading tour with other Guyanese writers based in Britain. At a packed reading in central London he read to an audience which included many exiled Guyanese – few of them, I'd guess, regular attenders of literary events. As he read from those poems that audience began to recite them with him – not to read them from a book but to recite them from memory; they were there etched in the memory banks, a part of their being, fundamental to their identity as Guyanese people. Few poets in our time – and fewer still writing in English – have made such an impact on the consciousness of a people.

And yet, as I say, his work is hardly acknowledged outside the Caribbean. Access to Carter's work has always been a problem for readers outside Guyana. Unlike so many colonial writers of his generation Carter didn't migrate to the metropolis to pursue a literary career, he stayed in the Caribbean, in Guyana. He was active in Guyanese politics one way and another throughout the forty years following his release from detention in 1953; disowned by and disowning in turns the two charismatic figures who dominated Guyanese politics in that period, Cheddi Jagan and Forbes Burnham. He served for while as Minister of Information in a Burnham government in the late sixties, at a moment when it seemed possible that a new, multicultural politics might be forged out of the old divisions. But that prospect proved illusory and Carter soon resigned, publishing a snarling poem which announced both his departure and his reasons:

> And would shout it out differently
> if it could be sounded plain;

But a mouth is always muzzled
by the food it eats to live.
('A Mouth is Always Muzzled')[2]

Carter's natural position seemed to be on the margins of formal politics; an outspoken agitator, his poems spoke to – and for – the conscience of the nation. It was a dangerous position to fill: he was a friend of Walter Rodney, the Guyanese historian and radical activist almost certainly murdered by Burnham's henchmen in 1980 and Carter was himself badly beaten when he joined a demonstration against the Burnham government's attempts to manipulate the constitution to try and keep themselves in power. After those – and other, similar, events – Carter seemed to stand back somewhat from the public struggle. As Rupert Roopnaraine, the Guyanese scholar and current leader of Rodney's party, the Working Peoples' Alliance, put it in his essay 'Martin Carter and Politics', included here, Carter

> embraced the pure practice of poetry as the only available practice for a seeker of truth in an era of degradation. He turned inwards and so did the poems. In the end, the truth of craft was all.

All his writing life Carter published primarily in local journals and newspapers, and for many years his work was only available in very fugitive, limited circulation collections. As George Lamming remarks in his discussion of Carter's career, he wasn't at all interested in self-promotion or developing a reputation, indeed he seemed 'philosophical' about the success or otherwise of his poetry in those terms to the point of complete indifference, trusting rather that time would sort the 'true poems' from the rest soon enough. The 1989 edition of his *Selected Poems*, again published in Guyana, quickly sold out and a revised second edition was published just a few months – as it turned out – before Carter's death, by the Red Thread Women's Press in Georgetown. It is a beautifully made book, illuminated by two leading Guyanese artists, but even that is a hard book to lay hands on outside of Guyana.

In many ways that early fame or notoriety set a misleading burden on Carter's reputation. His later work, while it never lost its political edge, was more oblique and cerebral than the overtly political poems of his youth, seeming to have more in common with the so-called magical-realism of many of his fellow South American poets than with the naturalism of much socially committed African-American and Caribbean poetry of the second half of the century. Consequently his later poetry didn't really 'fit' in terms of the prevailing orthodoxies and has not been read with the attention it deserves, has not found the kind of publishers and audience that might have followed it if it had been translated from the Spanish, say, with César Vallejo, Pablo Neruda and Octavio Paz. They are his contemporaries in every sense, his work is of that originality, force and stature.

This day
is an old one. It is as old

as a petal or a flower
or the rain or the still air
of a child's wild guitar
shuddering in the silence
of parents.
('Let Every Child Run Wild')

With the *Selected Poems* it is possible to read Carter's poems in the chronological order of their composition as a kind of testimony of despair, tracing a movement from the accessibility, optimism and assertion of those early poems towards the cryptic, world-weary meditations of his later years when that dream had been shattered by the intrigues and disappointments of Guyana's post-colonial and post-independence struggles for survival as a nation. There is no doubting Carter's despair over the betrayal of the possibilities that the end of colonial rule offered, or of his bitterness at the way Guyanese politics has been reduced to the self-mutilation of ethnic rivalry – the old colonial tactic of divide and rule internalised and exaggerated for perceived short term advantage. And that bitterness is certainly apparent in many of the later poems:

... I
keep working for a storm, some
kind of fury to write new dates
in our vile calendar and book.
('Some Kind of Fury')

But as many of the essays in this volume establish, such a reading of Carter's achievement is too simple, leaves too much out of account. Rather Martin Carter's poetry offers its readers the chronicle of a life – in its many facets – committed to *being*, in Guyana, through the tumultuous period his 70 or so years spanned. The poems provide a record of that fiercely intelligent, sternly poetic sensibility responding not only to the political turmoil but also to the personal and domestic claims on his emotions and energy – he wrote several beautiful love poems through his career – as well as to the spiritual and the elemental dimensions of life in Guyana. The later poems bear the evidence of that intense self-scrutiny in their pared down compression, in the pithy density of their language, in their lack of unnecessary ornament or dramatic pause. His poem 'Rice', for example, is much more than a complaint about rural poverty and exploitation:

What is rain for, if not rice
for an empty pot; and pot for
in a hungry village? The son
succeeds his father in a line
to count as he did, waiting,
adding the latest to the first
of his losses; his harvests
of quick wind padi...

Rather the poem is a meditation on the cycle of life and death and the futility of that necessary struggle in the context of an elemental time scale. Guyana is a place of immense natural forces – the sea, the rainforest, the rivers, the distant mountains, even the power of the rain when it falls, and like most Guyanese writers Carter was ever conscious of that contrast between the cruel grandeur of those elemental forces and the puny self-aggrandisement of mankind's ego. Carter was a great poet, one who 'dreamed to change the world' but came to accept, as he put it in one of his last poems,

> Here is where
> I am, in a great geometry, between
> a raft of ants and the green sight
> of the freedom of a tree, made
> of that same bitter wood.
> ('Bitter Wood')

Carter's influence is widely acknowledged but for a writer of such stature and reputation – sustained over so long a period, the serious criticism of his work has been sparse and all of it scattered through limited circulation literary magazines and Caribbean academic journals. The original intention of this book was to address that lack of an accessible critical text which would collect the best of the existing criticism and supplement it with major new essays focusing on aspects of Carter's work and its contexts not previously explored. With such a book, with the *Selected Poems* and with Nigel Westmaas's excellent special edition of *Kyk-over-al* (no. 44, May 1993) devoted to Carter's prose, then both new readers and serious scholars would have some solid foundation from which to begin to approach Carter's work. The finished book fulfils that ambition and does much more. The project was begun while Martin was still alive and we had hoped to present it to him as a token of the respect in which his work was held, but even at that time it was clear that any such volume would have to extend beyond the realm of the academic essay to accommodate the many poets and other writers who had important things to say about Carter's life and work. After his death that notion of the book as providing both a critical grounding *and* a forum for the remembrances, tributes and praise-songs for Martin by his fellow writers became more urgent. We have spent some time in collecting those pieces from far and wide.[3] I think there was only one writer I had tried to contact about contributing something to the volume whom I was unable to locate, and that for reasons that Martin would well have understood. The radical Nigerian poet Odia Ofiemun always cited Martin Carter among his influences, indeed in his volume *A Handle for the Flautist* he remarks,

> I cannot forget the Caribbean poet Martin Carter, whose *Poems of Resistance* helped me see poetry as struggle.

During most of the period this book has been in the making Odia Ofiemun has been more or less on the run in Nigeria, avoiding the attentions of the

Abacha regime which silenced – by one means or another – so many of the country's writers. Odia stayed in Nigeria and kept voicing his opposition despite the terror of the time, demonstrating by that commitment to place and truth the force of Martin Carter's example.

So the present book begins with an account of the historical, political and literary contexts of Carter's work, an overview which informs the readings of individual collections – and indeed individual poems – by a range of scholars addressing the work from sometimes very different perspectives. Some of the essays refer back to, and sometimes quarrel with, the earlier commentary, so having both collected here allows scholars to judge the merits of that dialogue. The focus of the book then turns to Carter's impact as a person and his influence as both a political figure and a writer. The section given over to the commentaries of his contemporaries includes memoirs by some of the great writers of the Caribbean – Derek Walcott, Wilson Harris, George Lamming, Jan Carew, Roy Heath, John Figueroa, while the list of younger voices commenting on his significance as an exemplar includes many of the writers who represent Caribbean literature on the international stage today, Pauline Melville, Fred D'Aguiar, David Dabydeen, Linton Kwesi Johnson, Grace Nichols, to name just a few of them. The book concludes with a small selection of the obituary notices published after Carter's death in December 1997. While, of course, most of those reminiscences and commentaries are finally very positive about his life and work, many of the writers insist on giving a rounded account of Carter the man, who was often troubled, sometimes difficult to work with and for most of his life engaged in various kinds of struggle – no-one ever pretended he was a saint. Indeed those warts-and-all accounts add an important dimension to our understanding of the social forces which bore on Carter through his lifetime in Guyana and against which much of his poetry can be read.

The importance of understanding this poet in his time and place is established in the essays which open this volume. Clem Seecharan's close historical contextualisation of Carter's life and work and Rupert Roopnaraine's detailed account of the political aspirations and intrigues of the period inform their readings of the poems, tracing the evolution of Carter's commitment to the notion of social justice, beyond the contagions of racial politics, to a fundamental integrity which characterised so much of his practice as both a man-in-society and as a poet. The pain of his realisation that the dream of a new kind of social order was being fundamentally undermined by the turn of political events in Guyana through the 1950s is vividly caught in Ivan Van Sertima's account of that period in the extract from his essay 'Astride Two Visions' that we include here. As Roopnaraine is at pains to emphasise, however, without wanting to make a simplistic separation between the political and the literary, it is as a poet that Carter's achievement must be understood and in the essays by Louis James, Samuel Asein, and Jeffrey Robinson some of the literary parameters within which Carter's poetry might be discussed are explored. Louis James's essay was first published in the Guyana Independence issue of the journal *New World Quarterly* that was co-edited by George Lamming and Martin Carter. Louis James was the leading metropolitan critic of Caribbean writing in the sixties and seventies and his book *The Islands In Between* represented the first sustained consideration of West Indian literature, so it is interesting to see how Carter's work looked to him at that time. His essay speaks of the 'cleansing indignation' that informs Carter's early poems, of the 'necessity' that such spirit find literary expression, but he is conscious of the fact that conventional metropolitan criticism cannot accommodate or do justice to such work, that it demands a different set of criteria for its explication and appreciation. The Nigerian critic Samuel Omo Asein's review of what he calls the protest tradition in West Indian poetry offers one alternative context, which locates Carter's work in a pan-Caribbean, indeed more broadly post-colonial tradition of poets using verse to raise and explore their own and their readers'/hearers' political consciousness. As Asein remarks, much of that work quickly becomes dated as the events to which it refers are superseded, but he admires Carter's ability to transmute 'the particular into the universal' a trait which, he argues, lends Carter's poetry 'its enduring value and contemporaneity'. Jeffrey Robinson's much-cited essay, revised for this volume, on 'The Guyaneseness of Guyanese Writing' would perhaps describe those particularities in rather different terms but begins from the assertion that Guyanese writers, including Martin Carter, have struggled to discover appropriate ways to represent a distinctly non-European experience. He reads Carter's work as 'a meditation on the nature of language and cognition' driven, in part at least, by that sense of the uniqueness of the Guyanese reality.

The essays that focus on aspects of Carter's poetry follow the chronological sequence of his publications. So this section of the book opens with Frank Birbalsingh's account of Carter's earliest work, the poems that predate the *Poems of Resistance*. Birbalsingh's essay reminds us of the extent to which a consciousness of race, class and colour permeated the colonial society, a fact which makes it the more remarkable that this precocious young poet, 'educated, brown, middle class' should so empathise – in his poem 'Three Years After' – with the experience of the Indo-Guyanese cane-cutters killed during the Enmore Plantation strike, people who were, Birbalsingh says, 'alien to him in almost everything except the fact of being born in Guyana.' Notwithstanding such empathy, that 'distance' between the poet and the experience of the people who are his essential subject inevitably produces a tension in that early work, a tension which the young poet was himself very conscious of and which emerges both in the tentativeness of some of those poems and in the stridency of others.

A perverse consequence of the British invasion of Guyana in 1953 and Carter's subsequent detention was to close that perceived gap between the poet and the mass of his society, at least for a while. Indeed Jeffrey Robinson persuasively argues that '*Poems of Resistance* made use of a rhetoric that assumes no gap between poet and audience.' Later in Carter's poetic career, as Robinson goes on to observe, the sense of a 'gap between speaker and hearer' is restored, though its nature is rather different from that his earliest work reveals. As the Jamaican novelist Neville Dawes remarked in his Preface to the 1964 edition of *Poems of Resistance*, reprinted here, those poems – 'University of Hunger', 'I Come from the Nigger Yard', 'This Is The Dark Time My Love' – and the others that have been so often anthologised, not only bind Carter to his local audience – his comrades in struggle, transcending issues of class and race in that period of national crisis and outrage – but also established Carter as a figure of especial respect among Caribbean intellectuals generally, wherever they might have found themselves through those decades of migration. As Dawes vividly paints it,

> Exiled poets (in stark London winters or within the hearing of African talking drums) who can tell you nothing about Carter's career or political views, remember and quote with deep approval lines like,
>
> Twin bars of hunger mark their metal brows
> twin seasons mock them'

The essays here by A.J. Seymour, Barbara Lalla, Rupert Roopnaraine, Kamau Brathwaite and Jeffrey Robinson offer readings of particular poems from *Poems of Resistance*, sometimes from very different critical standpoints. A.J Seymour's characteristically careful and sympathetic readings of 'I Come from the Nigger Yard' and 'University of Hunger' argue that these poems 'transcend bland socialist theory' and provide later readers with 'the true history of the period' in ways that other types of reconstruction never can. Seymour was, of course, a crucial figure in the development of Guyanese literature. An accomplished poet in his own right and through his editorship of *Kyk-over-al* and his Miniature Poets series of individual collections by Guyanese writers, which included the first poems of Carter's to gain much circulation beyond Guyana, he established both a platform where aspiring writers could be heard and a forum for the serious discussion of Guyanese writing. If his close reading of the poems – which is taken from one of several publications he produced that were intended as an aide to secondary school teachers – may seem a little mechanical to contemporary readers used to a more sophisticated kind of literary analysis, nevertheless these critiques are valuable both for their insights and for the sense they give us of the ways in which Carter's work was being discussed in Guyana. Coming at the poem from a very different perspective, Barbara Lalla's wonderfully accessible linguistic analysis discovers things about 'University of Hunger' that more traditional readings have felt but could not adequately explain. Like a literary archaeologist she uncovers the linguistic bones of the poem, noticing and explaining how Carter's utilisation of a linguistic ambiguity enables him to write in such a way that the poem is both available to an international readership yet also rings true to a creole speaking voice. One consequence of this technique, in the poem, is to allow Carter to challenge the orthodox presentation of a linear, closed, imperial history, as Lalla says:

> 'University of Hunger' rewrites history as incomplete, progressive and current – unbounded action that perpetuates the past in the present, and iterative action... that unlocks closure.

By so rearranging the way history is understood, she argues, the poem that begins in lament is transformed by its close into a statement of resistance and challenge. Rupert Roopnaraine's essay 'Re-reading Martin Carter' focuses similarly scrupulous attention to detail and nuance on another often cited but not so often fully considered poem, 'You are involved'. Roopnaraine's essay opens out from his linguistic and contextual examination of that apparently slight eight-line poem to engage with the full complexity of Carter's literary and philosophical project.

In 'Resistance Poems: the voice of Martin Carter', written before the publication of *Poems of Succession*, Kamau Brathwaite set out to demonstrate that there was much more to Martin Carter's poetry than the prevailing view of him as a 'protest poet' suggested. Brathwaite acknowledges and celebrates Carter's technical virtuosity 'as poet', develops the comparison that others have suggested between Carter and W.B. Yeats and responds to the electric surge of Carter's *Poems of Resistance* with an imagistic criticism of his own, as in this wonderful description of 'University of Hunger', 'with its long surf-like confident lines, and its epigrams moving within them like coralline resistors'. Echoing Louis James's comments more than a decade before, Brathwaite acknowledges that the particular circumstances and qualities of Carter's work makes 'conventional criticism hesitate... for lack of models of procedure.' Jeffrey Robinson's 'Root and Stone...' essay takes up that challenge, emphasising the complexity of Carter's technique, even in those early and seemingly direct poems of statement. Martin Carter was a profoundly serious poet but Robinson also demonstrates – and celebrates – the ways in which Carter would *play* with language, as only the great poets seem able to: layering, abusing, mistrusting language while at the same time shaping it into a poetry that, in Edward Baugh's words, 'distils the essential human anguish of its particular situation'.

One of the most remarkable essays in this collection is Eusi Kwayana's 'The Politics of the Heart', first published in the journal of the Casa de las Americas in Cuba and consequently less widely known in Anglophone circles than some of the essays that appeared in the English language literary journals. Written – self-consciously – as representing the perspective of a Guyanese 'common man', a fellow struggler for the cause, the essay suggests that some of the 'professional critics' of Carter's work fail to connect with, understand or adequately account for the *passion* that informed Carter's poetry and the responses it has generated among so many of its readers/hearers. Kwayana had been interned alongside Carter in 1953 and has been a prominent figure in Guyanese political life, so he is hardly a typical or 'innocent' reader, indeed – as Sydney King – he wrote the Foreword to the first edition of *Poems of Resistance.* All the same there is a distinctive quality to Kwayana's essay, a certain intimacy and insight, best expressed perhaps in his observation that:

> Martin Carter has always... seen himself in the vilest and most godforsaken of human beings... [and that he] can feel affinity with what he despises because he cannot separate himself from that social organism we call the Caribbean, and in particular, Guyana.

That sense of engagement, the 'lived struggle' which Kwayana feels underpins all Carter's work is, for him, the guarantee of that 'truthfulness' which distinguishes Carter's work for so many of his readers.

Kwayana's essay is revealing, too, in the portrait he paints of the Guyana into which Carter's *Poems of Affinity* was written, in the late 70s/early1980s, 'a police state' in which would-be readers of the more overtly political poems 'fear to be caught reading the volume at such a page, lest they be secretly noted.' Even that tension seems to be acknowledged within the work itself, as Bill Carr observes in his preface to the collection, 'the simultaneous presence of the public and the private' is a feature of these poems, fuelling their 'tragic lyricism'. Gordon Rohlehr begins his response to *Poems of Affinity* by locating the poems in the detail of that historical and political moment, invoking Carter's own description of the terror and the times in his famous 'Open Letter to the People of Guyana', in which he condemns the festering ruin of civil society that Burnham's Guyana had become. But beyond their importance as a response to 'the regime's perverseness', Rohlehr recognises the philosophical questing that these poems represent, exploring the most profound issues of being and meaning and faith as the poet confronts 'the neuter waste of time'.

The essays by Alan Persico, Stephanos Stephanides, Edward Baugh, al creighton and Michael Gilkes each develops that image of Carter confronting the desolation and despair of the period with desperate creativity. Indeed as Stephanides argues it is in that creative response that Carter remakes and redefines his reputation as a 'poet of revolution', a notion al creighton explores in his argument that critics have not been careful enough of the distinction between the role of the anti-colonial poet and the poet operating in a post-colonial – neo-colonial – context. Critics of Carter's later, apparently more 'private' poetry, creighton argues, need to work with a broader notion of what constitutes 'the political' if they are to understand the nuances of particular poems. His discussion of 'Proem' and 'Paying Fares', Baugh's reading of 'Ground Doves' and Alan Persico's careful attention to the resonances of 'Bent' in his essay, demonstrate the subtlety and complexity of these later poems. Taking that complexity on board Stephanides considers the nature of Carter's experiments with a poetic language that can speak to 'the dislocated subject's awareness of his place in the universe'. One quality of that poetic language is, as Barbara Lalla demonstrates in her analysis of 'University of Hunger', its subtle use of a creole inflection. Michael Gilkes notices that same 'cast' in many of Carter's later poems which, as he remarks, helps cement a verbal linkage between the philosophical musings of 'the poems man' – as one small girl dubs him – and 'the experience of the urban and rural working class'. Gilkes recalls that Carter was both amused and flattered by the girl's calling of him by his trade, accepting that it might have been an expression of awe at meeting this hallowed cultural figure or, as likely, that he was perceived alongside other such tradesmen: the milkman, the fisherman, the obeah man. Probably there was an element of both in the girl's recognition, suggesting, as Gilkes says,

> the poet's implication in the life and events of the city: Carter's personal involvement in the human condition about which he writes.

Ian McDonald's characteristically measured Introduction to Carter's *Selected Poems*, revised for the 1997 edition, reminds us of the importance of his domestic and family life to Martin Carter, both as a foundation stone of that 'human condition about which he writes' but also as a source of inspiration, a way of accessing 'the poetry that has informed the deep parts of his life'. That phrase, 'the deep parts of his life', recalls the several discussions of Carter as a philosopher in these essays. Eusi Kwayana writes of Carter's serious interest in Amerindian mythology, and speaks also of his wide reading in philosophy and human ideas from around the world. That openness is a characteristic of what some critics have called 'Carterite thought', as Kwayana memorably expresses it,

> (the theory of) surplus value and the motion of the stars are as real for him as the buried slave wanting to speak again.

Carter's poems become, as Mark McWatt suggests in his essay here, a channel for the poet-philosopher's engagement with 'the nature of consciousness itself'. In his fascinating essay on Carter's 'vision of land and landscape...' Stanley Greaves, the Guyanese painter who was a close friend and comrade in the creative struggle, alongside Carter, for many years, writes of the poet's experiments with what he calls 'philosophical couplets' in the working through and making of his poems. What is interesting is the sense we have from these several essays of Carter engaged in a sustained poetic and philosophical *process*, that the individual poems are part of a much more ambitious intellectual undertaking that went on throughout the poet's life, and that insofar as they function as commentary on political times in Guyana the poems serve, as McWatt puts it, to 'liberate the self from some of the terrifying encroachments of the phenomenal world'.

One has a sense of that kind of layering of priorities, the political and the philosophical, in Kwame Dawes's account of Carter's poetics. In the interview with Fred D'Aguiar that Dawes refers to, Carter seems not to want to answer the more straightforward questions put to him but 'hears' the questions differently and so answers in relation to his craft, his philosophy, rather than to his politics. This is not to deny the importance of the political dimension in Carter's work, rather it demands a more complex understanding of the relationship between philosophy, poetry and politics. In her essay on 'Carter's poetic essays in community', Gemma Robinson's reading of the *Poems of Resistance* demonstrates that even before the break up of the original PPP and the end of that dream of a socialist utopia, Carter's vision of a possible future society in Guyana was more complex than the simplifications of Marxist rhetoric acknowledged. Carter's notion of 'a free community of valid persons', implies, she argues, 'the triple dialectic of space, time and social being'. As her reading of the *Poems of Affinity* suggests, such a free community is no romance of peace and harmony but embraces the complexity, contradiction and conflict inherent in the make up of Guyana as a good, an enrichment, just so long as that triple dialectic is maintained in some kind of cultural equilibrium.

As George Lamming remarks in his interview here, Martin Carter was a stylish and provocative essayist as well as a poet, though much of his prose has been even more fugitive – scattered through newspapers, literary magazines and short-lived journals – than his poetry was. The Guyanese scholar Nigel Westmaas has done very important bibliographical, archival and interpretative work on Carter's prose, best represented in the special issue of *Kyk-over-al* mentioned above. In his essay here he remarks again the consistent seriousness of Carter's prose, not that his writing is without anecdote or what he calls 'creole wit', but that he looks 'sternly' at every issue, does not flinch from the uncomfortable argument or the 'difficult' resolution. We had intended to include a small selection of Carter's essays – and some of the interviews he had given over the years – in this book, but pressures of space make that impossible. However, we do intend to publish a larger selection of his written and spoken prose as a separate collection in the near future.

The rest of the volume is given over to memoirs by contemporaries of Carter's and tributes – including some poems – by younger writers to his achievement and the importance of his influence on their own practice. It would be foolish to try and summarise such a wide range of responses but I would just highlight some incidents and insights that strike me as particularly vivid. Remembering Neville Dawes's remarks in his introduction to the 1964 edition of *Poems of Resistance*, the fact that so many of Carter's contemporaries among the great writers of the Caribbean have wanted to contribute to this volume says much about the profound respect in which Carter is held, as man and as a poet, by that whole generation. Several writers recall the mood of optimism and camaraderie in that early 1950s period in Georgetown. Wilson Harris remembers the Anira group of radical intellectuals, 'serious… but not without its black humour' – hence the story of Jackson, sentenced, in jest, to hang if he should backslide on his avowed socialist principles. Characteristically, Harris sees more significance in this incident than those around him. Janet Jagan's memories of those times, in the years before the political trauma that so divided the country, reinforce Harris's account. Her memory of Martin Carter and Wilson Harris reading their poems at secret political meetings anticipates Harris's account of his having to read Carter's poems at a public event organised by George Lamming a few months later, while Carter was still under house arrest. Lamming's own account of Carter's spirit in the face of what he clearly felt was a kind of humiliation are poignant – though Carter clearly enjoyed the ironies of the situation Lamming describes when the new Governor of Guyana realised that he was swapping pleasantries with a proscribed 'subversive' at a party Lamming had organised. More revealing is Lamming's observation of the way Burnham and Jagan – both by now, around the time of independence, profoundly hostile to each other and at political odds with Carter – yet both retained a deep respect for him as a man of absolute integrity, and as a friend. Eric Huntley was another particular friend, among the group of activists interned with Carter in the wake of the British 'invasion' in 1953. His tale of the way that poems which would later be collected as *Poems of Resistance* were smuggled out of prison and printed on the government's own press at the New Amsterdam mental hospital is almost too good to be true. Jan Carew's description of those poems as being like 'street lighting that illuminates dark Guyanese skies at the beginning of the rainy season' is wonderfully evocative, while John La Rose's memoir reminds us that Carter's work and 'legend' quickly lit up other territories of the Caribbean, wherever the socialist/anti-colonial struggle was fermenting.

Huntley's memory of Carter as Guyana's first house husband is striking too, the radical ex-detainee, unable to get a job, changing nappies and doing the housework while his wife went out to work to keep their family. Perhaps that domestic experience informs what Roy Heath calls Carter's focus on 'the everyday' in his work; certainly Carter seems to have moved easily among the whole spectrum of the Guyanese people, from the most desperate to the most distinguished. David De Caires, among others, refers to Carter's notorious drinking bouts at various times in his life, driven to despair as one can easily understand but also, as De Caires suggests, as an expression of defiance. Derek Walcott comments that in the face of the kind of frustration Carter endured, his anger, expressed when he was in drink as verbal abuse towards those 'he might have called idiots' could be terrifying. John Figueroa's recollection of his encounters with Martin Carter at the Guyana Carifesta illustrates the many sides of the man: the poet-scholar able to recite from memory whole passages of the poetry of St. John of the Cross, in Spanish; the disruptive agitator loud in drink; and the political operator, coping with the pressures of 'the art of the possible'. He wasn't very good, by all accounts, at accepting that sort of compromise; his integrity, which so many of these statements by friends and commentators come back to, erupts in angry, bitter poems that sear through the well-mannered facade of social and political life in colonial Guiana. But as Walcott also understands, in other moods that integrity is expressed in the lyrical impulse, the soft-spoken tenderness that characterises so much of Carter's other poetry.

A St. Lucian poet of a younger generation than Walcott, Kendal Hippolyte remembers the impact of his first encounter with Carter's poems, which,

> brought the prosaic modern Caribbean into the realm of legend...the eternal war of good and evil.

For Hippolyte, like so many of the younger writers contributing to this volume, Carter's was, as Linton Kwesi Johnson puts it, 'an inspirational example.' I would pick out just three images from these pieces, each by a Guyanese writer recalling an incident from his or her childhood:

Mark McWatt's haunting description of the British warship anchored in the estuary of the Essequibo, announcing the arrival of the British forces and the overthrow of the PPP administration in 1953 to the curious boy whose father, a colonial official, warns him of the 'dangerous words' of the subversive poet; Sasenarine Persaud's painfully truthful account of the ways an Indo-Guyanese boy growing up through the turbulent years of the 60s and 70s almost inevitably saw Carter in terms of his racial background and apparent political affiliations; Karin King-Aribisala's memory of Carter's appreciation of civility, that in all the drama of his life he could find time to praise a child's display of good manners. Together those vignettes tell us much about the complex texture of the society Carter and these younger writers shared.

The contributions to this book, then, provide us with a wonderfully rich and varied response to Martin Carter's life and work. But this can only be the beginning. It is a familiar irony that the achievement of so many poets is only fully appreciated after they are dead. Indeed Martin Carter seemed to believe that this was the way things should be. Carter will, sooner rather than later, come to be recognised – as George Lamming puts it – as being 'in the very first ranks of the writers of the Americas' in this century. Future scholars then will be picking through these contemporary encounters with his work to inform and underpin their own critical responses. And there is plenty for them to be getting on with. The nature of Carter's work and the circumstances of his writing life, in conjunction with the fragile cultural infrastructure in Guyana means that much material that future – indeed present – scholars would treasure has been lost. Perhaps most crucially students of his poems are confronted with several versions of all his major poems, sometimes with quite significant changes between the published versions. The Demerara Publishers/Red Thread Press editions of the *Selected Poems*, while a magnificent and invaluable collection, does not actually resolve these questions, indeed if anything they exacerbate them. Carter is said to have 'meticulously checked the text of each of these selected poems and they now appear as originally composed'. Several issues derive from that assertion. In what form did Carter read the poems in: as they would be printed in the book, with standardised headings all in upper case letters, for example? I would be surprised if that were the case. As emerges from several of the close readings of the poems in this volume, Carter was meticulous about such things, he cared very much about punctuation and the arrangement of the text on the page, understanding very well the ways in which such details could change possible meanings. There are other more substantial textual queries about versions of poems included in the *Selected Poems,* some of which might be resolved if the poet's marked up proofs were available; but they seem to have been lost, or rather given away to an otherwise unremembered American researcher passing through Guyana who has not been heard from since. (If he or she should read this and still has those proofs, PLEASE get in touch with me!) And do the poems in the *Selected Poems* appear 'as originally composed' or in the final versions the poet wanted to put out? Not always the same thing at all. Then there are the uncollected poems and no doubt some previously unpublished poems and prose writings. So, all in all, there will be plenty for those of us who care about the details of Carter's work to chew on in future years, and scope for several further volumes of collected and variorum editions of his works, as well as critical and biographical studies. As Martin remarked on several occasions,

> The best poems write themselves, you know... But if they are produced in labour why should they be consumed in ease?

In this book we have taken up that challenge in the full, indeed desired, expectation that these will not be the last words.

Stewart Brown
Centre of West African Studies,
University of Birmingham.
May 1999

Notes

1. The first part of this Introduction is adapted from a memorial essay, 'No voice in the emptiness: the poetry of Martin Carter' which was published in *Planet: the Welsh Internationalist*, Aberystwyth, no.129, June 1998) The quotation in the title is taken from Martin Carter's remarks at the end of the first of his Edgar Mittelholzer Lectures, 'Man and Making – Victim and Vehicle', published by the Ministry of Information, Guyana, in 1971.
2. As al creighton and Kamau Brathwaite discuss in their essays here, there is some debate about the date of this poem's composition and the circumstances of its publication. Whatever the facts of that story it seems clear that, at one level at least, the poem does reflect on the pressures Carter was under during his tenure as a Minister.
3. I use the plural 'we' in discussion of the making of this book because, while I would take the editorial responsibility for whatever is included here, without the help of many people this material could not have been gathered together. I am grateful in particular to Ian McDonald, Anne Walmsley, Gemma Robinson, Gordon Rohlehr, Mark McWatt, Mervyn Morris, David Dabydeen and Jeremy Poynting for help in directing me to possible material for inclusion and for help in tracing and contacting writers. In addition Jeremy Poynting must be given full credit for his contribution to this book, serving almost as a second editor as well as the publisher. Without his deep knowledge of the Guyanese context, his enthusiasm for the project from the very first time it was suggested and his unflinching commitment to see the book through to publication, even as it grew in scale and complexity, it would never have appeared.

THE NECESSARY CONTEXTS

CLEM SEECHARAN

THE SHAPE OF THE PASSION: THE HISTORICAL CONTEXT OF MARTIN CARTER'S POETRY OF PROTEST (1951-1964)

The Colony's best poet is a Marxist leader of the PPP, Martin Carter. His ideology has given his work a passion and intensity.

Michael Swan (1955)

I see no substitute for passion, internally generated, and hard work.

Martin Carter (1960)

I
RADICAL PROMPTINGS OF CARTER'S IMAGINATION, 1939-52

Martin Carter was born on 7 June 1927 in Georgetown, British Guiana to mixed race parents – 'coloured' people as they are still called in Guyana. There was nothing extraordinary about the day of his birth in the colony, but the year is redolent of a measure of infamy. The Colonial Office, in league with the plantocracy and others of the old order, were manoeuvring to deprive the colony of its mildly liberal constitution and replace it with Crown Colony government – more nominated members; presumably more malleable. The pretext was that in the interest of colonial development it was imperative to give the Executive Council, presided over by the Governor and comprising primarily nominated officials and unofficials, greater control of financial matters. The truth is that vested interests in this backward colony had become paranoid at what they saw as an avalanche of potential subversives – popular leaders elected to the Legislature Council in 1926. Most of the representatives of colonial capital had been defeated.

The fear of change was imprinted on the year 1927, but the kindling of protest from diverse sources, also, was an inescapable fact of the Georgetown of 1927. Probably the most articulate protester, a formidable critic of the colonial condition, was Hon. A. R. F. Webber (1880-1932), a coloured publisher and politician seen to be incorruptible. His radical *The New Daily Chronicle*, founded in 1926, was a champion of the underdog; its iconoclasm was shaping a new self-confidence. On 8 June 1927, the day after Martin Carter was born, it carried a leader challenging the official premises for changing the constitution: Webber recommended 'a good, strong, imaginative Executive [Council], inspired by local knowledge and guided by a continuous policy, to take hold of the affairs of the colony...' A few weeks later his paper asserted that 'the quickest way to the realisation of [the political evolution of subject races] is not by suppression but by throwing open avenues of advancement

...'[1] The incipient nationalism would not have been lost on Carter's father, a junior civil servant.

Georgetown, in the hard times of the 1930s, was characterised by distinctly ethnic, quasi-political organisations: the British Guiana East Indian Association (founded in New Amsterdam in 1916), and the Negro Progress Convention (founded in Georgetown in 1922). Even the two main trade unions, the British Guiana Labour Union (founded in 1919) and the Man Power Citizens' Association (founded in 1937), tended to bear these features, reflecting the essentially ethnic division of labour which had evolved in the colonial economy since Emancipation. So that even the spate of working class protests from the mid-1930s, Carter's boyhood years, tended to harden racial proclivities.

This boyhood could not have eluded the procrustean claims of Guyanese racial articulation. Indeed, Carter's coloured or mixed race group, because of its comparatively elevated status within the colonial polity, tended to be most punctilious in its defence of that space. This bred a superiority complex, as the Guyanese writer, Edgar Mittelholzer (1909-1965), a coloured man from New Amsterdam, recalls:

> ... it was my own class – people of coloured admixture .... which looked down upon the East Indian sugar plantation labourers ('coolies' we called them, whether they were labourers or eventually became doctors or barristers or Civil Servants). It was my class which considered the Portuguese social inferiors because of their background of door-to-door peddling, rum-shops, salt-goods shops and pawnshops and their low standards of living. We, too, treated the Chinese sweet-sellers and shopkeepers with condescension because of their poor-immigrant status. We even looked with a certain distinct aloofness upon the young Englishmen who came out to serve as sugar-plantation overseers. We deemed them 'white riff-raff'. And as for the negroes, it goes without saying that they were serving people; that was an accepted tradition dating from slavery days. Only the pure-blooded whites could discriminate adversely against me and my class.....[2]

Carter's father, Victor Emmanuel, like many men from coloured families in British Guiana – the van Sertimas, Mittelholzers, McDavids, Westmaases, Sharples, Woolfords – had found a niche in the colonial civil service, below the British who were the heads of departments. Carter's people were also the first people of the book: they celebrated their European side and denigrated – denied, their African side. One could argue, therefore, that these twin pillars, European superiority on one hand, and coloured superciliousness in parading their Europeanness on the other, were what nourished the rebel in the young Carter in the 1940s.

Ian McDonald has remarked on the role of learning in the Carter household: 'Carter recalls arguments between his father and his friends about Spinoza and other deeply philosophical subjects. His mother, born Violet Eugene Wylde, also loved books and enjoyed reciting verses'.[3] Carter has also spoken of the bounteous influence of the Bible, its rich allure of language and allusions, its mythical imagery, seeping into his fluid imagination.[4] He had access, in

Georgetown, both to the Carnegie Public 'Free' Library and, until its destruction in the fire of 1945, the incomparable riches of the Royal Agricultural and Commercial Society Collection. Besides he would have read, regularly, the two excellent, if conservative, daily newspapers, *The Daily Argosy* and *The Daily Chronicle*, certainly their 'corners' for poets and short story writers. It is not far-fetched to argue that the realms of art, beauty and personal freedom to think and dream, fed by the universe of words, insulated him from the parochialism and what he would later refer to as the 'materialism and philistinism' of British Guiana. It also bred a passion for words: their elegance, subtlety, and the seduction of crafting them to give meaning to experience: a process which would have acquired some glamour with the publication of Mittelholzer's *Corentyne Thunder* in 1941, in England.

British Guiana, in the 1940s, provided a rich tapestry: this colonial backwater was stirring. Carter's education had taken him to Queen's College, the prestigious boys' school, in 1938 or 1939; he graduated in 1944. Deflection of the power of the dominant Imperial centre, during the War, bred a degree of local autonomy. This had been stimulated by the liberal Governor from 1941 to 1946, Sir Gordon Lethem (1886-1962), a Scot. Carter's most impressionable years were touched by the large sympathies and imagination of this able man, who believed that good government must transcend the old, insatiable demands of the sugar planters. Lethem was a resolute advocate of drainage and irrigation of the hazardous coastland, where over 90 per cent of the people lived; diversification of agriculture and support for small farmers; interior development. At every stage, however, the plantocracy tried to, and to a great extent were able to, stifle change. Such was Lethem's popularity, that people of all races in the colony petitioned the Colonial Office for him to have a second term. They were rebuffed. Carter's world at Queen's College and his early years in the civil service partook of the exhilaration (and despair) which crowned the Lethem years: an oasis on the weary road of colonial inertia.

Carter speaks often of the need for passion and hard work. Lethem's endeavours spoke of hope, shoots of possibilities, commitment – daring to change. One commentator's final portrait of the man could explain why he illuminated the lives of so many in British Guiana, possibly even Carter's, between the ages of 14 and 19:

> [Lethem] was a lion of a man – great-hearted, formidable when roused, of bounding energy and vitality. Large-minded and generous, he was the antithesis of everything petty, mean, meticulous, pedantic. The wide, rough colonial stage of his time was an ideal field for his qualities. His facility with languages and liberal and sympathetic spirit kept him in closest contact with high and low among the diverse peoples with and for whom he worked so devotedly and who in their turn loved and venerated him. His *vividia vis animi*, the faultless verbal memory and power of declamation; his humour and gusto, made him a fascinating leader and friend.[5]

Lethem's perceived purity of motives in British Guiana enlarged its peoples' sense of the possible, their potential for a fuller life. But this environment – a capricious landscape requiring water now, drainage soon afterwards; chronic malaria; the latifundist character of sugar – also bred a hurt and a radical temperament. High hopes and their abrogation during the Lethem years, coupled with the optimism spawned by the Moyne Commission Report and its advocacy of change (1945), expanded the rebellious spirit.

1945 was a pivotal year in Carter's life. He left Queen's College and got a job in the civil service, first at the Post Office, then as secretary to the Superintendent of Prisons, Samuel Baker – a man 'humane to prisoners and scornful of bureaucracy'; a 'great drunkard' and champion wrestler, from Wales.[6] All these features endeared him to Carter; but he was deeply aware that he was hemmed in. Very few colonials, even coloureds in the 1940s, could scale the heights of the civil service; besides, the job stifled initiative and crippled the imagination. But 1945 also brought a new day: A. J. Seymour, another coloured civil servant, founded the first literary journal in the colony, *Kyk-over-Al*. Its aims reflected a deeper ambition: 'an instrument to help forge a Guianese people, make them conscious of their intellectual and spiritual possibilities – build some achievement of common pride in the literary world – make an act of *possession* of our environment.... (emphasis added)'[7]

But the 1940s were marked also by an ominous rise in racial consciousness – a situation which was accelerated by the establishment of an Indian middle class with a base in rice, cattle and business. But even among Indian workers, their sense of their own possibilities had been buoyed by the relentless march of Indian nationalism in the 'motherland', India. Some, already by the late 1930s-early 1940s, were challenging the supremacy of Africans and coloureds in law and medicine. Theirs was something of a meteoric rise and this inspired fear. Carter was aware of this fear, and because he belonged to neither of the two main groups, he was acutely conscious of its destructive properties. Indeed, in 1944, fear of Indian dominance had led even the veteran African Guyanese trade unionist, Hubert Critchlow (1884-1958), to vote against adult suffrage in the legislature.

In 1946 Cheddi Jagan (1918-1997), an Indian, his American-born wife, Janet, H. J. M. Hubbard, a near-white communist trade unionist, and Ashton Chase, a young African trade unionist and assistant to Critchlow, founded the Political Affairs Committee (PAC). One of its aims was to establish 'a strong, disciplined and enlightened Party, equipped with the theory of Scientific Socialism' – a Communist party.[8] Cheddi Jagan was an American-educated dentist, but his roots in the sugar plantations coupled with his experience of American 'Jim Crow' institutions and rampant racism against African Americans, in the late 1930s-early 1940s, enraged him; but he lacked a frame of reference to comprehend inequality and racism. It was when he met Janet Rosenberg (born 1920), a communist of East European Jewish extraction, from Chicago, that he acquired the rudiments of a Marxist way of seeing. He absorbed it passionately, uncritically, with a convert's zeal.

Cheddi Jagan had found a religion; and he took it and his attractive, politically astute wife to his colonial backwater. He had a young man's enthusiasm and a facility for simplifying the message; oversimplifying it, the millennial vision. His astounding energy, personal charm and evident sincerity made him a hero of the underdog even among many Africans. Hubbard had moved towards Marxism earlier, around 1938-39, as a result of his exposure to the leftist books of two Scottish Presbyterian ministers in Georgetown. Maurice St. Pierre believes that Hubbard's Marxist ideas, ventilated weekly at a study circle in Georgetown, had permeated the Carter household by 1945:

> Reading these books was followed by a number of weekly meetings dealing with the translation of learning into action. Martin Carter, who was subsequently involved with the PAC, grew up in a home (along with his brother Keith who was later involved in the struggle) in which they were enjoined to think and discuss any issue freely. This experience, coupled with the marked propensity of the brothers for reading, soon led to a desire to ask questions and to seek answers about the nature of society, which sought to oppress the majority of the people.[9]

For the young Martin Carter, the analytical perspective and the optimism gained from a non-conventional reading – at variance with his Queen's College orthodoxies – fed the rebellious temperament. Cheddi Jagan and Janet, a first-rate organiser and editor of *PAC Bulletin*, dramatised this new hope; they epitomised the fledgling possibilities. The appeal of the PAC's radical politics was enhanced by Cheddi Jagan's election to the Legislative Council in November 1947, aged 29. For the first time a communist had won legislative honours and, overnight, he revolutionised people's conception of politics. Jagan recalls:

> Mine was the role of 'politics of protest', with the weapons of exposure and struggle. If the legislature was my forum, the waterfront, the factories, plantations, mines and quarries were my battleground. I brought a new dimension to the politics of protest. A continuity between the legislature and the street-corner; the legislature was brought to the 'streets' and the 'streets' to the legislature.[10]

Ian McDonald explains how Jagan's vision of freedom reached Carter, in Georgetown, in the late 1940s: 'He had become friendly with many of those, like himself, who had freed their minds and were determined to free their country. He had met the pioneering politician Cheddi Jagan when he heard that Jagan had a marvellous library and went to visit him and stayed to talk and talk'. Indeed, the Jagans frequently invited 'leading intellectuals' to their home to discuss a range of issues. Carter was one of them; he said that the group, deceptively called the Kitty Adult Education Association, was a 'communist front'[11]: it espoused Marxism.

In his first collection of poems, *The Hill of Fire Glows Red* (1951), appropriately, he seems to praise the speaking, guiding hands of Cheddi Jagan, his friend and mentor of those distant, spacious days of unsullied hopes and big vision. Carter recalls: 'Cheddi came back to Guyana in 1943 and began agitating. I used to hear about his agitation and became interested in the movement he had started. He had founded the Political Affairs Committee (PAC), and used to hold political meetings at the Kitty YMCA. I attended those meetings'.[12] This is from 'Looking at your Hands':

No!
I will not still my voice!
I have
too much to claim –
if you see me
looking at books
or coming to your house
or walking in the sun
know that I look for fire![13]

Cheddi Jagan's stature as the prophet of the new day was lifted by the Enmore shootings of 16 June 1948: five young sugar plantation workers were shot by the police – striking men who were among many demanding recognition for the Jagan-backed trade union, the Guiana Industrial Workers' Union. The *PAC Bulletin* covered the tragedy with this caption: 'WE ASKED FOR BREAD! ..... THEY GAVE US BULLETS!'[14] Enmore was the catalyst for the rise of the People's Progressive Party (PPP), a Marxist-led but a broad-based coalition of diverse races and classes. It was founded in January 1950. It superseded the PAC; and its organ, *Thunder*, replaced the *PAC Bulletin*. Carter became a member of the editorial board of *Thunder*.

Carter's imagery, in his early years in the PPP, fed on Enmore. The 'hill of fire', a transcendent feature of the plantation at harvest time, as the tall sugar-cane is set alight and the avalanche of fire consumes the cane-leaves, undergrowth, insects, snakes, etc., is the infernal motif for the pain, the hurt of slavery and indenture, and fountainhead of colonial being. But it also becomes the symbol of hope: it clears up, cleans, and allows for new shoots of cane, the ratoon, to sprout – the red hill speaks of a new day:

across the dark face of the river
the hill of fire glows red like fresh blood
like the blood of Quamina
flowing through the green forest
the green green forest.[15]

Quamina, the leader of the Demerara Slave Rebellion of 1823, gave his head to free his compatriots: it was displayed on a spike and left to rot. He will be a hero when the new freedom comes to Guiana, the poet is saying.

Carter, however, is declamatory. He mocks the lofty appellation, for British Guiana, 'Magnificent Province', 'Province of mud!/ Province of flood!'[16]

The Enmore motif, the bitterness of sugar, is branded on this land. The 'magnificent' is not him, 'with his torn shirt'; it speaks only of those 'in their white mansions' (the great house), 'by the trench of blood'. British Guiana is 'no El Dorado for me'; its catalogue of euphemisms cannot mask its brutal plantation heritage: the 'bruising and battering for self preservation/in the white dust and grey mud' – an allusion to sugar and the harsh coastal landscape of stiff, unyielding clay which imposes eternal toil, on slave and freed man. But he will no longer genuflect to poverty: 'now is long past time for worship'. No longer will he be 'kneeling'. He is now armed with 'this hammer of my hand' (the hammer and sickle) and 'this new science of men' (Marxism).[17]

The poet is 'listening to the land'. A voice is being shaped: he hears 'tongueless whispering', 'as if some buried slave wanted to speak again'.[18] He is preparing for the revolution; everyone will become soldiers of freedom – all will be involved:

> from the hospitals the lame will come
> the mad will be sane again
> for the revolution.[19]

But hovering over Carter's euphoria and undammable hope, the enormous gloom, the possibility of despair – from the beginning. It is as if his personal oscillation – his peaks, his troughs – could not leave the vision well alone. The Lethem promise, of pregnant possibilities and slim harvests, nestles ineluctably in Carter's poetic landscape, as in the following from *The Hidden Man* (1952):

> I stretch my hand to a night of weary branches
> feeling for leaves or any twig of blossom:
> But the branch is withered with no green leaf for me
> and the stalk is brown and has no petal for me
> and the root is tap root boring in equator.[20]
> [...]

The potential for the descent of man, the downward spiral, also, is vast.

II
Euphoria and Creeping Self-doubt, 1953-55: Poems of Resistance (1954) and their source

The years after Enmore (1948) and the General Elections of April 1953, the first under adult suffrage, were the fullest time in Carter's life. His dreams were not yet corroded by Guyanese racism and the demonic allure of power. The 'new science of men' fed notions of the weakness of chains, of the inevitability of freedom; most of all it made race an 'epiphenomenon', posing the evil away. The 'new science of men', especially in this potential cauldron of racism, could make one forget; it was a release into fantasy.

In 'All of a Man', in his *The Kind Eagle*, his other 1952 collection, the 'kind eagle' – no American eagle – batters the wall of unfreedom, freeing one suspects even the poet from the dead-end of the colonial civil service:

O strike kind eagle, strike!
Grip at this prison and this prison wall!
scream and accuse the guilty cage of heaven
hurling me here, hurling me here.

This antithesis of the American eagle, Marxism, has the strength and purity of motives, to enhance freedom, for total liberation: 'All of a man can fly like a bird'. Love and hope are the essence of the Carterian new man. The old certainties, the old religion, the whole colonial rationale which shackles – 'the guilty cage of heaven', is being shredded – the declamation of renewal is clean; the kind eagle *will* 'strike': 'The sharp knife dawn glitters in my hand'.[22]

Rupert Roopnaraine recently explained the depth of resolution of Carter's work in the early PPP days which fed the intensity of the poetry; the self-belief, too. Roopnaraine writes: 'Between 1950 and 1953 [Carter] and a few others did most of the party educational work in weekend classes. They worked along the coast. An important highlight of this effort was their study of the landlord system in the rice farming village of Golden Fleece, Essequibo. In this study and teaching the young activist was getting down to the anatomy of the estate system on the Essequibo coast. The activists found that there were elements of feudalism alive and well, that often the landlord was the miller and the shopkeeper as well as the moneylender. Carter's righteous anger at these conditions was not ideological in the narrow sense. These were among the discoveries and experiences he accumulated while doing political work off the platform while he was still a public servant. He taught with conviction the part played by labour in production. His scheme was not merely Marxist, but one reinforced with Carterian thought permeated with Guyanese history and experience'.[23]

These years of lofty ideals, in the early 1950s, had seen a trickle of radical sentiments in the PAC of the late 1940s flow with diverse, often discordant streams into the nationalist movement, the People's Progressive Party (PPP), an eclectic multiracial coalition with an anti-colonial mission. It was this, in conjunction with the suspension of the Constitution by the British, after 133 days, because of the PPP's alleged communist designs, which inspired many of the poems in Carter's finest collection. *Poems of Resistance* was published in London in 1954. It is here that Carter's Marxist vision and his optimism that the PPP could shape a free, coherent community from its disparate components, is discernible. It is here also that one can trace Carter's own quest for an authentic Guyaneseness, rooted in slavery. His great poem, 'I Come from the Nigger Yard',[24] is about the redefining of the past, and its reclamation as an instrument of renewal; the reassertion of one's humanity as a prelude to the building of the new day. The 'nigger yard' wrote the people out of history, but even there the quest for identity, for ancestral moorings to begin to reshape the present, had begun:

It was an aching floor on which I crept
on my hands and my knees
searching for dust for the trace of a root
or the mark of a leaf or the shape of a flower.

Carter's tale documents the pain, but does not despair. He shows us his rage leaping from the material and mental void, with 'coffin space for home' and 'priests and parsons fooling gods with words'. He screams; he is 'stubborn and fierce': he affirms himself; he becomes. The poem is permeated with hope. He spots 'a tiny star neighbouring a leaf/a little drop of light a piece of glass... like a spark seed in the destiny of gloom'. Like the quivering tension building in a drawn sling approaching release, the language is taut, redolent of aggravated strength; the 'nigger' will write his own history henceforth:

I turn to the histories of men and the lives of the peoples.
I examine the shower of sparks the wealth of the dreams.
[...]
From the nigger yard of yesterday I come with my burden.
To the world of to-morrow I turn with my strength.

Carter is reclaiming his African side; no bouquets here for the European side.

He did not feature directly in the short-lived PPP government of 1953; he did not even win the seat he contested, New Amsterdam. Roopnaraine observes that the seat was unwinnable but Carter 'used the campaign to deepen human relations and to educate people into thinking'. He resigned from the civil service after the 1953 elections, thus freeing himself to work more effectively for the PPP, both as a member of the executive and the editorial board of the party's organ, *Thunder*. Roopnaraine concludes: 'educating people into the habit of thinking may well be his most enduring contribution to our politics'. To Guyana.

Indeed, as the Robertson Constitutional Commission of 1954 reported, Martin Carter was one of at least six of the Party's 'most prominent leaders', who exerted 'a very powerful communist influence'. They elaborated: this group 'accepted unreservedly the "classical" communist doctrines of Marx and of Lenin: were enthusiastic supporters of the policies and practices of modern communist movements: and were contemptuous of European social democratic parties, including the British Labour Party'.[25]

The suspension of the Constitution and the incarceration of several PPP leaders, including Carter (for three months, towards the end of 1953), and the invasion by British troops, inspired some of the most overtly political poems in *Poems of Resistance*. Earlier, on 29 October 1953, as St. Pierre observes, some of these poems, including 'This is the Dark Time my Love' and 'I Clench my Fist', had been seized by British soldiers from the Magnet Printery in Georgetown. Apparently they had been 'so unnerving to the British' that they were the subject of a despatch from the Governor to the Colonial Office.[26]

Carter's imagery is angry; the hard edge is unforgiving in its denunciation of the British soldiers in the colony: 'All around the land brown beetles crawl about'. Speaking to his young wife, as several of the poems from jail do, they gain in intensity by the interweaving of the harsh political imagery with a pristine love for his wife and their child to whom she has just given birth:

Who comes walking in the dark night time?
Whose boot of steel tramps down the slender grass?
It is the man of death, my love, the strange invader
watching you sleep and aiming at your dream.[27]

He sees the suppression of the freedom movement in British Guiana as a part of the tapestry of imperialist repression wherever the battle for freedom is waged; but he does not despair. The spirit of his communist brothers and his ancestral brothers, African rebels, descendants of Accabreh, one of the leaders of the Berbice Slave Rebellion of 1763, feeds his zeal:

O wherever you fall comrade I shall rise.
In the whirling cosmos of my soul there are galaxies of happiness
Stalin's people and the brothers of Mao Tse-tung
And Accabreh's breed...[28]

But Carter, a man of intellect from the coloured middle class, could more readily assess the potential African-Indian confrontation with dispassion. Ominous clouds had settled over the PPP, during crisis week, after the April 1953 election victory, as Cheddi Jagan and L. F. S. Burnham staked their respective claims for supremacy. Carter could see that inherent in this fight were the germs of racial hate – not the nicety of philosophical disputations however persuasive. This probably accounts for the passion which he brought to his communist vision – an uncompromising path of economic democracy as the foundation for racial equality; no battle against racialism could be won amidst the greed of capitalism and rampant individualism.

Carter had argued in August 1954 against an American officer, Mr. L. E. Norrie, who had written in a local newspaper, *The Daily Argosy* (15 August), that Russia was the 'greatest colonial power on earth': it continued to dominate millions of colonial peoples. For Carter, in 1954, this was poison: the Soviet Union was *the* example – 'the star neighbouring a leaf'; 'the spark seed in the destiny of gloom'. He countered, in *Thunder*:

... in 1917 the people led by Lenin overthrew the capitalist state and instituted a system of Soviet Government which guarantees to the people a real chance to live like human beings. Because control of the means of production is in the hands of the people who decide how production should be organised, unlike the USA where the minority class controls everything, the Soviet Government is able to lead the people ever forward to a better life. And because again, the Soviet Union is a socialist country, a country which leads the world in the fight for freedom from imperialism and therefore from colonialism, it follows that Mr. Norrie's statement is viciously false and is cunningly calculated to deceive and mislead...[29]

Earlier, in May 1954, Rory Westmaas, Carter's close friend and junior vice-chairman of the PPP, who, also, had won the badge of communism from the Robertson Commission, had argued that the British suspended the Constitution because the PPP was not a 'reformist' party, like the parties of Manley and Bustamante in Jamaica and Grantley Adams in Barbados. These had 'placed themselves completely at the disposal of Imperialism'. Westmaas, like Carter, still believed that the PPP was fulfilling its task as the leader for national liberation: 'Our party in no way resembles these puppet organisations. The PPP, based on the strong working class-peasant farmer alliance with our small businessmen and intelligentsia, truly represents the interests of the entire people. Placing complete trust in it, the people had forged, in a matter of a few years, a sharp weapon for freedom and peace'.[30]

Carter's optimism, also, was not dimmed by the suspension. In a poem published in *Thunder* on 31 July 1954, 'If Today' (apparently never republished), he is still unrelenting in his hate of the soldier/invader, but the struggle sustains the hope:

If today our city is like a house of stone
rigid and cold, silent and still
It is because a soldier walks with a gun
Not even a friend of the dogs.

And if today the sound of the ocean on our shore
comes like a rumble of terror
It is because death rides at anchor in the sea
Watching until they sleep
waiting for hope to fade.
And even if today they try to stamp us down
flesh into mud, heart into stone
Are we not still a great generation of struggle
strong and uncountable
born to be free?

Carter's certainty of the political vocation in the PPP showed no signs of wear until the 'split' in February 1955, when L. F. S. Burnham, the most gifted African leader in the party, its chairman, and several others who had been designated 'socialists', 'essentially democrats', by the Robertson Commission, left the communist-led (Jagan) PPP. In fact, on the day of the fateful Burnham-inspired meeting in Georgetown, which consummated the split, Carter was still underlining the political vocation – a politics animated by the condition of the working class. The working class child, tomorrow's hope, was in an abysmal condition:

> ...he finds himself locked up in a huge cage of poverty where hardly any opportunity for real individual development exists. Any kind of gift or talent must be immediately sacrificed to the job of putting something in his belly from day to day. And, after a while the grind of life takes over, bright dreams become a bolt in a sugar punt – bent and rusty with the years.[31]

Voiceless people! As Carter would put it in the early 1970s, after he had resigned from Burnham's cabinet, 'the mouth is muzzled by the food it eats'.

By 1955, the rusting of ideals, the corrosion of hope, for Carter (and his friend Rory Westmaas) had begun. Burnham's departure signalled the ominous crystallisation and aggregation of deep-seated racial instincts, sectional prejudices, in this inchoate colonial polity. A united PPP had offered the best hope of stemming a slide into racial obscurantism. The menace of African-Indian incomprehension, fusing around the magnetic personalities of Jagan and Burnham, clouding out meaningful debate, led Carter to argue prophetically in March 1955, less than a month after the split:

> ... [that] it would be better for a person of Indian descent to support Mr. Burnham for ideological reasons than for the same person while agreeing with Mr. Burnham to support Dr. Jagan only because he happens to be an Indian. The same holds good for a person of African descent. For this would mean that the action was dictated by reason and not by racialism. In the long run reason would lead to the truth while racialism would lead to disaster.
>
> There is no separate salvation for Indians in Guiana, no separate salvation for Africans. There is only salvation for a united Guianese people fighting as a people against imperialism for National Independence.[32]

The resolve was beginning to crack in the Jagan-led PPP. Even the Marxist assertions were betraying a lack of conviction: catch phrases, dogmas were paraded to paper over the racial divide. Carter observed in September 1955:

> With all this burden in front of us, we tend to become pessimistic and retreat into silence. On the other hand, realising that the only profound solution is the creation of an equitable social order, we tend to repeat worn out clichés, until we ourselves stop believing in their value. Preaching is not going to help us much when all the raw causes remain. Be that as it may, however, one thing we must remember. Without racial co-operation in the face of imperialist menace, we go nowhere.[33]

Two weeks later, impelled probably by what he saw as the growing racism among some in the PPP, he remarked that fear was malleable; it could be embroidered upon, forged as an instrument to fan racial flames. Fear of the other's dominance, his capacity to bend you to his will, has the power of 'corrupting a man's mind, of twisting it into all kinds of shapes'. Fear in the arsenal of the racist in British Guiana, Carter explained, fed a perversion of hope and the liberating principles of Marxism. Inquiry, rationality, the quest for meaning, the shaping of broader loyalties by the reclaiming of history – all were neutralised by the poison of racism. Carter was very worried: 'Instead of going down to the *cause of fear, the racists accept fear and make it a cause* for antagonism... Especially since the split in February [1955], but even before then, these types have been practising their trade. Whether they occur in our Party or in any other Party, they should be dealt summarily, by expulsion on the one hand and exposure on the other'.[34]

By the end of 1955 the racial divide was hardening. A discernible uncertainty, then shoots of despair, crept into his work – the prose and the poetry. To repeat his stark admonition of September 1955: '...one of the strongest emotions that human beings experience is fear. Fear has the terrible power of corrupting a man's mind, of twisting it into all kinds of shape'. This angst spawned three poems which were published in *Kyk-Over-Al* in late 1955: 'Poems of Shape and Motion'.[35] The corrosive power of race, the death of reason and reflection pains him into self-reflection. He is 'wondering' whether he could 'shape this passion' as he pleases, 'in solid fire'; whether he could elude the slide into the racial abyss; whether 'the strength of my heart were enough'. 'Shape and Motion One' speaks of the corruption of ideals. He wonders if 'I could make myself/nothing but fire, pure and incorruptible'.

Carter is 'wondering' whether the primordial loyalties of race, 'the wound of the wind on my face', could be erased by the cause, the broader striving inspired by his politics, 'the work of my life', 'the strife of my days'. He is groping, hoping to find himself in the possibilities; that the 'space in my soul' may 'be filled by the shape I become'. Or is the racial fear too deep-seated, too cancerous ('the roots that spread out in the swamp'), to allow the seemingly untaintable, recent socialist ideals, 'the issuing flower', becoming anything but superficial, ornamental? Is the 'struggle' enough?:

I was wondering if the agony of years
could be traced to the seed of an hour.
If the roots that spread out in the swamp
ran too deep for the issuing flower.[36]

On 5 November 1955 Carter had reproduced in *Thunder* a poem 'Shatter this Age-long Shame', by the great Indian poet, the Nobel laureate for 1913, Rabindranath Tagore (1861-1941). He noted that it 'brings home to us the unity of suffering of all people who live under "the indiscriminate feet of dictators". It is a poem that could have been written in Guiana today'. It is tempting to read the poem and Carter's motives at another level, as a declamation against Guyanese obscurantism, the creeping racial scourge:

Lull me not into languish dreams;
Shake me out of this cringing in the dust,
Out of the fetters that shackle our mind,
make futile our destiny

Out of the unreason that bends our
dignity down...

By December 1955, when 'Poems of Shape and Motion' appear, Carter disappears from the pages of *Thunder*. He and his friend, Rory Westmaas, are already disillusioned with the PPP, clearly exhausted by what they saw as the atrophy of the higher principles. Dogmas were parading as thought. He had warned, at the time of the split, that 'no one should confuse politics as a social instrument for politics as a social disease'.[37] The latter had already claimed the politics of the land, including that of the Jaganite PPP: their inoculation with Marxist dogmas could not stem the virus of racism.

Writing as a private correspondent to *Thunder* on 28 July 1956, Carter exhorted all Guyanese leaders to treat the issue of race as a matter of urgent importance, central to the survival of the country. It was not enough to be committed to political and economic reform; it was essential to become preoccupied with 'the pure problem of ensuring racial harmony'. Carter advised:

> ...let us have an inward-looking, sincere and determined effort to accomplish racial harmony, and this effort should not be made only to aid political advancement in a general way, as is usually put forward in arguments in favour of it, but should be carried out as a task dictated by reason and by the sheer human necessity of creating and wanting a vital community in the deepest and widest sense of the word. For without a community to inherit the triumphs and victories, the most valuable achievements of the present generation will end up like cold night wind blowing through an empty house.

By late 1955, in 'Shape and Motion Three', the despair is growing, but there is still the possibility of redemption: the two are intermingled. The bleak imagery links the poet's identity with 'limping cripples', 'houses tight with sickness', 'dream without the sleep'; he hears himself in 'the loneliness of a child', in a 'woman's grief', 'in coughing dogs' at midnight. A morose imagery permeates the poem. Each stanza, bar one, begins with the line: 'I walk slowly in the wind': this repetition is evocative of one dangling, slowly in the wind. Yet the stanza in which this line does not appear casts the longest shadow of despair:

Cold huts of iron stand upon this earth
like rusting prisons.
Each wall is marked and each wide roof is spread
like some dark wing
casting a shadow or a living curse.[38]

A shaft of light – hope not yet extinguished – does, however, penetrate this bleak landscape of the imagination. He can still recognise himself 'in years and days and words that mean so much', in the history of human achievement. He is still able to claim the fruits of universal effort and vision: 'strong hands that shake, long roads that walk'. But the voice is becoming less certain, almost singular as it extends a twig of hope: 'a voice in the soul, a laugh in the funny silence'.

On another level this walk 'slowly in the wind' becomes an older voice, a mature, circumspect one. He concludes: 'I walk because I cannot crawl or fly'. He will not go back to the 'nigger yard' where 'I crept on my hands and my knees'; nor will he return to the illusion of the 'kind eagle', which 'soars and wheels in flight', the messenger of infinite hope: 'All of a man can fly like a bird'. The steps are now tentative, measured, laboured.

But by 1956 politics in British Guiana was becoming 'an empty house' with the loss of Carter – he never joined another political party – and his ideals of bridges across rivers of incomprehension and the perfectibility of humankind. His slide into despair and virtual silence was becoming eloquent. Ian McDonald reflects on the source of the despair: '[he] felt especially deeply, with no self-seeking fervour, the promise of that dramatic time. Thus when the degeneration of ideals and values, and the pettiness and corruption, slowly but surely overwhelmed the promise, Martin Carter's fall into disillusion, and sometimes bitterness, was bound to be deep. His style has carried the mark of this ever since'.[39]

III
The Cauldron of Race and the Crafting of Despair and Bitter Hope, 1956-62

Gordon Rohlehr has observed that life in the West Indies is 'sufficiently chastening to temper most rhetoric into reticence'. In Carter's 'Poems of Shape and Motion', he believes that 'doubt' was 'much more movingly shaped into poetry than his earlier oratorical commitment'. Rohlehr sees an inevitability in this process as 'our lives will from generation to generation be denuded slowly into grief, tiredness and silence'.[40] One is tempted to counter this, in the case of Cheddi Jagan, with the assertion that the rhetoric flowered the more the politics degenerated into aggregations of racial insecurities. Indeed, in September 1955 Carter had already cautioned that dogmas masked reality and crippled thought in the PPP.

While Carter's hopes drained away as racism grew, Cheddi Jagan, in his confidential address to the PPP Congress in New Amsterdam ('behind closed doors'), in February 1956, denounced him and his colleagues, Rory Westmaas, Lionel Jeffrey and Keith Carter, Martin's older brother. It was not until 22 December 1956 that Jagan's speech was leaked to *The Daily Chronicle*. (He was confined to Georgetown, so the speech was read to Congress). Significantly, he was silent on Carter's preoccupation with the race issue, while noting that he was one who had sought to change the Party's line on the West Indies Federation; Carter was in favour of joining. The speech was cluttered with extensive quotes from 'Comrades' Lenin, Stalin and Mao Tse-Tung.

Ironically, he accused Carter and his friends of suffering from 'left deviationist tendencies', of behaving in 'a mechanistic fashion, copying wholesale revolutionary tactics and slogans of left parties' in the advanced capitalist countries. They had not bothered 'to study carefully our concrete conditions and historical state of development'. Jagan deprecated their 'indiscretions of youthful exuberance', concluding that 'this tendency to left deviationism and adventurism must be combated'.

Jagan quoted from 'Comrade' Mao to underline the damage done to the PPP by 'left dogmatists' such as Martin Carter, before the suspension of the Constitution:

> We allowed our zeal to run away with us; we became swollen-headed, pompous, bombastic... We were attacking everybody at the same time. We tended towards what Mao Tse Tung called 'all struggle and no unity'. This is how Comrade Mao Tse Tung attacks the left dogmatists who during the 10 years (1927-1937) civil war period advocated overthrowing everybody. He said: 'You cannot overthrow those in power, so you want to overthrow those who are not in power. They are already out of power, yet you still want to overthrow those who are not in power...'[41]

Whatever the manifestations of Carter's 'youthful exuberance' in the early 1950s, his 'ultra-leftism' as Jagan labels it in *The West on Trial* (1966), by 1956 he was definitely focused on the 'concrete conditions' – what he saw as the engulfing African/Indian racism, rendering the ideological certainties nugatory. Indeed, it was Jagan whose politics was becoming constipated with a surfeit of indigestible Marxist shibboleths – ponderous dogmas to paper over, to wish away the slide into the void of race. His zeal allowed him to virtually pose the question out of existence; the fact that the PPP was permeated by an essential Indianness could be made to seem not to be so. He could tell himself a lie and see it as truth.

But Carter did not fall for the empty words. He shut up. He was a school teacher between 1954 and 1959; he then joined the British firm, Booker, which had deep roots in sugar in British Guiana, as Chief Information Officer. It was he who was free from paralysis of thought encrusted in dogmatic certainties. He was pragmatic enough to move to a successful capitalist enterprise led by a progressive chairman, Jock Campbell (1912-1994), who from around 1950 had inspired Booker to try to sweeten the bitter legacy of sugar.

Between 1956 and 1960 Carter published no poems; no definitive piece of self-assessment or retrospective profundity came from his silent pen. The odd piece of prose, however, was reasoned: the idealism was gone; the voice was older; reflective; circumspect. In January 1958 in an article which epitomised his outlook, 'Sensibility and the Search', he argued that the Guyanese sensibility was rooted in slavery and colonialism. Only the transformation of that sensibility could deliver a new people, and that would come only if the history of slavery, of self-hate, is forged into a source of self-identity: history as midwife; the 'nigger yard' as an instrument of redemption. He elaborates:

> ... this is no easy task. It will call for the emergence of men of genius, men who by a gift of nature are able to assimilate the experience of their heritage and transform it into meaningful symbols and images, so that all of us, on looking at these symbols and images, will be looking into a mirror and seeing ourselves for the first time.[42]

The reasoned, measured tone is evident also in a response on the role of the artist in Guyana. This is from *Kyk-Over-Al*, May 1958: '... the job of the artist and intellectual in the West Indies is no different from the job of the artist and intellectual in every part of the world. We are concerned always with the human condition and the establishment of value. Everything is to be taken in the hand and transformed and given meaning'.[43]

In December 1960, possibly reflecting on his own drought of imagery but relentless in his belief that new poems could not be forced, Carter argued that the notion that young artists should be 'encouraged', was flawed: 'Too often it means that with the best intentions we praise what is third rate and omit to point out that Art requires talent – real talent, and not mere literacy – in any medium. I see no substitute for passion, internally generated, and hard work'.[44]

Carter's drought came to an end in 1961: seven poems, 'Conversation' appeared in *Kyk-Over-Al* in December. By then Guyanese politics was deeply mired in the sterility of racial one-upmanship: Jagan's PPP dominated by Indians; Burnham's PNC by Africans. Presumed ideological differences became a carnival of words, so many masks for the stasis. The elections of August 1957 were won by Jagan; Africans felt excluded from the promise. In March 1960, at the Constitutional Conference in London, the British had granted internal self-government to British Guiana, with the virtual guarantee of independence after elections to be held in August 1961. The posing of the fundamental question of the transfer of power to a Jagan government, kindled old fears of Indian domination, of the death of African political endeavour. Race was the motif of this 'nation' on the threshold of independence; but Jagan's Marxist rhetoric did not wilt, nor that of the party's organ, *Thunder*.

Indeed, by 1959-60 they were animated by a big cause: the Cuban Revolution with its potent symbol of a fresh communist millennium taking on American imperialism – David and Goliath. The hopes were unconquerable. But the PPP's new cause ignited their enemies' flagging hopes. America's fears could now become Burnham's also: anti-communism would be engaged to fetch the real fears of Africans, Portuguese, Coloureds, Chinese (even Amerindians), feeding the will to stall the Indian march to their political Everest. The disastrous American invasion of Cuba to overthrow Fidel Castro, at the Bay of Pigs (April 1961), lent urgency, a discernible panic, to President

Kennedy's anti-communist crusade. This reached British Guiana through the American 'Crusade for Freedom', during the elections of August 1961; but the virulent anti-communism could not stem another Jagan victory.

Indian triumphalism, in their country-wide victory parade led by Jagan, deepened the pain and fear of non-Indians. By late 1961, it seemed as if the marginal demographic superiority of Indians had sealed their political control of an independent Guyana.[45] From this sterility, Martin Carter's reluctant voice speaks: 'A poet cannot write for those who ask / hardly himself even, except he lies'.[46] Liars are eloquent. As if responding to the Marxist rhetoric of the PPP and the undammable invective of race – the death of reason and the futility of words – the poet speaks of trying to speak, of wanting to understand, but failing: 'I barked!':

Speaking with one on a pavement in the city
I watched the greedy mouth, the cunning eye
I reeled and nearly fell in frantic terror
seeing a human turn into a dog.

Recovering, I studied this illusion
and made a stupid effort to be strong:
I nodded and agreed and listened close.
But when I tried to utter words – I barked![47]

All are consumed by the nullity: the Guyanese journey to nowhere. The despair permeates 'Who can share?'[48] also. Politicians, 'loud men who cry freedom and are so full of lies', are lumped with prisoners who rot in jail and drunks who 'dance like shadows'. They are all imprisoned – the politician, poignantly, by deceit, 'so full of lies'. They all crave one thing – freedom, and seem to enjoin the poet in lamentation, 'shouting to God'; but he does not see how God can help them: 'only souls that blaze and burn can win' this freedom. Freedom has eluded all of them; a total rebirth must take place. The authentic voice of freedom is likened to 'true poems': '...we who want true poems/must all be born again, and die to do so'.[49] There could be no hope in the present charade: 'There is no short cut to integrity'.

The times cannot be rescued by words, by rhetorical power however optimistic, possibly an allusion to his own exhausted words of hope. As Carter frames it: 'Trying with words to purify disgust'. The poet's inviolable craft cannot brighten the vacuous slide, the emptiness of language, the corruption of motives, the death of dreams:

...it seems I was mistaken
to substitute a temple for a shop.

To see a shop and dream of holy temples
is to expect a toad to sing a song.[50]

Prophetically, at the end of 1961, Carter sees 'a sound of conflict in the sky'. He sees hope only in rebirth: 'I wish this world would sink and drown again / So that we build another Noah's ark'. The big lie is everywhere;

fear stalks the land ('The frightened lizard darts behind a stone'); and time is *not* on their side ('... now is the wild assault'). Only the flood, rebirth, renewal, promise freedom: he hopes they can then 'send another little dove to find / what we have lost in floods of misery'. Ironically the poem is called 'So that we Build'[51]: like the poet's words, chiselled and refined over time, the quest for truth, for integrity, is a delicate, difficult process; it is repelled by lies.

Many years later, in 1973, reflecting on the extent to which 'the light of understanding' was put out by lies; how the man who lies to himself cannot discover truth; how lies are the only things he becomes capable of apprehending, Carter wrote:

> ...what a man believes is contained within the significance of what he consistently does; so that though his declarations of belief may point in one direction, the belief-meaning of his consistent activity may well point in another. While the latter may make clear what he really believes, the former may just be a habit of expression of the codification into acceptable terms of practices that are indefensible.[52]

IV
'Jail Me Quickly': The Guyanese Futility, 1962-64

By late 1961 President Kennedy was depressed: his obsession with what he saw as the infectiousness of Castroism in Latin America, especially after the Bay of Pigs disaster, rendered Cheddi Jagan's victory in August 1961 portentous. As recently-released U.S. documents show, this obsession fell on British Guiana as well. This colony of lilliputian economic significance to America acquired enormous significance because of Jagan's communism – the latter having been confirmed during the Kennedy-Jagan meeting on 25 October 1961, in the White House. So that although the British were prepared to take a risk and grant independence to Jagan, the Americans, after his visit, moved swiftly towards his opponents in British Guiana, L. F. S. Burnham and Peter d'Aguiar, the Portuguese leader – anti-communist alternatives.

In February 1962 Burnham and d'Aguiar launched a campaign against the Jagan Budget, ostensibly because its compulsory savings and capital gains provisions were anti-working class. Most see it now as a strategy of Jagan's enemies to bring his government down. Some see the hands of American trade unionists in the amazing unanimity and involvement of the local trade unions in this violent anti-Jagan campaign. Agitated by Burnham and d'Aguiar, the predominantly African crowds burnt down and looted many of the key businesses in Georgetown on 16 February 1962, 'Black Friday'. Buoyed by American fear of communism, Africans (and Portuguese) were now trying to make the place ungovernable in order to cripple the inclination of the

British to give Jagan (Indians) independence. The racial situation had deteriorated to the point where it warrants this crude formulation.

Strangely, in the heat of the moment, Martin Carter sees in 'Black Friday 1962', the first poem in his 1964 collection[53], *Jail me Quickly*, possibilities for renewal:

... I was with them all,
when the sun and streets exploded,
and a city of clerks
turned a city of men!
Was a day that had to come,
ever since the whole of a morning sky,
glowed red like glory,
over the tops of houses.

Carter sees the events of 'Black Friday' as cathartic, as bringing to the open issues which had been submerged by the hopes of 1953, especially race, which had stifled those hopes and fed the split of 1955. Yet, as often in his work, these shoots of optimism are intertwined with the creeping bleak vision:

And I have seen some creatures rise from holes
and claw a triumph like a citizen,
and reign until the tide!

If Carter does not see his optimism as misplaced, he does see it as transitory, 'until the tide' comes up. And in this cauldron of racial suspicion and stammered vision, lies apprehension for the tentative shoots. The clawing of the fleeting triumph quickly descends to the tomb of despair – a prologue to the hate and sterile rage in British Guiana in 1963 and 1964:

Atop the iron roof tops of this city
I see the vultures practising to wait.
And everytime and anytime,
in sleep or sudden wake, nightmare, dream,
always for me the same vision of cemeteries, slow funerals
broken tombs, and death designing all.

In British Guiana, men in despair, even the brightest, would turn to rum; often to the whorehouse, where the drinking was more important. It was not uncommon for fading men of ideas to pontificate incoherently to the urgent rum and fallen women. Carter draws on this slide for the despair which settled on his sad country, as the potentially cleansing burnings of February 1962 degenerated into an orgy of racial slaughter: blood and mangled bodies, bloated corpses in the river, profound racial hate with its universal signature: rape. The African-Indian incomprehension, in 1963 and 1964, brought Carter to a position of utter futility, to the cemetery of his dreams:

I know this city much as well as you do,
the ways leading to brothels and those dooms
dwelling in them, as in our lives they dwell.
So jail me quickly, clang the illiterate door
if freedom writes no happier alphabet.[54]

He blames no one person, no ideology. Blame is collective: history will not absolve us. He had pointed out at the time of the February 1962 riots that it had 'deeper social and psychological undercurrents'. Like the anti-Portuguese riots of 1856 and 1889, it stemmed from the perceived rise, by Africans, of a new group in the 'direction of the masters'. The riots of 16 February 1962 in which many Indian businesses were burnt to the ground, were rooted in the perceived ascendancy of Indians, late-comers, who, even less than the Portuguese, 'developed on the sidelines of the traditional fabric of relationships'. In 1962, virtually at the end of Empire, Africans feared that Indians would inherit the political kingdom. Carter's conclusion then has not lost its relevance to Guyana nor its urgency:

> None of the groups in Guianese society is prepared to have any other group ruling it. Not until each group is confident that no other group will rule will there be real peace in this county.[55]

But, as so often in Carter's universe, despair's edge is softened by a trace of hope, a subtle possibility. One week after the riots on 16 February 1962, he could see good coming out of these events when '... a city of clerks / turned a city of men!' The race question could be faced squarely:

> It is now that, for the first time in the history of the country, we have a chance to initiate things, and to fashion them to our purpose. And without in the least condoning the tragic events of February 16 and their unhappy consequences, it may be, after all is said and done, that what happened on that day is certainly not the worst that could have happened to us in this time and age. For now, at the very least, we know what can happen. And also that the old days are gone forever. The new days are for us to make. Are we good enough?[56]

Carter felt that 'we are witnessing the transformation of a whole society'. As noted above, in the poem 'Black Friday 1962', he is prepared for the despair; he even finds something redeeming in it:

> True, was with them all,
> and told them more than once:
> in despair there is hope, but there is none in death.[57]

Out of the events of 1962 Carter envisaged some compromise – a halt to the slide into the racial morass. This did not happen. By 1963-64, as racial atrocity cascaded upon racial atrocity, his 1962 imagery of 'vultures practising to wait' could well be seen as the central note of his imagination in *Jail me Quickly*: the harvest of the stench. The shoots of hope have wilted in one short year. In 'After One Year' he is resigned to the racial futility of Guyana: 'Men murder men, as men must murder men / to build their shining governments of the damned'.

Carter recalls: 'I had become convinced that this country would not get anywhere because of the racial division'.[58] Imageries of futility permeate the 1964 poems: '...squandered daylight mocks my deep remorse / for seeds that rot, for interrupted love / and hours spent digging hopes out of a grave'.

This is a land of 'sharp entanglements' (racism and the ubiquitous barbed wires, in 1964); 'angry streets'; 'frightened stars'; 'bleeding houses'. The whole of the country's being speaks of this futility. The poems ask: 'What can a Man do More?', 'Where are Free Men?' The poet is asking: 'What is the point of the effort?':

> How utter truth when falsehood is the truth?
> How welcome dreams, how flee the newest lie?[59]

The dream is greater than the effort: 'where are free men?'. In dreams only:

> And what in dreams we do in life we attempt.
> But where are free men, where the endless streets?
> Since we were born our wings have had no rest
> Our prison of air is worse than one of iron![60]

The rage; the declamation; the sometimes arrogant, assertive hope; the circumspect, tentative, even fleeting optimism; the eloquent despair interlaced with shoots of optimism; the cynical, seemingly resigned, but magisterial insights: the 'mouth is always muzzled by the food it eats to live' and 'the shame is greater than the victory'; the futility; the eloquent silences; his repellence by mediocrity and passion for mastery of his craft – they are all of a piece. He could not be diminished by the acquired labels: 'left deviationist', 'ultra-leftist adventurer', 'leftist dogmatist'. Carter's silence spoke more of the diminished quality of the politics and the 'mechanistic fashion' of he who did the labelling. Writing in January 1958, on 'the meaning of writing and reading... to the human condition', the voice from the drought asks his readers to ponder the words of Salzberger:

> Genius, the agent of the dialectical process of history, has to transgress against the laws of moderation which govern the lives of ordinary men, in order to bring to a crisis the conflicts of his age and restore a healthy equilibrium.[61]

The title of Carter's article was 'Sensibility and the Search'. This quote, therefore, may well contain the definitive motive of his art; his politics also: to provoke to reason and reasonableness.

But one tends to forget that sobriety has a place in Carter's passion. As the Chief Information Officer of Jock Campbell's reforming Booker, a redeeming chapter in the dark record of sugar, in some way he helped to make life better for plantation workers. The bitterness of sugar had inspired the art. Campbell was inspired by Carter's poetry of the early 1950s; it must have illuminated his reforming spirit. Now the poet himself was helping to sweeten the bitterness of sugar in the land he has called 'materialistic and philistine'. The pragmatism of his life and the despair of the art, also, are of a piece.

In January 1965 he became editor of *Booker News* and in an editorial soon after, 'On being a Guianese', he commended to his countrymen the response on the subject of one of his compatriots, E. R. Braithwaite, author of *To Sir with Love*. Carter writes:

> ...Mr. Braithwaite reported a conversation he had in Trinidad with a Guianese resident there. After chatting a few minutes he was asked which side he would be on when he returned to B. G. His reply was that he would belong to the side of British Guianese who were concerned first and foremost with the unity of all Guianese. Mr. Braithwaite's reply, in the context of the recent unfortunate years, should be pondered deeply by all who live in Guiana and identify themselves with Guiana.[62]

At the bottom of his art this is what one finds: the dream to make his country a 'nation' – where truth and standards do matter. Instead he has become 'so weary with time' – always trying to 'flee the newest lie'.

The final word on Martin Carter must go to his friend since the early 1960s, David de Caires. Here is his assessment taken from his piece elsewhere in this book:

> Martin Carter is a large man in every sense of that word. With his strong, brooding presence and his eternal bitter hope he has always represented for many of us a challenge to keep going and to do what we can and a proof of the enormous potential and possibilities in our Caribbean region. His bitterness and despair have been a measure of his hope. In his various undertakings, his trials and tribulations, his long depression he has retained a quality of spiritual integrity without which we would all have been much poorer.[63]

That is why this gifted, paradoxical man's work can transcend the politics, the time, the place, the people: the imagery is not strained; the statements are universal; the craft has been laboured at and refined; the effort springs from integrity.

Notes

1. The *New Daily Chronicle*, 3 July 1927.
2. Edgar Mittelholzer, *A Swarthy Boy* (London: Putnam, 1963), pp. 155-56.
3. Ian McDonald, 'Foreword', *Martin Carter Selected Poems* ([Georgetown]: Red Thread Women's Press, 1997, revised edition), p.22. Beyond here all references to this book are rendered thus: *Selected Poems*.
4. In 1989 Carter observed: '... when slavery was abolished in 1834 the greatest impact on the population in the sense of language was from the Bible because of the missionaries... So you would find in [the] speech of places like Guyana a tremendous influence of the patterns and vocabulary of the Old and New Testament and I must say of course that one could hardly find a better form to learn from', *Kyk-Over-Al*, No.44, (May 1993) ['A Martin Carter Prose Sampler', Nigel Westmaas (ed.)], p.144. Throughout this essay I have relied heavily on this excellent collection.
5. *The Times* [London], 20 August 1962. See also the issue of 16 August 1962 (Obituary).
6. See note 3.

7. A. J. Seymour, 'The Biography of a Magazine', *Kyk-Over-Al*, Nos. 46/47, (December 1995), p.18.
8. *PAC Bulletin*, No.1, (6 November 1946).
9. Maurice St. Pierre, *Anatomy of Resistance: Anti-Colonialism in Guyana, 1823-1966* (London: Macmillan Caribbean, 1999)
10. Cheddi Jagan, *The West on Trial: My Fight for Guyana's Freedom* (London: Michael Joseph, 1966), p.95.
11. See note 9.
12. Frank Birbalsingh, 'Interview with Martin Carter', *Kyk-Over-Al*, Nos. 46/47, (December 1995), p.218.
13. *Selected Poems*, p.39.
14. *PAC Bulletin*, No.27, 20 June 1948: 'At 3pm [on 17 June] the procession reached the cemetery. Here the human factor broke loose from its temporary prison and just stared you in the face and tore at your heart. Relatives and widows cried and wailed ... on May 7 the Central Demerara representative in the Legislative Council [Cheddi Jagan] tabled a notion asking for the appointment of a Committee to enquire into the dispute, the working and living conditions and into the profits of the Proprietors. Repeated attempts were made to get the Labour Dept. and the Govt. to intervene. The Labour Commission, however, in Olympian aloofness refused to admit that there was a strike...' (Eusi Kwayana [Sydney King] told me that he wrote this article.)
15. *Selected Poems*, p.36.
16. See 'Not I with this Torn Shirt', *Selected Poems*, p.33.
17. *Ibid*. See also 'Three Years After This' (Enmore), *Selected Poems*, p.38.
18. 'Listening to the Land', *Selected Poems*, p.42.
19. 'A Banner for the Revolution', *Selected Poems*, p.43.
20. 'I Stretch my Hand', *Selected Poems*, p.49.
21. *Selected Poems*, p.64.
22. 'The Kind Eagle, *Selected Poems*, p.63.
23. Rupert Roopnaraine, 'Martin Carter and Politics', *Sunday Stabroek* [Guyana], 8 June 1997. For a broader reading of Carter's poetry, beyond the politics, as reflected in one poem, 'You are Involved', see Roopnaraine, *Web of October: Rereading Martin Carter* (Leeds: Peepal Tree Press, 1988).
24. *Selected Poems*, pp.96-98.
25. *Report of the British Guiana Constitutional Commission, 1954* (Sir James Robertson, chairman), Cmd. 9274 (London: HMSO, 1954), p.36.
26. St. Pierre, *op. cit.*
27. 'This is the Dark Time my Love', *Selected Poems*, p.94.
28. 'I am no Soldier', *Selected Poems*, p.80. The other reference to Accabreh is in 'I Clench my Fist' (p.95):

    British soldier, man in khaki
    careful how you walk.
    My dead ancestor Accabreh
    is groaning in his grave.
    At night he wakes and watches
    with fire in his eyes

Because you march upon his breast
and stamp upon his heart.

29. Leader, *Thunder*, 28 August 1954 (*Kyk-Over-Al*, No.44, p.46).
30. Rory Westmaas, 'The People against Imperialism', *Thunder*, 8 May 1954.
31. Carter,'Politics and the Individual', *Thunder*, 12 February 1955 (*Kyk-Over-Al*, No.44, p.48).
32. Leader, *Thunder*, 5 March 1955 (*Ibid.*, p.51).
33. Leader, *Thunder*, 10 September 1955 (*Ibid.*, p.69).
34. Martin Carter, 'The Racists among Us', *Thunder*, 24 September, 1955.
35. See *Selected Poems*, pp.103-106.
36. 'Shape and Motion One', *Selected Poems*, p.103.
37. See note 31. This quote is from p.49.
38. 'Shape and Motion Three', *Selected Poems*, p.105.
39. See note 3. The quote is from p.24.
40. F. G. Rohlehr, 'West Indian Poetry: Some Problems of Assessment (Part Two)', *Bim*, No.55 (July-December 1972), p.144.
41. Jagan confirmed that the PPP was a communist-led party, as the British and the Robertson Commission had argued:

    Our party is unique in the history of national movements: from its very inception it as under left-wing, Marxist-inspired leadership, uncompromisingly championing the cause of the working class. The right wing, representing the middle and professional class and native capitalists, was in the distinct minority (*The Daily Chronicle*, 22 December 1956).
42. Carter, 'Sensibility and the Search', *The Daily Argosy*, 26 January 1958 (*Kyk-Over-Al*, No.44, p.80).
43. *Kyk-Over-Al*, No.23, (May 1958), p.20.
44. *Kyk-Over-Al*, No.27, (December 1960), p.106.
45. See the following for politics in British Guiana in the late 1950s-early 1960s: Jagan, *op. cit.* [1966]; Peter Simms, *Trouble in Guyana* (London: George Allen and Unwin, 1966); Thomas J. Spinner, *A Political and Social History of Guyana, 1945-83* (Boulder, Colorado: Westview Press, 1984); Maurice St. Pierre, *op. cit.* The latter is the most comprehensive on the role of the Americans.
46. 'They say I am', *Selected Poems*, p.109.
47. 'Groaning in this Wilderness', *Ibid.*, p.110.
48. *Ibid.*, p.111.
49. See note 46.
50. *Selected Poems*, p.112.
51. *Ibid.*, p.113.
52. Martin Carter, 'If a Man Lies to Himself, the World will Lie to Him!' (April 1973), *Kyk-Over-Al*, No.44, p.84.
53. 'Black Friday 1962', *Selected Poems*, pp.117-118.
54. 'After One Year', *Ibid.*, p.119.
55. Martin Carter, 'Recent Events Spring from Social Undercurrents', *The Daily Chronicle*, 23 March 1962 (*Kyk-Over-Al*, No.44, p.83).
56. *Ibid.*
57. See note 53. The quote is from p.118.
58. See note 12. The quote is from p.223.

59. 'What can a Man do More?', *Selected Poems*, p.120.
60. 'Where are Free Men?', *Ibid.*, p.121.
61. See note 42.
62. *Booker News*, 5 March 1965.
63. David de Caires, 'A Measure of his Hope', in this volume.

RUPERT ROOPNARAINE

MARTIN CARTER AND POLITICS

'His poetry was not a political instrument, but his politics was an expression of his poetry'
Eusi Kwayana

Look, look, she cried, the poems man
running across the frail bridge
of her innocence.
Martin Carter

From the beginning to the end, above and beyond all else, Martin Carter was the poems man. At once curse and consolation, voyage and refuge, poetry was his first and ultimate duty. When he finally turned his back on the streets, soon after the civil rebellion of 1979 and the murders of Father Darke and Walter Rodney, he embraced the pure practice of poetry as the only available practice for a seeker of truth in an era of degradation. He turned inwards and so did the poems. In the end, the truth of craft was all.

So if we now turn our attention to the narrow subject of how Martin Carter functioned as a political activist of the independence class struggle, it is in order to add another dimension to our understanding of the relationship between his poetry and his politics. That the poetry was throughout infused with the political, that the force that drove the poems drove the politics, has nowhere been better argued than in the 1984 essay, 'The Politics of the Heart,' [*Anales del Caribe,* 4-5/1984-85], by Eusi Kwayana, one of his closest comrades of the first hour and a loyal friend through the years. Kwayana writes: 'It is hardly to be expected that an intelligent poet living in a period of social upheaval will be aloof from it and unaffected by it, whether or not he chooses to be, or is chosen as, an actor in it, especially in the best traditions of the art,' Kwayana makes clear that he has in mind the Psalmists, Shakespeare, Dante, Byron, Shelley. Kwayana is right to stress the unity of thought, vision and practice underpinning Carter's activities, all interlocking facets of a single wholeness of being. It is, he says, 'Carter's naked sensibility, rather than his ideology that makes him both political and poetic.'

Those who listened to him on the public platform in the 1950s and paid attention to his writings, lectures and discussions over the years remember the thoughtfulness of his presentations, their 'peculiar meanings' (Kwayana). Eric Huntley, a fellow prisoner and rebel of the time, recalls the unsuccessful New Amsterdam campaign of 1953, when Carter was chosen as the candidate in the toughest constituency for the party, up against the town's favourite son, Mr Rudy Kendall, a conservative: 'He soon realised that there was no chance of his winning and therefore set about converting an election campaign into the People's University Square. Meetings at street corners became centres where Plato and the ideas of Toussaint L'Ouverture of Haiti were eagerly imbibed.' It seems that he used the Campaign to deepen human relations and to educate people, where necessary, into thinking. This educating people into the habit of thinking may well be his most enduring contribution to politics. He had resigned from the civil service to stand as a candidate and never sought to get back into it after losing the election. This allowed him to play an important part in the formulation and proclamation of party attitudes and policy. He made a strong impact on the workers and youth. Kwayana noted a method: 'Martin Carter would never seek to engage his hearers at the level of mere bread. He hated bread-lessness because with its absence people became more absorbed in hunting for it. He knew that in the long run there would be no human thought or creation without food... he would pose to his audience the most difficult question of the relation between ideas and concepts and life and he would glory in the answers he received, examine them and try to learn from them.'

As early as February 12, 1955, we find him applying himself to the fundamental issue: what does it mean to be political? He writes in one of his editorials (entitled 'Politics and the Individual') in *Thunder,* the organ of the People's Progressive Party:

> Of course, it must be stated here that whether the individual likes it or not, he begins taking part in politics from the day that he is born. Here it is only a matter of direct or indirect, positive or negative, conscious or unconscious activity. For the sake of clarity however, the word politics is used in a direct, positive, conscious and purposive sense.

But to return. From the argument above, it can be seen that far from politics being a hindrance to individual development, it is in fact the means whereby the individual may release himself and others from a crippling social environment. For political activity is not an end in itself, but only a means to an end, the end of social change.

Already, as early as 1955, the Carter manner announces itself; notably in the stubborn precisions of the writing and the rhythmic movement of mind. Thought itself is cadenced, musical even as it stalks the truth. The idea that human activity is political activity, that we are as condemned to the political as we are to the language inside of which we live is a familiar one. It was the creed of a generation of radical intellectuals in the Paris of the Second World War. The Editorial pursued its logic where it led. Politics, it argued, is as open to corruption as any other human activity, even more so:

> Of course people can corrupt anything and politics is no exception. As a matter of fact, because of its importance, politics attracts the best and the worst of men. What is necessary then, is that no one should confuse politics as a social instrument for politics as a social disease.

I am not alone among political activists of the Rodney generation who share Carter's contempt for the degraded notion of the 'politician', the successful one. After the narrowing circles of abstraction, he homes in to the heart of the matter in his very next *Thunder* Editorial, and exposes a grave weakness of the people:

> Because politics concerns everybody everybody has something to say about it. One very popular idea in this country, as in other countries, is that to be successful, a politician must be dishonest, must be tricky, smart, slick; must know to say one thing and mean something else, and do something absolutely different from what is said or meant. No one can deny, of course, that politicians by their words and deeds have done everything to create such an attitude of suspicion among the people.

And because it is Carter who is trying to come to grips with a human phenomenon which is not simply to be scorned and rejected, but to be understood, he goes on in the Editorial to examine it in its historical development. It is an orthodox materialist explanation. Locating the original dislocation in the arrival of slavery which broke the 'human grouping', he goes on to pull aside the politician's 'painted mask'.

> But why is it that politicians find it necessary to hide their real motives and intentions? Certainly not because they are ashamed of them; not because in themselves they are repulsive. Politicians hide their real motives and intentions because they want people whose interests may be different from theirs to support them, because they dare not show the cards in their hands, lest the people reject them. So rather than being open and clear, or unrealistic as they say, be smart and tricky and realistic as they say, and success will be inevitable.

So what manner of political activist was Martin Carter? What is most well-known is quickly told: an Executive Member of the original PPP, he was arrested, tried and jailed at the US Atkinson Field Airbase with other leading PPP militants (Sydney King, Rory Westmaas, Ajodha Singh and Bally Latchmansingh) after a demonstration during the state of emergency when Dr. Jagan was arrested in Mahaica for breaching the restriction order after the October 1953 invasion. Along with other comrades, he was jailed again a few months after being released from Atkinson Field, this time at Camp Street prison where he once worked as secretary to the governor. Not for the last time in the democratic revolution, police harassment, court trials and imprisonment were the order of the day for many of the front-line fighters, including Carter.

Close colleagues have testified that he did not babble in Executive Committee meetings and spoke only when necessary, that his contributions were always fully analytical, including practical knowledge of the people. He would always pose the issues in a debate and then proceed to make deductions. He was very active in the Executive Committee and editorial work of the party's newspaper. His editorials, which were signed at one stage, were outstanding both for structure and depth. He had a talent for invective and a fine sense of scorn: *'Starting off as a young war correspondent, he ended up as an old warmonger, betraying a consistency in this field which no one can deny.'* This of Churchill. *'In such surroundings moral principles are as stray dogs in a butcher shop.'* This of 'capitalistic and colonial society.'

Between 1950 and 1953 he and a few others did most of the party educational work in weekend classes. They worked along the coast. An important highlight of this was their study of the landlord system in the rice farming village of Golden Fleece, Essequibo. In this study and teaching, the young activist was getting down to the anatomy of the estate system on the Essequibo coast. The activists found that there were elements of feudalism alive and well, that often the landlord was the miller and the shopkeeper as well as the moneylender. Carter's righteous anger at these conditions was not ideological in the narrow sense. These were among the discoveries and experiences he accumulated while doing political work off the platform while he was still a public servant. He taught with conviction the part played by labour in production. His scheme was not merely Marxist, but one reinforced with Carterian thought permeated with Guyanese history and experience. Yes, Carterian. It is that distinctive.

He earns six mentions in Dr. Cheddi Jagan's celebrated account of the events of those turbulent years, *The West on Trial.* He first enters its pages as 'among the more ideologically developed party leaders (Sydney King, Martin Carter, Rory Westmaas, Fred Bowman, Eric Huntley) who had taken my side during "crisis week".' A few pages on, we find his name on the honour roll of the Robertson Commission, set up by the British to examine the state of the factious colony and duly boycotted by the PPP. He is named in the Commission's Report as among the 'at least six of the Party's most promising leaders' – the others were Dr Jagan, Mrs Jagan, Sydney King, Rory Westmaas and Brindley Benn – who 'accepted unreservedly the 'classical' communist doctrines of Marx and Lenin, were enthusiastic supporters of the policies and practices of modern communist movements.' Later on, he is part of the group which, in company with Dr Jagan, boycotts the historic Metropole Congress in February 1955 where the party suffered its first split. By the time we meet him again in the pages of the *West on Trial,* he is in bad odour. He is among a group – Rory Westmaas and Lionel Jeffrey are other named culprits – who have not heeded Dr Jagan's warning to 'guard against right and left deviationism and opportunism': 'These comrades,' writes Dr Jagan, 'through the Demerara Youth League and the B.G. Peace Committee, had taken some 'ultra-left' positions which opened the party to unnecessary criticisms and attacks from both the opposition and from the right-wing of the party.' Other crimes were dredged up, even those committed in the early pre-split days: 'In 1953, they had taken part in May Day demonstrations displaying banners of Stalin, and, contrary to the advice of the party, had picketed Princess Alice on her visit in 1952 with anti-British slogans such as 'Limey Go Home'.' Disagreements with the party line on nonviolence and civil disobedience during the occupation and on the question of the West Indies Federation were further aggravations to Dr Jagan. The 'ultra-left' split followed soon after the 1955 split. It is the last we hear of Martin Carter in the *West On Trial*. Out of the party, out of the narrative. It was the first of his two large political disillusionments.

In the period of political inactivity which followed and lasted for several years, Carter turned inwards and engaged in a long bout of self-interrogation. During this period, he took himself into the belly of the beast and worked as Information Officer and editor of the house organ for the multinational Bookers. Kwayana comments on this interlude: 'He at all times kept up a relationship with his old comrades and used his time to make a careful study of the multinational with whom he worked for a living.' He came back on to the barricades in 1962, on the side of what began as the workers' rebellion against the Kaldor Budget. To the consternation of many progressive people then and since then, he celebrated the energy let loose on the streets that Black Friday, day of riot and rebellion, 'when the sun and streets exploded,' when 'a city of clerks/turned a city of men.'

Re-invigorated by the new motion, he resumed activity in the nationalist movement, attended the pre-independence Constitutional Conference in London in 1965 and, after independence, served on the Guyana delegation to the United Nations in 1967. He returned to Guyana to join the PNC government as a technocrat Minister of Information, a position he held from 1968 to 1970. He was the Minister when Mr Burnham announced the discovery of Beria, an alleged Venezuelan spy, and chaired the Press Conference which escalated the hostile feelings between Venezuela and Guyana. Commenting on his new alignment, Kwayana writes: 'He did not lose face with those who knew him when he agreed to be Minister of Information in Burnham's government. The mood of the chief spokesman was very forward looking, with ideas of breaking through to the interior, the pioneer spirit, the cooperative movement, and especially the feeling that they were going to let a thousand flowers bloom.' Carter saw himself as an agent of reconciliation at a moment of maximum tension and deep division:

> The whole situation has to be carefully looked at. You had the racial conflict, very serious, this was the time of the riots, and your whole attitude was one of bringing about a sort of reconciliation between the races, between the Indian and the Negro... It was a touch and go situation at that time. I thought that anything that could bring about a defusion of tension was worth fighting for, because no one who had not lived out here could have imagined what was going on at that time. Then the very trees almost failed to sprout.

A high point of his tenure as Minister of Information was the February 1970 Caribbean Writers and Artists Conference held as part of the celebrations to mark the founding of the Cooperative Republic. We are indebted to Andrew Salkey, one of the prime movers of the Conference, for the vivid images he has left us of:

> the most relaxed and *simpatico* Minister of Government ever to appear in a Cabinet in the Caribbean, and ever to lead a cultural vanguard, anywhere, in the Area... He stood there, chatting to us and the invited audience of library officials and their guests, and looking, for all the world, like a romantic, imagist poet, hopped out of the fire and, now, dead centre in the flying pan. His words were tellingly chosen; his person, a gentle, tall, big man, a poet who may yet do a very serious injury to the sterile vocabulary and syntax of bureaucracy.

Even as he anticipated with relish Martin's subversion of the ministerial image, through which he 'would have emerged as the pioneer rediscoverer of the long-lost beating heart in anybody's politics,' Salkey hints darkly and, as it happened, prophetically, at the dangers awaiting the poet who dares to venture into the political arena; 'Yet,' he writes, 'who doesn't know how that ancient art of the possible tends to destroy the revolutionary poet who dares to change its atavistic brutishness into an effective human theory and practice?'

His sudden resignation in 1969 from the Ministry and government was dramatic. He made the famous poetic statement that 'the mouth is muzzled by the food it eats to live' which became almost a banner the moment it hit the Sunday press and is still quoted by contemporaries of his. His personal politics did not allow him to go on a campaign, but his friends knew and everyone sensed that it was aimed against manipulation and a level of corruption. The regime had just taken its first step on the road to absolute power. Twenty-two years of rigged elections were to follow, too many of them years of ruthless and even murderous repression.

His break with the Burnham regime marked Carter's second great disillusionment with the political leadership. He left the public stage but remained a powerful and influential public voice. Strangely, the more withdrawn he became, the more his authority seemed to grow, emerging at moments of illumination in mysterious, even oracular utterances. His lectures and writings over this period continued to reflect deeply on the society, chronicling its degradations and its fall into darkness and violence. He was happy to leave the battle against 'principalities and powers' to others. There were enough of us in the political struggle. Instead, recoiling from 'the treason of the spirit, ...the culture of petty deception, of trade off, sometimes of the traffic of another to the paymaster, all too noticeable among the upwardly mobile groups and those of broken faith... His battle is not merely against principalities and powers... As a poet he does not as a priority join the queue against those foes. In a way his fire is concentrated on their props, those weaknesses which make the road of an oppressor less dangerous: the self-pity, the self-hate, the meanness of rivals, the self-demotion of man, the subtleties of the lie and the many deceptions that form a big part of the interchange in human commerce. No wonder he resorts to intimate conversations with the wind, tuning each visible star into a chrysalis.' (Kwayana).

He was drawn to the streets by the mass protests and demonstrations against the Referendum of 1978 and was beaten for his pains, outside the Parliament Buildings. The outrageous attack on the person of Martin Carter that day at that place sent shock-waves through the Caribbean and had the effect of putting the region and the world on the alert: Guyana was becoming a dangerous land. He came out again exactly one year later, in the July 1979 demonstration outside the Magistrates Court when Walter Rodney, Omawale and I were charged with arson. [The Ministry of National Development and Office of the General Secretary of the PNC – a hated symbol of party paramountcy – had burned to the ground on the night of the first anniversary of the Referendum]. It was the demonstration when Fr. Bernard Darke, the photographer of the *Catholic Standard,* was stabbed in the back with a bayonet, in broad daylight, outside the Brickdam Police Station, a stone's throw from the Parliament Building. The murder of the priest drove him to the poem 'Bastille Day – Georgetown', and to his famous 'Open Letter to the People of Guyana', published in the WPA's *Dayclean Special* of July 1979, where he spoke of his role as citizen in a degraded society. It was his most comprehensive and direct indictment of the PNC regime in the last years of Mr Burnham:

> Like all other regimes of similar character, the PNC's main preoccupation is self-perpetuation. In principle the pre-occupation with self-perpetuation is understandable, since it accords with the fundamental idea of self-preservation. But while a truly democratic regime would try to ensure self-perpetuation by acting in a way such as would make it acceptable and needed by people, what does the PNC, which poses as socialist, actually do?
>
> The PNC's method of ensuring self-perpetuation consists of indulging in a deliberate policy of degrading people. And the reasoning behind this is that degraded people are incapable of effective resistance.

He goes on to give examples of the degradation:

> the rigging of elections in which many ordinary and by no means vicious people were cajoled into doing indecent things, and were thereby compromised. In corruption as a way of life, in which people were made to accept that stealing, cheating, lying, bearing false witness, informing on each other was a positive sign of loyalty to the regime; was what was expected of them, and were thereby further compromised...

He indicted the regime for the violence unleashed on the minds of the people through the

> rigidly controlled mass media, in which the very language used is perversion, facts falsified; threats against individuals and groups openly advertised; internal events of significance ignored; local events of significance suppressed; all contributing to the whole process of assault on moral and intellectual honesty, one end of which is to make mental independence a crime, and mental subservience to the regime the highest qualification in the land.

He saw that the greatest damage done was to the young people,

> who are led to believe that they can do anything, no matter how selfish, how

intolerant, how mindless, how coarse, since they identify this attitude with the attitude the regime underwrites.

The result is the warp of personality, the degradation of the spirit that is so much abroad in the society.

The 'Open Letter' of 1979 was a cry from the heart and a summons to resistance in the heady, danger-filled days of the civil rebellion. To us, combatants on the streets, it was validation, comradeship of a high order from a revered elder of the movement, encouragement in the truest sense of inspiring with courage. His response was not surprising to those of us who experienced the quality of his friendship. He has always been on the side of the fighting people, energised anew by every sign of their reawakening. It was to be the last revival of his spirit. 'The WPA,' he told an interviewer, 'made a change in this country. It made people aware that the world is a much bigger place than it seemed from the vantage point of Guyana, the WPA did very great work in this country.'

He was an early evangelist of national unity and ethnic reconciliation. And as the racial temperature rises around us in this bitter season, we would do well to pay the most careful attention to his findings. From among his many words on our most self-defeating division, I have chosen the following paragraphs which, though long, deserve to be quoted in full. They were written in March 1955, in a *Thunder* Editorial, after the split, as the masses of the people were polarising into their racial camps:

The PPP succeeded in uniting the people of Guyana because it showed that only unity among themselves would make them strong enough to fight the imperial government effectively. This was demonstrated at the General Elections when PPP candidates of African descent won seats in decidedly Indian constituencies against Indian candidates. That means if the people would only understand the major issue of the people's struggle against imperialism some good will be won. Thus it would be better for a person of Indian descent to support Mr Burnham for ideological reasons than for the same person while agreeing with Mr Burnham to support Dr Jagan only because he happens to be an Indian. The same holds good for a person of African descent. For this would mean that the action was dictated by reason and not by racialism. In the long run reason would lead to the truth while racialism would lead to a disaster.

There is no separate salvation for Indians in Guiana, no separate salvation for Africans. There is only salvation for a united Guianese people fighting as a people against imperialism and for National Independence. Let those who advocate racialism in any form among the people confute this.

Martin Carter contributed not only to the quantity of the national movement but to its quality. He educated us into the habit of thinking and proposed for our consideration a politics of decency rooted in the moral sense. Kwayana, finally: 'His politics comprises a general fury against all the forces, material and spiritual, subjective and objective, whether they are of the oppressor, of the oppressed, or of the groups between the oppressors and oppressed, which conspire against the human personality... For this reason he feels safer and less humiliated with acts of rebellion than with acts of surrender, even if these acts of rebellion are misconceived. It is enough for Martin as the beginning of wisdom to see the human spirit in an insurrectionary march against its own paralysis.'

The day we buried him at the Place of Heroes, before now reserved for Heads of State, the streets of the city were tense and teeming with angry protesters. Georgetown was once again in a state of turmoil following the controversial declaration of the 1997 election results. A roving band surrounded the entrance to the church compound where the funeral service was being conducted, thinking that the enemy was inside. Their chants rang out during the service. Some said it was a disgrace. I did not think he would have minded.

Cambridge, February 1998

THE LITERARY CONTEXTS

IVAN VAN SERTIMA

FROM ASTRIDE TWO VISIONS

If I were asked to name the two men who have had the most profound effect upon the thinking life of my generation, my community, I would not pause. There is no doubt in my mind as to who have thrown the longest shadows over the social and spiritual landscape of Guyana in the fifties and sixties. But before I commit myself I would like to say I want to enshrine no man as God or hero. I have no intention of erecting new monoliths, which, revolutionary and liberating as they may be at one stage, frozen into idols, prove tyrannical and oppressive in the end. I see these men more as agents through which something in the consciousness or unconsciousness of the community found its most dynamic expression.

These two men then to whom I refer, these great shadows and influences, are our ex-Prime Minister, Dr Cheddi Jagan, and our poet and novelist, Wilson Harris. To many this may seem an incongruous coupling – and in one sense it is – for these two men are far removed in the nature of their commitment and vocation, in the nature too and range of their capacity and impact. The effect of the one on the Guyanese community has been immediate and shattering, the effect of the other not so demonstrable, yet in the lives of the poets and men of sensibility of my time, it has been very marked and deep. To use an old metaphor, it has been like seed growing in the dark secret husk of the earth. To use a bolder, more original and more apt one, it has been like an underground nuclear device exploded in slow motion.

I will use these two men therefore – the vision of these two men – as poles or points of focus in my talk. For no Guyanese poetry in the last fifteen years – I mean, no significant Guyanese poetry – has come out of us, untouched by the repercussions of the bombs dropped upon our external and internal institutions by these two men. I myself have had the good or ill fortune to be caught on both occasions in what our nuclear scientists would describe as 'the annihilating blast area' of the bombs.

Annihilating, because like the man at Hiroshima, vaporised and photographed in an instant, I was left with only a stain or shadow of my former personality after both blasts. When I saw and heard Dr Jagan – I was only sixteen them – his stare and his voice startled me. The light in his eyes under the street lamps made him look like a mad dog. His voice grated and barked. It was harsh, violent with sincerity. And he spoke for hours, three hours without drawing breath. It was the monster of fury itself unleashed from a bitter century in those canefields. The effect of that voice and these eyes upon my impressionable soul was devastating. I went home from that meeting in a blaze.

And from one day to the next, as though that blaze had consumed a whole outer skin of childhood attitudes, all my major relations changed. My relations within my own home, my relations with my school, my teachers, my fellow-pupils. I would like to say what I mean by that in a little more intimate detail, not out of a desire to make public scandal of my family life, but because I want to give personal witness to the impact of Jagan upon the thought and life of a young man like myself in the fifties. Further, because what had touched and burnt me then was soon to become fire that would fall like rain over the consciences of youth everywhere in that country.

I was, until then, in desperate search of a father. Mine seemed to be moving away from me, breaking up before my eyes into an impotent and unexplainable rage every night and day. He was one of Guyana's foremost labour leaders. But a benign Dr Jekyll among the workers, he took on the features of a fiend and a Hyde in our home. His endless attacks on his enemies, real and imagined, kept us awake half the night. And in reaction to this – this hysterical dementia – I spat on his heroes – his Tom Paine, his Webbs and his Shaw, his Engels and his Marx. I saw them as secreters of some strange virulent poison that had deranged him. His political commitment, his sacrifices, at the expense of myself and my family, had seemed, until then, irresponsible and absurd. It was only when I saw and heard that demon from the backlands, Cheddi Jagan, that it made any sense at all.

[...]

Jagan stands discredited by many today, half-forgotten in the world outside, perhaps. I do not stand here to make a defence or apology for his years of administration. But what I do know is that in those early years he acted as a catalyst for the very best in our community. Men like my father, working in frustrated isolation for a quarter of a century, suddenly saw the disconnected fragments of the working class finally fusing. The People's Progressive Party, under Cheddi Jagan, united the urban and agricultural proletariat and the intelligentsia of that country. Race was no issue then. Class interest, ideological interest was all that mattered. And the men closest to Jagan, far closer than any of the East Indian leaders could be, were the militant African intellectuals. Never before in our history had we known such unity, such certainty, such hope. On that first evening in April, 1953, when we swept the polls and the whole town turned out, running and crying and singing in the streets, we felt then what the Haitians must have felt in their first ecstasy and flush of revolution. None of us was fool enough to believe such ecstasy could last but none of us, not even our enemies, could have dreamt that it would have ended so lamentably.

It has been said that our unity was no true unity, that what Jagan headed was a coalition of disparate elements. But a coalition does not negate a unity and there is no political union in any society, however homogeneous, that is not a coalition or coalescence of disparate elements. The point at issue was whether there was a genuine common ground to give credence and solidity to this coalescence of elements. That ground existed and it lay not only in a common enemy but, at its base, in common interests. A few peripheral elements, I have no doubt, could have fallen away as the movement and struggle entered another phase but the solidarity of the base elements – the African and Indian working class – was very real and profound. No one who witnessed, as I did, the sheer unbelief, the sense of shock and loss that smote African workers and Indian peasants alike after news of the great split, can question this. Such indeed was the feeling and conviction and vision of unity among Indians and Africans that they positively refused to believe in the reality of the split. Only those on the outside and a few in the inner sanctums of the Party took the news at its face value. Two years after it happened (and Jagan and Burnham were beginning to attack each other openly in the streets) the mass of Indians and Africans believed that they were still solidly united in secret but were only acting out some high-level diplomatic game of division to trick the British Government into relaxing its iron hold upon the country.

In other words, it was the division that seemed false and frail to the masses, not their unity, which remained for some time in suspension until that division hardened into an irrevocable and inescapable fact. Those who were not steeped in the heart of that time will blame our leaders for their fatal blindness and weakness. How could they, the jury of history will ask, let an opportunity like that, which may never come again this century, slip past? How could they betray the longing, the readiness, the capacity of the masses for such an essential marriage? Some will speak of the unbending extremism of Jagan, others will point to the private ambition of Burnham. But Jagan made many compromises. And Burnham beat his breast for months (sometimes in my father's drawing-room) paralysed and tormented at the thought of what it would mean if he did what he was being pressured and persuaded, against his own better instincts, to do.

That pressure was immense. The British Government made it clear in their white paper, and later spelled it out even more clearly through their agents... that they intended to disenfranchise Dr. Jagan, to disenfranchise all those who remained beside him, that they would never allow that party to go to the polls again, if its leadership remained unchanged. And then, to allow Burnham grace to organise at Jagan's expense, they left all his close colleagues free to go about as they pleased while they constantly harassed, imprisoned, searched, raided, and confiscated the books, records and correspondence of Jagan and his associates. Thus did they simultaneously threaten and seduce Mr. Burnham.

A great silence settled on that country for four years. One Black Friday morning the Chief Secretary, in his most unctuous tones, announced that THEY had decided to turn the clock back and WE would therefore have to mark time. It was in that period when our hope was made to stand dead like time itself trapped in a cell that my generation grew to manhood.

It was a reign of quiet terror. People who said brave things once turned on their words in fear. Reactionary politicians, beaten overwhelmingly at the polls, were nominated to rule over the people who had rejected them. All meetings were banned, literature seized and burnt, telephones tapped, mail opened, men detained indefinitely without charge or trial. Treachery to the spirit of the past became the means of survival.

But there were those who kept fresh for us the anger and high purpose of our yesterdays. The voice of the poet, Martin Carter, rang out in the darkness of that time 'like a blacksmith's hammer on its anvil when the morning is calm'. Martin had an enormous appeal to the youth of our country. The leading Party intellectual, it was he who had drafted the PPP manifesto. He was the first to be put away when the soldiers and the warships came. His poems from prison stirred and haunted us. Most of these poems, I feel, so blood-fresh and striking when they first appeared, have lost much of the urgency and magic with which they were once imbued when chanted by workers of a past decade. There are one or two, however, which transcend the time, which can never be forgotten, never be dated, such as his 'University of Hunger' which evokes the leaden misery and gloom of the peasants.

is the university of hunger the wide waste
is the pilgrimage of man the long march.
The print of hunger wanders in the land
the green tree bends above the long forgotten
the plains of life rise up and fall in spasms
the huts of men are fused in misery.

Martin was a voice and a legend to me for a long time. We only came face to face in the early months of 1958. My first impression was of a tall man with very elegant mesmeric fingers that tap-danced every now and then in his hair and along the rim of his spectacles. The keen intelligence in his eyes burned at times through the glass of those spectacles, at times they seemed to fade behind the smoke of his cigarette.

We met in a rumshop and the poet was high. He was the kind of man who only smouldered when sober and burst into flames when drunk. He was holding forth that morning on his favourite topic.

'To live here,' he said, 'to have our being here, denotes immediately a particular kind of sensibility, derived from the actuality of slavery, and a particular kind of status, derived from the actuality of colonial life. What I contend is that the sensibility of the slave and the status of the colonial make up *what we are* in the innermost meaning of the term.'

'Look at them,' he broke off, waving his hands over the ragged assembly of drinkers huddled at the tables, 'Poor brutalised wretches! They're walking still with their balls and chains and they don't know it. LISTEN' – he made a comical gesture with his fingers against his ears and bent forward, smiling confidentially – 'See if you don't hear the ancestral crackle of the whip on their backsides.

'You can't begin to understand what has been done to us. You can't imagine the real burden of the thing we're carrying. Just to emerge with a freeman's sensibility in this place is to achieve the impossible'.

He blew smoke straight into my face.

'For the essential meaning of slavery is the loss of self, the loss of identity. And what I mean by this is the loss of those relationships which allow of choices, the loss of those equivalencies between inward necessity and external situations. And I mean too the disruption of rhythm, the breaking down of the structure of the personality in which integration is lost and action remains action, removed from any possibility of being transformed into destiny.'

I remember during that meeting he was flanked on both sides by men who had played a prominent backstage role in our revolution. I am afraid I cannot name them but I shall refer to them in this talk as the Shadows. The spirit of these men had been broken. Their disillusionment seemed complete. They spoke now with almost no hope of a solution to Guyana's crisis. They attacked both factions of the Party with an acid viciousness. They saw the split that yawned now in the life of the country as a black pit into which would fall several generations of our people, helplessly, hopelessly. Hearing them talk and seeing them like clouds against the blueness of Martin's brilliance, filled me with foreboding.

I have seen Georgetown go up in flames twice in my childhood years. I think a wooden city on fire among the most beautiful and frightening things in the world, only a volcano can be as demoniacally beautiful and I do not think you can watch it from the safety of the streets. Even those who stood weeping for the loss of their homes and jobs were fascinated beyond grief by the spectacle. Yet in the morning, after the skies had burned all night in a livid magnificence of orange, blue-purple and gold, huge skeletons smoked in the places where our most illustrious buildings had been. I walked amid the ruins with hundreds of hungry men. Ash fell on our souls. Something of this came back to me, something of this feeling of desolation and loss after a vivid explosion, that day I met the Shadows.

It was this same black wind that was blowing over their souls that had killed my father. Less than two years after the suspension of the Constitution he died in utter despair, holding his head and bawling again and again: "What to do! What to do! What to do!". It is out of a sadness at this – this pessimism, this failure of nerve, this rout of all hope, and out of a conviction that what lay apparently subdued and beaten in the people was only in dormancy, that I wrote my poem 'Volcano'.

My heat
is nothing but a memory now
my cry
a terror of the long forgotten.
Time heaps high snow upon my passive flanks
and I stand muted with my furnace caged
too chilled for agitation
But mark me well
for I am still volcano

We were not, however, neither Martin nor myself, merely poets of protest. Martin's best work – beautiful little masterpieces like 'Voices', for example, are distinguished by a fine musical ear and an architecture of sensuous imagery, qualities that often redeemed his early raw poems of anger. One observes a startling leap and transformation in his poetry after *The Hill of Fire* collection and this may partly be traced to the influence of the Wilson Harris experiments with the dialectic of associations in 'Fetish' and *Eternity to Season*. Martin, however, I feel, achieves more striking impressionistic effects and is a much more accessible, if less original and penetrating poet, than Harris. There must be few poems in the region as a whole that can rival in pathos and beauty his 'Poems of Shape and Motion', from which I shall quote briefly at this stage.

I was wondering if the agony of years
could be traced to the seed of an hour.
If the roots that spread out in the swamp
ran too deep for the issuing flower.

Martin's disenchantment with the movement that had once inspired him gradually led to the kind of sterile nihilism I had found and feared in the Shadows. In his first attempt at the novel – which I was fortunate to read in manuscript – I became aware of the menace to his extraordinary promise posed by the philosophy of futility and despair.

In this novel we have a crude, illiterate figure – a poor fisherman casting his nets at the edge of the town – a man who in spite of his outward crudity has enormous internal reserves of power. Slowly as the action unfolds itself we see the injustice – he is wrongfully imprisoned – the castration – he is struck on his testicles by a policeman's club while attempting to escape – the whole paralysing, negating complex of his society which strikes continuously at the huge life of his instincts until the powerhouse blacks out. The lights stop flickering. Our hero is overpowered. Step by step his manhood is stripped away from him. Down, down to the last vestige. He is reduced, reduced to nothing. All his life-potential exploded. He becomes a cipher of tragic absurdity.

Author and protagonist become one in this unfortunate sense, that as the protagonist breaks up so does the work. Carter's powers were reduced, it seemed to me, to the same degree as he set out to reduce and overpower his hero or anti-hero. It was clear that this movement from idealism to nihilism was beginning to affect his development. This is not to say that art can only be fertilised by the one and not by the other – Camus and Beckett, I think, find nutriment for the black flowers of their art in the ground of nihilism. But for Martin this was a dead-end, not a growing point for new vision.

The energy and insights of his earlier work began to fade. The signals of collapse were there in his new poems which began to be filled with images of men drowning, submerging, reduced to nothingness, catching at a straw. He began to speak to us of a symbolic flood that would sweep away the whole hopeless wreckage of his society and civilisation. This was a far cry from his 'Poems of Shape and Motion' which participate compassionately in man's impotence and ironic hope and irremediable suffering. From these I quote again, finally...

I walk slowly in the wind
hearing myself in the loneliness of a child
in woman's grief which is not understood
in coughing doors when midnight lingers long
on stones, on streets and then on echoing stars
that burn all night and suddenly go out.

(Extract from the text of a talk delivered to the Caribbean Artists Movement at the West Indian Students Centre - September 5th, 1969 and published in two parts in the CAM newsletter)

LOUIS JAMES

FROM THE NECESSITY OF POETRY

Jean-Paul Sartre, in his essay 'Orphée Négre', wrote of the Negro poet as plunging into the dark void, using his instinct as a form of radar, to discover a fresh vision of the truth. 'I shall name this poetry "orphic" because this untiring descent of the Negro into himself causes me to think of Orpheus going to reclaim Euridice from Pluto.' One does not need to tie this, as Sartre does, to Césaire's concept of negritude: to break out of old patterns and recreate a new cultural sensibility has been the need of every nation in a state of evolution, whether it be India or Ireland, Nigeria or the nascent United States. As Shelley insisted a hundred and forty years ago in *A Defence of Poetry* (1820), 'poets are the unacknowledged legislators of the world.' Thus we have seen that in West Africa, Chinua Achebe's *A Man of the People*, Gabriel Okara's *The Voice*, and even lesser works such as T. M. Aluko's *One Man one Matchet*, played a part in creating the social and political realignment of the emerging Nigeria.

The writer's role as a poetic 'Orpheus' is peculiarly difficult in the Caribbean, subjected as s/he is to such conflicting influences, and competing cultural 'roots'. Nevertheless, in Guyana, A. J. Seymour, Martin Carter and Wilson Harris have each powerfully indicated different aspects of a writer's national significance. To begin with A.J. Seymour. Seymour has been one of those cultural catalysts, such as Frank Collymore in Barbados, whose importance to Caribbean literature goes beyond anything they have written. Seymour has been the centre of literary developments in Guyana, giving West Indian poetry a voice through his editorship of *Kyk-over-al,* and publicising it in his series of 'Miniature Poets'. His criticism has been evaluative, where independent judgement has been curiously rare. The choice of the name *Kyk-over-al* (a ruined Dutch fort) for the magazine is significant of Seymour's approach to his own poetry. As the vantage point overlooks the confluence of the Essequibo, the Cuyuni and the Mazaruni rivers in Guyana, so Seymour assumes, with a Yeatsian detachment, a position surveying both the nation's history and place. In his famous long poem, 'Over Guiana, Clouds', he focuses downwards from the eternally shifting Guyanese skyscape. The clouds provide an appropriate vantage point from which to view Guyanese history, continually changed yet unchanging, high above the land, yet intimately bound up with its fertility and seasons, responsive to its soil temperatures and forest vapours.

And they go rushing on across the country
Staining the land with shadow as they pass.
Closer than raiment to the naked skin, that shadow,
Bringing a pause of sun, over and across

Black noiseless rivers running out to sea,
Fields, pieced and plotted, and ankle deep in rice
Or waving their multitudinous hair of cane.

The clouds move across place and time, over the Spaniard invaders fighting the Indians, seen – an effective image this – as 'a cinema of rapid figures/ Thrown by wood-torches on the trees'; then they shadow the invading Dutch, Portuguese and English. The panorama of time and space is extended toward Africa. 'That thin old negro had beat the rhythm for years/The Ibu rhythm, learnt in African forests/From hands as proud as serpent veined as his'. The past acts as a focus for the present, leading to a meditative passage:

The flat peace of savannahs to the sea
With drifting statues of the animals
Cropping the country's peace with its sweet grass.

Moving to moral and social issues, Seymour envisages a group of prostitutes, and a service of Holy Communion. It envisages the future, as

The races fade into a brown stained people
And the Guiana Spirit arises, stretching
As a young giant begins to open his eyes.

How do we start to evaluate a poem like 'Over Guiana, Clouds?' The poem seems to me pleasing, readable, but limited both in technique and in its historical viewpoint. African drums are introduced, but in a somewhat *clichéd* way, and Seymour does not attempt a comprehensive and piercing study of Guiana's racial complexity. In style it is rather too much indebted to Whitman's *Leaves of Grass*. Conventional literary criteria, however, are not the only issues here. Auden once spoke of a poet's early writing as 'imaginary', that is, exploring a new field of experience through the imagination, and this is true of the writing of a new nation. It is not to be judged against accepted standards, for the standards are yet to be discovered. The writer is still doing that preliminary task outlined by another pioneer writer, James Fenimore Cooper, of illustrating the land and water which is the people's birthright. Seymour's poem was 'necessary.'

A certain stiffness we feel when reading some of Seymour's poetry is indeed intentional. He believes that to comprehend the patterns of life, one has to free oneself from the distorting effects of human passion. If one subjects oneself to such discipline and objective concentration, finally, a richer vitality will break out. 'Strip their beauty to the bone', he writes in 'Men Pruning Trees', 'Sun will bring those boughs alive'. Seymour's precept and practice chime with T. S. Eliot's search for an impersonal tone, and his attempt to subject passion to the refining fires of objectivity is particularly relevant to West Indian poetry, where indulgence in the emotions – anger, pleasure, or what-have-you – has unbalanced many a poetic sensibility. From the pruned branches, in Seymour's most successful verse, springs life, as in lines such as

Why must we wait until the blood runs slow
Through the old hired house, when property of eye
And ear and brain anticipate the night...? ('Truth')

A more directly passionate poem, such as the frequently anthologised 'Sun is a Shapely Fire', seems to me to work less well. On the other hand, controlled objectivity can be inappropriate at a time of national crisis. The sentiment that

There is no room to cry regret
No room for anger beating wild, fierce fists
Against the towering stone of circumstances ('Change')

can be evasion.

Martin Carter's poetry is in the poetic line of David Diop in Senegal, Dennis Brutus in South Africa, and the British Chartist poet, Thomas Cooper. Such writing is essential to any popular movement; its purpose is not to explore beneath the surface of reality to new spiritual and imaginative dimensions, it puts its back to the wall and inspires defiance. The distinctive quality of the verse in his book, *Poems of Resistance* (London, 1954 – banned in what was then British Guiana), is its cleansing indignation, which informs his whole vision of life.

Day passes like a long whip
Over the back of a slave...
Night comes from down river
Like a thief... ('Death of a Slave')

Martin Carter's first book of poems was published in 1954, and grew directly out of his participation of political resistance to British colonialism. It illustrates the way that social and political change requires new attitudes, a different poetry. Carter's verse however both embraced and transcended political protest. In 'I am No Soldier', he declares

I am no soldier with a cold gun on my shoulder
No hunter of men, no human dog of death.

The patriot dies, not only to crush the oppressor, but to witness to the power of self-sacrificial love, and speaking for such love, he cries, 'O wherever you fall comrade I shall arise.' Carter echoes the Haitian revolutionary poet Jacques Roumain as he claims kinship with the workers and the oppressed in Kenya, Korea, Russia and China; Roumain too, claimed fellowship with 'miner in Austria black miner in Johannesburg metal worker for Krupps... *(Bois-d'Ebene)* . Carter ends his poem with the remarkable line 'I am this poem like a sacrifice'. As I understand it, Carter is posing as an alternative to inhuman destruction, humane vision and pity, and the poem is so completely the expression of his personal struggle that he and the poem are one: 'I am this poem'. Such sacrifice is more costly even than bodily death. The latter requires physical courage. But the poet's transformation of political issues into human terms, his labour in fighting for freedom through appeals to reason and to the higher emotions, requires the most demanding self-offering of all.

Such a vision indicates the way forward from political violence that Carter explores in his poem, 'Till I Collect'. In a striking allegory of the rediscovery of a shattered identity, he sets out in a boat moved by passion – 'my mast of love' – and steered by self-awareness achieved through suffering – 'my rudder tempered out of anguish'. He fishes the deep for his lost self, but must do so with care, for a thoughtless search will only bring up the dead bones of past, broken and dead cultures.

> But my own hand I dare not plunge too far
> Lest only sand and shells I bring to air
> Lest only bones I resurrect to light.

However, fishing the subconscious, and the realms of the creative imagination, with rapt attention, the poet will discover a new identity, here unspecified, since it is yet to be found.

> Over the shining mud the moon is blood
> falling on ocean at the fence of lights –
> my course I set, I give my sail the wind
> to navigate the islands of the stars
> till I collect my scattered skeleton
> till I collect...

This is a highly successful poem, a fine balance of emotion and intellect within an imaginative whole. Carter's verse can be uneven, but his successes far outweigh any lapses. His verse is particularly effective in creating poetry of statement. In 'Letter 2', for instance, occurs this perfectly modulated account of what he was desiring while in prison:

> You think of green mornings
> Naked children playing in the rain
> And even fishes swimming in a pool
> A shop in a street and women passing by
> Walking from home to market in the morning
> A blind old man now tapping with his stick
> Seeing no one...

I would like to see more of this lucid, vividly simple, free verse. Martin Carter has his niche in the national evolution of Guyana: one hopes he will maintain the fire in his verse in less fiery circumstances.

Wilson Harris brings us to the exploration of mystical and spiritual reality in the emergence of a new nation. Harris's work, it seems to me, makes an interesting comparison with that of the Nigerian poet, Christopher Okigbo, who also creates a highly personal world of myth out of his national culture. Harris's main collection of poetry to date is *From Eternity to Season* (1954), a work that needs to be considered in the context of his fiction, for his preoccupations in the novels are clarified in the verse, and the poem becomes easier to understand with knowledge of the prose. A good point of departure for any new reader of Harris is the waterfall climbing episode in *Palace of the Peacock.* Here Harris magically introduces us into the experience normally met with only in moments of psychic hallucination, where one is simultaneously aware of external and inner worlds of reality. For Harris, time and space are exploded, and as in atomic physics matter is transformed into energy, and vice versa; a person may turn into a place, a place into an aspiration. Edward Brathwaite, in an excellent article in *Bim,* 'The Controversial Tree of Time', has pointed out how germane this vision is to the life of the Guiana jungles which Harris spent his formative years surveying, where all is continuous flux, transformation of matter to life, of life to matter. The flux is at once physical and spiritual. In Harris's words

> The living jungle is too full of voices Not to be aware of collectivity...
> ('Amazon')

> Untangled the trees mount to the sky
> and the silence is filled with a different wave like sound that alters dimension.
> ('Behring Straits')

Harris's vision is intensely personal, yet one inseparable from the Guyanese topography, probing deeper than does the more cinematic perspective of Seymour, who could not have written

> Broken shadows lift new sap front the ground
> Partake of a glowing sustenance, die and live again. ('Behring Straits')

Within and beyond this extends an immense and meaningful unity.

Eternity to Season is the exploration of the pilgrimage from the flux of 'eternity' to the 'season' of a meaningful moment within time Like James Joyce in *Ulysses,* Harris uses the Greek myths to reinforce his structure and extend his meaning. For him, symbols are universal and eternal, and, in T.S.Eliot's words, 'all is always now'. The classical legend of man leaving a decayed civilization (Troy), surviving immense spiritual and physical dangers through courage and ingenuity, and coming at last to harbour, becomes for the West Indian the voyage from the Africa or Europe, surviving the disintegration of the middle-passage and the exploitation of colonialism, finally achieving self-discovery. With Harris the integrity of the hero is of crucial importance. A heretic from both Greek and Christian points of view, he declares that creation, at least as far as man can know it, lies in the human will alone.

> Creation is the spirit and the courage and the wisdom men seek to employ.
> ('Laocoon')

Intellectually he stands in the modern Existentialist tradition, creating his identity against the void left by the alienating processes of colonial domination. Yet he adapts classical legend for his own purpose, transforming it within the specifically Guyanese context. The poem 'Canje' gathers together Ulysses, Tiresias, a Fishmonger and Achilles in the village of Cumberland at the mouth of the Canje river, a flood basin symbolising the meeting place of time and eternity, since there the river (time) alternates according to the season with the salt sea (timelessness). The names are classical, but the characters links with their originals can be tenuous. A projection of Harris's highly original concepts, they have little human characterisation. This limits the effectiveness of the poems. For if all is flux, time is collapsible, and all proportions relative ('The tiniest flake is a cliff, the merest trickle of water/a deluge'), the reader is desperately in need of something to hold on to. Harris's work can be uneven, even prosaic, as his words, to invoke Eliot's lines in 'Burnt Norton', 'crack and strain under the burden' of conveying his vision. Yet even in its relative lapses, Harris's work is unique, the creation of a poet's individual genius engaged in the historic task of forging the identity of his race.

A.J.Seymour, Martin Carter, and Wilson Harris, are each, in their very different ways, fine poets. But they should be read for a further reason. Each illustrates the significance of the writer to an evolving nation, and should reinforce the resolution that the cultivation of literature be given a central place in the era ahead.

(An edited version of the essay first published in *New World*, Guyana Independence Issue, edited by George Lamming and Martin Carter, May 26, 1966.)

SAMUEL O. ASEIN

THE 'PROTEST' TRADITION IN WEST INDIAN POETRY: FROM GEORGE CAMPBELL TO MARTIN CARTER[1]

The view has often been expressed that the poem must *be* and not *mean*; that the *raison d'etre* of a poem must be judged by the aesthetic quality of its interior architecture and artistic integrity. There is, of course, the contrary viewpoint which emphasises the social value of poetry and the functional relevance of the poet in society. These opposing views raise the perennial and controversial question about the responsibility of the poet (if he has any), his mode of operation and the nature of his art.

Poetry, to my mind, has an exhilarative social function in society in any age. The magnitude and the urgency of its function will depend on the historical circumstances; often bewilderingly possessive, in which the poet like any other artist is trapped. The ultimate value of a poem and the ultimate test of a poet's contemporaneity will be determined not only by the manner in which he has utilised and enriched the linguistic medium at his disposal but also by what Roy Fuller once described as 'the emotional situation' of the writer's age.[2]

The element of 'protest' which became prevalent in the West Indies in the 1940s and to some extent in the 1950s came as a revival of a fundamental trend in West Indian poetry. It had its generic roots in such oral forms as protest songs and work songs which not only formed an integral part of West Indian plantation culture but also survived through the post-emancipation period.

It was the recognition of this protest element which inspired the pertinent comments of a nineteenth century anonymous correspondent of *The Black Dwarf* who observed that:

> The negroes of the West Indies have among them various simple but beautiful songs, either embodying some mournful tale of love and affection, or the enthusiasm of liberty and patriotism... These people, when a little aroused, are so impatient of slavery, that the West Indian magistracy are very particular in the nature of their amusement.[3]

The writer went further to illustrate his point with a quotation which resonates with its self-explanatory topicality:

> ... when wild the war-pipes's breathing,
> Telling many a mournful story;
> When the frantic dance wreathing,
> Rousing us to deeds of glory;
> Vengeance, at the plaintive strain,
> Shall rise in arms again;
> Slavery burst its clanking chain,
> And sweet freedom live for ever.[4]

Such verses represent some of the earliest manifestations of that sense of outrage and unease which is an essential element of protest poetry. The Jamaican exile-poet Claude McKay shared this inheritance with his contemporaries of the Harlem Renaissance of the 1920s. With Claude McKay it was not a self-indulgent exploitation of vengeful rhetoric but an understandable response to the particular social realities in which the consciousness of most Blacks of his generation was rooted. It was the temper of the time which aroused the militant responses of the poets of this period. Seen against such a background, we are in a better position to appreciate the resonant protest in a poem like 'Enslaved':

> Oh when I think of my long-suffering race,
> For weary centuries, despised, oppressed
> Enslaved and lynched, denied a human place
> In the great life line of the Christian West;
> And in the Black Land disinherited,
> Robbed in the ancient country of its birth,
> My heart grows sick with hate, becomes as lead.[5]

The historicity which characterises McKay's poem recurs in George Campbell's work and has survived in the poetry of Edward Brathwaite and other West Indian poets in the sixties. For Campbell, 'No part of our past that is not/Part of our memory'[6]

The peculiar historical and social circumstances which the West Indian poet has lived through have thrust certain roles on him. It was an awareness of this social factor which, I am sure, helped to formulate Richard Wright's opinions on the responsibility of the Black poet *vis a vis* his social environment:

> The Negro writer who seeks to function within his race as a purposeful agent has a serious responsibility. In order to do justice to his subject matter, in order to depict Negro life in all of its manifold and intricate relationships, a deep, informed, and complex consciousness is necessary; a consciousness which draws for its strength upon the fluid lore of a great people, and moulds this lore with the concepts that move and direct the forces of history today;... a new role is devolving upon the Negro writer. He is being called upon to do no less than create values by which his race is to struggle, live and die. [8]

There is *no* doubt as to the relevance of this comment to the subject under consideration. For, whether the ultimate responsibility of the poet is to bridge the 'gap of communication' which exists between him and the community in which he functions as a poet, or to sail what Clifford Sealy, the Trinidadian editor of *Voices,* described as 'the uncharted ocean of self-discovery', needless to say that it is only a West Indian poet, with a sensibility committed to the West Indian situation, who can recreate for us the multiplicity of strands that have gone into the making of the *West Indian* consciousness. The poet can give vibrancy to this unique cultural and social heritage and revitalise his past in its relationship to the present. Therein lies the permanence and continuity of his heritage in his art within the West Indian context;

and only then, one might add, can the poet's work have for West Indians that exclusive referential value which T.S. Eliot had in mind when he spoke of the 'stubbornly national' quality of poetry 'in having a value for the people of the poet's race and language, which it can have for no other'.[8]

In the forties and early fifties, West Indian poetry came very close to having this exclusiveness. The new direction in West Indian poetry during those two decades was given a new impetus by the social upheavals of the late thirties and the resurgence of nationalist consciousness in the forties. These were momentous decades which John La Rose was to celebrate with deep affection, several years later, in 'Song to An Imperishable Sunlight', a touching statement of West Indian resistance:

We remember
  who fell forward
    in the dust,
writing the rueful story
    of our redemption..[9]

What in La Rose's poetry is an act of memory, was for the poets of the forties and early fifties a contemporary experience which most of them had to grapple with. New situations presented new challenges to which the poets responded with commensurate alertness, and often, militancy, a varying attitude which is reflected in the poetry of George Campbell and Martin Carter. In Jamaica, there was that generation of poets who were, as Edna Manley put it; 'involved and inspired by politics in the broadest sense of the word'.[10] About the same period also, there was in Guyana a 'growing school of Guyanese poets and writers' who were expressing a discernible 'feeling for Guiana'.[11] The socio-political chain of events which linked the South American mainland of Guyana with the islands in the Caribbean sea coexisted with the literary current which washed the shores of Campbell's Jamaica through the archipelago to Carter's Guyana.

With *First Poems* and a play in verse, *Play Without Scenery* performed by the Little Theatre Movement in 1947,[12] the young Jamaican poet, George Campbell established himself as a respectable literary figure whose reputation reached across the seas to the U.S. and Britain.[13] Not only did Campbell's collection break new ground with the range of his poetic sensibility and versatility, it re-infused into West Indian poetry the compulsive element of social protest. Two moods dominate Campbell's poetry: one is contemplative, the other a romantic excitable mood which is indicative of his social commitment. We notice the change from one to the other as we move from the submissive and almost ritualistic atmosphere of 'Magdalene' strategically located at the end of one section, into an entirely different conceptual world which is vibrant in its contemporaneity. In 'Magdalene', the situational verisimilitude and the self-denying passivity of the biblical figure give Campbell's lines a characteristic effect:

I felt secure
As I knelt at his feet
And had no fears
That at dead of night
I would hear the beat
In an outside room,
Creak of a door
And demand on my womb.[14]

This is a subtle reference to contemporary social vices and its moral overtones reflect a kind of social awareness. But it lacks the masculine vigour which informs 'Negro Aroused'. Here is an affirmation of a new rebelliousness reminiscent of Claude McKay in the twenties:

Negro aroused! Awakened from
The ignominious sleep of dominance!
Freedom! Off with these shackles
That torment, I lift my head and scream to heaven
Freedom! Now my blood rushes through my veins
And boils up in my head at their insult.[15]

Naturally, Campbell's new awareness led to a conscious search for racial roots and identity. It was this need for a cultural and racial point of reference which in turn encouraged his self-identification, albeit romantic, with Africa. This spiritual relation which Campbell sought to establish with Africa was not phenomenal in any way. Claude McKay and other Black American poets like Langston Hughes were articulating similar experiences in the twenties: '... am I not Afric's son,/Black of that black land where black deeds are done?'[16] seemed to be the prevalent question. But this spiritual quest often led to a realisation by the poet of his divided loyalty. Jose Antonio Jarvis, a West Indian poet from St. Thomas, exemplified this frame of mind in a poem which bears the suggestive title 'Atavistic':

I, whose dark ancestors played
Where the Nile's first drop was laid,
Have within me Nordic blood
Pulsing like the tide at flood.[17]

While in 'Africa Whence I Came' he recognises a racial link with Africa, Jarvis, like many others in his time, rationalises his rejection of the self-created primeval image of Africa basing his argument on an a-racial humanist ideology:

Africa fostered me
But I came
From the slime and the mud of the race
Which is man![18]

For Campbell, however, Africa was a spiritual home which he took possession of at the same time as he asserted and elevated the prototypical maternal figure. Hence in 'Mother' he transformed the obvious erotic connotations to give the poem a transcendental quality. The female figure no longer functions for the poet as a physically tangible and corruptible character but as the embodiment of an idea which fits into his pattern of romantic idealisation of his continental 'homeland'.

She sings of the African womb
Everlasting above the tomb
She sings of her island Jamaica
She sings of the glory of Africa.[19]

But when the purpose is scathing satire, Campbell deflates with comparable ease the female figure as in 'Smells Like Hell'[20] in which he directs his attack against youthful licentiousness; or, perhaps in the ungainly sketches in 'I Sung Democracy' of 'a pretty prostitute' with 'painted lips' and 'heavy hips'[21]. With a vivid stroke he presents a physical environment in which the squalid unnerving slums are shaded by the relief of the glamorous landscape like two contrasting faces of an ill-constructed social framework:

In the slums
Jewel staring eyes
Of human flies
Crowd the ruins
Of our social order. [22]

Campbell's comments on and criticism of contemporary Jamaican social and political realities suggest a strong influence of a Marxist-Splenglerean concept of history. The metaphors, even if stilted and simplistic, leave his message undisguised: 'Our country is now suffering/Slow is the day of Pain's long night'[23].

Underlying this topical overtone are Campbell's universalist views and concerns, especially in his poems of the war period. These poems reveal his anxiety about the threat to the infra-structure of contemporary values and the psychic trauma in a pervasive, stifling atmosphere of unease and suspicion: 'The sabotage of harmony/The utter distress/Of ugly war'[24]. Ultimately disillusion takes the place of illusion, with the revelation to him of an irreparable cosmic dislocation:

How can woman weep for daughter
Gathered in from the wide world's womb
And man in unnatural slaughter
Scattered back with his hands of doom.[25]

In fact, Campbell's poems on race and racial conflict are less precise. There are occasional references to this inbuilt interracial tension. But more often than not, as was the case in the socialist-inspired poetry of the period, the situational tension derived not from a black/white polarisation, but from a clash of values and biases; from the struggle of the new nationalist zeal against an exploitative imperialism. When the West Indian poet in the forties asserted his black identity he conceived of this assertion, often at the risk of dialectal logic, as a means towards the assertion of a fundamental humanity and solidarity with the 'downtrodden of the earth', pleading his human essence and individual integrity. We find this slant to the treatment of the theme of race in Claude McKay, and the problem which it posed for a later poet like Jarvis. The influence of Marxist internationalism can be traced in Campbell's work. It explains the universalist outlook and humanistic sentiments in such poems as 'Holy' and 'Let us Build':

In spite of Campbell's protest, there is a unifying conceptual framework which assumes a millennial dawn through purgation. Indeed, he saw himself in the enviable role of a committed artist whose duty it was both to warn and to prophesy. He reacted against those negative elements militating against the visionary world of his imagination, and was upset by the gap which separated that world and the contemporary decadent world. Consequently, we find in his work a progressive loss of faith and a bleak awareness of the futility of human effort:

Tomorrow is an outside world
It moves away from day to day
And leaves me in a futile world
I am the prisoner of my day.
But I can let my fingers touch
The ideal world I cannot clutch
And I can build for other men
Tomorrow I won't know again.[27]

Two years before Martin Carter's *Poems of Resistance*[29], Peter Blackman published a long poem *My Song is for All Men*[28] which had an affinity with Campbell's collection, not only in the choice of related subjects but also in its overt protest. Moreover, it anticipated in some respects the activist verse of Martin Carter. A staggering invective against capitalist exploitation and social injustices and a sustained racial identification, and assertion of black identity which he synthesised with a humanistic self-identification with working class groups, gave Blackman's poetry the characteristic tone of the age. There was the romantic idealisation of Africa and the Black Woman: 'She is the source of my pride, from her stem all my creations'[29]; the plaintive voice of the oppressed colonial trapped in a racial vortex: 'They say my features are coarse and repulsive/Too like the ape for man. Against these I have always to argue my humanity'[30]. Like Campbell, Blackman often took a critical look at the urban squalor and filth which contrasted glaringly with the luminous columns of modern architecture:

These you claim are only my just deservings
Rags and old packing cases fair receivings
For beasts such as I am so you say
Crabbed you would tend me manacled as madmen
Once crouched beneath your palaces. [31]

In place of self-pity and ineffectual pleas, Blackman emphasised a militancy in the manner of Claude McKay's more assured protest poems:

My case is not framed for plaintive complaining
Strong anger is knotted to my every desire
Bathing my limbs and refreshing the promises
Made for the reckoning
You will remember the reckoning.[32]

However when we come to Carter's poetry we find a powerful and eloquent statement of protest: 'in cold dark earth/time plants the seeds of anger'[33]; 'I take... my scorn/and fling it in the face of those who hate me'[34]; the same mood recurs as Carter speaks of 'the latitudes of anguish/ [which] pass through the poles of my frozen anguish, my regions of *grief*'[35]. This militant note has survived in West Indian poetry since Carter, especially in the works of poets like Lindsay Barrett, the Jamaican poet/novelist whose violent indignation becomes an almost over-mastering, but nevertheless creative passion: '... each line I write contains some fine particle of my hate'.[36]

Among West Indian poets of the forties and the fifties, Martin Carter was certainly the most vociferous. In his short poem entitled 'You Are Involved', Carter gives a terse symbolic formulation of the basis of social commitment:

Like a jig
Shakes the loom
Like a web
is spun the pattern
all are involved!
all are involved![37]

This is the voice of a militant writer, who in the late forties would stand at the city square in Georgetown and read his poems to a crowd of enraptured Guyanese. As far as Carter was concerned, poetry was a valid and necessary vehicle for social criticism and protest. He experienced, I presume, and presented that fascinating unification of sensibilities as a poet and as an activist in a single-minded commitment, which gave his poetry a distinctive tone. 'I am no soldier hunting in a jungle/I am this poem like a sacrifice'; but his was not always a simplistic programmatic statement of ideologies and manifestos:

These poet words have secrets locked in them
like nuggets laden with the younger sun.
Who will unlock must first himself be locked
Who will be locked must first himself unlock. [38]

Against the threat of the oppressor, Carter set his defiance and contempt: 'I clench my fist above my head: I sing my song of FREEDOM!'[39] In 'Death of a Comrade', the mournful tone changes to one of revolutionary exaltation: 'Death will not find us thinking that we die'.[40] Here we have an instance of the permanence of that protest tradition which Claude McKay's "If We Must Die" epitomises.

Because of his style and the militancy of his poetry, Carter has had a varied reception in the West Indies. Writing in 1960, Frank Collymore described Martin Carter as 'primarily a political writer whose rhetorical verse is one of the impassioned appeal for social reform', and pointed to the fact that he, like his fellow Guyanese A.J. Seymour and Wilson Harris, shared a common Guyanese sense of place.[41] Neville Dawes was more perceptive in his criticism of Carter which appeared in the preface to the 1964 edition of *Poems of Resistance.* Dawes summed up his claims for Carter's poetry with the approving remark that 'The present generation of New Guyana youth will need the inspiration of these poems in a time of crisis'. Certainly, the message of 'You Are Involved', and the engaged attitudes which various poets from the West Indies, especially the under-thirties, are beginning to give expression in their works have more than vindicated Dawes' claims.

There is no doubt about the characteristically explosive content of *Poems of Resistance* and 'Jail Me Quickly'[42]. The circumstances in which these poems were written provide the explanation for the mercurial content and the progression from the revolutionary idealism of the early period to an incredible frustration and helpless distrust of prevalent values in some of Carter's later poems. Carter's poems in *Poems of Resistance* are basically situational; intensely personal in the exclusiveness of the private experiences and responses, but representative and contemporary in their stunning reflection of a bleak slice of Guyanese history. For these particularised experiences and situations exposed for Carter an illumined spectrum of a universal predicament. It is this transmutation of the particular into the universal which gives Carter's poetry its enduring value and contemporaneity, outside its West Indian context.

There is the usual architectonic of protest poetry in a colonial situation; the resistance to an imperialist domination, and reaction against an exploitative and often depersonalising bourgeois social system. As in the poetry of some of his contemporaries in the West Indies, the polarisation of social values in Carter's poetry focused on the class more often than the race. Far removed from the mellow protest of Campbell, Carter, nevertheless shared with him an identical millennial vision, identifying himself, with the disinherited poor in an a-racial universalism:

> I shall come to the brave when they dream of the red and yellow
> flowers blooming in the tall mountains of their nobility...
> I will come to each and to every comrade led by my heart
> Led by my magnet of freedom which draws me far and wide
> over the sun's acres of children and of mornings...[43]

There is vituperation, but it rises above the level of self-indulgent protest; and, by far, more significant is the fact that Carter's indictment of contemporary social structure does not abandon us on a banal plane of mere documentation.

His language at his best has the freshness of the vital moment, with a concrete and consistent symbolic representation of those aspects of the social system which he abhors:

Here in my home my little child lies sleeping
Let freedom wake him – not a bayonet point.[44]

This haunting image of the prowling soldier becomes the dominant image in a rather obsessive way as he tries to recapture the mood of the emergency period. We are made to visualise more than once, 'A soldier marching with a long black rifle', [45] and elsewhere it is the sound of 'a soldier's bootstep/ marching [him] down the corridors of silence'[46]. The image is invested with a nightmarish significance and presence in 'This is the Dark Time My Love' as we see with the imaginative eye 'the man of death, ... the stranger invader watching [him] sleep and aiming at [his] dream.'[47]

In spite of this threat, Carter's response remained one of consistent and stubborn defiance which had its roots no doubt in his millennial view and in the optimistic concept that 'in despair there is hope'. He was convinced of the inevitability of 'the new day': '...I'll come alive again/And laugh again and walk out of this prison'[48] into a changed 'world of tomorrow':

This world's hope is a blade of fury
And we who are sweepers of an ancient sky
discoverers of new planets, sudden stars
We are the world's hope. [49]

In a moment of revelation the poet confronts the facts of his situation and abandons his dream for concrete reality; inevitably, his tone changes from anger and protest to a more intense concern with the human predicament. His conception of the universe becomes, as well, increasingly more sardonic.

So now obsessed I celebrate in words
all origins of creation, whores and virgins:
I do it with a hand upon a groin,
swearing this way, since other ways are false![50]

The response to protest poetry *is* understandably mixed at any one period. What in brief the reception of George Campbell and Martin Carter reveals to those who are familiar with their works, is the problem arising from the adoption of conventional critical norms in assessing their contribution to West Indian poetry and their consolidation of the tradition of protest poetry. Any attempt to put them in the proper place in this tradition will necessarily involve us in a re-examination of questions about the relation of the poet to his society, his obligations and his relevance or irrelevance to the society. For, in the final analysis, the specific question is whether or not these two poets were relevant to West Indian society in their time.

To fully appreciate the works of these two poets we must see poetry from a different perspective, and here the distinction which Hayward Keniston made between the poet as a social commentator and the social historian or political scientist becomes relevant and instructive. Keniston warns us that:

> The contribution which the poet... makes to our understanding of a society is of a very different order from that of the social scientist... the artist seeks to interpret the deeper impulses and motivations which determine the direction of social changes; he evaluates in terms of good or evil the trends he observes; he finds meaning in the tangled pattern of human conflict. Because, by virtue of his art, he is seer and prophet, he may recognize thus intuitively the wave of the future; he may even formulate the still unexpressed hopes and cravings of his contemporaries and thus help to determine the march of events [51]

We have tried in this survey to show George Campbell and Martin Carter as the two most fascinating representatives of the protest tradition in the forties and fifties, fulfilling certain roles which they considered relevant to the state of West Indian society. If we have invested their work with a new significance, it is in recognition of their contribution to the formulation of a West Indian consciousness and to the development of a particular trend in West Indian poetry. For, whatever the nature of our individual biases, we cannot ignore the fact that one of the most permanent features of West Indian poetry is its persistent reflection of the age, individual poet's social awareness and sensitivities, societal value and mannerism.

And when the mood of the age demands it, as was the case in the forties and fifties, this awareness and the articulation of the poet's experience inevitably takes on the garb of militarist commitment and protest.

Footnotes

1. Revised text of a Paper presented to the Commonwealth Literature Association Conference on "Literature and Society in the West Indies", held in Kingston, Jamaica, 2nd-9th January 1971.
2. Roy Fuller [Interviewed by Peter Orr] in *The Poet Speaks,* ed. Peter Orr (London: Routledge & Kegan Paul, 1966), p.67.
3. 'Letter to the Editor', *The Black Dwarf,* June 18, 1817, p.336.
4. *Ibid.*
5. Claude Mckay, *Selected Poems* (New York:, Harcourt, Brace and World, Inc., 1953), p.42.
6. George Campbell, *First Poems* (Kingston: Printed Privately, 1945), p.101.
7. Cited by Addison Gayle, Jr. in his essay, 'Function of Black Literature at the Present Time', *The Black Aesthetic* ed. Addison Gayle, Jr. (New York: Doubleday, 1971), p.418.
8. T.S. Eliot, 'The Social Function of Poetry', *On Poetry and Poets* (New York: The Noonday Press, 1961), pp.7-8.
9. Anthony La Rose, *Foundations* (London: New Beacon Publications, 1966), p.43.
10. Edna Manley, 'The Fine Arts', [A Group Discussion], *Caribbean Quarterly,* vol. xiv, Nos. 1 & 2, March-June, 1968, p.66.
11. *Annual Report on British Guiana* (London: HMSO, 1949), p.88.
12. *Annual Report on Jamaica for* the *Year 1947* (London: HMSO, 1949), p.75.
13. We are told of the favourable reception of *First Poems* not only in Jamaica but also in the United States and in Britain where some of the poems were broadcast from the B.B.C. *Annual Report on Jamaica for the Year* 1946, London, His Majesty's

Stationery Office, 1948, p.67. The report erroneously gave 1946 as the date of publication of *First Poems.*
14. *Ibid.,* p.26.
15. *Ibid.,* p.28.
16. Claude Mckay, op. *cit.,* p.38.
17. Jose Antonio Jarvis, *Bamboula Dance and Other Poems* (St. Thomas, Virgin Islands: The Art Shop, 1935), p.4 [In the Kraus Reprint volume which also includes Campbell's *First Poems,* Basil McFarlane's *Jacob and the Angel and Other Poems,* R.L.C. McFarlane's *Selected Poems,* Figueroa's *Love Leaps Here,* Blackman's *My Song is for All Men* and Harris's *Eternity to Season*].
18. *Ibid.,* p.5.
19. Campbell, *op. cit.,* pp.37-38.
20. *Ibid.,* pp.59-60.
21. *Ibid.,* p.63.
22. *Ibid.*, p.62.
23. *Ibid.*, p.74.
24. *Ibid.,* p.88.
25. *Ibid.,* p.91.
26. *Ibid.,* p.50.
27. Martin Carter, *Poems of Resistance* (Georgetown: University of Guyana, 1964), [Published originally in 1954 by Lawrence & Wishart of London.]
28. Peter Blackman, *My Song is for All Men* (London: Lawrence and Wishart, 1952).
29. *Ibid.,* p.7.
30. *Ibid.,* p.8.
31. *Ibid.,* p.9.
32. *Ibid.,* p.13.
33. Martin Carter, *op. cit.,* p.6.
34. *Ibid.*, p.22.
35. *Ibid.,* p.3.
36. Lindsay Barrett, *The State of Black Desire* (Alencon: L'Imprimerie Corbiere et Jugain, 1966), p.37.
37. Martin Carter, *op. cit.*, p.18.
38. Martin Carter, 'Words', *The Tamarack Review,* Issue Fourteen, Winter 1960, p.57.
39. *Poems of Resistance,* p.26.
40. ibid., p.8.
41. Frank Collymore, 'Writing in the West Indies: A Survey', *The Tamarack Review,* Issue Fourteen, Winter 1960, p.119.
42. Martin Carter, 'Jail Me Quickly', *New World Fortnightly,* No. 34, February 18, 1966, pp.19-25.
43. Martin Carter, *Poems of Resistance,* p.4.
44. *Ibid.,* p.23.
45. *Ibid.,* p.14.
46. *Ibid.,* p.12.
47. *Ibid.,* p.17.
48. *Ibid.*, p.11.
49. *Ibid.,* p.16.
50. Martin Carter, 'Jail Me Quickly', *op.* cit, p.21.
51. Hayward Keniston, 'Literature as a Barometer of Modern European Society', *The Humanities for Our Time,* Walter R. Agard et. al. (New York: Books for Libraries Press, 1968), p.27.

An edited version of an essay that was first published in *Jamaica Journal*, vol 6., no. 2, 1972

JEFFREY ROBINSON

THE GUYANESENESS OF GUYANESE WRITING

I was once asked by Mr. A. J. Seymour whether I thought there was such a thing as Guyanese literature and, if so, what were its characteristics. I replied that it seemed strangely mystical. I should now prefer to say that there is, in the major works by Guyanese writers, a similarity of theme and attitude. The theme is the relationship between the mind and the world and between both of these, considered as a dialectic, and time. The attitude is one that renders these relationships not so much as philosophy or theory but rather as riddle or mystery.

The relationship between mind and landscape is often such that the latter functions as a mirror, becomes, in short, the ground of dreams. John Hearne has written of the Guyanese landscape that it is 'one of the great primary landscapes of the world, and it can crush the mind like sleep. Like sleep it inspires the dreams by which we record the progress of our waking life.' Whether the ultimate source of this literature of dreams is indeed landscape remains itself a mystery to me.

At any rate, the formal concomitant of such emphases, mind and world caught up in time in a way that brings perception itself into question, is a more or less self-conscious art. For if art is vision and if the premises or the possibility of vision must be questioned, then art must question itself. This, of course, is a modern, rather than a peculiarly Guyanese, process. As Roland Barthes puts it in *Writing Degree Zero*, 'The ideological unity of the bourgeoisie gave rise to a single mode of writing... in the bourgeois periods (classical and romantic) literary form could not be divided because consciousness was not; whereas, as soon as the writer ceased to be a witness to the universal his first gesture was to choose the commitment of his form by either accepting or rejecting the writing of his past. Classical writing therefore disintegrated and the whole of literature from Flaubert to the present day, became the problematics of language.'

However, it seems to me that the writer in the Third World must confront the problem in an even more acute form because the undivided consciousness, the ideology implicit in the literary and linguistic traditions he must enter, may not only seem flatly opposed to his own divided condition but may even be said to subsist upon it. For instance, as Wilson Harris has pointed out, the concept of the person as a closed or complete entity wholly constituted by the attributes of a given plane of a given society seems to have little to do with the condition of the slave or, by extension, the materially and culturally deprived man.

It is at once comical and revealing that the best known poem in praise of Guyana, Walter McA. Lawrence's 'O beautiful Guyana', should issue from a poet who seems to be somewhere on the sea wall, his back resolutely turned to most of the eighty-three thousand square miles that are his ostensible subject, in rapt contemplation of the Atlantic Ocean. It is as if his absolute fidelity to a borrowed form drags up from his subconscious a content that undermines his patriotic intent by parodying both form and patriotism. To say this is not to complain that Lawrence was not several decades ahead of his time. The point is that form is not simply a container into which one can pour new thoughts. Also interesting is the unconscious subversiveness of the imagination; it is precisely in unconscious self parody that the glimmer of an awareness of a problem of language or a problem of form may appear, ending the illusion of a perfect understanding between writer and reader based on their common acceptance of 'universally valid' forms.

Martin Carter's *Poems of Succession* can be read as a meditation on the nature of language and cognition. The selections from *Poems of Resistance*, for the most part, belong to a tradition of public poetry which makes use of a rhetoric that assumes no gap between poet and audience. The later poems discover a gap between speaker and hearer, initially located in a specific social, political and historical context. In 'Groaning In The Wilderness', the poet, involved in a breakdown of community so complete that it entails the destruction of a social product, language, and thus of the humanity of the individuals in the broken community, finds himself barking. 'A Mouth Is Always Muzzled' seems to me much less specific in its historical and political reference even though it is usually taken to be about the politics of Guyana and nothing else.

A close analysis of 'A Mouth Is Always Muzzled' would show that the first stanza describes a breakdown first in speech and then in perception. In the case of speech, there is a movement from the self out into the world ending in disorder;

In the premises of the tongue
dwells the anarchy of the ear

The second movement is the reverse of this since it proceeds from the world to the self;

In the chaos of the vision
resolution of the purpose

In this case, there is a certain ambiguity; is it that the purpose orders chaos or that the purpose is founded, despite its 'resolution', upon chaotic premises? The second stanza describes two movements; one movement is speech which goes from the self out into the world and the other is the processes, eating, by which part of the world enters the self and actually becomes 'Self';

But a mouth is always muzzled
by the food it eats to live.

The two movements result in a kind of collision and in silence. The third stanza describes one movement from the world to the self with a benevolent, because man-made, interposition and one movement from the self into the world aided by human inventiveness:

> Rain was the cause of roofs.
> Birth was the cause of beds.

These are riddling statements that make the human powers of speech and cognition seem beset by difficulties everywhere in the environment. The final riddle grows out of this view of the human condition:

> But life is the question asking
> what is the way to die.

Greater than the demand for roofs and beds or, perhaps subsuming all such demands, is the need to live in such a way that the final absurdity, death, shall acquire meaning. The poem describes life more as a riddle than as a question, but then, says Carter in an earlier poem, 'If these are riddles, riddles write themselves'.

The order of time in the poems is frequently confused. Only the end of an experience can make complete sense of the experience 'Only where our footprints end can tell/ whether the journey was an old advance/ or a new retreat' so that one lives 'forward' and understands 'backwards'. This makes speech doubly difficult as time reveals new meanings 'So sudden, and so hurting/ is the bitten tongue of memory'. One normally bites ones tongue because something that lay in the future when one began to speak contradicts the intent. Carter has reversed the order of time by applying this to memory.

One poem brings together the question of the relation of self to world and the sense of time as running backwards in the order of cognition. It does so in the form of a dreamlike experience. 'About To Pass Me' presents the poet leaving a house (so that the experience of being in the house is in the past) and meeting himself approaching the house (when the experience of being in the house is in the future). One recognizes that the house and the person addressed are important to the poet and that the dreamlike experience expresses his own reluctance to leave. In other words, the contents of consciousness are being projected on to 'reality' so as partly to displace it. The 'practical' need to leave is seen in the poet leaving while the desire not to leave becomes the poet approaching. The double image is a curious balance of the pressure of internal and external or emotional and 'practical' elements and also a balance of past and future in a dream where 'faces that never lived stared at' the poet.

The poetry of Martin Carter undergoes a radical transformation after *Poems of Resistance*. This is usually explained wholly in terms of political disillusionment. Yet the consequences of so radical an exploration of the most basic premises of experience can only be a drastic alteration of form and a sort of difficulty best described as that of the riddle. In some cases the exploration comes to assume a political form without being wholly confined to the political context. It is instructive to compare 'Confound Deliberate Chaos' from *Poems of Succession* with 'Our Number' from *Poems of Affinity*. In the case of 'Confound Deliberate Chaos', the futility of trying to find out why 'canal beside a convent was Amazon to a boy' is a cause for celebration because it confounds all calculations. Scale in both time and space is always subjective, shifting and fluid, evading the rigidity of the mind that seeks to confine by calculation. However, scale in 'Our Number' becomes anything but a cause for celebration precisely because the 'we' of the poem have surrendered to 'a way of counting'. The last lines of the poem recall the elimination of individuality under slavery and indentureship. A slave, after all, is a statistic not a person:

Shrimp is our number. Is so
we stay. Is a way
of counting born we.

The use of the dialect at this point reinforces both the sense of deprivation (of language, in this case) and the tone of self-disgust. It is as if the poet joins the 'shrimp' while being distanced from them by the fact of knowing he is a shrimp. We are a long way from the compassion of 'The roofs of men are fused in misery' ('University of Hunger' in *Poems of Resistance*). Self-confined in 'a way of counting', we answer the political 'tide that naked skins us' only with impotent abuse. It would be difficult to describe more accurately the combination of private rage and public acquiescence inspired by the Burnham regime in many quarters. However, 'Census' lays the blame squarely on our failure to conceive of ourselves as valid persons, as subjects rather than objects:

Use the true mathematic
in a real counting.
Indite about strays
and such as those them.
Include the new others.
The big ones. The not so big
ones. That very big one
too. Then indict. Then add up.
Smaller count. Ampler measure.
True mathematic.

The irony lies, of course, in the very notion of including 'the new **others**' with the strays and 'those them' from whom they have sought to distinguish themselves (perhaps with expensive shirt-jacks and the inevitable Honda Accord). In a sense, though, such trappings create only the illusion of size, even in the case of 'that very big one', so that a 'smaller count' will suffice to include all, equally 'naked skin' at last. All are involved, including 'the new others' and, as Carter remarks in 'With that Loan' , 'a tick on the flank of a beast is itself a beast.' The relativism of scale that we saw in

'Confound Deliberate Chaos' returns with a terrible irony in the specific political context.

In eternity, riddles resolve themselves. *Poems of Succession* ends unexpectedly with a vision of the wise men of the mountains, the hsien, for whom 'a season is a midday.' The relation of the self to the world is one such riddle to which Carter returns in *Poems of Affinity:*

> Being, always to arrange
> myself in the world, and the world
> in myself, I try to do both. How
> both are done is difficult.

The puzzle is a puzzle only within one lifetime, however:

> Why,
> I have to ask, do I have to
> arrange anything, when every
> thing is already arranged
> by love's and death's inscrutable
> laws, mortal judiciary, time's
> doll house of replaceable heads,
> arms and legs ? In another
> house, not time's, time itself arranges
> mine and the world's replacement.

It is possible to see this optimism as a response to the failure of political hopes. To some extent, it may be but the problem of consciousness in its relation to time and the world has been central to Martin Carter's poetry since *Poems of Resistance*. The local, political and immediate experience is not so much supplanted by the eternal and universal as intimately bound up with it from the beginning.

The art of Wilson Harris is rather more obviously based on the dream like state. In *Palace of the Peacock*, the break between inner and outer world's is represented, in part, by the relationship between the narrator, whose closed spiritual eye is turned inward to a world of feeling, and the central character, Donne, whose seeing, material eye is turned outwards to the world of action. The literal journey into the interior of Guyana is the correlative of a spiritual journey to reverse this ancient 'dissociation of sensibility'. It is a journey into the past in the sense that the journey has been made before and the members of the crew are returning to the places where they died before in a 'mixed futuristic order of events'. Since the journey is a metaphor, it is possible to see all the characters as aspects of one character or, as Harris puts it, 'The crew that every man mans in his inmost ship and theatre and mind'. The novelist thus makes it clear that the tale is a kind of dream of a single mind. Indeed, I am told that the original title of the book was *The Dream of the Pilgrim*.

In *The Whole Armour*, Harris describes a journey simultaneously into past and future. The hero, Cristo, during his stay in the wilderness, goes farther back into the past than the time of Noah and imagines himself a monkey swinging from a tree (the cavalier fusion of Darwin and the Bible is characteristic). He also hears of a glass factory which did not exist in Guyana at the time Harris wrote. Within this curious temporal order, landscape then becomes a sort of mirror of Cristo's spiritual development. The same may be said of the landscape in *Palace of the Peacock*; the crew are actually journeying in pursuit of some Amerindian labourers, 'the folk' who have the 'only real devil of a title to the land'. They eventually find themselves pursued instead although 'the folk' never actually appear. The reason is that they are themselves 'the folk' as soon as they choose to be and so to pursue the folk is to pursue themselves. Thus the land gives back the terror and oppression they bring to it.

Few writers in English have mounted as concerted an attack on the traditional form of the novel as Wilson Harris has done. The point of the exercise is not to be exotic but to find a form appropriate to a reality very different from the one that English nineteenth century novelist lived in. I suspect that Harris underestimates both the power and the complexity of what he calls 'the conventional mold' but his sensitivity to the implications of borrowed forms is probably justified.

Edgar Mittelholzer's experiments with leitmotifs and 'telescopic objectivity' testify to his own, less systematic, interest in developing the form of the novel. In his novels, the dream state becomes the experience of the supernatural which, very often, mirrors the consciousness of the experiencing subject. In *A Morning at the Office*, a young woman thinking of having an affair, has her thigh pressed by a ghostly hand coming out of her desk. In *Sylvia*, the 'brown jumbies' taunt the heroine with her own sexual repression. Sometimes the landscape seems to have a personality, as in *Of Trees and The Sea*. Mittelholzer's interest in the supernatural can thus be seen as part of his interest in abnormal states of consciousness that are capable, at least partly, of displacing reality.

In Mittelholzer's case, the question of time appears as a sense of the weight of history. He is said to have written the Kaywana trilogy partly to give Guyanese a sense of their own history. The inanimate objects that contain their past like an electric charge, the key in *A Morning at the Office*, the Dutchman's map in *My Bones and my Flute*, indicate a way of looking at history that is quite different from, say, V. S. Naipaul's history of 'futility' or Kamau Brathwaite's African journey or the allegations of an absence of ruins. Mittelholzer repeatedly suggests that the past inheres in the present as a kind of potency released by human consciousness. This is not very different from the recurrence of the past in Harris's novels or from Martin Carter's poem 'What For Now?'.

The vision of the past as dream inherent in the present may also be seen in A. J. Seymour's well known poem, 'There Runs A Dream'. The poem has been criticized for expressing 'a romantic view of history'. The poet's obvious distaste for the rather sinister forest and tangled vegetation and his equally obvious appreciation of the 'trim dwellings' and broad fields are decidedly unromantic; no enthusiasm for untamed nature is allowed. However the vanished order persists mysteriously in the ancient symbol of time, the river, despite the anarchic jungle. The sense of mystery is conveyed by the 'black waters' because a normally transparent element has become opaque and dark; the past persists as mystery and dream just as it does in the art of Mittelholzer, Harris and Carter.

An extended version of the essay first published in *Kyk-over-Al*, no. 31, 1985.

READING THE POEMS

FRANK BIRBALSINGH

MARTIN CARTER'S EARLIEST POETRY

Martin Carter's poetry may be divided into three periods: firstly, poems in *The Hill of Fire Glows Red* (1951), *The Hidden Man* (1952), and *The Kind Eagle* (1952); secondly, the single volume, *Poems of Resistance* (1954); then his subsequent writing. This essay is concerned with the first period: Carter's first three volumes of poetry which are sometimes considered to be declamatory, rhetorical, even bombastic. To some extent, these strictures are also applied to poems in *Resistance*, where, however, they are seen as less damaging. Carter's subsequent work, meanwhile, is regarded as more reflective, low key, if not entirely spent of passion.

It was *Resistance* that first brought Carter to notice because it contained poems with stirring phrases, ringing tones, haunting images, and memorable lines: 'the university of hunger'; 'the nigger yard of yesterday'; 'broken land ripped like a piece of cloth'; 'whenever you fall comrade I shall arise'; and 'Death must not find us thinking that we die'. Why is the striking originality and frank, revolutionary power of such lines and phrases not found in Carter's earliest poems, or if they are, why are they not generally recognised?

At first one must admit to a basic difficulty in dating Carter's poems which may not appear in collections until long after they were written. A few poems in *Resistance*, for example, may have been written before 1954, at the same time as those that appear in earlier volumes. This is why, although the fluency and sustained power of many poems in *Resistance* entitle the volume to be placed in a special period of its own – there are many similarities in quality and subject matter between the pre-1954 poems and those in *Resistance*. What separates the pre-1954 poems is the fact that their political agenda – a peaceful, Marxist revolution designed to remove the most glaring evils in Guyanese colonial society – is not as expertly incorporated into their texts as in many poems in *Resistance*. Poems in the first three volumes successfully document colonial evils in Guyana and elsewhere, and passionately denounce them; but they are less successful in eliciting suitable images, or producing coherent structures and consistent statements to convincingly express the passion or outrage provoked by these evils.

'Three Years After This' from *The Hill of Fire Glows Red* is a typical early poem; it was written in 1951, three years after a strike which forms its subject. The strike occurred in 1948 at Enmore, a sugar plantation on the East Coast of Demerara, about twenty miles from Georgetown. Police shot and killed five workers, all Indo-Guyanese. The shooting transformed the strike into one of the most notable events in Guyanese political history, partly because it illustrated the historic struggle of Caribbean plantation workers against injustice, and partly because it had a profound influence on the career of Dr. Cheddi Jagan, (1918-1997) founder and leader of the People's Progressive Party (PPP).[1] The PPP, Guyana's first major political party, has always revered the Enmore martyrs, as the five strike victims came to be called, and it is not at all surprising that Carter, who was a PPP activist at the time, should find poetic inspiration in the Enmore strike.

Growing up in a British Caribbean colony in the 1930s and 40s, Carter was inevitably conditioned by the colour-based values of a society that was organised into broad groups: a small group of ruling whites, a larger middle class of brown, mixed blood people, (like Carter himself), and the largest groups – Afro-Guyanese descendants of African slaves and Indians, the descendants of indentured labourers brought from India, who formed just over half of the population. Both these two groups were preponderantly working class. However, since Indians lived mainly on sugar plantations in the countryside, Carter, who grew up in Georgetown, with its Christian ethos and Westernised habits and mores, could not normally be expected to identify with Indo-Guyanese who were largely peasants, with alien (Hindu or Muslim) customs and values, and different social and cultural practices, including speech patterns and food habits. The opening stanza of 'Three Years After This' depicts a geographical layout that hints at this distinction:

Enmore!
Twenty miles beyond the city
down the long red road.[2]

In 1948, when communications were less developed than they are today, Enmore was even more remote, geographically and culturally.

But remoteness does not deter oppression. When the authority of white plantation owners is threatened by Indo-Guyanese strikers at Enmore, the British colonial government quickly dispatches a lorry with armed police to restore order. Carter describes what follows: 'steel helmets rifles bullets bayonets blood/ and five men bleeding on the innocent grass' (p.10) Battle lines are clearly drawn. Since the police are employed by the government, they and the (white) British governor are seen to take the side of the plantation owners against the workers. The depth of outrage expressed by 'innocent grass' leaves no doubt about which side the poet is on: if the victims are innocent, then their victimisers are guilty. Carter's grief and implied revolutionary solidarity with Indo-Guyanese plantation workers appears to transcend the gap between his own educated, urban, brown, middle class background, and those for whom he is expressing sympathy, people who are alien to him in almost everything except the fact of being born in Guyana. Yet the gap is not transcended by other citizens in Georgetown:

and yet, and yet my city had no shame
my city with a prison for a heart

city of dust and silent streets
city of street preachers... (p.10)

Here the poet indicts Georgetown, centre of the colonial administration, for its uncaring or repressive attitude toward Enmore; but the force of outrage implied earlier by 'innocent grass' is not completely matched by his rather tame indictment of Georgetown as shameless, prison-like, dusty, and silent. One would expect murderers to be denounced more sharply, and this discrepancy arouses suspicion either about the integrity of Carter's political convictions, or about his skill in implementing these convictions in his poetry. Not that the poem betrays false feeling or sentimentality necessarily; it is more that the poet's ideological identification with Indo-Guyanese victims of oppression does not appear to be corroborated in the poem, by the social history from which he comes.

At the same time, there is no denying, at least in an emotional sense, that Carter's early poetry is genuinely inspired by outrage over the divisiveness, exploitation and general injustice of colonial rule in Guyana. It is undeniable too that in dealing with this subject, he cannot ignore an Indo-Guyanese working class which forms virtually half the population, and is the backbone of the colony's main industry – sugar. But Indians only began arriving as indentured labourers in Guyana in 1838. For centuries before that, African slaves sustained the sugar industry, and they and their descendants formed a majority of the Guyanese population until the early decades of this century. If by the 1940s, Afro-Guyanese, white and brown Guyanese constituted the bulk of the colony's urban middle class of teachers, civil servants, office clerks, and professionals, that still left a sizeable Afro-Guyanese working class whose lot in the cities and villages was not much better than that of their Indo-Guyanese counterparts on the sugar plantations.

This is why another poem from *The Hill of Fire Glows Red* invokes the name of Quamina, leader in a failed slave rebellion that occurred in 1823. The colour red is dominant through frequent references to blood and fire in this poem 'Like the Blood of Quamina'. In the first stanza, a sugar cane field has been set alight to make the field ready for reaping, 'flame like a smouldering hill of fire' (p.8) Since the fire is not completely out, its destructive potential implies defiance of the sugar plantation proprietors, the perpetrators of slavery, which is linked to a similar potential in the blood of Quamina:

the hill of fire glows red like fresh blood
like the blood of Quamina
flowing through the green forest (p.8)

This final stanza is a call for liberation through revolutionary action such as the rebellion mounted by Quamina. Yet the link between the defiant, avenging power of fire, and the resurgence of Quamina's legacy, is hardly more convincing than Carter's professed solidarity with Indo-Guyanese victims of oppression in 'Three Years After'. The image of the blood of Quamina flowing through the green forest refers to revolutionary activity one hundred and thirty years earlier, and its link with events in 1948 appears slightly far-fetched. This failure to realise the revolutionary agenda with full conviction opens these early poems to the charge of being merely rhetorical or bombastic.

While other poems in *The Hill of Fire Glows Red* expose limitations and injustices in colonial Guyana in similar fashion, and propose apocalyptic redemption by means of a messianic, Marxist call to arms, most poems in the 1952 volume *The Hidden Man* tend to ignore the possibility of a new heaven on earth, and devote themselves to documenting details of colonial oppression. Poems like 'Who Walks a Pavement' and 'O Where to Hide', for example, are dominated by images of darkness, entrapment and confinement which cannot be evaded despite strenuous resistance. The first poem evokes the horror of prison, and describes a man 'who walks a pavement, walks and disappears'; the second has a persona who is upset by persistent drumming and stamping, and is eventually overcome by fear and trembling: 'God the face of earth is moving!/where to hide? O where to hide?...' (p.32) Although the persona is completely disoriented and cannot find refuge anywhere, his/her disorientation is concretely observed and quite credible. This at least is more persuasive than any shrill announcement of political nirvana that never comes.

The images and ideas in poems from the third volume *The Kind Eagle* tend to be more concrete and realistic like those in *The Hidden Man*, and altogether they represent an advance in technique over the uncorroborated, utopian longings and forced imagery that we have seen in some poems in *The Hill of Fire Glows Red*. 'O Human Guide' from *The Kind Eagle* evokes typical images of pain, harshness, and discomfort. The atmosphere of suffering and adversity is established from the very first lines of the poem which set the tone of what is to follow:

> In the burnt earth of these two years
> I dip my hand, I dip my hand. (p.35)

The image of burnt earth is potent. Up to the 1950s, huge mounds of loose earth and clay used to be built and then set alight for days so that the finished – burnt earth – could be used as construction material for resurfacing roads in rural areas in Guyana. But the poem does not refer to the constructive qualities of burnt earth. By dipping his hand in burnt earth, the poet is recalling bitter memories, which he later describes as 'the furies of this world' and 'painful flowers'. It is true that the final stanza attempts to balance the impact of these negative references with more positive images, but the final lines of the poem confirm its gloomy message while still containing an image of powerful resistance:

Each day I ride a wild black horse of terror
and every night I lock him in my bosom...! (p.35)

Between 1950 and 1953 Carter played a very active role in the PPP, at one time editing the party newspaper *Thunder*, then standing as a candidate for the party in the 1953 elections, and later going to prison for his political activity. All this, including direct contact with workers and other party activists undoubtedly increased his political maturity. Because we cannot be certain about the date of composition of each poem, it is not possible to demonstrate a consistent development in Carter's verse, either of his political ideas or poetic technique. All we can say is that *Resistance* contains more successful individual pieces than any of the earlier volumes.

Some of Carter's best poems are found in *Resistance*, not because he has lost his revolutionary fervour or changed his Marxist ideals, but because he has learnt, by 1954, to express his fervour and ideals with more skill. One of the best poems in *Resistance*, 'Death of a Slave', deals with the same subject as the poem on Quamina but in the later poem the observation is solid, factual, objective, down to earth. The diction as well is simple and smooth, and the expression fluent and coherent. After outlining the history of slavery on sugar plantations with all their brutality and injustice, the poem predicts that such humiliation is likely to breed retaliation and nourish a spirit of resistance and liberation. Hence the final stanza:

In the dark floor
In the cold dark earth
time plants the seeds of anger. (p.50)

Conviction is total. The adjective 'dark' has been repeated several times, and hints of resistance are scattered throughout the poem, so that the final images of seeds of anger planted in the earth comes as an expected (not predictable) conclusion. Here is no drift into dream or false rhetorical hope; for it is perfectly natural that well planted seeds should germinate, grow, and generate new life. The image is realistic, literally down to earth. Nor is there any ideological rhetoric or forced encouragement of ill-matching associations and links. The final note of optimism is concrete and firmly grounded, and the overall effect of the poem is one of sureness of touch and great power.

If *Resistance* contains far more poems which reach this level of assured achievement, it should not be thought that even Carter's first collection is without such poems. 'Looking at Your Hands' in *Hill of Fire Glows Red* remains one of Carter's most memorable poems. It ends:

And so if you see me
looking at your hands
listening when you speak
marching in your ranks
you must know
I do not sleep to dream, but dream to change the world. (p.11)

These lines may not bring heaven down to earth, but as a mere statement of intent, they pack a powerful punch in terms of confessional solidarity, revolutionary zeal, and uplifting hope; and their youthful energy, disarming candour and fresh optimism make for a stimulating conclusion. They celebrate human solidarity when it is enlisted to promote an ever present human need for change and reform.

Any comprehensive account of Carter's performance as a poet must consider the uniqueness of the social, ethnic and political conditions in which he lived in the 1950s. Poems like 'Three Years After This', 'Do Not Stare at Me', and 'Like the Blood of Quamina' reflect the arduous task of forging Indian and African aspects of Guyanese ethnicity into a single nationality. The task is even more arduous when nationality has to be forged on the basis of a peaceful socialist revolution which was the agenda of the PPP. If Carter is not consistent in successfully representing this agenda in his poetry, it is not because of false feeling or drifting into dream, it is because of a fundamental difficulty of representing ideology in art. This difficulty persists whether it is the political variety faced by artists in the former Soviet Union, or the religious kind faced by Graham Greene in his lifelong struggle with orthodox Roman Catholic belief. As Greene struggled with the artistic implications of Catholic orthodoxy and the Roman church in his novels, so does Carter struggle with the artistic demands of his socialist faith in his early poems. As a rule, it appears that poems which merely trumpet the rewards of his faith, or announce the imminence of a Marxist millennium, without adequate corroboration, tend to be less successful than those which translate their ideological longings into credible human reactions, concrete images, consistent statements and coherent structures.

So far as Carter's place in Caribbean poetry is concerned, if Walcott is lauded for stimulating and insightful reflections on the dilemma of West Indian identity, and Brathwaite for conferring overdue dignity on African components of West Indian culture, Carter deserves no less praise for celebrating an undying, human spirit of resistance against oppression and a persistent, equally human desire for freedom. Indeed, it might be argued that Carter deserves greater praise since this spirit of resistance has unique historical resonance in a region where slavery/indenture lasted for four continuous centuries, right up to the time of World War One. Comparison between Carter's 'Death must not find us thinking that we die' and Claude McKay's 'If we must die, let it not be like hogs'[3] illustrates the prevalence of a spirit of resistance in West Indian literature and a desire for freedom that is as fundamental to West Indian experience as the issue of identity, or the reclamation of African cultural inheritance. Carter's preoccupation with politics in his early poetry should not devalue his artistic achievement, any more than Yeats's preoccupation with the colonial politics of Ireland in 'Easter 1916' damages his poem's reputation as one of the finest in modern Irish literature.

For in paying homage to heroes who 'dreamed and are dead', Yeats celebrates the same undying human desire for liberation that is expressed in Carter's unforgettable line 'I do not sleep to dream, but dream to change the world.'

Notes

1. C. Jagan, *The West on Trial* (London: Michael Joseph, 1966), p.109.
2. Martin Carter, *Selected Poems* (Georgetown:, Demerara Publishers, 1989). All subsequent quotations from Carter's poetry are from this text.
3. Claude McKay, 'If We Must Die' in Paula Burnett, Ed., *The Penguin Book of Caribbean Verse in English* (Harmondsworth, Middlesex: Penguin, 1986), p.144.

SYDNEY KING

FOREWORD TO *POEMS OF RESISTANCE FROM BRITISH GUIANA*, 1954

You are about to read poetry which is significant for oppressed people, and particularly for Guiana and the whole Caribbean. Added significance resides in this poetry because Martin Carter approaches the world from the profound humanist standpoint of a Communist. The increasing grandeur of his work shatters the philistine belief that art is a pose divorced from real life, that bringing reality into art is the death of art.

Every man has a world outlook. Every artist, as a man, has a world outlook. Shakespeare can no more escape this than Accabreh the slave rebel. T.S. Eliot can no more escape than Mayakovsky. This world outlook cannot be non-tendentious, non-party. A world outlook is the most highly partisan thing. But readers must be warned that it is easy for an artist who conforms with 'custom', with 'the established order', to masquerade as non-party, as neutral.

It can be said in criticism of Martin Carter that at times in earlier stages this poet has produced works which are no more than 'critical realist', that is to say, a critical exposure of reality. But they were critical from a revolutionary standpoint, a new type of criticism. And little wonder. He was charged with the task of establishing a realist tradition, you might say, in respect of many periods of our history. His was the heavy task of speaking for the African slave, for the American Indians, and remaining faithful to the world proletarian cause. Even in recent times, in *University of Hunger* in which he arouses our anger at the leaden misery of the peasants, although we can see that the picture is drawn by an artist of profound humanity, we are not dragged out of the gloom. 'The clocks of dawn stand up and crow like bugles'. And after this we return to see the moon die, to 'the unbelievable' and 'the shadowless'.

Perhaps what the poet was doing was to begin to tear the veil from our eyes at the time when the working people of Guiana were first beginning to move. When the people began to display their young vigour, Carter turned his attention to nurturing the forces of the radiant future, to sustaining the people in their struggle, till he could write in *I am no Soldier*, 'I am my poem, I come to you in particular gladness'.

Strangely enough, as the reaction becomes more brutal, Carter's poems take on a more decided optimism. And small wonder. For the reaction is becoming more brutal because the certainty of the people's victory becomes more and more evident, because the consciousness and fighting condition of the workers are rising and because international warmongering is losing out. The repression occurred in Guiana because Anglo-American imperialism saw people standing up to their full height, growing conscious of their humanity.

In a colony there is no room for 'intellectuals'. Everyone must be an activist. Here, where bombs have never been dropped, complacent people have not yet realised the significance of the worldwide movement for peace. Those who understand the profound economic, political and cultural consequences of war are in the front line of the fight for peace. Those who associate with the imperialists and American business agents, enjoy the 'peace' of their own pseudo world. It is not surprising, therefore, that Martin Carter was the first of us to see the necessity for a peace movement here, and was elected by our people Chairman of the Guiana Peace Committee at a public meeting in 1951. In his poem to the dead Stalin he invites us to swear, 'Earth will be guarded like a little child – peace will be won'.

In another poem, not published here, he warned peace partisans, 'Guard well the peace and save the grateful years'.

The imperialists know quite well the influence of artists. That is why Martin Carter was put in detention camp with a strange hedge of barbed wire and a gate of bayonets. That is why his *Poems of Resistance* were banned in Guiana.

He is never satisfied with the standard of his work. Constantly enriching our cultural experience, constantly refining and humanising our emotions, boldly adding rich West Indian image and idiom to the English language, the poet continues his task. His poetry means everything to our people. It gives them courage, confidence and pride in themselves. It encourages them in their struggles for peace through national self-determination. His words ring out in the country air among the workers like a blacksmith's hammer on its anvil when the morning is calm.

The message of these words is clear and easily understood.

Georgetown, British Guiana, January, 1954.

NEVILLE DAWES

PREFACE TO THE 1964 EDITION OF *POEMS OF RESISTANCE*

The post-war generation of West Indian writers, holding various and sometimes strange political opinions – or none at all – regard Martin Carter with special respect. He is a poet with a unique place in modern Caribbean Literature. Exiled poets (in stark London winters or within hearing of African talking drums) who can tell you nothing about Carter's career or political views, remember and quote with deep approval lines like,

> Twin bars of hunger mark their metal brows
> twin seasons mock them
> parching drought and flood.

or

> In the cold dark earth
> time plants the seeds of anger.

or

> I do not sleep to dream, but dream to change the world.

This is the most living tribute a poet could hope for.

Poems of Resistance, originally published in 1954 established Martin Carter's reputation and distinguished him as an outstanding poetic voice in the awakened, explosive questioning of our mental and physical environment and bondage. His poems are in a line of literary resistance which may be said to begin with Claude McKay of Jamaica; (non-literary resistance goes back to the slave revolts but our history has not yet been written so as to make this absolutely clear). Certainly, 'Death must not find us thinking that we die' has close affinities with McKay's continuing landmark:

> If we must die – oh, let us nobly die...
> Like men we'll face the murderous cowardly pack,
> Pressed to the wall, dying, but – fighting back.

But there is a new note of militancy in Carter,

> I take again my nigger life, my scorn
> and fling it in the face of those who hate me.

and of universal awareness:

> ... to-day in the middle of the tumult
> when different voices join to say the same
> and different hearts beat out in unison,

so that the tears of alienation and suffering caused by slavery become the fierce tears of happiness at the dawn of the reconstruction of the complete human personality. Here Carter is at one with the Martiniquan poet, Aimé Césaire:

> Make not of me that man of hate, for whom I have only hatred,
> although I set myself down in one single race,
> you know my tyrannical love
> you know that it is not out of hate for other races
> that I demand to dig for this single race,
> what I want is for universal hunger,
> for universal thirst.
>
> (*Cahier d'un Retour au Pays Natal*)

The universality of a poet's statement has most validity when it is firmly based on his specific experience. And the poems collected here may be regarded in one way as a single poem of resistance to the special oppression of 1953, one eloquent refusal to be dehumanised by imperialist bayonets and colonial prisons. Where Martin Carter's voice rises to angry rhetoric, the tone is appropriate: daring rhetoric has greater power to free men from bondage than 'curling arabesques.' At the same time, even in the difficult circumstances in which these poems were created, there are areas of controlled calm, as in this lovely movement:

> Over the shining mud the moon is blood
> falling on ocean at the fence of lights.
> My mast of love will sail and come to port
> leaving a trail beneath the world, a track
> cut by my rudder tempered out of anguish.

That, simply, is the work of a genuine poet.

But wherever oppression exists (in 1964, for 'Kenya' read 'Angola', for 'Malaya' read 'Vietnam') poets like Martin Carter will raise their voices in resistance, will sing for freedom and will be willing to make their shirts into banners for the revolution.

Martin Carter was in his early twenties when he wrote *Poems of Resistance*. The present generation of new Guyana youth will need the inspiration of these poems in a time of crisis.

A.J. SEYMOUR

A COMMENTARY ON TWO POEMS
(from: *Studies of Ten Guyanese Poems*, 1982)

"I Come From The Nigger Yard"

The nigger yard of yesterday – this is a powerfully evocative image. The 'nigger yard' is a West Indian term linked with the slavery of the sugar plantation. The novels of C. L. R. James, Roger Mais and Orlando Patterson – especially *Minty Alley* and *Brother Man* – revolve around the nigger-yard reality, as well as those of Sam Selvon and Jan Carew. In Guyana, the nigger-yard of the slave plantation later became the 'bound yard' where East Indian immigrants in the 1840s were housed before allocation to estates was made. The term is synonymous with the conditions of open pit latrines and often bathing in the open under the standpipe which becomes the centre of talk and gossip. Martin Carter invokes in the short story 'Out, Out, the Fire', the atmosphere of the nigger-yard.

Historically, few physical evidences may remain of the nigger yard, except in Rastafarian settlements. As soon as indigenous governments took over at Independence, they tried to improve housing conditions and to remove the yard. In Guyana, in the 1950s, Sir Alfred Savage used the period of the Suspension of the Constitution to build houses of better quality for lower-income groups, and these superseded the nigger-yard logies.

– *the scorn of myself* – this describes one of the most shameful legacies of slavery and the plantation system; the African slave was continuously conditioned to feel inferior with a chain-association of lack of freedom, poor living conditions, ignorance and the lack of education, inadequate speech systems and merciless and oppressive working conditions. These internalised the external circumstances into 'the scorn of myself'.

Not all independent governments have seen the wisdom of changing as soon as possible the education systems inherited from the past to work upon these images of self-contempt, and lack of esteem enshrined in the mind of the African slave's personality and his descendants. The Rasta movement seems to thrive still upon this element while in 'Western civilisation', the black-skinned peoples are feared and oppressed wherever they live.

– *the agony of the dark hut in the shadow* – not as simple as other images, like 'days of cruelty and nights of pain' this is a very important image embodying lack of sunshine, lack of facilities, alienation from light and heat and power and including the brooding nature of inferiority in sickness and poverty. Notice also how the poet links it with the next line in the 'hurt of things' where the addition of an 'r' as a letter philosophises the negative nature of existence, and adds an attractive element to the poetry.

– *'leaping I come,...will hear'*. This is very dynamic and menacing at the same time. It carries the images of crowds of black peoples thronging the 'wide streets of tomorrow' with angry shouts. In this phrase is packed the fear of white cities, that the ghettos will break loose as projected by C. P. Snow and invade the T.V. viewing rooms.

The first stanza is like an introduction to a long piece of music, proclaiming the themes that will follow, and stating the power of the poem.

The second stanza sets out the birth and childhood of the nigger-yard infant child. As 'nakedness', note that not only is the stone invoked, but the star, which is matter endowed with power and radiance; nothing clothes the star nor the slave, but the slave may have the same brilliance and power as the star.

In these eight lines, various images emerge. The days are blind, the cradle rocks back and forth in time, but with the feeling of the skin torn from the back of a slave. Even the floor is aching. Note that the child is looking at the dust for patterns – the root and its trace, the leaf and its mark, the flower and its shape. These are all organic and growing symbols; the message here is that even the child has expectations of organic development in the growing process, and the reader must expect the child wants it too.

The third stanza finds the nigger-yard child 'walking with bare feet'; this world is a world of fever-images or distorted dream symbols. The faces are strange and terrible, the world is upside down, the hearts are torn and wounded, groaning cries come to the ear within the wind. Because the faces are strange, one is warned that there is no sense of mother's or familiar features appearing and therefore alienation and possible hostility are in the feelings of the child stemming from the strangeness.

Fortunately life always has compensations. In the fourth stanza, in the first half, music is one of these compensations; true it is sad music, there is the bugle, alerting the reader to the presence of soldiers and police and militia to keep order and project the existence of guns. The drum is also a sign of the forces of disciplined order, but there are overtones of an African past to be found in the drums and celebrations of dance and village festivities. Voices of women bear with them the images of worship services or funeral observances. To the child's ear it is far away – in the distance in a church or burial ground, or a sign for later experiences in his life in 'pauses of silence, then a flood of sound'.

In the second half of the stanza these images are dismissed as 'ghostly' or wind-spirits only insubstantial, the reality is agony and torture – 'born in agony', rhyming with 'torn in torture', the leaves twisted and broken, obviously by the fingers and hands of unfeeling men. The world is cruel as it spins from day into night into day outside of the room and the building when the child is situated. Notice also the stained sheets on the hungry beds and the awakening to discomfort.

What is remarkable about the fifth stanza is that the element of hope is introduced. The child is now grown up, or is growing up. The time is twilight. The place is near to trees, there is seen a star, 'a tiny star neighbouring a leaf' – observe that it is the 'I' of the poem who sees the star, 'notices' it. We can say that the 'prospect pleases and only man is vile'. What is this star? A drop of light, a piece of glass, a spark seed that shows heaven may grow in the destined gloom. It becomes an image of the dream of the human being conquering darkness, a dream nourished in the heart, rejecting the sorrows, struggling against the world of sorrows, changing the colour of leaves from green to the blue of happiness as the sun goes down. The giant shadows are still menacing but the dream is powerful.

The stanza that follows describes the city in which the narrator finds himself. We have passed from the developing world to the ghettos and slums of developed cities which have a third world in their midst. Described as a slum, the image is that of a coffin, linked with prisons and hospitals. The Law and the Church which we would expect to be stabilising influences are described as scornful and blasphemous and the narrating 'I' is like a mangy, hungry, dusty dog, angry and screaming. The only image that is optimistic and that swims against the negative tide is 'a river running' – an element of cleansing in this slum-world.

'It was a child born from a mother' – this stanza, like the previous one, creates an extension from the sugar plantation memory into that of the slums of the so-called developed world. The focus is on the growing lad – bleeding clots, painful experiences that mark the child's face and brow with patterns of alienation. The foundry section, like all manufacturing sectors, is of unfeeling hard cold, icy substances, like hammers to inflict blows and anvils to reduce the hammered objects to powder or distortion. The foundry days are possibly the period when the growing mind is hardened against the unfeeling elements in home, and church, and society in a hopeless, helpless manner.

The narrator now feels himself one of the large, miserable crowds and mobs. 'Owning the land' can mean several things – the power of the proletariat, or in the majority as against the elite, few in number, or part of the production process in field and factory. We find music again, dancing of women bought for money, throbbing jazz from trumpets and trombones. The last three lines are questioning and challenging, even slightly menacing in the phrase, 'challenging fire'.

With a leap, we come to the present time. What is the time of the writing of the poem? The world is convulsed with change, the tumult is half way through and won, the face of the land is changing. Most important, the poet feels that the shifting earth is 'twisting into shape'. Again, we are at the mercy of an image. 'Different voices joining to say the same', may mean the winds of change blowing through the world, the independence of former colonies, the growing popularity of socialist policies, the hope of better things implicit in the North-south dialogue, the third world expression of solidarity among oppressed peoples everywhere.

In the second half of this stanza, the narrator returns to the feeling of the first stanza of the poem. He is full of the strength of his manhood. 'Linking his fingers, welding his flesh' into a power that will lead to freedom.

The final stanza sums up, but with a sense of maturity, what the poem has been saying all along, the note of menace is there. 'I come to the world ... fury in my hands'. This is linked with the wounds on his body and the scars upon his soul. But there is a rational element. The 'I' personality' is reflective and will read the histories of the peoples and their lives. He will see the 'shower of sparks'. These will include the dreams and visions that come from encounters in events and the wealth of the dreams. Life is a mental and spiritual affair, not only physical. The glories will give him pleasure and the riches will enhance him, but he will be saddened by the sorrows and diminished with the losses.

In the last two lines, the narrator points out that the past had the heavy burden of distress and anguish, but that the future is a period in which the world must reckon with his strength as a factor for helping to shape it.

'From the nigger yard of yesterday I come with my burden. To the world of tomorrow I turn with my strength'. So strength is the image that reverberates as the poem ends.

For many readers in Guyana, the Caribbean and the Third World, this poem 'I Come from the Nigger Yard', shares with one other 'The University of Hunger', pride of place among Martin Carter's poems, since they provide words, like guns, in which he speaks for all colonials everywhere, and for all oppressed subjected and deprived people living in slums in big cities. This poem comes in the second phase of Carter's poetry when the stirring call of revolutionary anti-colonialism to be found in *The Hill of Fire Glows Red* was replaced by dark anger, a sense of waste, and of personal suffering coming directly from his detention in prison in 1953 after the Suspension of the B. G. Constitution. His words become a vision shaped by anguish and indignation in a personal defiance that gathers together and enshrines the true history of the period.

"University of Hunger"

Of the poems of Martin Carter, this is perhaps the most outstanding.

The title gives us a lead into the poem. 'Hunger' here is the desire for necessary things to feed the body, mind and spirit, a desire that is not met and that becomes therefore a deprivation. It is a Third World feeling expressed against the developed countries, and at the same time, it is also partly the expression of people who live in slums and ghettos in developed countries.

It is a poem with the spirit of trade union protest in it and therefore penetrates and transcends bland socialist theory.

'University' denotes the place where immature and questioning intelligences have a chance to satisfy their needs in a situation which helps them to learn in an organised way from other workers and from leaders who are teachers, in the same way as university dons guide undergraduates. It also says that the people who enter the University of Hunger will graduate with deep understanding of life and events and class situations.

The first six lines lay the scene in a static way. The first word, 'is', carries with it its implied subject 'it', but it brushes that pronoun aside to affirm strong existence; the first two lines indicate images of learning, deprivation and waste, and show men as embarked on a journey that has its inbuilt destination, a pilgrimage. Not like the pilgrimage to Canterbury, this is an organised, measured, joyless and determined protest, men on the move in multitudes, for their rights.

'The print of hunger wanders in the land'. Here we have physical evidence, like the rubber stamp, of desert conditions passing from one part of the country to another. There are long forgotten things – maybe graves, waste canals, abandoned plantations, and ruined houses. The green tree is bending perhaps like a body in weakness over the lost assets. Rural areas are suggested here. The land is buckled by the parched drought, rippling like the spasms of hunger in a starving man. The places where men live, their huts, are seen to have come together, to be fused in misery, as the men and women who live in them huddle together to share their deprivations. There was a saying once in Scotland, 'It's as easy for two to starve as one'.

This is the only static stanza. All the others have measured involvement in them, linked with the rhythm of the lines, and there is a growing menace of men approaching. The second stanza introduces the mule, the strong bastard animal with flaring nostrils and patience and determination and a certain stubbornness. Men are following the mule prints and in this march we know that since the mule will get to its destination, they will reach there also. This is implied in the line. 'Passing the ancient bridge'. The bridge has linked two places for a long time in history over a dividing canal or trench, and it is a symbol of stability, but along with it are images of dead pride and sudden fear in 'terror and the time'. People have fled over this bridge but the men here are bunching together and moving slowly in the poem.

The third stanza seems to identify the poem with the Guyana coastland – 'the distant village of the flood' such as a village in West Coast Berbice which used perpetually, it seems, to be under tide water. The marching men have travelled at night through 'the common hours of nakedness' when men seek personal privacy as at night time. The change from middle air to middle earth suggests the loss of idealism and that a stoic realism is being born. They are generally farmers and peasants who know intimately the two alternating diseases of Guyanese agriculture: either too much water, or not enough, flood or drought. In a sense, the duality of these twin seasons are embodied and reinforced in their two eyebrows, hardened to metal by disaster and hunger.

We have, following this, another affirmation. 'Is the dark ones'. These are people of African or Indian descent, blackened and browned by the blazing sun. Their feet, as they move them, are accustomed to sink below the surface of the soil, they seem 'half sunken in the land'. They have little or no influence on the way things are organised. They have no voice, are unrepresented in any council and the three deeply negative words that follow show that they have no fullness, no conviction and no shadow to throw as they move.

But they are on the march, these people; they come 'treading on the mud floor of the year'. For each of the twelve months of the year, these dull peasants and disheartened farmers walk on mud as a floor both in field and hut. They do this in the midst of the sound of the sea and the sight of the regular flood waters, backing up in the roads of the village and in the canals. The bat, symbol of their life, is blindly flittering in the neighbourhood, in houses, rafters and in trees. And the poet suddenly becomes lyrical in the philosophical and anguished statement of meaningless life, with men wanting to know the meaning of existence; the song rises, 'O long is the march of men, and long is the life and wide is the span'. The wind blowing off the sea is cold and cuts through one's rags, and the cutlass and fork and hoe remain unused in the soil, as one has little strength to use the hoe.

The sixth stanza borrows images from the shore – the sea and the air and the sand. Not all are images of despair. The marching men are like the sea birds flapping and following a boat, but the sky is blood purple with its sunset, like blood of torture, and resembles flakes of fire powdered on the sky as the sun goes down.

But notice the element of hope –'water melodies of white foam' sounding from the sand, even though that sand is wrinkled, as if with age.

With stanza seven, we go back to the marching men. The streets of night along which they travel hold their desire like the bare thighs of a woman. They move on and on along these long streets and underneath is the sexual image of a lover moving his hand up his beloved's body.

For the first time, we come on the image of the drum beating. The overall shadow of night seems to tell us the men must rest, so the drum stops beating. The men who haven't shaved at least since the beginning of the march and have beards of differing lengths, fall down (almost too dramatically) and go to sleep. But soon the early roosters are welcoming the daylight and these bugle calls awaken them.

The final stanza describes that awakening to march again. They see the moon go down in the east. They hear the conch shell blowing and the clanging of iron, almost like an army being stirred awake. Three lines repeat emptiness, lack of voice, lack of conviction and lack of influence. Then we have the repetition of man's marching through a life that seems to have no ending and the wide span that starts with a man's birth and ends with his death.

The poem leaves an impression of rural, disheartened men who have little, who are hungry, who are marching to the capital city in their multitudes to demand in confrontation some redress, as their human right from the authorities. All they have is their hunger and deprivation, but they are men. We need to repeat at the end the first stanza with its lack of movement, in order to end on the same note with which we began, and to summarise the content of the poem.

BARBARA LALLA

CONCEPTUAL PERSPECTIVES ON TIME AND TIMELESSNESS IN MARTIN CARTER'S 'UNIVERSITY OF HUNGER'

Martin Carter's 'University of Hunger' is about arrival and about the formation of a mind, the collective mind of a people, by the circumstances of that arrival. It is therefore a historical vision. However, in 'University of Hunger' only the last verse is Standard English past tense, with the single exception of line 20. (A copy of the poem is appended at the end of the essay.) On the other hand, Creole may convey reference to past time without marking past tense, and the time reference of some verbs in the poem is therefore ambiguous. If the poem echoes with voices in both codes, it may well interweave past and present vision, and, in so doing, refocus our view of history. Thus, an important issue in interpreting this poem is its multidimensional time reference. In a phrase like *they come, come* may be present or past, depending on whether the voice is English or Creole. The linguistic situation of the Caribbean enables Carter to address an international audience through the widely comprehensible code of Standard Caribbean English, but, at the same time, to counter traditional poetic discourse by intercepting Standard structures in a number of ways.

To begin with, if we view his first line as Standard English, we assume from the punctuation that it is a statement but from the constituent order that it is a question. If it is a statement, it is mutilated by subject deletion, and it omits a comma between complement and appositive. From the outset, then, if we assume a Standard English voice, Carter tampers with the conventions of traditional literary discourse. The fact is that the structure is more recognisable as Creole. However, he yokes the Creole sentence patterns, familiar in oral discourse, to literary diction unfamiliar in the vernacular. The tendency to frustrate reader expectations continues throughout the poem, which departs from linguistic norms not only at syntactic but at lexico-semantic levels *(print... wanders)*. However, anomaly at the lexical level creates no anxiety; it is the usual stuff of metaphor.

The subjectless sentence is the sole, though recurrent structural feature that the reader can immediately link with Creole, and at first glance the poem would seem to make sparse use of Creole diction. The use of one feature consistently may reflect selectivity aimed at a representational effect, even in the presence of non-Creole structures such as the passive *(are fused)*. At the same time, familiar trappings of traditional Standard English literary discourse reveal their own discrepancies on examination. This second verse contains a normal Standard English subject *(they)*. However, the pronoun has no identifiable referent. Again and again, features that would orient the reader are suppressed or frustrated.

The limited number of Creole features is not an argument against the reality of a Creole voice. Orality in literary discourse is a function of representational features in any case. As any transcript of spoken discourse readily shows, it would be impractical for literature to mirror actual speech with its hesitations, false starts, incomplete sentences and pauses for feedback. Moreover, literature that represents speech in a code other than the official written code usually samples features of that unofficial code. The writer selects a workable balance of features. Most should be well enough known to be easily comprehensible, but some must contrast strongly enough to the official form to remind readers of the code they represent.

Representation can be subtle in the Caribbean. Representing the Caribbean voice need not mean producing an array of Creole features in contrast to English features. Such representation may mean exploiting features which are ambiguous in the sense of having one meaning in Creole and another in international English. This ambiguity is often lexical, but it can also be grammatical, as in *come,* where time reference depends on the code involved.

Manoeuvring between past and present involves a shifting vision. So does departure from 'normal' discourse – deviation from features that accurately represent the more usually selected code. Writers have adopted Creole (or their idea of Creole) for the purpose of shifting vision of the Caribbean over the past two hundred years.

Early writers, who had limited (if any) experience of the Creole and who attempted to represent Caribbean speech, were steeped in presuppositions about the ungrammaticality of Creole. They were unaware of its integrity as a separate system. Assuming that Creole was a corruption of English, they represented Creole speech essentially by departing from English. They hardly sought features that accurately represented Creole. The purpose of the code shift was then, as it continues to be, an indication of a shifting vision. However, representation as corruption indicated a shift to an ill formed or limited vision. The aim of such representation was not primarily representation of a *bona fide* voice at all, but a signal of unfamiliarity – the strange, the quaint, the savage. Indeed it was a signal of non-representation of the norm, the accepted, the well-formed, the civilised. (For fuller treatment, see Lalla 1996.)

Current writers who are in a position to accurately represent both Creole and English speech actually sample the Creole for features that will signal a code shift in the voice they represent or a code shift from one voice to the other. Where the composite vision to be reflected is educated, highly analytic, culturally refined, sensitive to socio-historical information available to a well-read or even erudite speaker, the shifts are subtle, mainly semantic. The shifts may play on ambiguity between Creole and English syntax.

What Carter is saying about history in the poem may well hinge on how the speaker views time. The link between the poet's voice and the speaker's vision is an interesting one. Gerald Prince (1987) distinguishes Voice (the narrative rather than the grammatical category) from Vision, by associating Vision with perspective (point of view) and Voice with the instance of narrating. Voice, he describes as a set of signs that characterise the narrator, that provide information about 'who speaks'. Voice includes but is not limited to person. Prince distinguishes Vision as a set of signs about 'who perceives'. Thus there may be vision from behind (omniscience), vision with (limited, internal) or vision from without (limited, external).

This distinction between Voice and Vision is not universally shared among narratologists. Without the distinction we can categorise psychological perspective as above. However, perspective involves other aspects of focalization besides psychological orientation. For example, we might suggest that 'University of Hunger' conveys a non-locatable, indeterminate, all-seeing position of omniscience (zero focalization). We would then be positing a perceptual perspective that combined psychological orientation with spatial and temporal orientation. Any discourse conveys spatio-temporal perspective through such indicators as adverbs, tense, person, and so on. What does *they come* imply about the spatio-temporal dimension of the speaker's perceptual orientation?

Perceptual perspective, which Fowler compares to viewing position in the visual arts, is normally conveyed by elements of language that indicate position, in space and time, of the speaker relative to the events, characters or situations to which the speaker refers. However, the speaker's orientation in time is conveyed both by deictic features (those that point in a direction) like tense, and by non-deictic features like aspect. (Aspect conveys the distribution of the action in time as complete or incomplete, as recurrent, as habitual, and so on. So *they come treading* is present tense and progressive aspect.) Because the poem accommodates both Standard English and Creole, and because these codes mark tense and aspect quite differently to each other, ambiguity arises regarding the position of the speaker in time in relation to the events and situations observed.

Present tense usage must refer to events that are current, but may refer to events that include but extend beyond the current situation. The first two lines of 'University of Hunger' appear to be timeless, to be as unlimited by particular time reference as they are by particular space reference (lines 1-2). In fact, the dimensions of space and time are entangled by the adjective selected. The *long* march extends through both space and time – indefinitely from past, through present, into future. The Creole perspective identifies that which is being observed or contemplated in the *is...* sequences rather like that of the following sentence: Is the sequence of phrases the English question. The opening simultaneously questions and answers. Either way, it conveys stasis.

The next four lines also present an observation of what must be present experience but may extend beyond the present (lines 3-6). First there are two continuous situations, wide ranging marks of hunger and the bending tree, and, again, each is linked by implication to the past by semantic components of words like *print* and *forgotten.* What is sometimes termed the simple present in the next action is not particularly simple in that it conveys unending, probably iterative motion, a rise and fall that extends back into *the long forgotten* and indefinitely on along *the long march.* The passive also conveys a present situation resultant from past circumstances. However, it is one from which the actor (the real subject of *fuse)* is suppressed. The line is not about 'who to blame', about the agents of the misery. The line is about situation and experience, about those who inhabit the misery.

Into this sketch of a timeless, ongoing situation the observer introduces *They,* a pronoun without identifiable reference – except, perhaps, to the men whose huts are *fused in misery* (lines 7-11). *Come* implies movement from a point remote from the speaker and his surroundings **towards** the speaker and his surroundings. A series of progressives *(treading, passing)* are present if the main verb is present but past if the main verb is past. Semantic components of some words in the sentence (like *hoofmarks* and *ancient)* maintain implied reference to both present and past.

Where does *come* fit, in terms of time reference? In Standard English, *come* may be narrative present, used for recounting an event as it occurs, an event that is continuous and progressive. Recurrence of *come* in subsequent verses suggest that it is also iterative, endlessly repeated. At this point it becomes clear that aspect has been ambiguous earlier, in lines 3 to 6. In the context of the lines that follow 3 to 6, it is clear that the discourse in 3 to 6 may be descriptive – static, timeless, continuous – or they may be narrative. The subject of *come, They,* could be entering the situation for the first time or for the umpteenth time. On the other hand, from a Caribbean Creole perspective, *come* is also, easily, past perfective (complete) in its reference. Finally, it could be Creole present perfect, particularly if it refers to the men whose huts are fused in misery and accounts for their presence, tells us where they come from.

The second set of *is...* sequences identifies *they* as *the dark ones, the half sunken in the land.* The first unambiguous past time reference is in line twenty, *is they who had no voice.* This unambiguous past tense raises, by implication, a definite contrast with the present. At the time of speaking, the *no voice* situation is presumably at an end.

Each additional *they come...* sequence may be a new phase in the events recounted in narrative present, or it may be a parallel set of observations to the first, merely additional information about the ongoing, progressive action. An interminable struggle forward is implied by the refrain (lines 26-27). *Is* conveys the timelessness of a generic statement. The repetition of *long* again refers both to spatial and to temporal distribution. Uncertainty about precise location in time and space is reinforced by ambiguity about the subjects of certain actions. This ambiguity of subject extends far beyond the Creole *is...* structures and beyond the uncertain pronoun references. Ambiguities of reference turn up in a variety of sentence constructions. What, for example, is the subject of *mingling?* Is it *they?* Is it, by implication, the sound of the *treading? the mud floor of the year? the year?* Absence of a comma means little in a poem in which commas never occur, in which phrases and clauses fuse in a procession of parallel structures whose boundaries remain unmarked. Again, sentences that have *they come* as their main clause, in which time reference may be ambiguous (depending on code), frequently contain dependent participles like *mingling.* Such participles supplement our information on action but, not being finite, they do not establish tense.

Creole structure in *is...* and *they come...* sequences are never maintained, but, similarly, the structures of the official language are intercepted by nonstandard features, *is they who rose..., is they who heard..., is they who had no voice...* Then comes the contrast in register again, the formal, ceremonial refrain of *O long is the march...* Parallelism and repetition reinforce the reader's sense of time distribution as iterative. So does the alternation between the stasis of circling *is...* phrases and the delayed action of verbs in the last two verses *(move, returns, fall down, stand up* and *rose).* In the last verse, three verbs are unequivocally marked for past tense *(rose, heard, had).* However, even in the second to last verse, several verbs have plural subjects, are therefore unmarked *(move, fall down, stand up),* and may be Standard English or Creole. Up to this point, the end of the poem, the speaker's position in space and time, relative to what he observes, appears to be unlimited, transcending the length of the march and the width of the span.

Although most narrative is prospective, in that the events tend to occur chronologically moving towards the position of the speaker, most narrative is also retrospective in that the speaker recounts events that are past at the time of narrating. However, narrative can also be simultaneous (as in a running commentary) even as events progress. In this poem, if *come* is English, the speaker recounts ongoing events that may be read as progressive or as iterative. It is in this sense that the poem can be read as a narrative, as a sequence of linked events. At the end, still observing a present situation, the speaker makes contrastive references to past events and situations.

But what if *come* is Creole? Creole *come* may refer to a specific event, a particular arrival in the past, in which case the narrative is retrospective rather than simultaneous. Alternatively, Creole *come* may account for the presence of *the dark ones* (present perfect), for the observations expressed in the *is...* sequences. Perhaps the speaker tells us where the human figures on the landscape *come from,* just as *rose, heard,* and *had* in the last verse identify characteristics of the subjects in the *is...* phrases. *Come,* then, describes or defines the identity of those who people the viewer's landscape. On this plane the poem is not narrative but lyrical.

The fact that finite verbs in 'University of Hunger' can be read as referring to past even while they can be read as referring to non-past facilitates simultaneous reading of the poem as narrative and lyrical. In either reading, the poem conveys a perceptual perspective that is limitless, floating in space and alternating in temporal orientation. These narrative and lyrical discourses need not be independent of each other.

It is possible to distinguish multiple voices. One voice identifies the characters of the landscape and the quality of the landscape in an unrelieved series of *is...* phrases (lines 1-2,18-22, 28-31, 33-35, 42-44, 51-56). Another voice (or others) may break in to unfold origins descriptively (present perfect) or in narrative that accommodates past time reference to a series of events (Creole *they come from...)*. At the same time, this discourse retains the immediacy of the simultaneous narrative (English *they come...)* and conveys identity of the characters by applying the present simple to 'timeless' reference. Spatial dimensions of the poem are cosmic, in keeping with the geographical and emotional magnitude of the journey, but there is a definite and continuously reinforced sense of direction towards this speaker. One of these voices, or a new voice, or a chorus, raises the refrain that links identity with history three times in the poem, and, at these points, the verse shifts from the spatially locatable view of the speaker who says *they come.* The text thus accommodates reading of narrative and lyrical subtexts. In addition, the structures that accommodate Creole statements and Standard English questions simultaneously convey a multiple voice with the right to declare and interrogate at the same time.

This poem therefore presents **either** alternative perspectives **or** alternating perspectives. Either way, the complex perspective increases the angles in time from which the landscape and its inhabitants can be observed, and so enhances the vision. In addition, a further dimension of perspective enlarges our experience.

Psychological and spatio-temporal orientation regulate perceptual perspective, but perspective can also be conceptual, ideological – the attitudinal orientation of the speaker to the subject, event, character, situation or setting. Features that regulate perceptual perspective can also contribute to conceptual perspective.

Like perceptual orientation, conceptual orientation is affected by both ambiguity of tense (present vs past/non-present) and ambiguity of aspect (perfective/imperfective; complete/incomplete; isolated event/iterative; bounded/non-bounded). A detached, objective Creole voice conveys a description that implies stasis *(is...* sequences), supported by gap-filling references to the provenance of the arrivants (perfect, *come from)*. This lyrical description runs parallel to narrative that can be read as simultaneous and immediate *(come,* Standard English simple present). Alternatively, the attitude to events is more remote, retrospective *(come,* Creole past). The retrospective references accommodate a view of arrival as collective (one expanded explanation), or as divisible (innumerable arrivals which occurred parallel to each other or in series. They can only be recounted linearly, even if they were simultaneous with each other.) The flexibility in perception suggests a concept of the Caribbean situation as open-ended and dynamic. Internal change in this situation is conveyed both in expression and content.

As the poem concludes, the action gradually becomes more aggressive, more militant. At first, by context or contiguity, the *march* shares the same tempo as *pilgrimage, wanders, rise up and fall down, come treading, come in long lines.* However, at the end, again by context or contiguity, the *march* partakes of the tempo of *stand up and crow like bugles, rose early, shell blow* and *iron clang.* Not only does the march quicken, but the refrain that suggests lament in the context of the opening may, at the end of the poem, imply a subtle, parting challenge. Reinforcing this possible shift in tempo and tone is another development. A number of conceptual landmarks that distinguish the discourse as Caribbean (what one might call the iconography reflected in the work) produce contrasts in connotation at the beginning and end of the poem.

The vision is marked as Caribbean partly by code choice and code shift but also by selection of content. The Caribbean is implicated by reference to common and definitive elements of Caribbean experience such as journey, poverty, twin seasons, oppression and resistance. References to actual objects or to visual images of widespread familiarity accumulate. These are objects of immediate relevance and significance to a common, shared background and to a current condition in the region. Some (like a glimpse of the coffle) summon up the deep past of transportation from an ancestral land (the long march, the distant village). Others verbalise common impressions of past oppression and endurance *(metal brows).* Familiar images, of deep symbolic significance to the region, stud the verse: the mule, dark ones, the huts, the hoe in the ground, sea, boat, sunset, white foam on wrinkled sand, the beating drum, shell blow – images of immediate and poignant effect. In addition to conveying a rich sequence of visual symbols, the poem echoes with sounds of equally stirring significance. The silence of despair and oppression *(no voice)* and the monotony of *treading in the hoofmarks of the mule* mingle with sea sound and water melodies, but are broken by the beating drum, cock crow, shell blow and iron clang.

Visual and aural imagery of resistance accumulate at the end where dynamic and completed action *(stand up, rose, clang)* counters the stasis of repeated *is...* and the incomplete slow motion of *come treading).* In some Caribbean discourse, through not necessarily in all parts of the region, *shell blow* may not only refer to the conch that marked plantation routine but may also suggest a call to revolt. The clang of iron rises louder than the friction of chains and echoes the clash of the machete.[1] At the same time, patterns in the verb phrase change towards the end of the poem. At first, passives *(are fused)* and statives (*is…*) suggest lack of participation in any action but journey *(they come)*. Where verbs convey action rather than state, the verbs are often intransitives. There is no patient to the action of *come*. Only at the end does *they* occur in transitive verbs *(heard the shell blow)*. At the same time, the tone throughout is one of certainty. No modal verbs suggest uncertainty about the truth of any observations in the poem. Only the orientation of speaker to subject remains unfixed and conveys plurality of meaning rather than uncertainty. Even as the verb becomes more active and increasingly transitive, an iconography of oppression (the mule) gives way to an iconography of resistance (the beating drum).

A speaker's attitudinal orientation emerges through features (such as modality, transitivity, lexical choice) that regularly mark ideological perspective. Conceptual perspective on the history of the region also emerges partly through the presence or absence of features that we have noted as marking spatial and temporal perspective. To the observer, the place from which *they come* is remote *from, distant.* The speaker is poised in a point of time that is unspecifiable, so that the time of observation is achronal.[2] Whether the account is timeless present, past perfective, or any other possibility of tense or aspect, and whether this account is simultaneous or retrospective, the account that constitutes this poem groups situations and events on the basis of principles that are non-chronological – a representation that constitutes what narratologists term *syllepsis.*

In fact, the 'University of Hunger' approaches history in a manner that counters the familiar approach of traditional, imperial history. Imperial history recounts past events in a set of relations in which chronology is paramount. Imperial history foregrounds causal links (defined by the conceptual perspective of imperial discourse). It takes the interests of the powerful as its point of departure. 'University of Hunger' rewrites history as incomplete, progressive and current – unbounded action that perpetuates the past in the present, and iterative action (*rise up and fall in spasms, move up and down, returns and dies away*) that unlocks closure. It also presents suffering as causeless, a range of is-circumstances unconnected by any term implying causal linkage. This is the big picture – vast landscape and seascape, vast movements of people over geographical space, irrational suffering of cosmic dimensions. Once, briefly, midway, and then again, at the end, this sweep of collective simultaneous history is intersected by contrast to past circumstances: *is they who had no voice.*

For an instant there is a glimpse of a past that is bounded, contrasting with the present. It is to this boundedness of the past that the poem returns near the end *(is they who rose; is they who heard; is they who had no voice),* before the final echo of the refrain. So the history has time depth even in the situations that the present perpetuates. The simultaneity of collective history is one dimension of the account; the actual past of inhabitants in the timeless landscape is another. Where the past is marked in unambiguously Standard English fashion, two aspects of the past seem pertinent and entangle perceptual and conceptual perspective. The past was non-participatory; but, also, non-participation is past. The verb phrases negate participation (*had no voice in*) only for the past, then they convey the perception of action (*rose watching, heard the shell blow and the iron clang*). At this point, the energy of the sexual imagery invigorates the second to last verse and continues to the next. The poem's view of history locates the speaker geographically at the point to which vast global movements are directed. In the temporal dimension, history is both a matter for retrospective narration and for lyrical description, where it is expressed as past, present or timeless; complete or incomplete; discrete, continuous or iterative. History relates a current situation (stasis) to a past of eternal relevance, and it presents the identity of a people as a fusion of the current situation and of the events that have produced that situation.

The effect of a fractured vision, of alternating glimpses from different angles, is a composite picture, fuller in its totality than any single perspective could have produced. Moreover, the vision matures as the poem progresses. In the context of voicelessness as past, the present contrasts and the future is open to contrast also. The refrain opens the end of the poem beyond lament over past oppression, beyond an observation on the timeless present and illimitable endurance, and onto a speculation on opportunity in time to come. Carter rewrites history through shifting perceptual and conceptual perspective so that the collective response to Caribbean experience is transformed between the beginning and end of the poem from lament to challenge:

> long is the march of men and long is the life
> And wide is the span.

References

1. Ian Robertson notes that, in Guyana, clanging a piece of metal marks stages in the routine of a work day, for example at a construction site.
2. Prince defines achrony as 'an event deprived of any temporal connection with other events'.

Carter, Martin, *Poems of Resistance,* London, Lawrence and Wishart Ltd., 1954.
Lalla, Barbara, *Defining Jamaican Fiction: Marronage and the Discourse of Survival,* Tuscaloosa: The University of Alabama Press, 1996.
Prince, Gerald, *Dictionary of Narratology,* Lincoln and London: University of Nebraska Press, 1987.

University of Hunger

is the university of hunger the wide waste.
is the pilgrimage of man the long march.
The print of hunger wanders in the land.
The green tree bends above the long forgotten.
The plains of life rise up and fall in spasms.
The huts of men are fused in misery.

They come treading in the hoofmarks of the mule
passing the ancient bridge
the grave of pride
the sudden flight
the terror and the time.

They come from the distant village of the flood
passing from middle air to middle earth
in the common hours of nakedness.

Twin bars of hunger mark their metal brows
twin seasons mock them
parching drought and flood.

is the dark ones
the half sunken in the land.
is they who had no voice in the emptiness
in the unbelievable
in the shadowless.

They come treading on the mud floor of the year
mingling with dark heavy waters
and the sea sound of the eyeless flitting bat.
O long is the march of men and long is the life
and wide is the span.

is air dust and the long distance of memory
is the hour of rain when sleepless toads are silent
is broken chimneys smokeless in the wind
is brown trash huts and jagged mounds of iron.

They come in long lines toward the broad city
is the golden moon like a big coin in the sky
is the floor of bone beneath the floor of flesh
is the beak of sickness breaking on the stone
O long is the march of men and long is the life
and wide is the span
O cold is the cruel wind blowing.
O cold is the hoe in the ground.

They come like sea birds
flapping in the wake of a boat

is the torture of sunset in purple bandages
is the powder of sunset spread like dust in the twilight
is the water melodies of white foam on wrinkled sand.

The long streets of night move up and down
baring the thighs of a woman
and the cavern of generation.
The beating drum returns and dies away.
The bearded men fall down and go to sleep.
The cocks of dawn stand up and crow like bugles.

is they who rose early in the morning
watching the moon die in the dawn.
is they who heard the shell blow and the iron clang.
is they who had no voice in the emptiness
in the unbelievable
in the shadowless.
O long is the march of men and long is the life
and wide is the span.

Rupert Roopnaraine

RE-READING MARTIN CARTER

(from *Web of October: Re-reading Martin Carter,*
Leeds, Peepal Tree, 1988.)

YOU ARE INVOLVED

This I have learnt:
to-day a speck
tomorrow a hero
hero or monster
you are consumed!

Like a jig
shakes the loom.
Like a web
is spun the pattern
all are involved!
all are consumed!

This short poem is one of the best known and most quoted of Martin Carter's poems. It is the final poem of his best known collection, *Poems of Resistance* published in 1954. This little book of eighteen poems was an inspiring cultural expression of the Guyanese people's fight against colonial rule. Branded 'subversive literature', it was seized in a police raid during the repression which followed the landing of British troops and the suspension of the constitution in October 1953.

Why does this particular poem end the book?

To answer this question, we have to understand how the poem works and what it means. The title of the poem is 'You Are Involved' and it is usually taken to be a poem about involvement, more, a poem urging commitment and involvement, usually in a struggle for justice.

But there is much more to this little poem, as there is much more than a call to arms in *Poems of Resistance,* although there is that primarily.

Indeed, 'You Are Involved' can be said to be pointing in the direction of that aspect of Martin Carter's poetry – some call it private or non-political – which did not escape the notice of his best readers.[1] This area of his concerns as a poet has become more and more insistent in the dense and difficult poems of recent years. 'Proem', written in 1974, provides an illustration.

PROEM

Not, in the saying of you, are you
said. Baffled and like a root
stopped by a stone you turn back questioning
the tree you feed. But what the leaves hear

is not what the roots ask. Inexhaustibly,
being at one time what was to be said
and at another time what has been said
the saying of you remains the living of you
never to be said. But, enduring,
you change with the change that changes
and yet are not of the changing of any of you.
Ever yourself, you are always about
to be yourself in something else ever with me.

It is not necessary to argue that this little known and less quoted of Martin Carter's poems which opens the 1977 collection *Poems of Succession*, is involuted, dense and complex. By comparison 'You Are Involved' is model of austerity and simplicity. But the preoccupations of 'Proem' – and they are the preoccupations with the coming into being and activity of poetry itself – are not new. They were always there, less obsessively and more tentatively, but they flicker from time to time through the youthful songs of protest of the anti-colonial revolution. They are the preoccupations that are inscribed at the heart of 'You Are Involved'.

The title of our poem, 'You Are Involved', has some unusual features, and it is with these that we must begin.

It is not a line lifted from the body of the poem itself, but it is, in its construction, exactly like lines 5, 10 and 11, the closing lines of the two stanzas. Consisting *only* of words that occur in these three lines, the title is locked into the poem and implicated in the pattern of its motions and therefore in the logic of its meaning. This emerges only as the poem unfolds, as its repetitions or echoes, begin to register.

It is reasonable to say that the poem invites us to treat its title as part of a whole. Indeed, it is only when the title is treated as the first line of a poem of twelve lines that the balance of its stanzas is asserted and their symmetry revealed: six:six instead of five:six.

We can see how the title participates in the central pattern of the whole:

YOU ARE INVOLVED
....
....
....
....
you are consumed!
....
....
....
....
all are involved!
all are consumed!

But because it is the title, of course, it is not in the same register as the poem proper, even though it seems to be at one with its tone and feeling.

While outside the poem proper, it may be either where the poem began, the line that first im-pressed itself on the poet and forced itself out through him; or, it may be what came after the fact, outside of the poetic experience altogether and after its embodiment in language, but what sums it up: either a point of departure or a point of arrival.

At the beginning of his analysis of Keats' 'Ode to a Grecian Urn', Leo Spitzer writes that he feels justified in beginning as he does by 'the title of the poem, 'Ode to a Grecian Urn', which though located outside of the poem proper still belongs to it and contains the orientation intended for us by the poet, who as is always the case, *speaks in his title to the public as a critic*' (my emphasis).[2]

In the case of our title, it also has this difference: whereas the poem proper consists of what is spoken by a narrator created by the poet for this purpose, the title comes from the poet himself, speaking in his own voice, unmediated by the narrative *persona*. After all, according to what turns out to be the logic of the poem itself, only the poet can be capable of utterance after the final line of the poem since the narrator, having dissolved into the all who are consumed, has been to all intents and purposes snuffed out. That he speaks to his public 'as a critic' is the *sign* that marks the poet's triumph over the experience which is of death and dying: he has extricated himself symbolically through the creation of the poem and, within it, of a proxy who speaks 'from the other side': the 'I' of line 1.

Let us next note that the 'you' that greets us right here at the outset is a word of great complexity and range of function. First of all, the 'you' is a duality: it contains a double reference – it is used to address both a single person and many persons, that is, both singular and plural. Important implications flow from this simple fact. In his brilliant 'philological' analysis of an American advertisement, Leo Spitzer has demonstrated how this very ambiguity of the 'you' was exploited in the strategies of advertisement.[3] (The verbal text of the advertisement under scrutiny – it also has a visual text – is the famous one promoting a particular brand of orange juice: 'From the sunkist groves of California/Fresh for you'.) Drawing on the philosophy of grammar to uncover the nature of the 'you', Spitzer writes:

> 'You' is a startling word: it calls up the dormant ego in every human being: 'you' is in fact nothing but the ego seen by another; it also suggests someone outside of us who is able to say 'you' and who feels akin to 'us' as a fellow man. [4]

Perhaps its most notorious example, footnoted by Spitzer, is its use in the wartime enlistment poster by James Montgomery Flagg: 'Uncle Sam needs YOU for the United States Army'. This cartoon, more so than any other example, effectively exploits 'this personal susceptibility of the individual to any address which is intended generally.' The English 'you' can do this, Spitzer argues, because it:

> ...enjoys an ambiguity to a degree unknown in the main European languages, which are characterised by greater inflection; it is equally applicable to a singular or a plural audience, and in advertising, this double inference is fully exploited: the advertiser, while preparing his copy for the general public, thinks the 'you' as an 'all of you' – but intends it to be interpreted as a 'you personally,' applicable to individual A, B, or C, ... *Though he is only one of millions, every single individual is individually addressed and flattered.* (my emphasis)

The 'you' of our title works in a somewhat similar way. That is, it has the effect of actively drawing the individual reader into a wider community of persons, or, as the poem will demonstrate, into a wider community of victims.

Our first word singles out an individual from all of humanity (the reader) who then proceeds in the company of the narrator to merge his individual being into humanity as a whole. In our own case, though he is only one of millions, every single individual is individually addressed and implicated. The title beckons to the reader to approach, step in and live out the poem's experience of annihilation.

Now while it is true that the 'you' is ambivalent and is applicable to a singular and plural audience, that is, to one or to all, it is as a singular that it first presents itself and makes its appeal.

Unlike in the case of Spitzer's advertisement, our 'you' is the first, not the last word. This is why our 'you' contains its plural reference *only as a potentiality* when it first hails us. It is not until after we have accepted the invitation and entered into the poem proper and travelled down to the final 'all' of the last line that one of the important motions of the poem is revealed, or better, is activated: the plural 'all' reaches back to the singular 'you' of the title and triggers its plural content. This is to say that the 'you' which began only as an address to a single individual has acquired through the process of our experience of the whole poem, a plural audience: all of humanity. There is a suggestion of circularity, with 'you' and 'all' being different points on the circle. This circularity is linked to the idea of eternal recurrence, that tragic sense of time that haunts the poem.

It is important to realise, however, that the initial movement from the particular 'you' to the universal 'all' is not direct. It reaches there by first passing through the 'you' of line 5, the only other time that this pronoun occurs in the poem's eleven lines. Now, in spite of the exclamation mark that punctuates the end of the line, suggesting an insistent directness, the 'you' of line 5 has taken on a more impersonal – or, more strictly, an 'indefinite personal' and generalised sense, like the French *'on'*. (This use as an indefinite personal pronoun is one of the special uses of the pronoun 'you' noted in the *Oxford English Dictionary* and is for denoting 'any hearer or reader: one, any one'.) And it acquires this impersonal and generalised meaning because the 'you' of line 5 is the culmination of a sequence: *speck-hero-monster-you.* This sense of the 'you' as more impersonal and generalised than personal and particular, is reinforced by the switch from the 'you' of line 5 to the 'all' of lines 10 and 11. A definite distance separates the 'you' of the title from the 'you' of line 5.

As we shall see later, the 'you' of the title and the 'you' of line 5, as subjects in both the grammatical and philosophical senses, also govern two different verbs and processes: 'are involved' and 'are consumed'.

'Consumed' is obviously not simply the restatement or repetition of the idea informing 'involved'. It is an advance on it.

What we find is that the distance that separates the 'you' of the title from the 'you' of line 5 is matched by that which separates 'involved' from 'consumed':

you are involved
\+ +
you are consumed

The narrator (the 'I' of line 1) is caught up in a similar movement as the reader/s: *I-you-all-all*. It is the same movement from the particular *I* to the universal *all*. (But we will return to the narrator later.) It is important to our argument that these movements we are describing be understood as taking place *within* the experience of the poem: they constitute part of the process, its coming into being. And, most importantly, it is a process which is activated by the presence of the reader and the act of reading.

Our little poem belongs in the company of those works of art, like impressionist paintings, which exist *in statu nascendi* (in a state of being born).[5] They are not closed and finished things, but require the activity of the reader or spectator to bring them to life and completion, to finish them. From the very first word of the title, the reader is implicated, not only in the dark time of the world, but also in the labour of the poem itself.

There are five verbs or verb structures in the poem.

Two are repeated: 'are involved' and 'are consumed'. All are rooted in the present. Even 'have learnt' is in the perfect tense. Not 'I learned', which would have been preterite. Whereas the preterite would have cut the links between the present and the past, the perfect anchors the past into the present. The sense of the present contributes to the urgency pulsing through the poem. I will return to this idea later.

Of the five verb structures, four involve the past participle.

Contrast this with 'Proem', that other poem of process, where there is an overwhelming frequency of the present participle (*saying*, *questioning*, *being*, *living*, etc.).

What is the effect of this preponderance of past participles in the poem: involved, learnt, consumed, spun? They suggest that we are in the realm of the done, even the done for. The accumulated sense is one of fatality, doom and powerlessness to affect the state of things. Which is why the poem is not one of militancy and exhortation, but of anguish and a certain stoic calm.

But the more important effect of the past participles is to set up, within the poem's logic of meaning, an opposition between the stasis of the done, in the domain of the object, and the movement we have described above, in the domain of the subject. This opposition is an important source of the poem's tension. That is, it is another motion within the poem.

And within the world of the past participles that is static in relation to the mobility of the pronouns, there is movement – from 'involved' to 'consumed' – that is the poem's key movement, the source of its deepest drama.

Note that, in a poem of so few words, 'involved' and 'consumed' each occurs twice, and in the most strategic of places, at the beginning and at the end. They mark the beginning (involved) and end (consumed) of the first stanza and constitute the final crescendo of the second: they announce the opening and closing of the poem's two movements in the musical sense.

What of the verb not containing the past participle?

There is only one: 'shakes' in line 8. Working actively, transitively and intransitively, it occurs in the first of the poem's two similes:

Like a jig
shakes the loom.
Like a web
is spun the pattern

The similes constitute the body of the second stanza. The one follows the other in immediate succession; they resemble each other and seem to be symmetrical. They are in fact different and enter, through their very differences, into complex relations with each other:

1. jig : loom
2. web : pattern

Clearly, 'web' is to 'pattern' differently from 'jig' is to 'loom'. A web *is* a pattern; it is like it in itself, it is spun like it. The relation of 'jig' to loom', on the other hand, is wholly dependent on the operations of the verb 'shakes'. There is no relation of likeness other than those established by the verb 'shakes'. And how does 'shakes' operate? It operates *actively,* transitively and intransitively.

It is transitive when it is the action of the subject 'jig' in an unabridged clause: 'A jig/ shakes the loom'.

'Jig' is a word of uncertain origin and is used to mean two different things in the poem:

(i) a mechanical contrivance that activates another machine, like a loom;
(ii) a dance.

When 'shakes' is intransitive, it is governed by the subject 'loom' following its verb: 'shakes the loom,' or, prosaically, 'the loom shakes'. 'Shakes' establishes the likeness which is of the movement of the loom to a jig. In this intransitive operation of 'shakes, 'jig' is being used in its second sense.

Depending on whether 'shakes' is working transitively or intransitively, important differences also arise in the use of the relational 'like' within simile 1. When 'shakes' is transitive, 'like' works as a conjunction to introduce the unabridged clause: 'a jig/shakes the loom.' When, on the other hand, 'shakes' is intransitive, 'like' works as a preposition to govern a noun: 'a jig'.

As the only verb of *activity* within the body of the narrator's story (that is, from line 2 to line 11) 'shakes' is in striking contrast to the verbs containing the past participle, which express an accomplished state. Whether in its transitive or its intransitive function, 'shakes' is the only verb in the poem which expresses the principle of *activity.*

In simile 2, 'like' also enjoys a dual function, that is, it works here also both as a preposition governing a noun ('like a web') and as a conjunction introducing an unabridged clause. But in simile 2, this conjunctional use is concealed, or retracted. This is so because the verb of the unabridged clause is suppressed:

Like a web [is spun]
is spun the pattern

The retraction of one of the two functions of 'like' brings about a contraction of the simile as a whole. It is now a simile in transition to a metaphor. An encyclopaedia of poetics states the difference:

> Whereas metaphor is a mode of condensation and compression, simile through its descriptive function readily leads to diffuseness and extension, even to the digressive development of the figurative scene, action or object as an object of beauty.

This compression of simile 2, especially after the very extended behaviour of its predecessor, is expressive of the movement that has been demonstrated in the poem's other verbal arrangements.

So from simile 1 to simile 2, the ground has shifted: one of the two grammatical functions of 'like' is retracted, the objects of the comparison are alike in and of themselves and result from the same activity – spinning. And most importantly, we have passed from the realm of the active ('shakes') into the realm of the passive ('is spun'). This movement from activity to passivity is one of the two motions within the second stanza.

But the two similes do not express simply a movement from one state to another, or two distinct and separate stages of a single process. A rare punctuation mark, the poem's only full stop, is there to keep them apart. Yet they are joined. For even when confined in its transitive function by the subject 'jig' and the object 'loom', the verb 'shakes' exerts its 'intransitive' influence, that results from its subject's activity: the spinning of the loom, on to the *web* and *pattern* of simile 2. It reaches into the second simile and invites us to think of a web set trembling by the slightest movement on any single one of its strands.

The web that is spun and the loom that shakes like a jig are confirmed in their connection when we note that 'loom' and 'web' were once synonymous poetic usages, now obsolete. As in H. More in 1647:

> Like spider in her web, so do we sit
> Within this spirit and if ought do shake
> This subtile loom we feel as it doth hit

So the 'loom' of line 8 is both the instrument for weaving together separate strands and is itself webbed, or stringed. Even while one simile follows the other in immediate succession, a standard enough technique for multiplying likenesses, the second moves in the direction of passivity and prepares us for the movement within the poem's two final lines, its central motion. But it does so without quite leaving behind the activity principle of the loom as the creator of patterns.

And what is this pattern that is spun?

The loom is the great Loom of Fate which binds all together, that strengthening and realisation of the whole which is simultaneously a losing and negation of each individual part. The pattern that it weaves is the cosmic tapestry which expresses the idea central to fatalism: man is at the mercy of the gods. As in blinded Gloucester's cry of anguish: 'As flies to wanton boys, are we to th' Gods: They kill us for their sport'.

Such is our 'web' of line 9. The effect of the similes, and of the motion between them, strengthens the view that this is a poem of despair, almost Greek in its austerity, its sense of eternal recurrence, and the hopelessness of its vision.

The exclamation marks, three in all, bring to a close stanzas not overly disturbed by punctuation, and are the graphic signals of the poem's apocalyptic direction. In the loom shaking like a jig there is a suggestion of arbitrariness, of artlessness and heartlessness, with things falling as they might. It is an infernal machine. And there is after all, at the heart of the design, an element of chance and wilfulness, an absurdity under the circumstances.

This haphazardness of things, or contingency, is expressed more openly in the rapidity with which a 'speck' may become a 'hero,' a 'hero' a 'monster,' although the day of the monster is not named but is beyond tomorrow. But the Great Web is democratic: there is and will be room for all.

Involved, consumed, you are involved, you are consumed, all are involved, all are consumed – the refrain tolls through the poem and is choric in its function.

The movement from 'involved' to 'consumed' is the first and the last of the poem's movements, that which was in the beginning and which is at the end. It dictated the motions of the 'You' and of the 'like'. It is the poem's central motion, that which governs all its other motions and into which all other motions are drawn and converge.

In the drama of consciousness and utterance that is the poem, 'involved' and 'consumed' signify the two stages of the process of knowing. The moment at which *and within which* we pass from one into the other is the moment of truth and of the knowledge of truth. In the language of speculative philosophy, it is the point at which the 'for-itself' of consciousness encounters the 'in-itself' of the world and act out their courtship and their conflict.

This zone of transaction where subject and object meet is what George Whalley, borrowing from the vocabulary of physics and neurology, calls the 'interface'. The interface is the zone of truth and reality, where all values reside. 'To be 'involved' at the interface is to be 'real', to engage in reality', says Whalley. And the task of the poet, whose involvement at the interface most resembles that of the mystic, is 'to reveal 'what it is like' at the interface'.[6] The poet does this by engaging in an 'event of reality', in experience of such potency and depth that it drives him to apply the means of escaping the pull of its abyss which, because he is a poet, are means that are available to him. It is his mode of affirmation.

To such an 'event of reality' Whalley offers the word *paradeigmatic:*
This term has two implications:

> (a) the form or archetype of human experience is to be found in paradeigmatic experience and not in the experience of everyday man in the workaday world; and
>
> (b) that this order of experience is its own argument, carries its own proof within itself, is at once an event of value and knowing... paradeigmatic experience is the responsive feeling of naked collision with reality: an intimate penetration into, or immersion in, reality.[7]

The poem is what springs from the experience of a paradeigmatic event. And the space between the event and the finished poem is where the activity of poetry takes place, where the poem is born and shaped.

For Whalley this is the saving contract, the act and art of 'symbolic extrication':

> Symbolic extrication is the activity by which the poet extricates himself from an intolerable reality (the paradeigmatic event) by transferring his feeling for that reality to a system of symbols. The poem is not merely a by-product of that withdrawing movement but the necessary condition of it.[8]

In reproducing the passage from involvement to consumption, the poem does so in a way that suggests that the passage is ineluctable and somehow perilous. It has to be gotten over and gotten over with. This, I believe, is the source of the urgency which pulses in the poem. Expressing itself through particular organisations of language, this urgency has what can be called a psychological basis in the poem. In the re-enactment of the drama of consciousness that is the poem, it is the urgency driving the narrator to draw the conclusions out of his experience before it is too late: 'This I have learnt'.

By making 'this' the first word of the poem proper, a dislocation of the normal word order, the emphasis falls immediately on the lesson itself – he plunges us without ceremony in *medias res.* The 'I' is then jettisoned. It does not reappear in the rest of the poem. In the sense suggested by the poem, it *dissolves* away. The narrator is enacting the urgency of the poet to rid himself of the terror of the paradeigmatic event. The experience of the event that is the origin of the poem occurs in the space just prior to the dissolution of the subject into the object. It is the subject's last act. It is the space of perception, the space of a final transaction between the subject and the object before the subject is devoured ('consumed') by the object. This consumption by the object is a consummation for the subject, something for which it yearns. ('Consume', in another obsolete usage, was once synonymous with 'consummate'.) This compulsion of the subject to be one with the object, in all its loathsomeness and fascination, is a shudder that runs through the poems of Martin Carter and is the subject matter itself of certain poems. It is the compulsion that sets the imagination in motion and provides the site of its unique drama: the subject/self poised, defiant and sentient, on the brink of its engulfment by and into the object/world, mute and mineral.

'To make a work of art,' writes Whalley, 'is for the artist an urgent and clamorous need: it is his only means of withdrawing from reality, and the work of art faithfully – ruthlessly – made is the only condition of his returning into contact with reality again.'[9]

When we speak of the poem being one of process, and call it dialectical, it is because it is made up of a webbed system of language, a complex of active and mobile language elements in dynamic interplay. Such a poem will yield a sense of itself as poem and tend to present or lay bare the play of its artifice and its stratagems. Even while conveying the most sombre of visions, it will speak for the interconnectedness of all things. The motions within such a poem will express and derive from the motion of all things.

Nothing is separate from anything else, there is no identity without relationship, we are implicated in every relation to the real world of our fellow human beings and of nature, and we are condemned to the surroundings made for us by our history. And when we speak of the poem being one of truth, and call it art, it is because it is the necessary and shaped utterance of an experience of reality so potent and terrible that it is relieved only by its expression through and in the poem itself. Such a poem is born out of the death-wish of the subject.

'You are involved' is, in the last instance, a philosophical and religious poem that enacts the drama of its own creation – at once its genesis and its revelation. Coleridge says somewhere: 'to read Dryden and Pope, etc, you need only count syllables; but to read Donne you must measure *time,* and discover the time of each word by the sense of passion'. It is this sense of passion charging each word that burns so brightly in the slightest song of Blake and accounts for its radiance and its lyrical power.

It is not to be precious that we invoke the names of Donne and Blake and Coleridge. Nor is it merely because these visionaries of reality, with Dante and Yeats, are among the most revered of Martin Carter's poets. 'You are involved' comes to us out of an experience of reality that is essentially religious in the intensity of its conviction, in the humility of its frail humanity and in the spirituality of its concerns.

In the concluding arguments of his study of the advertisement, Spitzer shows how the 'for you' that ends its text is the re- emergence, in secular and laicised form, of a phrase:

> ... which can perhaps be traced back directly to statements of dogma made from the pulpit... When the pastor declares that 'Christ has suffered death for you, for the liberation of your soul from sin', he is presenting this divine intervention as working for each individual separately and 'you' is interpreted by each of his listeners as a 'for me personally'.[10]

To call the poem philosophical and religious is also to say that it has a powerful ethical dimension. The narrator is, in fact, expressly created in his pitiful shivering humanity and speaks to and for us all out of human fellowship and human suffering. He stands for man in his human sensuousness who saves himself in that only human way, through the *logos* that was in the beginning and always is, through the altogether human and social act of language.

The narrator of 'You are involved' is sensuous suffering man crouched, like Blake's Newton, over the object of his original suffering. He is man in the 'abomination of desolation'.[11]

In 'You are involved' the landscape is empty. Nature is nowhere to be seen or felt. Unusually in 11 lines of Martin Carter there is not a tree nor a stone nor a sky to be seen.

He is fixed in no place, this 'I'. And because he occupies no particular place and can be anywhere, we are free to imagine him everywhere, within and without: he is archetypal.

'Man is an objective sensuous being, and because he feels what he suffers,' Marx writes in the *1844 Manuscripts,* 'a passionate being. Passion is the essential force of man energetically bent on its object'. And language, through which we are saved, Marx says of it: 'the element of thought itself, – the element of thought's living expression: language, is of a sensuous nature'.[12]

To return briefly to the verb 'shakes', we can say that, in its transitive use, it is the only instance in the poem of something acting on something else: it is the action performed by the jig on the loom.

As such it raises up the problem of causes and of the first cause: who moves the jig that shakes the loom?

The absence of an originating agency, like a human hand, suggests the inhuman and so joins in the sense of fatalism that the dancing loom suggests when 'shakes' is intransitive. But this mysterious activation of the loom also opens in the empty space of human agency, and activates the ethical dimension of the poem. It is the place within the poem where we can enter the domain of the ethical, the domain of human action.

The ethical argument of the poem may go as follows: we are condemned to be involved because we are the active creatures of nature and of history and we can ignore or repudiate but not alter or undo the fact of that condemnation to involvement. Our every act is an intervention into the world of other human beings and alters (shakes), however minutely, the disposition of forces (web/pattern) that exist in the real world.

Human activity is transforming activity. At least one ethics of political commitment says that because this is so, human actions must be responsible and conscious actions and are most humanly directed when enlisted in the service of human freedom against forms of oppression and human suffering.

Human activity is transforming activity not because we choose it to be so: it is its lot. Actions based in such an understanding of ethics may – the fatalism of the poem suggests that it does and always will – lead to disastrous interventions which may be as private as the broken promise of a lover or as public as a political catastrophe. These failures, for our consolation and recuperation, we interpret or transform into instances of the eternal human condition, points on the wheel of history: in the moment of the most felt failure, time loses its linear way and turns into a circle. Repeated failure can tempt us, in self-defence, to turn fearful of intervention itself, except in the most mediated of ways, through acts of the mind which – if you are also a poet – may in the end be the truest and purest acts of all and the only true acts available.

This, if you like, is the ethics of the poem.

And it is an ethics of stoicism.

But we would do well to go beyond this, into the poem's deepest zones. We do this by following the poem where it leads. And it leads us by its words. Attempts to confine the poem to a statement about, or even to an experience of, an event of politics in the narrow sense, deprive it, or what is more our loss, make it deprive us of what are its most pressing dimensions and its own expressed urgencies: we narrow its range and limit its power. And it closes itself to us.

What we prefer to say, in this regard, is that in an environment of militancy and passion and discovery, in the bleak days when reaction and unreason held dominion over reason and revolution, or when the revolution lost dominion over itself and fell into unreason, a young poet brooded deeply and creatively about the large eternal things: truth, being, the one and the many, knowing and doing, birth, life and death.

At the heart of the brooding, whether sparked by the stem of a broken flower or by the turret of a gunboat, in its deepest depths, were sadness and dejection, a sharing in the lost hopes of a hopeful time.

In a season that promised birth, the generation of 1953 lived through the anguish and bitterness of the stillborn: This we have learnt.

To return now to the question with which we began these observations: why does this particular poem end *Poems of Resistance?*

I believe it is because it puts a certain stamp of completeness on and crowns and transfigures the *experience of the making of the previous poems,* many of which also have their dark and private spaces. Because, too, it is a poem of rupture and transition, an end and a beginning.

The dense, self-absorbed poems of Martin Carter's recent years are the destination, or better; a stage in the way (since the poet is still growing) of a poetic and philosophical journey that began at the beginning, in those militant and apparently least private poems of those so public days. And that which is encoded deep inside the early poems is to emerge more and more boldly, more and more insistently, in the later poems. Set down with such suppleness and lyrical confidence a quarter of a century later, 'Proem' is a meta-poem, speaking to us of its own becoming: the 'you' of 'Proem' is the poem itself.

The young poet-militant, from within the frontline of the people's freedom struggle, placed this spare and elegiac little luminous poem at the end of *Poems of Resistance* because, being a poet of truth and scruple, he could not but qualify the hope and temper the optimism of the battle songs. All was not light. And of all the sensitive fighters around him, it was he who looked most intently into the nightmare of our history and, in occasional flashes of darkness, he made his report of what he saw there. And in the nightmare of the present he has gone on reporting. It is why his friend Wilson Harris can say of him: 'Beneath the flamboyance, flag or shirt for the revolution, lies mingled horror and hope'.[13] And it was precisely in the moments of most intense darkness that he reflected most intensely on the act of poetry itself and registered its passion and its glory.

From the outset a poet true to his calling, Martin Carter has never been deaf to the siren-song of poetry itself, whispering above the clamour, as it has whispered down through the ages, that 'its political mission is to refuse any political mission and to continue to speak for everyone about things of which no one speaks, of a tree, a stone, of that which does not exist'.[14]

The siren still sings in his ear.

Today, in a bleak tune, her song comes piercing the wind. It is pure and clear.[15]

Notes

1. See for example, Wilson Harris, 'The Place of the Poet in Modern Society: A Glance at Two Guyanese Poets,' in *Explorations,* ed. Hena Maes-Jelinek, (Dangeroo Press: Denmark, 1981); William Carr, 'Introduction' to *Poems of Affinity* (Georgetown, Guyana: Release Publishers, 1980).
2. Leo Spitzer, *Essays on English and American Literature* (Princeton, NJ: Princeton University Press, 1968), p. 72.
3. *Ibid.*, p. 251.
4. *Ibid.,* p. 271.
5. This useful distinction is made by Ortega in his quirky but symptomatic 1925 essay, 'Notes on the Novel': 'A novelist must proceed in the same way as the impressionistic painters who set down on canvas such elements as the spectator needs for seeing an apple, and leave it to him to give this material the finishing touches. Hence the fresh taste of all impressionistic painting. We seem to see the objects of the picture in a perpetual *status nascendi*'. He contrasts this to the 'finished' and 'mummified' presentation of the objects of non-impressionistic, i.e. representational painting. Jose Ortega y Gasset, *The Dehumanisation of Art & Notes on the Novel* (Princeton, NJ: Princeton University Press, 1972), p. 64.
6. George Whalley, *Poetic Process, An Essay in Poetics*, (NY: Meridian, 1967), p. 31.

   'Let us imagine that man and nature (or 'subject' and 'object') meet and embrace each other at an interface, the interface being a pliable and permeable membrane extending infinitely both upwards and on either hand. The membrane is to be regarded as a medium joining, not separating, subject and object... In actual life, subject and object interpenetrate each other; but since for purposeful action we must pretend that subject and object can be separated, the interface also represents this assumed separation'.
7. *Ibid.,* p.31.
8. *Ibid.*, p.31.
9. *Ibid.,* p.105.
10. Spitzer, p. 274.
11. In the words of Jesus:

    But when ye shall see the abomination of desolation, spoken of by Daniel the prophet, standing where it ought not, (let him that readeth understand,) then let them that be in Judea flee to the mountains.

    MARK 13:14; MATTHEW 24: 15-16.

    For Blake, the 'abomination of desolation' resides in man's reasoning power, his capacity for abstraction which can become hostile to humanity when substituted for reality:

    And this is the manner of the Sons of Albion in their strength: they take the Two Contraries which are call'd Qualities, with which every Substance is clothed: they name them Good & Evil; from them they make an Abstract, which is a Negation not only of the substance from which it is derived, a murderer of its own Body, but also a murderer of every Divine Member: it is the Reasoning Power, an Abstract objecting power that Negatives every thing. This is the Spectre of Man, the Holy Reasoning Power, and in its Holiness is closed the Abomination of Desolation. (*Jerusalem* 10:7)

    To these abstractions, Blake 'opposed the Visions of Imagination' (*Jerusalem* 74:26)
12. Karl Marx, *The Economic & Philosophic Manuscripts of 1844* (New York: International Publishers, 1976), p. 182.
13. *Explorations,* p. 8.

14. Hans Magnus Enzensberger, 'Poetry and Politics' in *The Consciousness Industry, On Literature, Politics and the Media* (New York: Seabury, 1974), p. 81.
15. The question that now arises is why does this little poem disappear. It is absent from the selection from *Poems of Resistance* which reappears in *Poems of Succession*, forming one of its parts in the architecture of the whole. The answer belongs to the story of *Poems of Succession* which is yet to be told. Suffice it to say, for now, that 'Proem' holds the key.

KAMAU BRATHWAITE

RESISTANCE POEMS: THE VOICE OF MARTIN CARTER

Martin Carter is one of the few authentically optimistic English-writing Caribbean poets. Not a personal optimism based on a private garden/plot, although there is/was that too; but a more general political anticipation of and confidence in the future of anti-colonial struggle. Like Campbell[1] and Reid[2] in Jamaica, Telemaque[3] in Trinidad, the early Walcott[4] in St. Lucia, Seymour in Guyana, Martin Carter expresses the postwar West Indian certainty that the former colonial territories would soon attain political independence, and that there was, or soon would be, a national identity of which we would all be proud. This would be based on love/possession of landscape, as expressed by Derek Walcott:

> If we know anything, we know we can have a better
> Island, bright as advertisements let it lose its litter
> Of hovels, hunger, and let there be no loss of anger
> Infectious in the peasant, which is the worse danger.
>
> Almost impossible and absurd the distant love for
> England. Love is here, and luck under your
> Feet; the world is green outside, you rot in rooms [5]

and/or on mass consciousness, as in A.J. Seymour's

> They are all heroes. They make history
> They are the power in the land.
> And the children grow
> Force their way out of the slums into the professions
> And stand up in the legislature.
> Today they hope
> But tomorrow belongs to the people.[6]

Carter himself has little of landscape – at least in the physical sense of local colour – in his poems. In his work we have no poems about, and few references to, Georgetown houses, Stabroek market, kokers, rivers, etc., that we find in Seymour; no sense of the world-creating jungle that pervades the poetry of Wilson Harris. 'Old Higue'[7] is his only folk poem – and one of his weakest:

> Old higue in the kitchen
> peel off her skin –
> mammy took up old higue skin
> and pound it in the mortar
> with pepper and vinegar.

But from his first published booklet, *The Hill of Fire Glows Red* (1951), No.4 in Arthur Seymour's Miniature Poets series, we find the then only

24 year-old Carter already centrally concerned with anti-colonial political action, and the dynamics of revolutionary peoplehood:

I tell you and I tell no secret –
now is long past time for kneeling
with clasped hands at altars of poverty.

How are the mighty slain?
by this hammer of my hand!
by this anger in my life !
by this new science of men alive
everywhere in this province!
thus – are the mighty slain![8]

The people's destiny is to destroy the bastions of power and privilege. But Carter, coming clearly from an area of some privilege himself, is still able to preserve, at this stage, a sympathetic tension between the opposing forces:

Do not stare at me from your window, lady,
do not stare and wonder where I came from –
Born in this city was I, lady,
hearing the beetles at six o'clock
and the noisy cocks in the morning
when your hands rumple the bed sheet
and night is locked up in the wardrobe.

My hand is full of lines
like your breast with veins, lady –
So do not stare and wonder where I came from.
My hand is full of lines
like your breast with veins, lady,
and one must rear, while one must suckle life.[9]

One gets the feeling, though – though one can't blame him – bliss was it in that dawn to be alive – that Carter was at this point rather pleasurably seeing himself as the people's revolutionary poet; their cultured street preacher:

if you see me
looking at books
or coming to your house
or walking in the sun
know that I look for fire![10]

and it was rather 'nice' was it not, to be so recognised by the common man:

I am most happy
as I walk the seller of sweets says 'Friend'
and the shoemaker with his awl and waxen thread
reminds me of tomorrow and the world.[11]

It is the voice of Revolution without the Revolution. And yet, better this hope, lilted voices, out of the morass of colonialism, than smugness, ignorance of reality, directionlessness or alienation:

This is my hand
for the revolution...

that night there will be thousands of torches
from the hospitals the lame will come
the mad will be sane again
for the revolution.[12]

II

The poems that make up *The Hill of Fire Glows Red* were published *(1951)* soon after the formation of the People's Progressive Party (PPP), an anti-colonial alliance (East Indian and African; Cheddi Jagan and Forbes Burnham) committed to constitutional independence from Britain, national integration and development under Marxist/socialist principles. Carter was himself a member of this party which was, in the words of one of its historians, 'the first organisation with real political party credentials ever to have existed in British Guiana.'[13]

In 1953, the PPP won an overwhelming victory at the polls – the last, as it turned out, to be held under the old Crown Colony system. Not tomorrow but now, all at once seemed to belong to the people. But Cold War conquering US was not so sure or too happy. Jagan's 'doctrinaire' Communist programme was seen as a soft-under-belly South American threat. Local and expatriate Guyanese Big Businesses couldn't have agreed more. Within six months of the popular victory, the constitution was in suspension. British troops patrolled the country, the PPP government was splitting and out of office, and Carter (along with certain other militants) was in detention camp with, as his friend and colleague Sidney King (now Eusi Kwayana) put it, 'a strange hedge of barbed wire and a gate of bayonets.'[14]

This is what they do with me.
Put me in prison, hide me away
cut off the world, cut out the sun
darken the land, blacken the flower
stifle my breath and hope that I die![15]

You think of green mornings
Naked children playing in the rain
And even fishes swimming in a pool...[16]

It is not easy to go to sleep
When the tramp of a soldier marches in your brain
You do not know whether to sleep or wake:
When a rifle crashes on the metal road...[17]

With this imprisonment, Carter's poetry enters its second and for many its finest phase. The young fiery optimism of *The Hill of Fire* disappears as sudden as a match blown out; and in its place is anger and a thickening sense of waste in *The Kind Eagle* (1952), *The Hidden Man* (1952), and *Poems of Resistance* (1954): [18]

It was a city and a coffin space for home
a river running, prisons, hospitals
men drunk and dying, judges full of scorn
priests and parsons fooling gods with words
and me, like a dog tangled in rags
spotted with sores powdered with dust
screaming with hunger, angry with life and men.[19]

I stretch my hand to a night of weary branches
feeling for leaves or any twig of blossom:
But the branch is withered with no green leaf for me
and the stalk is brown and has no petal for me

and sleep is time that hides me from my labour
and rest is death that rids me of my panting
and dogs and branches and dim rooms of distress
are living worlds that populate my dark.[20]

The 'Letters from Prison', then, and the extracts from the two poems just quoted, illustrate Carter's description of and reaction to his detention. From here, he appears to take two courses. One set of poems, coming to mental grip with his environment, may be said to be his prison carvings:

A prison is go back, go back, go back,
lash of two things, shell which is the heart
and heart which is the shell – the hollow tear.[21]

These lumps of hardened air
invisible drums are beating at my head:
I hear drum drum drum
loud drops of wax falling from time's black candle.[22]

It is in this group that we come upon the fine controlled images of:

City moon clad, black tree domestic, dreary doormouth gaping
earth no mother, sky no father, space no home in comfort:
No mark, no madness like this sanity[23]

is air dust and the long distance of memory
is the hour of rain when sleepless toads are silent
is broken chimneys smokeless in the wind
is brown trash huts and jagged mounds of iron.[24]

But there is also a shift in the contrary direction – another understandable (?) reaction to imprisonment – the drift into dream and (false) rhetorical hope: into images of resurrection and monumental cosmos: 'the kind eagle soars and wheels in flight'.[25]

I make my dance right here!
Right here on the wall of a prison I dance!
This world's hope is a blade of fury

and we, who are sweepers of an ancient sky,
discoverers of new planets – sudden stars
we are the world's hope[26]

O wherever you fall comrade I shall arise.
In the whirling cosmos of my soul there are galaxies of happiness
Stalin's people and the brothers of Mao Tse-tung[27]

O come astronomer of freedom
Come comrade stargazer
Look at the sky I told you I had seen[28]

It is as if, comparable to the moment, mentioned above, that the young Carter, in his red of dawn, saw himself in the role of revolutionary; that now, at a time of reversal of those dreams, he saw himself in the role of victim or sufferer:[29]

It is not easy to be free and bold!
It is not easy to be poised and bound!
It is not easy to endure the spike!
So river flood, drench not my pillar feet[30]

Ego becomes foremost:

In the burnt earth of these years
I dip my hand, I dip my hand.
I plunge it in the furies of this world.
I find the lake whose source leaks from a river.
I splash the pool that feeds my painful flowers.[31]

And exclamation:

O beauty of air like a glad woman!
O fringe of grass always so ever green!
O sloping ocean, sloping bed of love!
O trophy of my search! O human guide.
Each day I ride a wild black horse of terror
but every night I lock him in my bosom ...[32]

Although you come in thousands from the sea
Although you walk like locusts in the street
Although you point your gun straight at my heart
I clench my fist above my head; I sing my song of FREEDOM![33]

These last two poems are clearly propaganda or ideological pieces, written in anger at the arrival of British troops, come to support the imperial takeover of the constitution:

You come in warships terrible with death...
I know your finger trembles on a trigger
And yet I curse you – Stranger khaki clad.

But fortunately, even though the pressure and perhaps even the temptation must have been there, Carter, in *The Kind Eagle*, even though he gives us rhetoric, seldom gives us such plain bad verse. Compare, for instance, the gun/heart image, quoted at 33 above with say, 'This is the dark time, my love':

Who comes walking in the dark night time?
Whose boot of steel tramps down the slender grass?
It is the man of death, my love, the strange invader...
watching you sleep and **aiming at your dream**.[35]

It is in the gun aiming at **dream**, rather than **heart**, that the cool source of poetry resides; and Carter's is no exception. Yet it would be a mistake to dismiss his self-regarding rhetoric too quickly, since it is an essential part of his political stance which in turn is/was an intimate component of his poetry. Further, as we shall see, it is this very rhetoric which is at the base of his finest achievements, when he attains a tension/equilibrium, in his own words, both poised and bound.

III

The movement towards this begins in 'Till I Collect'[35] where we find, perhaps for the first time, a reticence or countervailing gesture coming to confront the erstwhile one-way wordage:

The fisherman will set his tray of hooks
and ease them one by one into the flood.
The net of twine will strain the liquid billow
and take the silver fishes from the deep.
But my own hand I dare not plunge too far
lest only sand and shells I bring to air
lest only bones I resurrect to light.[37]

In 'I am no soldier' [38] we see its development because here the reticence of ego (impotence of incarceration) is caught – and released – within a tactile circumambient landscape:

But now the huge noise of night surrounds me for a moment
I clutch the iron bars of my nocturnal cell
peeping at daylight.
There is a dark island in a dark river

This is intensified in 'I come from the nigger yard' with

It was me always walking with bare feet,
meeting strange faces like those in dreams or fever

which connects with but is extended into

And there was always sad music somewhere in the land
like a bugle and a drum between the houses
voices of women singing far away
pauses of silence, then a flood of sound.
But these were things like ghosts or spirits of wind...[39]

What is even more remarkable is that Carter's prison experience gave him not only new rhythms:

A prison is go back, go back, go back[40]

I hear drum drum drum
loud drops of wax falling from time's black candle[41]

earth no mother, sky no father, space no home in comfort[42]

but a whole new formal shape of poem: 'You are involved'[43] and 'Death of a slave'[44]: which correlate in line and language, with the barred, controlled, formal cell and structure in which he found or imagined himself:

This I have learnt:
today a speck
to-morrow a hero
hero or monster
you are consumed![45]

And it is in 'Death of a slave' that Carter first reaches the kind of metaphorical equilibrium which, given the kind of poetry he was writing then, is one of his most significant achievements. The poem does not begin like 'Death of a comrade'[46] with his typical long, singing: 'Death must not find us thinking that we die.' Instead there is the rare (as in 'Involved'), sparse:

Above green cane arrow
is blue sky –
Beneath green arrow
is brown earth –
Dark is the shroud of slavery
over the river
over the forest
over the field.[47]

'Slave' here is a prisoner to oppression of man, history and landscape, finally of time. But he is also implanted in the landscape and through his heart and seed of blood/ death comes to possess it:

In the dark earth
in cold dark earth
time plants the seeds of anger[48]

So that the death of the slave creates life, while time (in which this death is subsumed) creates anger. Anger and life are therefore equated, and from here on, ('This is another world'), the poem begins to move into outer and inner time, outer and inner space, in a cycle that becomes, like Harris', both eternal and seasonal, universal and particular in reference:

Day passes like a long whip
over the back of a slave ...

Night comes from deep forest
in a boat of silence [49]

And yet, by the time the poem comes to its close, Carter has done even more than this; for he has contracted the life of the poem back to the image of the dying slave and is able to re-enshroud the verse with an apparitioned end-stopped finite sense of death; the enormous root and wheel of time, hidden under the body of its blood:

The slave staggers and falls
his face is on the earth
his drum is silent
silent like night
hollow like boat
between the tides of sorrow.

In the dark floor
In the cold dark earth
time plants the seeds of anger[50]

It is in this context, with this background, that we can come to 'University of Hunger', regarded by many as Carter's finest poem, with its long surf-like confident lines, and its epigrams moving within them like coralline resistors:

They come like sea birds
flapping in the wake of a boat
is the torture of sunset in purple bandages
is the powder of fire spread like dust in the twilight
is the water melodies of white foam on wrinkled sand...

O long is the march of men and long is the life
and wide is the span.[51]

IV

Yet, ten years later, this fine extended hope was in ruins. The political optimism of the 50s had never come to life. Each Caribbean territory of British rule had decided – some reluctantly, some selfishly, the rest because they had no choice: one from ten, as Eric Williams had said, leaves nought – to continue the difficult process of decolonisation on their own. There would be no federal West Indian nation, but the old colonial fragments, each flying its own strip of flag. Within the wider Caribbean, too, there had been failure. Cuba under Castro, had dared to burn the nest of the high-flying American eagle; the West Indies had joined the boycott against the incendiaries. In Guyana, where this fear of communism, brought nearer, many thought, by the presence of militant Cuba, had already crippled constitutional development, there was further regression. The 1955 factional split in the once-nationalist PPP, had become two parties, Jagan and Burnham, based on race, on slave and indentured servant. So instead of fighting the oppressor, the country began to fight itself. By 1962, nothing less than a race war was raging in the country. The politics of hope had become the politics of hate. Carter, traumatically bewildered and wounded, held on to his original PPP/nationalist/anti-imperialist comradeship for as long as he could; resigned, retired (1956), but reappeared when Burnham's 'African' party came to power in 1964. But it wasn't the man who had written 'Tomorrow and the world' [52] and 'Cartman of Dayclean'. [53] Now it was

All, all who are human fail,
Like bullets aimed at life,
or the dead who shoot and think themselves alive![54]

In 1971, the Minister of Culture, as he had become, resigned again from power. For many, he long before that had resigned himself from poetry.

V

This, as we shall see, was/is very far from being the case. But between, *Poems of Resistance* (1954) and Carter's next published sequence of poems, *Jail me Quickly* (a set of five that appeared serially in *New World Fortnightly* late in 1964 reprinted together in *NWF* 34 (1966)) there appears to have been the most dramatic loss of faith yet recorded in our literature. There is, of course Aimé Césaire's revocation of communism in 1956. But Césaire has gone on, since *Lettre a Maurice Thorez*, to write most of his major plays,[55] in addition, among other pieces, to the collection of poems, *Ferrements* (1960). Carter, on the other hand, has written very little[56]:

True, was with them all,
and told them more than once:
in despair there is hope, but there is none in death.
Now I repeat it here, feeling a waste of life,
in a market-place of doom, watching the human face![57]

It is a measure of the difference in their worlds. Césaire, the expatriate gallic creole, can make a creed of rhetoric. For the native Caliban, sooner or later the line and image have to match the ruined stone and language of the environment.

VI

This is why we were so interested in those tight cellular poems in *Poems of Resistance*. From 'You are involved' and 'Death of a slave', Carter had a choice: towards 'imagism' and perhaps a more direct correlation with experience; or a continuation of the long rhetorical line: marvellous vehicle for hope, fire and anger, but less efficient in the aftermath of ash and ruin. But habits and old skills, gestures of past successes, die hard. And Carter, although acutely aware of the changes in both his inner and outer self, seemed unable or unwilling to vouchsafe the pristine mask

O rain and fire, hopeful origins!
O rust and smoke, only enduring end!
I almost stumble underneath the waste
while squandered daylight mocks my deep remorse...[58]

Behind a wall of stone beside this city,
mud is blue-grey when ocean waves are gone...
And I have seen some creatures rise from holes
and claw a triumph like a citizen,
and reign until the tide![59]

Is this really Carter's voice or is it, as he himself puts it, the 'childhood of a voice':

The familiar white street
is tired of always running east,
The sky, of always arching over.
The tree, of always reaching up.

Even the round earth is tired of being round
and spinning round the sun. [60]

We do not know what really 'happened'; but in terms of his poetry, we are aware that by 1964 Carter had, for his own purposes – retreat? disguise? failure of his own rhetoric? – acquired a persona; borrowed a voice:

... think you I do not know
that love is stammered, hate is shouted out
in every human city of this world?
Men murder men, as men must murder men,
to build their shining governments of the damned.[61]

The music, the associations here are with that other young/old disillusioned/ hopeful revolutionary, W.B. Yeats:

Many ingenious lovely things are gone
That seemed sheer miracle to the multitude...[62]

The blood-dimmed tide is loosed, and everywhere
The ceremony of innocence is drowned;
The best lack all conviction...[63]

O chestnut-tree, great-rooted blossomer,
Are you the leaf, the blossom or the bole?
O body swayed to music, O brightening glance,
How can we know the dancer from the dance?[64]

Carter's creatures rising from the holes, clawing a triumph like a citizen, and reigning until the tide ('Black Friday', see above), have clear, close connection with Yeats' 'The second coming': 'The blood-dimmed tide' (above), and the 'vast image out of Spiritus Mundi', that rises out of the desert sands. There is nothing more specific than this; but the echoes are there. Compare Carter's

> Now there was one whom I knew long ago
> And then another to whom I paid respect:
> The first I would salute, the second praise
> But all is gone, all gone, the murderer cried.[65]

With the Irishman's

> I have met them at close of day
> Coming with vivid faces
> From counter or desk among grey
> Eighteenth-century houses.
> I have passed with a nod of the head
> Or polite meaningless words...
> And thought before I had done
> Of a mocking tale or a gibe
> To please a companion
> Around the fire at the club,
> Being certain that they and I
> But lived where motley is worn:
> All changed, changed utterly:
> A terrible beauty is born.[66]

My explanation for this is based on the notion of *sympathetic models.* There is much in the early revolutionary/colonial Yeats that would have attracted Carter; and the Irishman's later old-man's impotence theme, would have tolled bells in Carter's post-1962 disillusionment consciousness. Also, they were both great bards, great creators of rhetoric.

But the significant thing is that Carter does not appear to reach back and across to this literary connection until after 1962: *at a time when, instead, one would have assumed him to be moving closer and closer into his own thing.* Why this was/was not happening can only be a matter of conjecture, without some intimate knowledge of Carter's biography.

My guess is connected with a point I made earlier, to the effect that Carter's work has dealt little (directly) with his landscape: physical and socio-cultural. In formal terms, there is no nation language (dialect), no 'nancy forms'; (compare, for instance, Carter's 'Old Higue' with Wordsworth McAndrew's; or even better, with a poem like Lorrimer Alexander's 'Moongazer'). When the bottom fell out of the (international) long-lined rhetorical world, there were only two possibilities: a development of the survival structures like 'Death of a Slave', or a reversion to sympathetic models. With his non-dialect literary education and instinct, the latter was perhaps the most certain choice for Martin Carter. It gave us the single voice crying from the pages of *Jail Me Quickly*:

> And how to leap these sharp entanglements
> or skirt this village of the angry streets?

How utter truth when falsehood is the truth?
How welcome dreams how flee the newest lie?[67]

VII

Now, crossing the divide towards 50, Carter will begin to write his most difficult, probably his most beautiful poems; his – what he has in fact called – *Poems of Succession*.[68] Not now from the hill of dawn, the running streets of noon, the afternoon of prison; but from the greenless, almost wordless wilderness itself:

Trying with words to purify disgust
I made a line I simply can't remember:
For hours now I've poked through memory
A desperate child in a jam-packed garbage can.

It should have been a line with nouns and verbs
Like truth and love and hope and happiness
But looking round it seems I was mistaken
To substitute a temple for a shop.

To see a shop and dream of holy temples
Is to expect a toad to sing a song.
And yet, who knows, someone may turn translator
When all these biped reptiles crawl again.[69]

In *Savacou 3/4* (March 1971), there is even evidence of a return to the survival model:

In the premises of the tongue
dwells the anarchy of the ear;
in the chaos of the vision
resolution of the purpose.

And would shout it out differently
if it could be sounded plain;
But a mouth is always muzzled
by the food it eats to live.

Rain was the cause of roofs.
Birth was the cause beds.
But life is the question asking
what is the way to die.[70]

From this kind of utterness, most West Indian writers would have turned back from, or gone on into un/peaceful silence. Carter's *wake* is that out of the existential residue of his illuminations, he is still creating stark from ash.

If these are riddles, riddles write themselves
And where we end no starting indicates:
Your eyes that sparkle teach me how to mourn
For all our deaths are certain as our births.

And making this today I test the burden
Then free myself, but not to weigh you down
What we call wings the birds can give no name
To heaven is their flight, on earth our sin.[71]

Or as he says in 'Proem':

Not, in the saying of you, are you
said. Baffled and like a root
stopped by a stone you turn back questioning
the tree you feed. But what the leaves hear
is not what the roots ask. Inexhaustibly,
being at one time what was to be said
and at another time what has been said
the saying of you remains the living of you
never to be said ...[72]

By any standard, despite the few qualifications one might retain, this is a major achievement: a poet writing so plain, so true, so nearly harshly peaceful, that conventional criticism hesitates (so little has been written on this man) for lack of models of procedure. Our critics deal with dance (the 'life' of the poem) or dancers (the poet as maker). But with Martin Carter, how can we know the dancer from the dance...

Footnotes

1. See George Campbell, *First Poems* (Kingston: private publication, 1945).
2. V.S. Reid, *New Day* (New York: Knopf, 1949).
3. See H.M. Telemaque, 'In our land', In *Caribbean Voices* (ed. John Figueroa) I, p.58 (1971), and other anthologies. See also some of the poems in *Scarlet* (Georgetown: 1953).
4. Derek Walcott, *25 Poems*, (Port of Spain: author, 1948).
5. Derek Walcott, *25 Poems* (Bridgetown: author, 1949) p.19.
6. A.J. Seymour, *The Guiana Book* (Georgetown: 1948) p.42.
7. Carter, *The Hill of Fire Glows Red* (British Guiana: 1951), p.5.
8. Ibid., p.3.
9. Ibid., p.4.
10. Ibid., p.9
11. Ibid., p.11.
12. Ibid., p.14.
13. Leo A. Despres, *Cultural Pluralism and Nationalist Politics in British Guiana* (Chicago: Rand McNally, 1967), p.4.
14. Introduction (p.2), *Poems of Resistance* (London: Lawrence & Wishart, 1954).
15. 'Letter I', *Resistance*, p.10; all references are to the 2nd edition (1964).
16. 'Letter 2', ibid., p.12.
17. 'Letter 3' ibid., p.14.
18. *The Kind Eagle* and *The Hidden Man*, both published in Georgetown in 1952, are subtitled 'Poems of prison', and 'Other poems of prison', respectively. The pages of these books are unnumbered. *Poems of Resistance* was first published in London (1954) with an introduction by Sidney King (see above), and again

in Georgetown (University of Guyana, 1964) with an introduction by Neville Dawes. It is interesting to note that Carter's first 'Poems of prison' were published a year – or so it seems – before he actually went to prison – unless, of course, there is an error in their dating.
19. *Resistance*, p.21.
20. 'I stretch my hand', *The Hidden Man* (Georgetown 1952). There is no pagination.
21. 'Who walks a pavement', *The Kind Eagle* (Georgetown, 1952). There is no pagination.
22. 'O where to hide', ibid.
23. 'No madness like this sanity', *The Hidden Man*.
24. *Resistance*, p.1.
25. 'The kind eagle' from *The Kind Eagle*; reprinted as 'The knife of dawn', *Resistance*, p.16.
26. Ibid.
27. *Resistance*, p.4.
28. Ibid., p.5.
29. For Carter's discussion of the artist as victim in Caribbean society, see *Man and Making – Victim and Vehicle*, The Edgar Mittelholzer Memorial Lectures, Fourth Series, (Georgetown, October 1971)
30. *Resistance*, p.16; the version in *The Kind Eagle* reads 'drown not my pillar feet'.
31. 'O human guide', *The Kind Eagle*.
32. Ibid.
33. *Resistance*, p.26.
34. Ibid.
35. *Resistance*, p.17, my emphasis.
36. 'The hidden man'; *Resistance*, p.24.
37. Ibid., my emphasis.
38. *Resistance*, p.3.
39. Ibid., p.20.
40. *Eagle*.
41. Ibid.
42. *The Hidden Man*.
43. 'Eagle'; *Resistance*, p.18.
44. *Resistance*, pp.6-7.
45. 'Eagle'; *Resistance*, p.18.
46. *Resistance*, p.8.
47. *Resistance*, p.6.
48. Ibid.
49. *Resistance*, p.6.
50. Ibid.
51. *Resistance*, p.2.
52. *Hill*, p.10.
53. 'The hidden man'; *Resistance*, p.25.
54. 'Black Friday 1962', *New World Quarterly*, no. 34 (1966), p.21.
55. *Christophe* (1963); *Une saison au Congo* (1966).
56. This essay was written before Carter's *Poems of Succession* (1977) which suggests that Carter was writing, though not publishing very much.
57. 'Black Friday', op. cit.
58. *NWF* (1966), p.23.
59. 'Black Friday', op. cit.
60. *NWF* (1966), p.25.

61. *NWF* (1966), p.22.
62. W.B. Yeats *Collected Poems* (London: MacMillan, 1952), p.232.
63. Ibid., p.211.
64. Ibid., p. 245.
65. 'Conversations', MS dated August 1965.
66. Yeats, op. cit., pp.202-3.
67. *NWF* (1966),p.23.
68. Martin Carter, *Poems of Succession* (London, POS: New Beacon Books, 1977), 117 pp. This most welcome collection (appearing after this article was written) contains selections from nearly all Carter's published pamphlets and sequences: *The Hill of Fire Glows Red* (1951), *The Kind Eagle* (1952), 'Returning' (1953), *Poems of Resistance* (1954), 'Poems of shape and motion' (1955), 'Conversations' (1961), 'Jail me quickly' (1963), plus 41 poems written since 1963 – representing some, but by no means all, and certainly not all the best of the poems that Carter has been writing recently. Also missing are selections from *To a Dead Slave* (1951) and *The Hidden Man* (1952).
69. 'Conversations', op. cit.: printed in *Succession* (p. 64) where Carter dates the sequence 1961 (cf. n.64, above).
70. 'Occasion', *Savacou 3/4* (1970/71), p. 171. In *Succession* (p.85) the title is 'The mouth is always muzzled.'
71. 'Anonymous', *New World Quarterly, Guyana Independence Issue* (1966),
72. *Succession*, p.9.

First published in *Caribbean Quarterly*, vol. XXIII nos. ii & iii, 1987

Jeffrey Robinson

THE ROOT AND THE STONE: THE RHETORIC OF MARTIN CARTER'S *POEMS OF SUCCESSION*

'Proem' as a theory

Between the conception
And the creation
Between the emotion
And the response
Falls the shadow
T.S. Eliot (from 'The Hollow Men')

'Proem', the first of *Poems of Succession*[1], can be interpreted in more than one way. What remains constant is the sense of a disjunction between intention and act similar to the one referred to in 'The Hollow Men'. On the most obvious level, the poem is about poetry and, specifically, about itself.

Not, in the saying of you, are you
said. Baffled and like a root
stopped by a stone you turn back questioning
the tree you feed. But what the leaves hear
is not what the roots ask.

To attempt a paraphrase, we may say that no reading of the poem is definitive, its capacity to generate meaning cannot be exhausted. Yet, though the poem has an autonomous existence, it remains part of a human world, a natural (like a plant's growth) process of radical exploration of the world 'out there' which inevitably becomes an exploration of its own origins in human consciousness. The word 'stone' is here charged with associations of silence and coldness expressive of the infinite mystery of the world not yet humanised by culture. The task of humanising is complicated because a gap or disjunction opens up between what is said and what is heard, between our capacity to receive, on the one hand, and all that is offered by our exploration on the other. The poem, since it is language at the highest level of organisation, is our 'root' in the sense that it is organically a part of what we are as human beings, that it is the sensitive tip of our exploration of the universe and that it is one of the means by which the external world becomes assimilated to the world within.

Inexhaustibly,
being at one time what was to be said
and at another time what has been said
the saying of you remains the living of you
never to be said. But, enduring,
you change with the change that changes
and yet are not of the changing of any of you.

The poem is both one and infinite. It arises out of the intention (what was to be said) and the creative act (what has been said) yet is limited neither by the poet's intention nor by his first articulation or understanding of it. It acquires meaning only in experience which endlessly modifies its own readings.

Ever yourself, you are always about
to be yourself in something else ever with me.

The poem exists and yet is always pure potentiality, realising itself in infinite variety as that process of exploration which is itself unchanged.

The disjunction between what is said and what is heard can be a cause for either dismay or rejoicing. Dismay arises out of the inevitable imperfection of communication through language, (one thinks of Eliot's 'words strain/ crack and sometimes break under the burden/ ... Decay with imprecision, will not stay in place,/ will not stay still.'). Rejoicing is occasioned by the fact that this 'untrustworthiness' of language may well be a necessary condition of the existence of poetry. For poetry is not simply communication of the poet's ideas and feelings; it can generate meanings never consciously intended by the poet and this is partly because language is not the private possession of the poet but a social product. It brings hosts of associations to bear on his intentions so that its indiscipline, its refusal to stay fixed like mathematical or logical symbols, is part of the reason the poem escapes the poet in the end and becomes a potentiality.

The two voices of Martin Carter

In the poems published between 1951 and 1955, one is aware of two voices; that of the rhetorician and that of the maker of complex images. Examples of the former abound in *Poems of Resistance* (1954).

If I do not live to see that day
My son will see it.
If he does not see that day
His son will see it.
And it will come circling the world like fire.
It will come to this land and every land
and when it comes I'll come alive again
and laugh again and walk out of this prison.

The poem depends heavily on rhetorical patterning for its effect, on the repetition of 'not' and 'see' and, later, of 'come' in 'it will come', 'it will come', 'it comes', 'I'll come' and then 'alive again/and laugh again', so that the emotional climax of the poem is created through the orator's favourite device of anaphora. However, examples of the complex image can also be found in *Poems of Resistance;* the following is from 'Cartman of Dayclean'.

The cupric star will burn as blue as death.
His hopes are whitened, starched with grief and pain.

The 'cupric star' suggests copper sulphate or blue vitriol and 'vitriol' takes us naturally to acid and thence to burning which is also an attribute of blue flame. The star of the morning suggests Lucifer and thus hell from which idea comes both the flame and the 'grief and pain'. The star burns as blue as death, although death is normally either white or black and, indeed, the transition from blue vitriol to acid or from blue flame to white heat takes us to rigor mortis and so back to death. The poem achieves its effect not by repetition but by the complexity of its vision.

The voice of the rhetorician is generally clearest in the overtly political poems. Perhaps this is because those poems seek to give a voice to the voiceless, the politically and culturally deprived. Such poetry seems to be based on a fairly simple view of communication.

'Cartman of Dayclean' has many possible levels of meaning; one sees, for instance, a man, representative of the working classes and at the same time, Man, struggling with the 'granite burden', which probably reappears years later as the stone in 'Proem', and, at the same time, the poet endlessly wrestling with that which is about to be itself in something else ever with him (in connection with this last level, the familiar tag *'ars longa, vita brevis'* may apply).

What is interesting is that, after 1955, little is heard from the rhetorician who was so much in evidence in *Poems of Resistance.* Instead, one finds references to gaps between the real and the ideal. Eventually, the idea appears that these gaps may not be as tragic as they seem at first sight. Perhaps the disappearance of the rhetorician has to do with the co-opting of the rhetorical/political poems in *Poems of Resistance* by the most unlikely political interests. Such poems, after all, are less organised as vision and tend to suffer rather than generate meaning. My present concern, however, is with the correspondence between the theory expressed in 'Proem' and other poems on the one hand and the two voices on the other. In the course of *Poems of Succession,* one finds an increasing concern with time and with the effects of time on words; this, of course is part of what 'Proem' is about.

After Poems of Resistance

Related to the gap between intention and act is that between the ideal and the real in 'Shape and Motion One' (1955)

I was wondering if I could find myself
all that I am in all I could be.
If all the population of stars
would be less than the things I could utter

In 'They say I am', from *Conversations* (1961), the sense of the autonomous existence of the poem appears.

> A poet cannot write for those who ask
> hardly himself even, except he lies;

In 'Groaning in this Wilderness' from the same collection, the specific political and cultural context of these discoveries about language and the world is made clear.

> Speaking with one on a pavement in the city
> I watched the greedy mouth, the cunning eye
> I reeled and nearly fell in frantic terror
> seeing a human turn into a dog.
>
> Recovering, I studied this illusion
> and made a stupid effort to be strong:
> I nodded and agreed and listened close.
> But when I tried to utter words – I barked!

The poem explores the poet's difficulty as a man of language when language is ceasing to be itself (dehumanised in a 'wilderness of silence'.) In the context of a breakdown of community, the poet's material, language, whose whole life is community, becomes even more suspect. Again, in 'To Substitute a Temple', the poet tries with words 'to purify disgust' but, though he should have written 'a line with nouns and verbs/like truth and love and hope and happiness', he realises that 'To see a shop and dream of holy temples/is to expect a toad to sing a song'. The most important words in the language becomes 'nouns and verbs'.

Nine years after *Poems of Resistance,* 'Childhood of a Voice' from *Jail me Quickly* (1963) tells us

> The light oppresses and the darkness frees
> a man like me, who never cared at all:
> Imagine it, the childhood of a voice
> and the voice of childhood telling me my name.

If the 'childhood of his voice' is the 'voice of his childhood (as a poet), it may be telling him his name because he has increasingly abandoned the stance of poet-as-orator whose words are supposed to be clear windows on a reality outside of themselves (the light); instead he has become a maker of complex images whose words are increasingly opaque, calling attention to themselves not only as signs but rather as icons. The oppressive aspect of the light may well be the susceptibility of some of the earlier poems to a sort of political manhandling. I take the line 'a man like me, who never cared at all' as referring to the growing detachment of the poet's voice. In the course of *Poems of Succession,* one ceases to be addressed by a recognisable personality or persona (revolutionary or, as in 'On the Fourth Night of a Hunger Strike' or 'I am no Soldier', ideal sufferer) by the poem itself; in other words most of the poems after 1955 are statements that generate their own authority instead of deriving it from an implied speaker.

In 'Words' (1957), the focus is on the words themselves as icons.

These poet words have secrets locked in them
like nuggets laden with the younger sun.
Who will unlock must first himself be locked.
Who will be locked must first himself unlock.

The words are now a standard men must meet rather than the other way around – not because the words are non-human but because they are ideally human ('jewels dug from dung or speech from flesh/still bloody red') which is why the decay of speech leaves a poet barking.

Quite apart from the specific political and cultural context, the detachment of the poet from the poem is seen as a necessary process in 'What we call Wings' ('If these are riddles, riddles write themselves/And where we end no starting indicates') so that the reader is enlisted in a common process of discovery in 'Rain Falls Upward' ('Someone, somewhere, shall know one day/more than I read of what I do'). At the first appearance of 'A Mouth Is Always Muzzled' (1969), the poem was generally taken as being about the difficulty of political expression. It also consists of a series of images suggesting disjunctions between inner and outer worlds:

In the premises of the tongue
dwells the anarchy of the ear;
in the chaos of the vision
resolution of the purpose.

The first two lines refer to the movement from consciousness to the world outside and the breakdown that occurs in the course of that movement. The next two lines refer to the movement from the world outside into consciousness and to another breakdown. Speech issues as Babel at the other end of the line of communication; cognition, whether it be a disordered perception or a perception of a disordered reality, is internalised, ambiguously, as 'resolution of the purpose' (this may mean, on a straightforward reading that consciousness can order reality or, more ironically, as in Conrad's 'good, stupid kind', that the capacity to act often depends on a limited perception of life's complexities).

The second stanza again refers to disjunction between inner and outer worlds.

And would shout it out differently
if it could be sounded plain;
But a mouth is always muzzled
by the food it eats to live.

Speech issues from within to the world outside and is baffled by external conditions. Food, conversely, is that part of external reality that we most obviously internalise and make part of ourselves. Yet there is a collision between the two movements just as the root in the process of seeking nourishment, comes up against the stone and turns back to the tree it feeds.

Rain was the cause of roofs
Birth was the cause of beds.
But life is the question asking
what is the way to die.

Both roofs and beds are aspects of the man-made world, the humanisation of the environment. Roofs are used to stop the movement of rain from the environment to our bodies and here the interposition or break is beneficial. Beds are used to reproduce our kind, a movement from the self out into the world. These two humanising creations are a *response* to the demands of the organism and the environment. (Rain *was the cause* of roofs) but, as the first two stanzas have suggested, they are not a complete answer. The form of the concluding riddle makes death itself part of the question suggesting a possible reformulation; death is a question to which life is an answer in the form of a riddle. Death, the final absurdity, can be given meaning only by life which, however, must be so ordered as to constitute an answer. The first two stanzas pose the problem of the ordering of chaos. At the moment, answers cannot be 'sounded plain' (so much for the rhetorician).

The first stanza of 'Even as the Ants Are' (1969) describes a break affecting cognition itself and, to the break in communication, opposes an image of natural and humble reaching out, perhaps a glimpse of an alternative:

And no one will ever know how we came to possess
and possessing are not allowed to speak
not even as the ants are, crossing from my cup
to your spoon.

Yet in 'Endless Moment World', the problem of communication becomes a cause for a kind of ironic celebration. In 'Tradition and the West Indian Novel',[2] Wilson Harris has written about the 'kinds of overriding advertisement and persuasion upon the writer for him to make national and political and social simplifications of experience'. In the first stanza of 'Endless Moment World', Martin Carter, presumably with tongue in cheek, says

But finding out I had to tell
to all what my intention was
learnt wherefore certain things are done
and just for so put in my name.

One supposes that the description, 'Guyana's National Poet', must sometimes be an unwelcome kind of praise. The poet, however, is Proteus and is not to be held in such a snare.

But knowing now I need not tell
at all what my intention is
I romp this endless moment world
returning, reshaping, rejoicing

Language is not only sound; it is meaning but the reader need not know the poet's intention for the meaning has moved out into the world. The poem is an endless moment (enduring and changing as in 'Proem') and the poet is both speaking and silent and thus, in the last stanza, both fish and fowl like Proteus.

In 'How Come' (1972), the celebration is muted to a sense of wonder.

So now
how come
the bafflement of speech?

So now
how come
the long delight of air
the sense of power
and the sense of passion
created by the dead and wooden
crutch of the spirit
and tongue?

Apparently the connection between cripple and poet is a paradoxical awareness of both power and limitation. Speech is both baffled and baffling in the sense that one's own words seem, on the face of it, intimately a part of one's nature, expressive of one's individual personality and yet they so often, after some time, appear alien and even acquire a life of their own. This is especially, but not exclusively, true of poetic utterance. As an answer to the purely personal need for expression, speech is imperfect. Only a private language could ever answer that need exactly but a private language would be incomprehensible to others and so, by definition, fail to be language. Speech, as we have it, is a substitute for the unattainable ideal. A crutch is a substitute for a limb, as necessary and intimate as speech, which, however, remains paradoxically alien.

The mystery lies in the fact that 'the crutch' of language is a source of power. The sense in which it is alien to each individual speaker (created by other people for other purposes) is a necessary condition of the power of poetry to acquire objective value; it can reveal truth even to the poet and its merit is not simply a question of its relevance to his personal needs.

Indeed time continues to upset certainties and bring about painful revaluations of 'what was to be said', as in 'In the When Time' (1973).

It remains possible to glimpse morning
before the sun; possible to see too early
where sunset might stain anticipated
night. So sudden, and so hurting
is the bitten tongue of memory.

The temporal order is here so complex as to suggest a labyrinth. Morning is a beginning and sunset an ending but both are subject to the uncertainty of a limited foreknowledge; there is only a 'glimpse' and the sunset 'might' stain. The phrase 'too early' suggests that, in addition to the effect of sunset on night, we have to consider the reverse effect of night on sunset; the word 'too' implies that the foreknowledge alters our perception of the present. The 'bitten tongue' suggests, again, foreknowledge, since one may bite one's tongue in mid-sentence, having suddenly foreseen the possible effect of the words. Yet the poet speaks of 'the bitten tongue of memory' as though the confrontation with the past were a re-enactment of the moment of decision when the event was still in the future. The existentialist 'freedom' with its accompanying 'anguish' (in the Sartrean sense) seems to return although, of course, the peculiar horror is that, in the case of memory, the freedom is illusory and only the anguish is real. The phrase 'the bitten tongue of memory' is particularly interesting in the present context since the metaphor narrows the application of the Existentialist view of human freedom to the specific area of speech or language.

In the course of *Poems of Succession,* an entirely coherent theory of language is worked out in the poems. At this point in the collection, an Existentialist view of freedom is being used to examine the limiting effect of time on cognition in general and language in particular. The old argument about *The Four Quartets,* that Eliot's thesis about the inadequacy of language is belied by the success of the language in which it is expressed, can perhaps be applied to Carter's poems as well. The present writer does not share all of the opinions about language that are being abstracted from the poems. The point is rather that Carter's poetry undergoes both a formal and a theoretical evolution and that the theoretical base, an increasing distrust of language, is an explanation, not necessarily sufficient, of the formal change from oratory to cryptic and condensed statement. This is certainly not to deny that there is a political context in which the formal changes occurred.

Even the necessarily relative vision of one who must live in time is seen in a context of celebration in 'Confound Deliberate Chaos' (1974).

> Stark and stay dance in mineral air
> master in the sky. From the plantation earth I cry!
> And it is futile trying to find out now
> from a house-top or a clock
> why canal beside a convent
> was Amazon to a boy. Besides,
> just facing about will make
> what led follow; and what followed, lead.

Here the relativism is again temporal although it is surely a relativism of value as well. The situation of the viewer is determined by time. He is on a house-top, higher than the canal and higher than the vantage point of youth; the clock is both a symbol of time and spatial metaphor. To attempt to regain that vantage point is futile. The illusory 'freedom' with respect to the past, noted in 'In the When Time' has been abandoned; so, however, has the anguish, the 'bitten tongue of memory'. The poem is both a dance and a cry from the 'plantation earth', a phrase that carries both the pain of slavery, past and present, and inevitable associations of growth and renewal.

The last poem in the collection, 'Two In One' (1975) calmly pictures the men of the mountains, the hsien, who are able to see events almost *sub specie aeternitatis* so that 'a season/is a midday,/ a voyage/but a stroll!' Thus the power of time to revalue poetry (and everything else) is not, finally, a tragedy; it 'confound(s)/deliberate chaos, all calculations'. In fact, it sets the poem free and time is the dimension in which its freedom (like the hsien, it is immortal) shall develop. This development towards acceptance appears also in those poems which explore the gaps between speech and hearing and between intention and act. The disjunction between inner and outer worlds is seen in 'The Child Ran Into the Sea' (1974) as one that the organism and the environment continually seek to break down.

The child ran into the sea
but ran back from the waves, because
the child did not know the sea
on the horizon, is not the same sea
ravishing the shore.

The child, like the root, must explore, thrusting deep into the world even though at the limits of its reach it finds a different sea (symbol of chaos; like the stone, not yet humanised). Meanwhile,

...on the shore
nearby, at the feet of every child
shallow water, eating the edges
of islands and continents does little more,
little more than foam like spittle
at the corners of the inarticulate mouth
of some other child who wants to run
into the sea. into the horizon.

The untamed world, with respect to the child, is itself a child facing another (internal) horizon. Once again, the poem presents two opposed movements, from the human out into the world and from the world deep into human consciousness. The difference between 'The Child Ran Into the Sea' and 'A Mouth is Always Muzzled' (their publication dates are five years apart) is that the two movements produce, not a collision but a yearning in the former poem.

Poems of Succession and, especially, those poems taken from *Poems of Resistance,* offer a number of temptations to the critic. It is easy to forget that the material is presented as poetry to be experienced and valued as such (the questions of whether art is an order of value *sui generis* and of the relation between poetry and politics need not detain us if we agree simply that a poem may be a political manifesto without being reducible, qua poem, to its political content) and to make the value of the poetry equivalent to or commensurate with the correctness (however such a thing is judged) of the political attitudes contained therein. One does not need to share the political opinions of a poet to value his poetry any more than, as a prerequisite for appreciating 'The Wreck of the Deutschland', one needs to believe in a God who drowns women to make a point.

On the other hand, a number of motives may drive the critic to deny the importance of the specific political context of some of the poetry, adopting a kind of New Critical approach. Since this kind of approach has obvious political implications once one moves outside its own range of assumptions, my difficulty in the foregoing analysis has been that the theory of language I find in the poetry is not at all what one would expect given Martin Carter's high standing with Guyanese Marxists.

It may be necessary to distinguish between Carter the poet and Carter the political myth. The former seems to me far more complex and paradoxical than the latter. Carter's poetry is not simply one political device among many, an occasion for the critic to make his own political stand on the side of the angels, nor is the political content arbitrarily chosen. Art and political statement in some of the poems may both be seen as aspects of a commitment to truth. Poetry is a matter of vision and there are times and places in which merely to have seen clearly is already to have performed a political act.

Notes

1. Martin Carter, *Poems of Succession* (London: New Beacon, 1977).
2. Wilson Harris, *Tradition, The Writer and Society* (London: New Beacon, 1967) p.30.

This essay was first published in *The Journal of West Indian Literature*, vol.1, no., 1, Oct. 1986, p. 1-12.

BILL CARR

FOREWORD TO *POEMS OF AFFINITY* (1980)

This present collection of new work by Martin Carter confirms – if indeed further confirmation be needful at all – what most of his readers have long felt: namely, that Carter is the finest poet writing in Guyana today. And I think one can say, without reservation, that he is the finest of all Guyanese poets. You will note where my stress falls, upon 'finest'. The term 'national poet' is fundamentally meaningless. In fact it might be considered a term of opprobrium insofar as it is susceptible to use by the unscrupulous: the devil, as it were, citing Scripture for his own nefarious purposes. At best the term is an inexplicit sentimentality likely to be employed in a slovenly fashion by persons more interested in the possible implications of 'national' rather than in the questing and complex implications of 'poet'. Only Jamaica, as far as I am aware, went many years ago to the absurd lengths of crowning a poet with a wreath of *lignum vitae* and proclaiming him 'Poet Laureate'. One does not apprehend Carter in this way and he himself objects to a title that has merely been foisted off on him.

I have spent a little time on this apparently minor matter because clearly the imposed title is an irrelevant growth from the title and significant political content of his volume *Poems of Resistance* (1953). The poems in that volume achieve the unique effect of speaking to us in a voice which is at the same time public and private. My grammar is not confused here. It is merely a simple way of drawing attention to the dialectic of Carter's poems. The public and the private are at the same time simultaneous and yet separate and so the poems and so we, as his readers, are preserved from the barren echoes usually to be found in what is frequently described as 'political Poetry'. This is also a misleading expression. If a poet (or Poetaster) makes a resounding statement on a public and political issue then he is, it would seem, a 'political poet' (in fact he may not really be a poet at all) and in any case the 'poem' is likely to perish as the issue or issues recede into the turbulence of political history. The private assertion, however, (explicit in the craft) guarantees the life, and also the integrity, of the poem. There are some poems in the 1953 collection which might cause a reader some moments of uneasiness. But it is not part of my business to direct the reader's attention to them now. My business is to focus *Poems Of Affinity*.

In this collection there is only one explicitly political poem in which the content is available even to the reader who does not know what is being mourned. This is the poem Bastille Day – Georgetown, 'Bastille' sets up the context in which a cruel event took place in Georgetown on the 14th July, 1979; Carter gives the date at the end of the poem and he himself was present when the event took place (the murder in broad daylight of a Roman Catholic priest).

Not wanting to deny, I
believed it. Not wanting
to believe it, I denied
our Bastille day.

The taut phrasing of the paradox surely precipitates the reader into the bewildered horror of that day. To deny would be to lie but at the same time Carter does not want to believe it. And there is the additional irony of Bastille Day. Instead of storming the scowling prison we are now all its prisoners by virtue of the horrid act and the apparent equanimity with which it was accepted by those in authority. 'All, all are involved/ All are consumed', says Carter in one of the finest and most familiar of his shorter poems, and that poem is surely echoed or (perhaps enlarged upon) here:

I have at last started
to understand the origin
of our vileness, and being
unable to deny it, I suggest
its nativity.
In the shame of knowledge
of our vileness, we shall fight.

One notes the constructive adhesiveness of Carter's relationship with his fellow men ('our vileness' – without that kind of awareness what do you really have?) and one notes also the precise irony of 'nativity'. As far as I am aware only one birth has ever been called that and Carter, at the same time, is no Pontius Pilate with the timid acceptance of what is palmed off as the inevitable.

What might the implication of the title be? The reader might wish to ponder. I have already spoken of the simultaneous presence of the public and the private in Carter's poetry. It is the hallmark, the sterling guarantee, of Carter's abundant and angry humanism. Affinity with what, though? Affinity with his fellow men, of course. But affinity also with the sun, with trees, with water and clouds. This affinity is juxtaposed with a disaffinity with time, for it is through our allotted time-span which we do not know that we experience so deeply our suffering, our defeats and losses. Sun, trees, water and clouds – these are the roots from which the human condition grows. But it is time which contains, which conditions. The sun can be eclipsed. Drought will deny us water, trees and living things. But time is an absolute and impersonal process, eternally.

Every day is as old
as a new day is. Time
represents itself.

The paradox is inevitable. In time everyday is the same as every other day. We are time-ridden.

> ...I,
> unapologetic, remember why every
> day was once a new day. As new
> and as old as my childhood roaming
> among grass. The world is a cold
> wind. It is a glass of sweet water
> in a grim place of thirst.
> Farewell rain. When again shall I
> taste your high cloud?

The last three lines of this poem had me puzzled for some time. And I may be entirely wrong in what I propose now – although it is perfectly possible for a reader to contribute to a poem, to relevantly perceive something the poet himself may not have seen and intended. My difficulty was resolved, I hope, by the two poems which deal with the Latin American poet Cesar Vallejo. There is something in Vallejo's poetry to which Carter urgently responds. Hence the two poems addressed to Vallejo in this collection. There would be an obvious measure of fatuity in describing Carter as a Latin American poet or even as a South American poet. Carter is an English speaking poet but his homeland is situated in the North-eastern shoulder of Latin America. I blush to state the obvious. But one needs to remember the differences between Guyana and the islands in the English speaking Caribbean. Guyana shares much of her historical and social experiences with the islands but in size and terrain she is unique by comparison. So is Carter's poetry. His work is quite unlike the work of Walcott, E.K. Brathwaite or Mervyn Morris. What relates his work to theirs is a shared and serious concern for craft. But the sensibility his craft expresses has no obvious meeting place with theirs. The small islands have never had to undergo the traumatic shock of politics in Guyana, beginning in 1948 till the suspension of the Constitution by the British in October, 1953. I have already mentioned terrain. In Carter's poetry sun, clouds, trees, water are almost: impersonally used. There is nothing of intimate personalisation and realisation of nature in his poetry and this, I think, is a consequence of space and terrain. Man is sharply present in his poetry (sometimes as an odious commonplace) but man nevertheless is impersonally dwarfed and Carter's creative humanism, diminishing man's sense of his own scale in the universe, is anthropomorphic. The true sense of his scale assists towards some approximate to religious faith and, of course, its antithesis:

> ...Having betrayed
> old gods in an old day, we seek
> now to betray new ones
> in a new day.

These are the concluding lines of the poem. I think of the 'Conquistadores' and Walter Raleigh's own gods '...old day'. Carter, by the way, has a responsible and serious interest in the indigenous inhabitants of Guyana, the Amerindians – 'betray ours'? I take this as pointing to the tragic nature of Guyanese history over the last thirty years or so. Or often now, Carter has experienced this tragedy. It has assisted at the forging of his craft and it is central to his private life. Indeed in this collection he has accomplished the rare feat of writing tragic lyric poetry. The lyrical quality is controlled and tight (one can think of the art of the woodcarver) and so one experiences the essence, the nature of the tragedy but never with any nagging monotony or repetitiousness of tone.

I will conclude with one further poem:

> This morning is new, but the sun
> that made it is old. New and old
> is the face of the world's great grief,
> a kind of music we listen to and hear
> when the toil of silence builds
> our house of language in this wind's
> throat, the grim larynx. A green leaf
> on the branch of a tree fingers
> our time's disgraceful space. We
> are its measure.

There is not a word that has to explain its presence. The words appear to slip into their proper places. (Though anyone who actually feels this knows nothing about poetry). It should be clear that the search for words to accurately express meaning and experience has been and is, a strict and disciplined one. And the final attestation is the tense elasticity of the movement of the poem entirely lacking strain or superfluous pressure.

My final pleasure is to hand these poems over to their best guardians – their readers.

EUSI KWAYANA

THE POLITICS OF THE HEART

It is not hard to understand the source of much of the academic rebellion against the poetry of social concern, the so-called political poetry. When such critics look back on the poetry of the past, they seem to have no difficulty with Shakespeare, Byron, whom it is true many perhaps dislike. They do not wince at Hazlitt, Shelley, William Morris, Dante or the various poets of the Bible. Distance lends enchantment to the politics of the past and it becomes epic, patriotic, ethical or religious and all they see in it is the high emotion, the fascinating language and the constellation of images. They are far away from the conflict, so far that they see it as a higher Peace. The political economy of those days is not pressing on their kitchens. The political economy of past days does not challenge them to disturb the comfort of their nests. Many look only for a psychological explanation, of the main direction. This is all very well, but it is not the whole story.

The time is overdue for a reader's response to Martin Carter's poetry. Noteworthy are the poetic soul, the poetic method or the method he employs in his art, the poet's postures, for he has postures, just as a batsman has postures and stances. This is quite different from accusing him of posturing, which to him is the highest evil. One cannot read Carter, either, without being made alert to the relationship between poetry and politics. It will be useful also to see how the poet functions or used to function as a political activist of the independence class struggle, his particular interests and the kind of speeches he made. Generally, out of this examination will come some idea of what I perceive his world outlook to be. And this will not be discussed in terms of this or that school or ideology.

To avoid suspense, we should note at once that Carter's 'Shape and Motion Two' is a very close description of his sense of himself, whether he intended it or not. He walks 'slowly in the wind watching myself in things I did not make'. He sees himself in jumping shadows, in 'houses tight with sickness', in 'coughing dogs when midnight lingers long'. In short, he is a part of everything, material and spiritual, and everything else is a part of him. In this respect he has not to 'mature'. He was also there in the 1950s.

Some of the finest images of the Bible are in Psalm 144: 'the sea saw it and fled: Jordan was driven back./ The mountains skipped like rams and the little hills like young sheep...' But it is in part a poem dealing with the liberation of the Jews from Egypt, 'from a people of strange language'.

Another well known psalm now adapted into reggae poetry and song is – 'By the waters of Babylon I sat down and wept/ When I remembered thee, O Zion!/As for our harps we laid them up/On the trees that were nearby/They that took us away captive required of us a song in our heaviness/ Sing us one of the songs of Zion/ How can we sing the Lord's song/In a strange land?' A singing of this song never fails to moisten the eyelids.

Psalm 104, on the other hand, is almost pure nature poetry containing what is to this day, the working material of most genuine poets, quite apart from the world outlook found in their poems.

It is hardly to be expected however, that an intelligent poet living in a period of social upheaval, will be aloof from it and unaffected by it, whether or not he chooses to be, or is chosen as, an actor in it, especially in the best traditions of the art.

The categories of natural science do not trouble Martin Carter, although he understands them and respects them very intelligently. Yet the more he understands them, the more he is convinced of the oneness of life. The origin of this outlook is not known. It was certainly enriched and sharpened by his study of the exponents of humanist thought like Marx's materialism; but he was much freer than they to carry understanding of nature to its logical conclusions.

So in his philosophy are woven the all-pervading spirit of the Hindu, the universal empathy which Robeson claimed for the African, the objectivity of Europe as represented by Marx and the uncanniness of the folk in whose wisdom he revels. Thus surplus value and the motion of the stars are as real for him as the buried slave wanting to speak again.

As a political activist and poet in the past, he put a peculiar meaning on his discussions, lectures and speeches. The bland statement was never enough. He was never satisfied merely to raise class issues without dealing with the subjective state of the members of the class. He would say something like this to a meeting, large or small: 'Now I am sure you all agree with me that this colony called British Guiana is a jail. Now, why is it a jail? It is not because you and I are in some cell with an iron bar and a big key. No, it is not that kind of jail. Why is it a jail, then?' Martin Carter would never seek to engage his hearers at the level of mere bread. He hated breadlessness because with its absence people became more absorbed in hunting for it. He knew that in the long run there would be no human thought or creation without food.

He would pose to his audience, especially, but not only a small gathering, the most difficult question of the relation between ideas or concepts and life and he would glory in the answers he received, examine them and try to learn from them.

Is it true that the more political poems, as Bill Carr suggests in his masterly foreword to *Poems of Affinity,* are the least enduring? We can revel in the poetry of the coming and passing of Arthur, and detach ourselves perhaps, from the essentially political issues involved in the epic. What is more political than the old order passing and 'yielding place to new' with God fulfilling himself 'in many ways lest one good custom should corrupt the world'? No one sees the ghost of dialectical materialism here although it leaps out of the lines. The professional critics must examine whether in many of the landmark poems, as well as other works of art of a certain period, it was not a question of the artist employing means available to him or her either to reinforce the existing social order or to hold it up to ridicule or scorn or earn for it a well deserved condemnation. The fact that we are looking at these poems at a range of five hundred years and more does not make them less tendentious or political than Auden's underestimation of a 'dull, dishonest decade' or Martin Carter's 'defiance of darkness'. And when we talk of a social order, how can we separate it from the values it upheld, sought to destroy or those that upheld it or sought to destroy it?

Poetry is in fact, more political, or more concerned about man's lot, than most manipulators of the existing political machines have managed or dared to be. At another level, Shakespeare's understanding of the political process can still be a good model for the highly certificated political scientists of the present day. The people's cry for brakes on the executive in the seizure and piling up of public resources in their strong boxes is still answered by the maximum headers with Cassius's opportunism: 'in such a time as this it is not meet/that every nice offence should bear his comment'.

In approaching Martin Carter's poetry, while it has matured from the concerns of public mobilisation, we must be aware, as he is aware, that he is writing not in a social vacuum, but in a world in which after ages of development there is a state which, in all countries, has assumed responsibility to a greater or lesser degree for placing limits on those forms of human destitution and human misery and that this destitution is capable of economic description. A poet who returns again and again to such themes is qualifying for the hemlock, whether or not he joins or supports a party or any formal cause. I am not arguing for political poetry, nor suggesting that the finest poetry is political. I am arguing that readers and critics should not disqualify poets or artists in whole or in part because they betray or proclaim political concern, if only because many of these critics genuflect before the old masters like Dante, Shakespeare, Goethe, Lope de Vega, writers in the Gita and the Bible without allowing themselves to be deterred by the link between the art and public attitudes, state power or any social power and the lot of human beings in the distant time.

THE HILL OF FIRE GLOWS RED

'When you see me coming to your house [...] Know that I look for fire'. Fire among all material things was the central value for the poet. From it he draws strength, encouragement and hope. Perhaps it was the power of fire to purge without losing its own beauty which draws it to him or him to it. He was also attracted to the fire of human feeling because he felt that when men and women were afire, they burn true and there is no guile or deception in the character. He would never confuse noise or fury with fire.

Many progressives will wonder why he gloried for example, in certain aspects of the so-called Black Friday 1962 and has published his poem on it. Martin would applaud, despite the political implications, when on Black Friday 'a city of clerks/turned a city of men'.

The Hill of Fire Glows Red was perhaps his first published collection. Several of the streams of thought and feeling which were to develop later, and to multiply themselves in the poet's life and art could already be felt in this volume of the Miniature Poets series, made possible by the efforts of that poet of all the poets, A. J. Seymour. It was the pure fire of a young rebel whose hatred of death and misery was as noticeable as his feel for nature in motion and his defiance of the complacent mind, which he has always considered a great danger. 'Do not stare at me from your window, lady/do not stare and wonder where I came from/Born in this city was I, lady/hearing the beetles at six o'clock/and the noisy cocks in the morning/ when your hands rumple the bed-sheets/and night is locked up in the wardrobe'. The contrast is sharp, politely bold, giving no ground, when he invites her: 'Stare at the slums in the south of the city/Stare hard and reason, lady, where I came from/and where I go'. But although she needs to be made aware, as Victor Hugo might say, of the existence of mankind, she is not a human enemy and he can again smile with her at another level: 'My hand is full of lines/like your breasts with veins, lady/and one must rear, while one must suckle life'.

Already too, he is ready to lend a hand to anything aimed at changing the world. His technique of the triurn (a word borrowed from my church days) process rather than the dual; not 'I do not sleep to dream, but dream to sleep' but: 'I do not sleep to dream, but dream to change the world'. This method is prevalent in Martin Carter and sometimes it takes on an even more material form as an expression of the multiple or better the plural reality of things. The method gets stronger in 'The Kind Eagle'. It is not a unique method, but its use in his hands is unique: 'And only hope, hope only,/the kind eagle' is one example. 'Freedom is a white road with green grass like love'. A thing is not only like another thing of the same tendency, but like another surprising thing of another quality, in one movement it is like a road and in another it is like love. The 'noisy cocks in the morning' is a phrase that serves the contrast the poet seeks to establish between himself and the lady of the window in whose wardrobe night is still 'locked up' at six in the morning. She, poor woman, does not hear the cocks, since at that hour she is buried in bedsheets.

Thus far, in what way is Martin Carter a political poet? Is there any justification for the supposition that his political awareness, for such it is, spoils his poetry, or hinders it, or perhaps inspires it?

From what we have seen so far it is Carter's naked sensibility, rather than his ideology that makes him both political and poetic. His taste for nature, his keen knowledge of everything that lives around him – the shades of colouring on the leaf, the time of the beetles' chorus, the star neighbouring the leaf at twilight, the delirium of fever, the nakedness of a stone, the white waxen glory of the frangipani, the way, as Solomon would say, of a snake on a rock – are familiar ground. But seldom does he have the leisure to revel in them for their own sake. He puts them at the service of man. Another sense in which the poetry is political is the way it often permeates itself with social relations. In 'On a Child Killed by a Motor Car', one of the most beautiful of his tragedies, note the fidelity of the social relations in all stages of the brief lament. There are some five examples of this in the seven short lines of a well crafted poem. The concern with human labour, the human attributes given to the 'wheat that made the loaf', the whole realism of a little child being sent to a shop for a mere loaf of bread; the climax of the images of how 'in this field of the heart's ploughed land/you were threshed'. The poem is so brief, painfully satisfying, that it is given here in full:

Child, a moment of love ago
you danced in the eye of the woman
who made you. Within another moment
like the innocent wheat that made the loaf
of bread she sent you for
in this field of the heart's ploughed land
you were threshed!

In terms of period, *The Hill of Fire Glows Red* is an image of the hopes of a colonised mass of humans, organised into the barracks of international capital on the mudflat and the sands of our homeland. He was intolerant of 'colony' as a human class. It was the same as 'prison', 'grave' and other impositions. It was the dead end of human society. In *The Hill of Fire Glows Red,* as it announces, is the poetic image of a rebellion that is building up. He senses it and knows it as unavoidable and he ceaselessly seeks out and encourages every member, looking at your hands, listening while you speak, marching in your ranks, 'looking for fire'. This is the politics of the stirring of the 'dry bones', the politics of germination, of a coming to life which imbues his poetic efforts.

In the later period of the *Poems of Resistance,* to be discussed later, man is beautiful because he is taking on the world, and the political process of challenging our own humanity; the armies of a military power are failing to quell the spirit of his unarmed people. Because of this he can glory in the political process. At any point when the political process becomes a thing in itself and for itself, it appals him and he produces images to trouble the souls even of those who are callous in the manner of his frontal question in the later period of the sixties: 'or do you think/the impartial bullock cares whose land is ploughed?' *(Poems of Succession)*.

The 'impartial bullock' can be a kindly personification of the political process bereft of ideals and also of those who are its practitioners. He warns about the coming disenchantment of the masses who are no longer on the offensive, but have yielded to the impartial bullock: 'so jail me quickly, clang the illiterate door/if freedom writes no happier alphabet'. The bullock has touches of the idiom of Marx when he says in reply to a question, 'If a man were an ox he could turn his back on the sufferings of mankind and consider his own skin'. Yet the bullock ploughing the fields was part of the Guyana landscape until the coming of the tractor. It is still seen in a few places, but at any rate it is a live Guyanese image. It is impartial under the yoke and it goes where driven, dealing with all farmers equally. As bullock, however, the politician or administrator takes on more personal responsibility for his actions. He tramples on all targets equally.

This is not to say that hope is dead. It springs as yet from the eternal fount. But there is the danger that in the conflict between the irrepressible energies, victory may not advance the human cause. There are forces which are 'mocking great dreams' and 'wrong deeds' which are becoming the order of the day.

Since it is not the work of the reviewer to read for the reader, it is enough to point out how the poet does not shrink from the ultimate judgement that in his own city, men murder men to 'build their shining governments of the damned'. The mention of governments may distress those who make a distinction between poets of the past and poets of the present, and those who fear to be caught reading the volume at such a page, lest they be secretly noted. But no poet of the present age can ignore the influence of governments even on the environment, to say nothing of the lives of people. Nor can the poet ignore the fact that government-making is a modern enterprise which many have reduced to the level of a joint-stock company of the rulers.

The Hill of Fire Glows Red was the work of a very young poet in the making whose personal study and search for truth had already given him a world outlook. His sensitivities had already been sharpened by attendance at the leading boys' school, the physical and mental straight jacket of the civil service, his discovering of world literature, his ceaseless enquiry into the past of the Amerindians and their condition, his interest in slavery and its offshoot indenture and his quest to discover the real being of those two captive peoples, his keen and particular study of Guyanese history including the significance of little incidents recorded in the memories of the aged. He also knew friends like Wilson Harris, at the time with Sidney Singh and others, a rebel philosopher in his own right who had also developed an authentic world outlook, whose faith in the Caribbean was already a fundamental factor in his thought. Harris used to muse with his friends through the night and while on the one side they talked of the working class, he would represent the impending cataclysm in his own vision and idiom.

'...the dark energies, let us call them the anonymous forces, they are at work and they will create a culture that will astound the world...' *The Hill of Fire Glows Red* did at the level of art what the wage earners were doing in little patches, resuming the struggles of the early quarter of the century. It raised up a tower of intellectual rebellion. That tower was on fire against sloth, blindness, smugness, self-satisfaction, complacency and submission to the fate of a colonised people. It was not seen by many people. It was read at people's gatherings. It was seen by the curious members of the intelligentsia. For them it made the struggle against dead ways no longer something only to be found in the intellectual creation of foreigners, though it was to be found there too, but something of which Guyanese artists, thinking and feeling people, men and women, were potentially capable. Why, here was one who was not merely revelling in the safe beauties of rapturous nature and the attractions of women, but looking at where man was going and concerned that men be alerted. *The Kind Eagle* was the title of the second collection which he published on his own on a small scale basis through one of the many printers about the city in those days. I dimly remember the proof reading and the bold italic type on the front cover.

The spirit of the poetry does not lose any of the original purity of passion to be found in *The Hill of Fire Glows Red.* Already there is the striving to see himself in what is around him, to stitch realities into one. The scope of interest is wider and the concern more particular.

It is a very private statement of one who is also a very public person. The private statement of a conscience that is a public conscience is the happy fusion that Bill Carr is willing to embrace. Martin's creative method has never allowed him to write a party song. His poems are not written as trumpets or bugles. Many of them turn out to be that because the poetic vision is so fused with human destiny. What is private, in certain of its moods, also throbs with public concern. Also what is non personal becomes personal through the same process, so it is non personal, and then internalised and then returned as non private.

The particular poetic fantasy created in the title poem of this volume, which I do not have near, is so lifelike that it ceases to refer to a single prisoner and has implications for the wider prison of the colony: 'I make my dance right here/Right here on the wall of prison I dance.'

It is still the concern of many not insensitive persons whose station in life has brought them to some comfort, how the general population can enjoy or appear to enjoy carnivals, when there is so little to celebrate with and so little to celebrate. The image of the prisoner's dance may not be out of place or as isolated as it seems. He can dance on the spiked wall that imprisons him, and in dancing think he sees hope. The problematic future is clear to him. His weapon is going to be the 'sharp knife of dawn', all very consistent with the private wishes of a prisoner surveying his captivity.

Though already a revolutionary, he has not because of that lost his artistic method or craft. Nor should a revolutionary who discovers his own creativity suffer in either because he has two trades instead of one.

The film *Terror and the Time* did not lose sight of the cinema potential of this poem. Those prisoners who through their ventilators at the top of the cell could see more above than below, are they not 'sweepers of an ancient sky/discoverers of new planets, sudden stars?' The world's hope lies partly here in suffering and in the knowledge that sometimes comes from its pain.

The artist makes his point, and, unless an actor or singer tarries not for answer, does not expect to be applauded or followed, or understood in the way he intended the meaning. This is not the way of the political agitator who fails if he does not get an overwhelming response, now or later – else is the preaching vain. The poet's triumph is in creation. If there is an immediate response to his work the artist is surprised. The more there is a mass response, the poet may even be disturbed. The more lifelike the work is, the less the poet 'knows' about its creation, since it also sweeps him along and the more he may hesitate about proclaiming it. Because of the very political economy of art, the poet, unlike the calypsonian, is satisfied to begin with a small audience. He knows that it is not the people's fault that they would not be summoned with a bell, for a bell crier cannot do justice to a poem. Still he knows that the production is one of the agencies which will affect the appreciation of art; that in some pre-modern societies, art has a central place and is appreciated and that in the modern and post-modern societies it is less unanimous.

The agitator must not undertake his task unless the aim is to stir the unaware, or those who stand near to the pit of hopelessness.

It was kind of the eagle to soar in the view of the damned, symbolising hope and freedom, a hope that is uplifting and a freedom that is above the baseness and corruption attendant on the captive condition and its personal politics. This is the hope of the anti-colonial struggle of the masses. But thirty years later the poet's spirits are sinking, as his compassion is pained at 'our vileness' *(Poems of Affinity)*. The architects have not kept their sights on the eagle. Many of them had never sensed her sheer dignity on the wing through the prison bars, from which the eagle can be seen to best advantage.

The Kind Eagle, in one of its meanings, on reflection, was a film-worthy vision of the attractive human possibilities, once the colonial prison was broken and left behind, mourning its captives. The poem is very private, though not in the same sense personal in origin. It contains fine poetic form for us in the Caribbean. It has much of the unavoidable politics of much genuine poetry or art. It comes out of a man who could draft a handbill for agitation against some public wrong. It does not come out of Carter's personal prison experience. It is written while he is a civil servant employed in the prisons in the clerical service, a job he dismissed suddenly. He was to return to the Camp Street Prison some years after as Her Majesty's guest to suffer in person what he had suffered through other wretched. The remarkable thing is that, as I wrote in 1954 in the preface to *Poems of Resistance,* these poems strike an instant chord in the hearts of the ordinary people walking about, then as now in the bigger prison.

In a matter of months after our joint release, with Ajodha Singh, Rory Westmaas and Bally Lachmansingh from preventive detention at the U. S. Air Base, Atkinson Field, Martin Carter, like other comrades in arms, was to become at Camp Street Prison, Georgetown, 'A man who walks the pavement, walks and disappears'.

What is poetic vision? What is poetic genius, not in the sense of the genius of a prodigy, but genius in the sense of insight and sensitivity. It is seen in those creations of the artist, in which the artist is burning out the spirit in pieces and creating what is very private to him and at the same time what, either today or tomorrow, will strike a chord of sympathy in a wide cross section of the human species. In reference to poetry, this is poetic vision or poetic genius. A poet is a certain kind of person with a certain attitude, a certain extra sensitivity in certain areas of being. Thus the artist is not someone who consciously makes himself into an artist. True, he may not be able, like the Minister of Health of Guyana Dr. Van West Charles, to visit Guyana Water Authority with his stethoscope in ear and decide what is needed is a 125 hp pump and not a 100 hp pump. Art cannot aspire to magic. What can be made and perfected is the craft of the artist. The more the artist perfects this craft, the more effective is the artist. Thus there are many who have perfected learnable skills to a high degree without the quality of art. There are also thousands of persons everywhere with the sensitivity and feeling of artists who never practice any art. The social relations of production – that is of any given economy – have a lot to do with how many artists blossom into practitioners of an art. Some cultures are able to accommodate large numbers of musicians and dancers, for example, who are serious, feeling artists, but whose conditions of life did not make them widely known. As the society grows more specialised, so also become the chances for practice among genuine artists.

As it becomes more literate or bookish, this achievement of literacy is more necessary. It raises an additional hurdle for those gifted in a certain form of artistic sensitivity. For this reason, unless they satisfy a precondition of literacy to a given standard, they may never be recognised as being among the people's artists. For indeed artists do not make themselves, nor are they made solely by their parents. So it is we come back through materialist reasoning, and we have no apology for this, to the very 'self discovery' of the religious mystic in this narrow area of art.

No one can, with as little scientific and intellectual equipment as most of us have, say with near certainty what factors went into the fashioning of Martin Carter as an artist and why he became a poet and not a musician or a sculptor. More easy to achieve is the reason why he became for most of the time a man of the people and not a man against the people, or a man 'between' the people.

The Caribbean character is highly complex in its personality manifestations – how people see themselves and how they want to be seen. The calypsonian who sings of how West Indians quickly become English or American in tone or accent is saying this in more striking form.

One thing the ruling intelligentsia of the late 1940s and early 1950s learned from the leaders of thought in our society during those years was noncommittal and non-commitment, not only as a road to very material promotion, say, in the expatriate firm or in the civil service, but as a way of intellectual promotion among the intellectual community. It was the pose corresponding to those in Shakespeare's time 'who only therefore are reputed wise for saying nothing'. In our case it was those who were reputed wise for believing nothing.

No need to throw a flower, throw
a petal. Rain is a cousin
of air, the blood of parents.

To move along with Carter in his poetry one must have some sense of the line or the mode of travel. If the method of this poet has matured over the thirty years or so he has been publishing, it is in the mastery of techniques for telling of the unity of life. Telling, not preaching, lest it should be thought this is an attempt to turn Carter into a soap box orator, except that in the fullness of his life, when duty lay in doing that function, he did not shrink from it. Even on the soap box he never gave up the struggle to show life in all its interconnections. As a politician he was impatient with the finality of political formulation but he also sympathised with the need for a start of common definition and identification of wrong. As a poet he was uneasy with the finality of political formulation. Still he always saw the practical need to start with a commonly agreed definition of wrong.

As to some of his poetry being political and causing unease among critics, this unease may be due to their own limited view of beauty. A poet who is revolutionary is drawn to the struggle because of its beauty. It is a limited but not a separate activity: the beauty of the vision that inspires human beings to raise weapons of all kinds against oppression and degeneracy is no less a proper subject for poetry than the beauty of flowers, or the beauty of character. The ugliness of oppression also calls forth in many hearts the effort of rebellion, in an unspoken affirmation of the beautiful potential of life.

In reality, however, Martin Carter is a deeply political poet; this is another way of saying a deeply human poet, because in the broader aspects of man's freedom, the precondition of individual freedom is political freedom, just as many must first of all assert their individual freedom in order to break away from the bondage of fear and fight for political freedom. Thus, as a prisoner in 'The Knife of Dawn', he could rise above the prison condition – a real prison, by the way, – and 'dance on the wall of prison'. Dawn is a time of day, and it is also new after each night. It is a sharp knife glittering in his hand; it is the world's hope, a blade of fury. Its kinship to the 'Kind Eagle' must not surprise, for this is the unity of all things in the economy of Martin Carter's world and thus it is that a blade of fury and a kind eagle are equal to the same thing: hope.

The switching of image while retaining unity of theme, often in one breath, and the switching of perspective form two of his favourite devices.

Every day was once a new day. 'As new/and as old as my child-hood roaming/among grass. The world is a cold/wind. It is a glass of sweet water/ in a grim place of thirst'. Childhood is itself new, but the poet's childhood is a memory since it was a long time ago. 'The world is a cold/wind' is a momentary truth, an idiom telling some narrow or rather single aspect of the world. It is also 'a glass of sweet water in a grim place of thirst'. A thread of imagination can stitch the two images together. In our atmosphere, a cold wind hardly leaves a burst of rain far behind. The accidental collision of his language with what rings from 'the huts' of the rasta is a measure of his closeness to the popular culture of the outcasts among us and those who cast themselves out.

Revealing the sameness of things which appear to be different is another way in which the poet knits together a pattern of the world. Vision is translated into sound, but it is the same idea, the same principle. 'New and old is the face of the world's great grief,/a kind of music we listen to and hear' as if there is a natural computer of truth translating light into sound and a grieving face into corresponding music.

And how does 'the toil of silence build our house of language in this wind's throat, the grim larynx'. These sentiments are hardly hidden. He is so uplifted by the throwing off of what appears to be the passive mood that seemed to have settled on the population. But his perceptions are not blunted by his enthusiasm. He can distinguish those who are truly alive from 'the dead who shoot and think themselves alive'. He has seen 'some creatures rise from holes/and claw a triumph like a citizen/ and reign until the tide!' There is hope in despair; it is in death that there is none. So the convulsions of the desperate are not to be scoffed at.

Within the set of poems titled *Jail Me Quickly* are streams of concern continuing from *The Kind Eagle.* The metaphor of colonial humanity rising above the grime of the colonial condition is not a far-fetched reading of the adventures of the eagle flying over the prison and of 'homeless birds flying to the forest'. It is an upward, human mobility, not the mobility that aims at leaving others earthbound, but the mobility that wants all humanity to rise. This is the winged urge and necessity that takes hold again in 'Where Are Free Men'.

It is not as though he goes through one phase of development, sheds the idiom and the philosophy of that phase and then moves on without traces to another phase.

It is tempting to see Carter as developing in a straight line, to see his poetry and his mind maturing to the point of his ideal of affinity in the 1980 poems. This is not how his poetry developed. As early as 1955, the idea of the identity of all life and the identity of the poet with it found expression in 'Shape and Motion Two'. Already he watches himself in things he did not make: 'in jumping shadows and in limping cripples/ dust on the earth...' He hears himself in 'the loneliness of a child/in woman's grief *which is not understood*/in coughing dogs when midnight lingers long'.

Martin Carter has always, and the more mature he grows, the more so, seen himself in the vilest and most godforsaken of human beings. And although his perspectives for man are limitless, he has never found arrogance to the rest of the animal kingdom justified. Nor does he make any rigid distinction between the various manifestations of life. We are life in a special form, but we are not all of life. So the volume *Poems of Affinity* is dedicated 'to all children, flowers and dogs, in that order'. This is also a warning to his fellow humans and especially his fellow citizens that the order of dedication is not fixed.

I have been careful not to read critiques of this volume except Mr. Bill Carr's, which reading suggested to me my own attempt, as a response to his views on 'political' poetry. I have pointedly not read Mr. Gordon Rohlehr's, which I heard of when well advanced, because I do not want to be influenced by what the professionals are saying, valid as it is. There is already quite a lot in Carr that I see as valid, despite his profession.

When we come to *Poems of Affinity* Carter is astonished at the apparent peace in the midst of intense injury. He is convinced that at this point of time, in this phase of their existence, the dominant trend in humanity as judged from its behaviour is complicit in its own destruction. 'Badly abused we fail to curse/ *Our* fury pleads'. The emphasis is crucial, for true fury should be fire!

The genius of Martin Carter, the distinctive feature of his politics is that he can feel affinity with what he despises because he cannot separate himself from that social organism we call the Caribbean, and in particular Guyana. The volume is therefore one theme, endlessly varied, and worked in all its facets so that its wholeness, its influence, its seemingly pervasive presence, that is, its presence everywhere is not ignored, disguised or misunderstood. He can do this without worship of the supposed all-powerfulness of the dominant class. And this is one of the points at which Carter breaks rank and breaks lances with other members of his social formation.

He is a link between the mere man of science and the mere humanist and a link between both of these and the artist. Try as he might, perhaps under the impact of new emerging social formations, and the breakdown of old values, or through his own internal development in response to the human environment, he cannot avoid pleading the human cause, the cause of life.

There are several images in the collection *Poems of Affinity* which bring out his view of life as a unity. These are not chance images, nor are they of forced design, although an artist must design. They flow from a deep-souled concern not with man only, but with every expression and form of life. He is a singer of truth in the age of conscious science. He is a musician of creation, a keen perceiver of motion in atoms and of atoms in motion and of things in the atoms of all things: a *singer of the unity of being.* If I misunderstand this, then I am of all readers most mistaken.

In *The Hill of Fire Glows Red* the young poet shows an awakening of senses and instincts which are to grow more alert and more active with years and events. Even in those years he can see the map of water underneath the stars and the map of stars above the mass of water, where 'shines the beauty of my darling in her laughing eyes'. Writing from memory, some of the lines that struck me then strike me now – but he, the poet, has matured. One of these passages is in the poem: 'do not stare at me from your window, lady,/ do not stare and wonder where I came from/ Born in this city was I lady [...] hearing.../... the noisy cocks in the morning'. It is this apostrophe that he tells the smug socially unaware lady, 'stare at the wagon of prisoners/ stare at the slums in the south of the city/stare hard, and reason, lady, where I come from and where I go' – exactly what every young rebel wanted to say to every complacent looking person. Unfortunately, it was the dainty ladies that to us for some time seemed most complacent.

Another loveable poem was one that appealed to rural instincts because of its deep fraternity: 'as I walk the seller of sweets says 'friend'/and the shoemaker with his awl and waxen thread/ reminds me of tomorrow and the world'. In this first publication what came out was the young poet's response to the human environment. 'This city with a prison for a heart/ city of dust and silent streets/city of street preachers'. He was becoming impatiently aware of suffering in the midst of relative non-suffering and also of the wider prison.

His lament on the Amerindian destiny was a biting comment on what colonialism had made of Amerindian civilisation: 'Not hands like mine these Carib altars knew/nameless and quite forgotten are the gods/and mute,/ mute and alone/their silent people spend/a ring of vacant days/ not like more human years/as [...] their rivers flow away'. Martin's interest in the Amerindians was remarkable, as already discussed and not missed by Carr. His method of trying to get into their being is unique. He reads every scrap of paper written on them, sees them when he can, listens to stories about them, including those intended to degrade them and notes their ongoing response to the onslaughts on their dignity and well being. Here is a very rich example of what Carr points to in his very professional critique as the 'voice that is at the same time public and private'. It is a very, very private statement, but who can ignore the implications?

In 'Playing Militia' he turns away from the fascination of the leaves and flowers in the graveyard; in their variety of shapes and shades, the poetic raw material of which he holds a stock without limit is to the signs of militarisation on the street. The imagery of the sewing machines sowing a new drill and the drooping uniforms 'like the wet feathers of a crow's wing/ over secret carrion' warn us that this craftsman does not depend on mere inspiration. He knows his environment in detail, because he has studied it in detail. It is also so it seems, an article of faith with him that things are related by matter, spirit and motion and that he too is connected with them all. The notion of secret carrion now more secret because of the shelter it enjoys, the patent lack of purpose displayed by the marchers raise hopes that the concern is not about the militia playing but even more about the chances that the militia may be or become the plaything of others.

In 'I Still Stare' comes out another area of maturity and competence in which he can afford to revel at leisure. It is in the understanding and use of the popular idiom. He need not break the texture of his well carved syllables to introduce Guyana talk. In two short phrases 'Title Different. Signature equal' he gives the essential mood behind what can be a form of creole words, of the same order as 'wrong wuk' or 'bateau'.

This issue arises again in 'Our Number' and is much clearer here. This poem is a salute to the folk philosophy, the folk attitude and towards the end to the folk language. Through and through it is shrimps' language, only apparently in English. 'Irregular the horizon' is full of deliberate contempt for 'render the horizon irregular'. It is the folk in all countries that make these poetic leaps of language, like 'hard ears', 'own way' and a host of cases. Yet at the same time the poem is not pure folk. In folk idiom it seeks to elevate mathematics to a central place in the explanation of being: 'Is a way of counting born we'.

In the same lines the double entendre will strike all those acquainted with the folk idiom in matters of sex and reproduction. Although Carter's preoccupation with science and scientific method is present all through his poetry, he seldom promotes the claims of mathematics as he does in this poem. The pins, the tide, its regular rhythm, the seagull 'proportioning' a catch and the fisherman's wife 'counting fish'. Just to show how human animals are, she is 'another seagull'. Are we not also then like animals in our economy and our behaviour? Our number is also our nature. Its mystic show-windows are mere irony, or perhaps an elfish concession to a fortune-telling culture in which everyone knows what leaders visit what obeah men and obeah women.

The images have many little faces, as all good images have. There is the posture of surrender with the telling consequence that we 'denizen an epoch of abuse' from all pervading foe – 'the tide that naked skins us'.

Another example of Carter's closeness to and respect for the folk idiom is the image of the 'mouth' in 'In a Certain Time'. All the hatred of the folk for corruption, especially the corruption of the police. He is also 'defying the dark'. In a land of material and moral gloom he has no alternative. Among the most contemptible forms of behaviour he finds that 'ugly is the weak/coward mouth which having advantaged/advances'. In this poem he moves from one image to another to show that on some things he can no more be silent than the owl hooting (by hindsight) 'to startle the vile eye of a toad/and initiate its own defiance of dark'. The image is of the mouth 'eating' – in West Africa 'chopping' – for the corruption of public office at whatever level is very popular. It is not only a most despised practice, but one which has great corrupting power, setting in motion a whole tide not only of resentment, but disenchantment and in the end disbelief and readiness to walk in the footsteps of the damned so as not to be out of step, not to be thought stupid or impractical.

When the cultural weakness of the PPP became strident in the late 1950s, when there was seen a notable lack of moral strength and a lack of creativity, that was the major moment of loss, when the rivals reached a pinnacle of power.

He did not lose face with those who knew him when he agreed to be Minister of Information in Burnham's government. The mood of the chief spokesmen was very forward looking, with ideas of breaking through to the interior, the pioneer spirit, the cooperative movement, and especially the feeling that they were going to let a thousand flowers bloom. In this sense the absence of hard ideology was seen as an advantage and was seen as a suitable mood for grouping again the forces of the nation. There was talk of a new deal for the Amerindians, mainly because ASCRIA has never hidden its commitment to Amerindian Freedom and lost no chance to raise the Amerindian issues.

By 1969 he had had his second shaking of the faith in political leaderships. His distinction was to resign from the Burnham cabinet when it was on the road to increasing its power. The question will be asked whether he was complicit in the election rigging of 1968. I do not know what his role was in those elections. As a chairman of a marketing board myself, I had been asked to play only one small part in those elections, namely to speak on the Essequibo coast (Suddie) constituency at two or three meetings on election eve; nothing else. It would not surprise me if Martin Carter had been asked to do even less. It was well known that we were not election birds. Even I, as the more political of the two 1953 pioneers, had never been part of PNC riggery.

He cannot hide the humiliation which he feels at the treason of the spirit. This is the culture of petty deception, of trade-off, sometimes of the traffic of another to the paymaster, all too noticeable among the upwardly mobile groups and those of broken faith. These tendencies are unwelcome and disquieting, but not unique in a pre-revolutionary and even revolutionary situation. His battle is not merely against principalities and powers. He feels that there are enough people in the political struggle, outdoing one another in effort and lack of effort. As a poet he does not as a priority join the queue against those foes. In a way his fire is concentrated on their props: the self-pity, the self-hate, the meanness of rivals, the self-demotion of man, the subtleties of the lie and the many deceptions that in his concern, form a big part of the interchange in human commerce.

No wonder he resorts to intimate conversations with the wind, turning each visible star into a chrysalis.

Whereas the political activist, including the revolutionary, must stress and calculate on the revolutionary and progressive aspects of the culture, not the political poet. He feels in the folds of his own soul the abrasions of the hundreds of thousands living double lives, disguising their real soul until it resembles the disguise rather than the original. It is not for his art to deal with the formative rebellion. To him the soul suffers even more if it does not meet present insolence with present response. This is the sign of humanity he seeks. And while as a historian he well understands the accumulation of anger and rebellion, to him, without the sparks from the wire there is no life in it. So he complains, 'There is no riot'.

Those who have the good fortune to know Martin Carter do not spend hours in endless regret at the loss of a comrade. No such loss has taken place or ever took place. He prefers to work for the future of man. We never find him glorifying force, or mere force, or worshipping power. It is when a comrade shifts to that ground that we see one, at least, of the symptoms of loss. He has never been there.

In his young days he was misunderstood by shallow people and also unknowingly added to the misunderstanding of me in an incident in my office in my days as a minister in the PPP colonial government of 1953, which Martin and I regarded as the 'people's opposition'. He was visiting me at the ministerial building. The discussion lasted some time and as I never used the air conditioning and he was smoking, he felt thirsty. A bureaucrat of the old colonial administration, still in the service and posted in the ministry I served, heard him ask for a glass of water. As I rose to get it he intervened and said, 'I'll get it'. Now Martin had been a clerk in that very civil service and had been a constant rebel against the whole administrative culture. When I heard Mr. Kranenburg offer to get him a glass of water in my place – and I was generally seen as the naked and ignorant black boy from the country – he said with little restraint: 'Kranenburg getting water for you? Power!' The point of his remark was misunderstood and in fact it went around that class somehow that I had ordered the gentleman to fetch a glass of water.

He must prove all things. His art, his philosophy, his images as such, each one of them, must be informed by total experience. He professes knowledge of how the unfortunate women of the city think and feel. He is very eager to understand what makes them who they are. He has spent many hours in the joints in which the priests and priestesses of the subculture and the sub-poor spend their abundant leisure, always probing their wisdom, learning their speech, picking up the music of their inflexions, the rhythm of their sighs and their whole make-up. He must know what they eat and how their hunger spaces itself out. And in his seasons of drinking, he must drink at least as much as they and try perhaps to see the world from the perspective of an outcast.

He comes back every now and again – in fact he never really leaves it – to his theme of the succession of failures at the public (political) level. 'Title different, signature equal' or the 'identical flaws in the space between light of lost long ago lamps'. In this the blackouts represent the assaults on the hopes of the people. Without any burst of song he makes the whole world attend on our plight, as the very human raindrop near a leaf hesitates to waste itself on our land: 'near a leaf, a raindrop pauses over a dead land' with the force of a giant thunderbolt. This whole sigh of regret at hopes lost and of a mission bungled confounds those who see him as a dead soul who is 'doing nothing' or who has switched off his past of the 1950s.

In course of time, he declares, without setting out to satisfy or to please anyone: 'In this foul age of a new/and recurring despair, I/keep working for a storm, some/kind of fury to write new dates/in our vile calendar and book'.

In the poem 'Inventor', which because of its brevity has more impact and momentum than Mark Twain's 'Soliloquy of King Leopold', he takes on the vileness of him who makes all things vile and shows how rejection breeds rejection.

His politics comprises a general fury against all the forces, material and spiritual, subjective and objective, whether they are of the oppressor, of the oppressed, or of the groups between the oppressors and oppressed, which conspire against the human personality. It is not the politics of the platform for which he has both due respect and due contempt and in which he has taken part and may again take part. For this reason he feels safer and less humiliated, with acts of rebellion than with acts of surrender, even if these acts of rebellion are misconceived. It is enough for Martin as the beginning of wisdom to see the human spirit in an insurrectionary march against its own paralysis.

'We Walk the Streets' is a fine example of this private public statement of the poet. In the first four lines it gives no hint of any significance beyond the poet and the reveries of the 'supine hours'. Its ultimate concern with man comes out in the news that the hours, cut into pieces, 'pile up into history'. This is what is political in this poet: his inability to ignore man's agony. Note also the close similarity of image between lines in this poem and the theme of *The Kind Eagle*. In the earlier poem, 'The sharp knife of dawn glitters in my hand'. This is the hope of colonial man consistent in the dark, as a slow moving cart takes him through the night of material necessity to the marketplace of modern times. In the second poem he is dreamily 'lighting a flick knife in my wind's awkward hand'.

The boldness and certainty, of the earlier days, for him, are gone, and disguise of his feelings is not one of his virtues, either on paper or in life. It is no longer, regrettably, or wisely, the sharp knife of dawn glittering in his hand.

An important development in Carter's being is that the optimism of the 1950s is gone. This perhaps deepens the nature of his politics since in spite of the inertia with which the dictatorship sits on the land, he keeps his partisan commitment to man.

It is not beside the point that Carter has known two big disillusionments in the political process as such. Like many poets outside of the Caribbean, Martin Carter has been from his twenties a full fledged freedom fighter, at one time listed as a Marxist revolutionary. He was a serious organising worker and political tutor in the fifties as a founder member of, the PPP, at which time he was already becoming known as a poet. He was a very close acquaintance of, among other persons, Wilson Harris and for his unconventional attitudes was disliked, though respected, by official society.

In political life he was a candidate in the 1953 General Elections in the constituency of New Amsterdam, the toughest of all constituencies for the PPP against a veteran townsman accepted as 'awee boy', the late Mr. Rudy Kendall, a conservative politician. He used the campaign to build up a considerable following among the workers and youth in that town assisted in the political work by Rory Westmass.

Carter remained with the so-called Jagan faction after the split in 1955, but became disaffected and withdrew during the months of the withdrawal of the 'ultra left' or 'adventurists' as Dr. Jagan has variously called them during 1957. Before that, he along with four others was detained without trial from the time of the suspension of the constitution in October 1953 and held at the US base at Atkinson Field. After his release, he, like others, endured much police harassment, court trials and imprisonment. He was imprisoned in the very prison where he first worked as a civil servant, the scene of the poems of prison, including *The Kind Eagle.*

'At the time of the 1953 elections he was already married and while in detention writing some of the *Poems of Resistance,* he mentions in 'Letter...' 'and the young one... is he well and mischievous as ever?/... I send a kiss to tell you everything'.

He went inactive politically and for a long stretch went through much introspection about all aspects of life, a function he considered a duty. He worked for some of this time as Information Officer and editor of the house organ for the multinational Bookers. In these days Bookers dispatched to Guyana specially chosen theoreticians to measure the political motion.

He at all times kept up a relationship with his old comrades and used his time to make a careful study of the mind of the multinationals with whom he worked for a living.

In 1962, he and urban associates, most of them former members of the PPP, included stalwarts like Eustace Sam, a conscious worker who was a phenomenon in his class. Eustace Sam is still at work and has borne the full brunt of prison, persecution and all the ills of all regimes. Martin Carter and his associates were on the streets with the worker's rebellion against the 1962 budget. His chief interest seemed to be that 'a city of clerks/turned a city of men'.

There was what Walter Rodney had called a 'honeymoon' between the Burnham government of the PNC and a number of Caribbean progressives, which Rodney pronounced to be 'over'. During these hopeful years Martin Carter, without joining the PNC, became a technocrat Minister of Information. He sat on the cabinet and with his customary keen observation must have compiled a rich document of the mentality he was associated with. Martin left the cabinet as suddenly as he had joined it, but of his own will.

Despite the apparent pessimism – a label which needs revision – of much of his work and pronouncements, he has never failed to support with enthusiasm any sign of the reawakening of the masses. Thus his whole spirit revived considerably during the civil rebellion of 1979 spearheaded by the WPA and Walter Rodney.

His brother Keith had been for some time a political associate and something of a mentor of the whole left faction of the PPP and he made very early judgements of the limitations of Jagan as a leader. His pronouncements are always readily embraced by the Guyanese people. Two of them spring to mind. In one public lecture he tried to lay bare 'the paralysis of the spirit' affecting his fellow Guyanese. In the other he warned that there was a lot of talk from the present regime about 'discipline', but what it really meant was 'regimentation'. He has never set out to be accepted by his audiences, but rather to serve them uncomfortable truths for future health.

In his poetry Martin does not make photographs of nature. Yet his love of the Guyanese landscape is deeply rooted, whether on coast, river or interior, sky, trees, canefield or water. They form a natural backdrop in his communication and he may pause to include some special and relevant feature, natural or man-made. His pen does not wait for marvels to paint, but will dignify the Cartman of Dayclean, which forms the prelude of the film *The Terror and the Time* (Victor Jara Collective). In this poem 'broken land ripped like a piece of cloth', 'sea of dayclean washing on the shore', 'brooding city like a mound of coal' is as important as 'hidden cartman fumbling for a star'.

I have seen no poems of Kaieteur by him. There is Seymour's grand 'legend of Kaieteur'. But, 'in the ladder from the cave the rungs of time/ bend like the working roots that eat the soil'. This view of Carter and the poetic soul of a revolutionary is nowhere better supported than in one of his own earlier poems, published in *The Hill of Fire Glows Red* and undeservedly forgotten. In it he sets out to declare, as other artists have done, that mere nature-love was unsatisfying, while the beauty of humanity itself was being, as he believed, deformed by agents of force. The poem speaks for itself more eloquently than any reviewer can.

Shines the Beauty of My Darling

If I wanted
I could make pictures of night
the map of stars above the mass of water
the mass of water underneath the stars
the beauty of my beloved
like a flower bringing dawn light into dark.

Yes, if I wanted
I could close my eyes right now
and bring these things like life into my brain.

but new are these times

and no matter where I turn
the fierce revolt goes with me
like a kiss –
the revolt of Malaya
and Viet Nam –
the revolt of India
and Africa –
like guardian

like guardian at my side
is the fight for freedom –
and like the whole world dancing
for liberation from the slave maker
shines the beauty of my darling in her laughing eyes.

Through the agency of Mrs. Janet Jagan, many of the poems of *The Hill of Fire Glows Red* appeared in a publication, *Masses and Mainstream,* a cultural magazine in the USA in the early fifties.

The picture of the map of stars above the mass of water is a night scene from the rural areas during a flood of the coastal pastures, where since the Venn Commission report after the Enmore shooting, extra-nuclear housing schemes have been built. There are not only the wide sweeps of territory, rivers and forest, but the plantation high bridges, the moon on the 'shining mud', light and shadow, and the bent back of a struggling old woman.

If the Caribbean poets had been as bold as the poets of Latin America and many areas of the world, like the Middle East and like many of the poets of antiquity and many of the poets of African rebirth – perhaps the feeling of belonging to a nation may have been more highly present or deeply present in the Caribbean. But one may rightly ask whether the national sense does more to produce the poetry than the poetry to produce the national sense.

In arguing from past poetic models to explain Martin Carter's poetic vision, one recalls 'The Masque of Anarchy' of Percy B. Shelley, a lifelong rebel. Some of its stanzas may be placed side by side with those of the poet we are studying and it will be readily seen who was the greater rabble-rouser of the two.

Shelley had heard of the massacre of his countrymen and women in Manchester in 1819, while he was in Italy. He very deliberately set out to reflect on the killings through the 'visions of Poesy'. His treatment of one of the guilty politicians, Castlereagh, and the whole ruling class is exemplary:

I met murder on the way –
He had a mask like Castlereagh –
Very smooth he looked, yet grim;
Seven bloodhounds followed him:
All were fat; and well they might

Be in admirable plight,
For one by one, and two by two,
He tossed them human hearts to chew,
Which from his wide cloak he drew.

and later his address to his distant compatriots:
Rise like lions after slumber
In unvanquishable number
Shake to earth your chains like dew
Which in sleep hath fallen on you –
Ye are many – they are few.

We may wish to compare this with 'Here is my hand for the revolution'. Or

If you see a smile of bitterness on my mouth
You must not think some joke amuses me
It is only the fury of my heart changing to scorn
At the sight of a soldier searching for me.

Dante, revered nowadays as an inoffensive classical poet, was much offended in his own time and gave much offence in turn in his quest not only for justice but for influence. Some of his political motives will not appeal to the class conscious or purist minds of the present, but he was for most of his adult life an active fighter for very immediate causes. He is even said by some writers to have switched sides in pursuit of some public principle. His *Comedy,* which later became *Divine Comedy* long after his death, was not an epic divorced from life. Professor McAllister finds that 'it is peopled with Dante's contemporaries and, particularly in the materialistic realism of the *Inferno,* it is torn by issues and feuds of the day, political, religious and personal. It treats the most universal values – good and evil, man's responsibility, free will and predestination; yet it is intensely personal and political, for it is written out of the anguish of a man who saw his life blighted by the injustice and corruption of the times'.

One of Martin's most controversial and little understood poems is 'Demerara Nigger' which appeared in the *Caribbean Contact* in May 1983. He refers to Farinata's presence in Hell, Dante's Inferno, where Farinata maintained his noble bearing and refused to be depressed by the depressing conditions.

In this poem, Carter is holding up Farinata as an example, on account of his will to 'withstand' for what 'withstands' also 'stands'.

The moment of truth is the moment of realisation of the poet. He realises but only very late, 'until the sudden/ fumble of the premonitory wing/ of the bat on the roof' that mortality was not 'a thing to be endured'. The stirring of the bat signifies lateness in the day or lateness in time, perhaps, very much like Minerva, the bird of wisdom who flies out at evening. With this new experience of life in a living hell, what is to be one's attitude to life? Now that hope and fear are equal emotions? Would it be so if no messenger rode? But a messenger rides.

The two hells, Dante's and his, can be compared. But as Farinata has shown, the mind can rise above such a fate. 'This foot for instance. This shoe/Step. Floor. Book, for instance.Lamp.' – a series of signs that reaffirm life and activity. But it is not easy to make this self-reassurance. The words are 'tortured out like a turd'.

Who is the riding messenger? None other than 'Demerara Nigger, / Downward through the horse' into hell, of course.

In normal times, the 'way and cause' could be sufficient justification, 'right if not an ending'.

Is it not better to be a bat, to lose the gift of art, but to be able to see in the darkness, 'barter talk for sight' and to confuse clocks; from a human point of view to turn night into day and day into night!

This is how he had to make his exit from the human race like Farinata 'scorning and demanding'. Thus there seems to be advantages in leaving 'mortality' and becoming something else within the whole field of cosmic energy where both the hell-bent horse and its ride make sense.

Still, mind is the supreme value. The singular mind has great possibilities, as shown by his own freedom to contrast 'nigger and Ghibelline'.

The Rodney poem is restrained lamentation. The poet's laments for those he respects in a special way are dignified and controlled. It seems to be an overriding and studied humility in the presence of death. In his poem on the death of Ivan Edwards, he declared that since they would walk and speak no more together 'then let me take a patience and a calm/ for even now the greener leaf explodes'. The keen reader will smell here the popular proverb: 'green leaf a fall an lef yellow wan a tree' which is repeated up and down the country when a young person dies.

In the presence of death he does not orate, drama or go into convulsions of grief. In the case of Walter Rodney and the manner of his death, he is content to level the enemy with the deadly barb of art, not with the readily sensed abuse. It is even possible that as in the 'Demerara Nigger', this poet is at times deliberately obscure. This reflects the nature of the police state in which he is working and has worked before in the colonial days, though policing of the spirit is now a much better organised government service.

Summing up a whole aspect of Rodney's work, the beauty of his communication with masses of people and the spread of the spirit of freedom which he inspired, he calls them 'assassins of conversation' which he sees as Rodney's weapon, and says with superior irony, they are so foolish as to bury the assassinated voice in the grave.

The sense of awe is total, but controlled, like one trying to get accustomed to an unexpected storm which breaks over the land. He is in the awesome presence of rain and 'the sky's wild noise'. He knows he is in the presence of some 'who not only, but also kill/the origin of rain'. Their actions assault nature herself. The faculty of judgement is lost. Their 'feet' bear up 'the ankle of the whore' and they decorate their bodies in noble robes as though pursuing a struggle in the interest of humanity. 'Conversation' – in the situation where oral, face to face communication is the most popular and most effective, the 'assassins of conversation' has far reaching meaning and is a telling indictment.

What then are his weaknesses as a poet? His name has a very wide appeal, much more so than other poets in this region. The special quality of his political activity in the anti-colonial movement made his name a household word. He is quoted by one and all and is in this way available to every group that wants to refer to a poet to illustrate a point. His poem 'All are involved, all are consumed' is famous for the many ways in which it has been manipulated.

He came into compulsory public notice again when for a brief turn he served as Minister of Information in a Burnham Cabinet, with the agreement of some of his friends, and dropped out as suddenly as he had dropped in, with the admonition that 'the mouth is muzzled by the food/it eats to live'; a snippet carried in the *Guyana Graphic,* which made much more sense to a wide cross section of Guyanese. I remember more than one elder quoting it to me in conversations on the street, in particular one Indo-Guyanese man who dismounted from his bicycle to exchange notes on the times.

Here is a man then, with the popularity of a star batsman, or a cinema actor, or a favoured political leader, whose craft is none of these but the craft of poetry. He does not always write for the wide cross sections who wish to read him.

In his earlier poems, there was, even there, the strong private idiom, which however, partook freely of the popular idiom turned to other purposes, like 'Just listen, and you know'. There was the practice of using a very popular object, like one of the high bridges in a plantation, and centring it amidst thoughts and concepts only dimly related to it, which knowledge of the bridge itself would help to make clear: 'passing the ancient bridge/ the grave of pride, the sudden flight/the terror and the time .

He knew quite well the elemental force of such words as 'time' among the ordinary folk, even those more oral than literate, so that such a word had a double meaning always. It conveyed one sense to the folk who had lived through a certain experience and another meaning to readers personally removed or remote from that emotion.

Similarly, in: 'Nigger Yard' when he talks of 'the hurt of things' or 'It was a child born from a mother full of her blood' when he talks of the lessons of human history and is 'pleased/with the glories and sad with the sorrows/rich with the riches, poor with the loss' – these are lines into which old women will read rich justification for their outlook on their lives.

In other places too, like 'here is my hand for the revolution' and the idea of the lame coming from hospital, the mad being sane for this great event, those who cannot read learning to read, not only is the language simple, but the fantasy is also very popular. He is amalgamating many trivial dreams into one great dream. The popularisation of such verse justifies this fantasy and results in value formation. Who does not understand the encouraging cheer in the lines:

As I walk, the seller of sweets says 'friend'
And the shoemaker with his awl and waxen thread
Reminds me of tomorrow and the world

There was definitely a period in his life when he lost faith in the mass movement and began to identify the crowds with the leaders, the 'impartial bullocks' who led them. It would seem that philosophically he freed himself of all assumptions and began anew to turn to the lives of persons rather than peoples, to examine afresh, to penetrate, to probe, to examine the spirit, to test whether his own dreams were valid. He went back on a loftier plane to his old, direct confrontation or better, encounter with people, not seeing them through this or that philosopher, this or that organisation.

What happened then was inescapable. His images were specialised and what he struggled to achieve was internal consistency, until he would break out of the bounds of that image and consciously choose another until his vision alone and the trained imagination became the link between image and image, until we are faced, as discussed briefly above, with the image of an image of an image.

Night fakes
the rule of stars; as we fake
light's good pencil. A child's
chalk ridden blackboard. Alphabet
of hope in a season of insects

And that is the problem. The free verse to which his early readers are accustomed is still there, but the craftsman is keeping a tighter hand. Both his craft and his philosophy, in a formal sense are maturing.

The object of the interest has not shifted. It is still 'the pilgrimage of man, the wide span' and the long march. But the vision is like a fly's, multifaceted, no longer satisfied with formal simplicity. These elements were always there in the making: the simple affirmation was never true, never satisfying, or if it was true, it was not the whole truth. This is where he breaks with the mere revolutionary and treats what may be suspected as a single focus as a new level of blindness.

For these reasons, many Carter lovers have difficulty lapping up his meaning in many of his poems with the ease of capillary attraction and without labour.

One cannot say to him, 'Martin, are the serial images really necessary? Will it not be more simple for the people to read if you will just let them off with only part of the process of your truths?'

Such a mission would be even more absurd than that of the citizen who asked Martin Carter to write a poem for an anniversary!

And in reply to my proposal I can hear the response, 'The best poems write themselves, you know... But if they are produced in labour, why should they be consumed in ease?'

(First published in *Anales del Caribe* (Cuba) no. 4/5, 1984/5)

GORDON ROHLEHR

'ASSASSINS OF THE VOICE': MARTIN CARTER'S *POEMS OF AFFINITY* 1978-1980

When I first met Martin Carter in December 1980 – I'd known his work for twenty years and taught it for ten, but had been living outside of Guyana for nineteen years – I could hear these poems in the way he spoke. He seemed to be trying to communicate the urgency and meaning of a horror which he had seen. He was spasmodic of utterance, cryptic and fragmented, as many of these *Poems of Affinity* are, yet electric and warm and able to make the fragments cohere, as many of these poems do. It was only six months since Walter Rodney's death, the culmination of a series of violent political events, some of which Carter had witnessed, once in the intimate capacity of a victim.

In June 1978 Carter had been attacked and beaten while he was demonstrating against the Referendum, by which the People's National Congress (PNC) in Guyana sought fifteen additional months in office, the time necessary to draft a new Constitution which would bestow on its leaders absolute dominion and eternal life. He had also been in the July 1979 demonstration when the Roman Catholic priest, Fr. Bernard Darke was murdered in broad daylight, an incident which gave rise to his poem 'Bastille Day – Georgetown', and to his 'Open Letter to the People of Guyana', where he defined his role as citizen in a degraded society. The cameras of Trinidad and Tobago Television focused briefly on his shell-shocked face during the funeral of Walter Rodney, where Lamming in his oration quoted Carter's bitter condemnation of the regime as 'assassins of the voice.'

Carter's 'Open Letter to the People of Guyana' provides the perfect context for his latest collection of poems, *Poems of Affinity* 1978-1980, a slim, stark volume which, along with those courageous Working People's Alliance (WPA) Newsletters, provides us with depressing testimony as to the quality of life in the Co-operative Republic. Carter writes in the 'Open Letter':

> Like all other regimes of similar character, the PNC's main preoccupation is self-perpetuation. In principle the preoccupation with self-perpetuation is understandable, since it accords with the fundamental idea of self-preservation. But while a truly democratic regime would try to ensure self-perpetuation by acting in ways such as would make it acceptable and needed by people, what does the PNC, which poses as socialist, actually do?
>
> The PNC's method of ensuring self-perpetuation consists of indulging in a deliberate policy of degrading people. And the reasoning behind this is that degraded people are incapable of effective resistance.

Carter then proceeds to cite examples of such degradation: the rigging of elections, the reduction of honest people to a norm of cheating and lying, the regime's rigid control of

> mass media in which the very language used is perversion; facts falsified; threats against individuals and groups openly advertised; international events of significance ignored; local events of significance suppressed; all contributing to the whole process of assault on moral and intellectual honesty, one end of which is to make mental independence a crime, and mental subservience to the regime the highest qualification in the land.[1]

The result of this Carter defines as 'warp of personality and degradation of spirit.'

Two questions are posed by this context where perversion of the word leads to perversion of thought and deed, and ultimately to subservience and degradation of spirit: (i) what perspectives for political action and involvement does Carter perceive in a scenario of growing absolutism and (ii) how does the Muse, the spirit of poetry, sensibility and honest utterance survive in such an environment? The relevance of these questions is , of course, by no means limited to the Guyanese scenario.

Carter in the 'Open Letter' answers the first question by suggesting two necessary lines of political action; (i) 'Resistance to the brute fact of degradation itself. Resistance to the exploitation of this degradation by the regime' which should take the form of 'individual repudiation and civil disobedience.' (ii) Exposure of the regime's 'ideology of self-perpetuation.' Carter's answer to the second question has involved a definition both of the situation of the artist and of his active responsibility in a context of both political and existential exigency.

In a statement entitled 'The Location of the Artist' Carter describes art as a form of 'negative productivity [which] presupposes a process of positive productivity as its environment'. He goes on to explain what he means:

> The first consideration to be dealt with concerning art and the artist has to do with satisfaction and fulfilment. This satisfaction and fulfilment has to do with the development of self-consciousness. Self-consciousness itself is an issue, itself subsumed by the issue that subsumes all issues: human fate. The artist cannot change the nature of this fate: all he can do is endure it. At the same time it is his society which has to provide the conditions that make this fate endurable. It is in these senses that art is described as negative productivity and positive productivity suggested as the required environment of the artist. Where there should be interaction of negative and positive productivity we find instead only the contiguity of two negative productivities, one seeking to retain its integrity through independence and autonomy, the other attempting to assimilate this independence and autonomy into a system which, since it does not have the requirements of positive productivity, is not in a position to offer co-existential status.[2]

The artist's responsibility in this context is defined again and again in *Poems of Affinity*. These poems are often about politics, and do offer a perspective of 'resistance' and 'exposure'. But they are also about time, endurance and people's unfulfilled abuse of their grim time. If politics is constant degradation of peoples' sensibility, a diet of decaying language, and ultimately an assassination of the voice, time is a neuter process in which all life is caught. If resistance to corruption of the word and its corollary, clarity of utterance, are a political imperative for the citizen, resistance to the riddle of fatality, time and death through constant exploration of Self in Cosmos and Cosmos in Self[3] becomes the existential responsibility of the artist.

'Our Time', the first poem in the collection, explores both the political and the existential situations. Here Carter notes the failure of people to create their 'time'.

> The more the men of our time we are
> the more our time is. But always
> we have been somewhere else.

'Time' here means a particular historic moment. People create their time by investing their historic moment with the energy of effort. Meaning and identity are connected to, and grow from the quality of creative sensibility, the oneness of our response to our moment.[4] 'But always we have been somewhere else.' Here, as elsewhere in the collection, time and place are equated, and the word 'place' could easily replace the word 'time' in the first two lines.

In order to illustrate our abject failure to create our time. Carter employs an image drawn from the Guyana landscape: that of the crab holes[5] which become visible when water drains out of canals, and ooze slime and muddy bubbles as the crabs emerge or hide. Thus, the people who should articulate their resistance loud and clear are heard:

> Muttering
> our mouths like holes in the mud
> at the bottom of trenches

The corruption of the voice, the rot of the word, is suggested in the phonic similarity between 'muttering' , 'mouths' and 'mud'. Our failure to be people of our time is related to a failure in articulate statement, here given an implied quality of putrescence and suppuration. And this failure is the result of a failure in resistance.

> Badly abused
> we fail to curse. Our fury pleads.

Carter returns to this theme later in the collection in 'Our Voice Betrays', where, 'Caring too little,' the people surrender their birthright to a parvenu regime – symbolised by a voracious stray dog – and blindfold themselves rather than face the truth of what they have become. The fact that Carter there says 'Everything blindfolds' rather than 'Everyone', indicates that the people, 'caring too little,' have reified themselves, or allowed the regime to reify them.

The consequences of apathy and self-evasion are explored in the next poem, 'Playing Militia'. Carter in his 'Open Letter' had cited as an example of degradation:

> the militarisation of the people in which poorly fed children are made to march in the sun like soldiers, playing militia at the expense of their lessons: in which paramilitary forces enjoy a spurious social prestige at the expense of the rights of their fellow citizens; thereby putting a premium on authoritarian bullying in clear mirror image of the behaviour of the leaders of the regime; all serving to bring about in the consciousness of people and their children that parading is more important than learning. And uniforms more important than a respect for law.[6]

In 'Playing Militia' Carter presents the various military and paramilitary groups as examples of a loss of individual personhood. A people has acquiesced in its own degradation and pays the price in a devaluation of their uniqueness. He also notes that the children are being robbed of their childhood and of their innocence ('girls unbreasted, boys ungamed'). Loss of uniqueness is presented as being contrary to the very spirit of nature which allows each object, leaf, flower or fruit, its originality and distinctness. Even in the cemetery where things are equal, they are also separate. The Guyana regime, then, has actually outdone Death; they have succeeded in making an entire nation indistinct, an undifferentiated mass of faceless uniforms which can scarcely conceal the inner festering.

> The sleeves
> of uniforms droop
> like the wet feathers of a crow's wing
> over secret carrion

Here the scorn is conveyed by a power and precision of image. 'Droop', for example, captures both the ill-fitting appearance of the uniforms and the jaded spiritless exhaustion of these children, whose tiredness is the nation's. 'Secret' captures the very quality of the regime, who have made accomplices of these cruelly misguided children. It is a quality of suspicion, a secretiveness out of which flowers scandal.[7] At the centre of each secret is decay.

There is also the beginning of a kind of wordplay, extreme in poets such as Brathwaite and Questel and frequently evident in Walcott, though absent from earlier Carter.

> the phalloid needles of sewing machines
> have sown a new drill

'Phalloid' is overdone, but it does imply the rumour that sexual exploitation of young women has occurred in National Service camps. True or false, such allegations are a natural result of the secretiveness with which much is done in Guyana. 'Needles' suggests that the people are being inoculated with some loathsome serum or sperm. One notes, too, the subtle shift in spelling and meaning from 'sewing' to 'sown', the latter word definitely implying the mechanical insemination of the people by water and the word, semen and propaganda. Then there is the more obvious wordplay on 'a new drill' where 'drill' is both the green khaki of uniforms and the military exercises of these fake soldiers, as well as the monotonous catechism of State propaganda, by which children and adults are made ready for the new life. Such wordplay enables the poet to explore several layers of meaning at the same time and in an economy of space.

The counter-poem to this, 'Let Every Child Run Wild', comes very late in the collection. In this moving exhortation, Carter reveals a Blakean sense of the sanctity of childhood, whose destruction evoked the bitter 'Playing Militia'. 'Let Every Child Run Wild' has a freer movement and is less laconic than most of the *Poems of Affinity*. The wild freedom of children in the rain suggests the elemental, the primal, the ancestral.

Rain is a cousin
of air, the blood of parents

The children's freedom, endorsed by the poet's imperative 'Let every child' suggests guitar music.

Let every child run wild, or stop,
or stop the way men journey
through the earth's loop, the freedom
of a guitar

The alternatives are to permit the young the joy of their youth, or stop the wild guitar melody of their freedom by en-trammelling them in the noose of the adult world. It is for having done the latter that Carter condemns the regime and the poem leaves us with a vision of freedom curtailed:

... the still air
of a child's wild guitar
shuddering in the silence
of parents

'Shuddering' is powerfully suggestive of the sudden terror which overtakes the children as their parents interrupt their game in the rain. As in Blake the parents represent experience, authority and the inhibitions imposed by centralised authoritarianism. The 'parents' are the regime's censorship of peoples' freedoms, a censorship which is exemplified by their attempts to commandeer even occasions for celebration, depriving them of the spontaneity which gave them point and imposing on them the rigid paramilitary monotony of the State's 'new drill.'

Carter frequently asserts the need for vigilance or active rebellion.

In this foul age of a new
and recurring despair. I
keep working for a storm, some

kind of fury to write new dates
in our vile calendar and book.
('Some Kind of Fury' , p.53)

Here the connection between assertive rebellion, the act of making and the redemption of debased time is made explicit. What, however, is the fate of those who aren't obviously in step with the regime?

'Paying Fares' provides us with the answer. Here Carter describes the results of that loss of uniqueness and individuality noted in 'Playing Militia'. People who have so abjectly acquiesced in their own depersonalisation, lose the capacity to value the uniqueness and survival efforts of others. In this poem, we see the people waiting for the bus of collective deliverance, the poem taking place between their waiting and the bus's arrival.

Waiting for the bus
they see him, the powerful crab
edging sideways through the silt
of their lives.

If in 'Black Friday' the crab was a symbol of the brief triumph of the citizens' rebellion before the high tide of repression obliterates them, here it is a symbol of survival, cunning retreat, aloneness and a saving instinct for resistance. The crab's triumph here is to have remained itself in a time when everyone is expected to jump or is coerced into jumping on the collective bandwagon.

The shell of the crab, the armour of irreducible personhood within which and behind which the poetic vision dwells, the shuttered 'flags' of his window blinds which allow him to see through the regime without being seen, are the targets of the system's instinct for destruction. The word 'flags' mocks the State's anthem-and-flag nationalism. The questions 'What, they wonder/does he eat, and who/his obeahman?' are grimly humorous. The first refers to the regime's tendency to victimise its opponents by denying them employment. The crab survives such spiteful meanness and menace. The second refers to the legalisation of obeah in Guyana,[8] by which the State sought to appropriate one of the survival mechanisms of those driven to desperation by the extreme psychic distress which life in the co-operative republic has inflicted on people. The powerful crab is agnostic and lives without such a prop.

Carter fully understands that to live without the moral muck and silt of the regime's patronage is to invite its reflexive viciousness. Nor are the people on the poet's side. They are more likely to turn in fury and spite on the isolated rebel whose courage is also the measure of their own cowardice, and whose independence of spirit becomes a symbol of the fineness which they have denied in themselves. Rather than bear the shame of admitting this, they adopt a victim-making psychology, and willingly become henchmen and assassins for the regime. They plan to set his house afire:

but cloth
can burn they mutter, paying fares

There is, it should be noted, an almost opposite line of interpretation of 'Paying Fares'. In this simpler, but quite feasible analysis, 'the powerful crab' becomes Burnham; his 'edging' and oblique movement would then be the menacing secretiveness of his relationship to citizens whose material and moral existence he has reduced to muck. The citizen as lesser crab wonders about the private life of his leader. Does he indeed, as it is rumoured, savour the finest of local and foreign cuisine while reducing their diet to silt? By what mysterious necromancy has he sustained his relentless grip on power? The 'flags' of his curtained windows could then be the tawdry nationalist sloganeering to which political vision and public understanding have become reduced; while the final bitterly muttered threat 'but cloth/ can burn' would then be the people's as yet unarticulated resentment as they reluctantly pay yet another price hike for goods and services which, like the mythical bus, never arrive. 'Paying fares' can refer generally to the price the nation has been paying for the ride on which their leaders are taking them. Carter itemised this price in the 'Open Letter' quoted above. One notes, however, that in Guyana, 'fares' is the name given to a prostitute's fee. Carter may be implying that those who do the regime's dirty work are undergoing a most peculiar whoredom, in that they pay the very regime which has reduced them to a prostitution of spirit, for reducing them to such prostitution.

The daylight murder of Father Darke was the most glaring example of such prostitution of spirit. Carter's witness of this barely credible crime led him to the bitterest condemnation of his people.

I have at last started
to understand the origin
of our vileness, and being
unable to deny it, I suggest
its nativity

His use of the word 'nativity' is an act of deliberate desecration, by which Carter seeks to convey his perception of the murder as a kind of monstrous birth, a reversal of the Incarnation in which the Word was humanised, the diabolical genesis of 'vileness'.

The title 'Bastille Day – Georgetown', is bitterly ironic, since its aim is to locate the Guyanese struggle in a context of international proletarian revolt, thereby exposing the former as a nauseating insult to the history of the working class. Guyanese sans culottes don't rise up against an aristocracy of corruption; they murder for a mess of pottage ('a pot of rice'). Yet Carter declares, hope issuing out of the depth of such hopelessness.

In the shame of knowledge
of our vileness, we shall fight

Shame can indeed be a source of revolutionary defiance, since it requires the consciousness of a sense of limits, the recognition of a point beyond which behaviour ought not to be allowed to deteriorate. Carter holds open the barest perspective for the rebirth of consciousness and conscience out of shame, and with consciousness/conscience, the will to fight.

But the will to fight is only the beginning. The real issue is whether the confrontation between the people and the regime will result in the positive transformation of the society. For that to happen, both the people and the regime must experience shame, a sense of limits and sanctions leading to a rebirth in consciousness. If shame can result in a strengthening of people's will to struggle, it ought ideally to result in a recognition by the regime of the necessity for compromise and imaginative flexibility in its dealings with people. Compromise will involve here what Paolo Friere termed consciencization: a recognition of the people's right towards participation in defining both their objectives, and the means of deploying their energies and labour in the attaining of those objectives.

The picture of the regime which Carter has painted in *Poems of Affinity,* includes no evidence that it is capable of shame, or will recognise any sanctions except those which it has itself imposed on the people. Nonconformity, as we saw in 'Paying Fares', is greeted with ferocious recrimination which, more than any absence of shame or conscience, is what keeps Guyanese apparently passive, and positively afraid of the active and visible defiance which Carter advocates. Their resistance tends to be passively subversive – as in the peasant who deliberately under-produces, hoping thereby, obscurely, to starve out the supporters of the regime – or escapist, – as in the thousands who have migrated to the West Indies, Suriname, the USA and Canada, some of whom have been seeking the status of political refugees in the countries of their adoption. Thousands of highly skilled people whose unmolested existence in Guyana the regime couldn't permit, have revolted by leaving, the stories of their escape providing lively testimony of the real ingenuity of the people in sidestepping degradation at the hands of the regime. Hundreds of smugglers, hustlers, hucksters, are part of an alternative subsistence economy which, in fact, challenges and undermines the regime's rigid economic sanctions, but ultimately at the expense of the proletariat, who have to pay hugely inflated prices on the black market for commodities which the State can neither afford nor supply.

Carter never acknowledges the quality of passive resistance which the Guyanese people have revealed. It is, in his opinion, not a means of fighting for transformation, but a type of evasion, a being 'elsewhere' ('Our Time') when our historic moment calls for confrontation. But he is aware of the possible consequences of the people's confrontation with a regime that has time and again signalled its preparedness to employ the various military forces at its disposal against the people whose 'farcs' have paid for those forces. Carter's response to the State's potential for recriminatory overkill is verbal defiance, a bitter scorn which, while it conveys resistance also implies political impotence.

This scorn is communicated through his application of feral imagery to the regime. In 'In a Certain Time', he contrasts the regime's abuse of the mouth – 'old jaws and a toothless snarl' – with his own use of language as resistance and vigilance.

But as an owl hoots
to startle the vile eye of a toad
and initiate its own defiance of dark:
I also speak. Having despised
all fangs, I neither have nor want
a time to bite.

If this sounds a bit extreme, like an echo of the 1953 Carter, it is worth pointing out that soon after this poem was written, the regime acknowledged its own saurian nature when it adopted as part of the insignia of the Guyana presidency, the cayman, a particularly voracious black crocodile.[9] No shame there at all; no capacity for consciencization; only the persistent signalling through word and symbol, of a potential for naked ferocity: only a perversion of language and sign which deepens in proportion to the degradation of consciousness.

II

As we have already seen from our examination of 'Our Time', the political poems of this volume are generally about other things besides politics. One of those things is time. In 'I Still Stare' we have a characteristic poem on this theme. The poet emotionlessly stares at his future (death) through the window of vision. His unillusioned stare 'beyond a pattern of stars' is in no way connected to earlier dreams. 'Pattern' suggests that the future has been prearranged and astrologically fixed. Beyond the pattern is impenetrable void in face of which the act of writing becomes a motiveless reflex.

Our hands have
written. They will continue to write
always the same.

Everything, including his writing, will be absorbed in 'the time beyond sundown.' 'Being Always' is a similar sort of poem. It begins,

Being, always to arrange
myself in the world, and the world
in myself, I try to do both.

The strange syntax – a characteristic of these poems – suggests Carter preoccupation with the ontological/existential problem of the nature and implications of being. 'Being' involves (a) perpetual location, what Carter calls 'arrangement' of Self in Cosmos and (b) constant 'arrangement' of Cosmos in Self. The word 'arrange' suggests falsification, fabrication, the deliberate invention of otherwise nonexistent relationships between things which are utterly 'other', totally separate.

Such fabrication is, of course, second nature to the poet, particularly to the twentieth century post-romantic, post-symbolist, post-everything poet. But Carter takes no comfort in what he arranges, because he feels that life itself is an arrangement in which men are time's puppets:

> time's
> doll house of replaceable heads
> arms and legs

to be assembled or discarded like the world itself, when its time comes. Ultimately, both ontological and existential questions, as well as aesthetic ones, lose their point. Here we are as far as possible from Carter's passionate avowal of the necessity for political confrontation.

There are less hopeless and more complex poems on the same theme. 'As New and as Old (I)' and 'As New and as Old (II)' or 'With That Loan' posit a far more complicated relationship between man and time. The first of these begins with a riddling statement:

> Every day is as old
> as a new day is

'Old' and 'new' mean the same thing in the neuter process of time. Night and day are twin illusions, the one ruled by stars, the other by the sun. But the difference is false, since both are manifestations of time as neuter process. Writing too is illusion; but it is also an act of desperate and utterly necessary faith in a time and place of crawling things and people.

The last lines of the poem pose some difficulty since initially they seem unrelated to the rest of the poem:

> Having betrayed
> old gods in an old day, we seek
> now to betray new ones
> in a new day

They suggest that the avowal of faith and the reality of betrayal are, like everything else, part of a fixed pattern. Carter seems to be questioning the strength of his political commitment in the face of his existential despair. Full of self-recrimination and self-doubt, he discloses a nakedly honest, driven, unillusioned and unhoping self beneath the political one. This self caught up in the neuter process of time, experiences what T.S. Eliot in 'The Dry Salvages' described as :

> the trailing
> consequence of further days and hours,
> While emotion takes to itself the emotionless

Years of living among the breakage
Of what was believed in as the most reliable –
And therefore the fittest for renunciation.[10]

Carter is if anything, bleaker, more 'emotionless' than Eliot in the grip of the succession of new/old days, and his sense of man's continual betrayal of his faiths.

The second poem entitled 'As New and as Old (II),' starts with nearly the same riddle, one that could have been taken from *Ecclesiastes* whose theme is the cyclic sameness of time, and the unnewness of things under the sun.

This morning is new, but the sun
that made it is old

There is a connection in both of these 'As New and as Old' poems, between the sense of being ridden by a vast impersonal process, time, and the development of (i) a stoical toughness shot through with anguish (ii) a sense of the undifferentiated sameness of all things – good/evil, happiness/grief, truth/falsehood, faith/betrayal: (iii) a capacity to affirm and negate in the same breath, or to negate what one has affirmed.

So Carter listens to 'the world's great grief' which, like his confessed tendency towards betrayal, is both new and old.

a kind of music we listen to and hear
when the toil of silence builds
our house of language in this wind's
throat, the grim larynx

The 'music' Carter listens to and hears, is of a decidedly starker quality than Wordsworth's 'still sad music of humanity'; for the things in which Wordworth had faith – Nature, harmony, a process of reconciliation, the consolation of philosophy when elation waned – are all, despite 'Let Every Child Run Wild', more normally rejected as impossible props in Carter's vision of the world. Carter suggests both the inner ordeal of making ('toil of silence') and the fierceness of external stimuli ('this wind's throat, the grim larynx') against which his voice must assert itself. This dialectic of introversion and extroversion, elsewhere illustrated by the extreme tension between existential and political concerns, gives the poem its severity, its fiercely affirmative quality.

As with the first of these poems, the final focus is as much on society as it is on the poet. The 'our' of the penultimate line assumes a communal quality which it did not have earlier in the poem, even though the 'We' is still the poet.

A green leaf
on the branch of a tree fingers
our time's disgraceful space. We
are its measure,

'Our' here refers to society; the word 'disgraceful' makes this clear. 'Disgraceful' and 'vile' have become favourite words with Carter for describing Guyana. The 'green leaf' here is not the symbol of explosive rebellion that it was in 'Death of a Comrade'.[11] It is, rather, an example of renewal in Nature; an illustration of the cyclic movement in life, the naturalness which in 'Playing Militia' Carter describes his society as having insulted.

We emerge from this poem with two notions of the poet's commitment: (i) in the very process of making he listens to, shapes and defies the cold neutrality of time and (ii) when he looks outside of himself at his society, he measures the degree of its disgraceful abuse of the wider waste of its time.

In 'With That Loan', Carter begins with an even more puzzling riddle, whose relationship to what follows isn't immediately obvious.

A tick on the flank
of a beast is also
a beast: as every answer
creature of a question.

Its implication is that everything is generically related to its apparent opposite: the parasite to its source of nourishment, the victim to his oppressor, the answer to its question. The poet's relationship to time is that of a lesser parasite to a greater. He derives nourishment from a process which is slowly devouring him. The poet, then, is simultaneously trickster hero and inevitable loser, Anansi, the web-spinner of riddles, himself caught up in time's snare.

...In
this world time is a snare
and I am masticated
by its jaws. All I could have
and have done was to borrow
its tongue. With that loan
I have gained a mastery
of the language of our negative yes.

Kamau Brathwaite[12] correctly sees this poem as being representative of the spirit of the entire collection. Carter's universe, abandoned by old gods and new becomes, like Eliot's, subject to time. But whereas Eliot struggles to relocate God at the centre of his universe and so redeem time and resolve paradox, for Carter time remains eternally present and unredeemable.[13] The result is that for Carter, each act of affirmative faith is also an act of negation; and each act of choice returns him to the opacity of a neutralising process which confounds both lucidity of vision and the faith implicit in all choosing. So that he says 'yes' and 'no' in one and the same breath.

This results in a poetry of constant paradox which is characterised by what I have termed the 'riddle'. The riddle is an attempt to give concrete shape to a perception of ambivalence. It depends on a correspondence between an image and its 'meaning'. We must be able to move from an image – often one that describes the 'behaviour' of an animal, plant or object – to some human or general situation. The riddle here is like the proverb in traditional African folk tales, with the difference that the proverb is a condensation or concretised summary of the story which precedes it, while with the riddle we have no elaborate tale; only the crystallisation of paradox, of trick, of spell, of rune. What Carter does is to present us with imperfect riddles; riddles in which the image doesn't quite correspond to the idea which it seeks to convey. This gives many of his later poems a cryptic quality, even an incoherence, since at times the reader is confronted with a succession of apparently unrelated images, or of images unhinged from their suggested 'meanings'.

In 'Rice' the peasant, like the poet, is caught in time's and nature's riddle; the apparently pointless alternation of seasons neither of which fulfils hope. Here again we have the vision of *Ecclesiastes:* son succeeds father, new moon full moon; but nothing changes. The cycle is unhallowed by any ritual which might give meaning to its implacability. What replaces the circle of meaning is paradox, whose archetypal form is the riddle or the rune. Hence the poem begins with a riddle as the poet/peasant seeks words which will at least describe the trap of time. Borrowing time's language of paradox where yes and no complement each other, the poet becomes, like time, an equivocator.

The peasant, caught in what is really the same paradox, waits in drought for rain to grow his 'harvests of wind padi' – itself an image of unfulfilment – a harvest of grainless husk, analogous to the poet's futile harvest of time's language. The peasant, like the poet, questions not only his own waiting for rain, but the whole process of time. His first question/statement is a simple riddle, to which he supplies a simple answer

What is rain for, if not rice
for an empty pot

One notes, though, that the suggested answer to the first riddle is itself stated in question form, and leaves open the possibility that rain might well be for something else... Flood, for example. It could be a destructive as well as a regenerative force, as Carter noted in early poems such as 'University of Hunger' and 'Not Hands Like Mine'.

The second riddle, though, asks 'What is the use of a pot when there is no food in the village?' This is the question for which we were being set up. There are no illusions here about a fostering Nature or a loving Providence; only a sense of trap and pointlessness. So the peasant like the poet, imitates time. He too becomes trickster, Anansi, master of the riddle.

In his calculation
his yield was the share he would reap
when he cheated, like the moon and the sea.

The riddle, then, is the form which man creates when he perceives paradox and his helplessness in the face of cosmic incongruity. The trickster emerges when he pretends an illusory mastery over a fickle universe.

In 'Beans of God' the poet assumes the peasant persona. Society is indifferent to the poet's toil as is Nature to the peasant's. The poet works in an indeterminate twilight between the sunlight of reality and the moonlight of a waning illusion, just as the peasant is caught between and mocked by the twin seasons of drought and flood.[14] The poet also works in the poorest of ground – the hard blank foot-trodden concrete pavements of the city, in whose cracks only the toughest weeds survive. He is planting, of all things, the beans of God.

On the pavements
of the feet of cripples I plant
the green pods of the beans of God.

Glowing and alive, these are the most affirmative lines of the entire collection. They attest to the sacredness of the poet's role, despite its apparent futility. Beans don't grow on concrete and even if they did, could scarcely survive the trampling crippled feet of his society. Yet the poet – no longer trickster but the related figures of magician and wise fool – plants his song, a challenge to the system's concrete.

We end this essay with an examination of three poems, 'Our Number', 'Bent' and 'Ground Doves', each of which offers a different clue as to how Carter perceives his role and responsibility as poet in a degraded society. 'Our Number' is an attempt to connect image and idea in a less riddling manner than, say, 'With That Loan' or 'Too Much Waiting'. The scene is the foreshore at low tide. The focus is on a shrill-tongued fishwife counting shrimp. One of the ideas that emerges is that the people are shrimp in the hands of their leaders – the abusive fishwife – and have been born out of 'a way of counting,' an economic and totally materialistic system. 'Census', the penultimate poem, wittily connects this 'way of counting' with rigged elections.

The poet responds to and transforms the objects which he perceives outside the cranium's bare space. One notes an extreme compression of syntax which includes the use of adjectives and nouns as verbs ('irregular' in line one or 'denizen' in line eight) and the omission of words ('the tide has gone [and left?] them bare'). This last image is most certainly a reference to Carter's poetry in which the language is for the most part pruned of rhetoric and bare and clean. The fisherman, who in 'Till I Collect' had served as an image of the poet as dreamer, has here brought home a meagre catch.

The poet is resigned to both the barrenness of imagination and the squalor of politics. Yet there is still the effort at defiance. He shares in the seagull's and the fishwife's desperation, in their querulous struggle for food and their defiance of 'the tide that naked skins us.' Tide here is both the abstract process of time and the political regime which flays (skins) us and leaves us naked. The fishwife who with relation to the shrimp may represent the power of authority to falsify the accounts and census lists is herself fragile and helpless in the grip of time and tide.

In 'Bent', what strikes one immediately is the stark clarity of the image, the naked brilliance of light in which it is seen:

On the street, the sun
rages. The bent back of
an old woman resurrects
the brimmed bucket of this world's
light and insupportable
agony. A damage of years

Here there may be the faintest echoes of 'The Fabulous Well' sequence from Harris's *Eternity to Season*, [15] though Carter, it must be stressed, normally displays little of Harris's interest in the mythic, the ancestral, the primal, or his sense of the possibility of reconciliation. The old woman is the Muse. She has endured in spite of the 'damage of years' and has something of the eternal quality of Wordsworth's Leechgatherer, as well as his bent hoop-like shape, 'feet and head/Coming together in life's pilgrimage.'[16] The Muse as fetcher of water resembles the slave of antiquity, yet her servitude brings light, and her task is a redemptive one. She is Carter's Agonistes, the artist/victim whose agony is 'light' in both the adjectival and the nominal senses, because he has willingly chosen to bear it, and because he seeks the halo of illumination which it bestows.[17] But the agony is also 'insupportable' because the burden is cosmic. It is 'the world's light,' the sun reflected in the circular mirror of the full bucket of water, which she 'resurrects.' This connects her with Apollo, sun god and patron of music and poetry, Atlas the world-bearer, and Christ the resurrected son/sun of God. The word 'resurrects' is itself ambiguous, and reconciles the paradox of intolerable Sisyphean ordeal and transcension, because it can mean both 'lifts again and again' and 'rises again from the dead'. The second meaning also accords the Muse victory over injurious time.

The impulse towards art is a driven need, an incredible thirst in the spirit, the primal necessity for grace (water). It is

the crushed cloud
of an incredible want

which has drawn the ageing, crippled Muse, Legba's sister, out into the sun's inferno. In that fierce heat and stark light, she's both caught and apotheosised, and enduring, partakes of the cosmic. The eternal sky, 'blue and ever,' imitates her; shares her curved state and perhaps her blues. She is finally both the victim of a hostile cosmos and a paradigm from which the universe devises its own curvature and bent. This is, perhaps, the poem in which Carter best reconciles the two responsibilities which he outlines in 'Being Always', that of locating Self in Cosmos and Cosmos in Self, or, as he states it elsewhere, that of going through the open-ended process of becoming that identity is: 'a process and becoming in which even without a conscious intention on the part of the human agent, the objective world is humanised and the human world objectivised.[18]

In 'Ground Doves' the Muse, here imaged by the doves which in Guyana are known as God-birds, seeks refuge from 'our time's new wind.' Here, as in 'Bastille Day – Georgetown' and 'Bent', the imagery is religious. Grace, holiness, the Word of God, the Paraclete, here associated with a quality of sensibility, faces asphyxiation in an atmosphere of the perverted use of language and sign. Our degradation begins with the corruption of the Word. Attempting to escape, the doves, who are anima, irreducible spirit, seek their element, the air. But then, tragically,

On electric wires
which stretch from nowhere
to somewhere, they perch to perish
with singed feathers

The refuge which the doves seek is dislocated in space, rooted nowhere and stretching towards an indefinite somewhere little different from that nowhere. Those stretched high-tension wires have featured in several twentieth century poets[19] as an image of neurosis, the mind's short-circuit. The choice offered is to live in and through the foetid swamp of society and politics, or alienation in a nowhere region where the soul's electricity short-circuits, and the mind snaps under its hypertension.

There is a faint suggestion of hubris and fall, but this is outweighed by the presentation of the doves as true though fragile souls. They are 'ordinary and average, identifiable as 'you and I.' They are, in fine, the attainable goodness of the average person, which becomes fugitive in an oppressive ethos. The poet, part of their community of fear, advocates a duty of compassion.

We shall have
to pick them up. And burn our hands.

The victims' lives can be given meaning, their efforts to preserve humanity rendered more than a dead letter. If those of us who once shared in their timidity participate in this final act of retrieval. The price of such participation is a vicarious suffering – imaged by the singeing of the hands – sustained in an act of rendering meaning to our pain: in an act of compassion, a consciously chosen fellow suffering which is absolutely necessary, if we are collectively to survive the broken wind of unchange in our 'swamp of vapours'.

Carter as poet of a society which he considers degraded, frequently finds himself in the dilemma of the anti-hero of modern confessional fiction: how to castigate a society for a degradation which one often recognises within oneself. His position is that of Camus's Judge-Penitent of *The Fall,* Jean Baptiste Clamence, who assumes the role of his biblical namesake, John the Baptist, but modifies it considerably by describing himself as a shabby prophet for shabby times. Carter summarises his problematic position in a phrase from one of these poems: 'Accursed, I curse.' Clamence's claim is that he is conscious of his own degradation and that it is this which earns him the right to castigate his supine brethren. Carter redeems and justifies the poet who 'makes a victim of himself'[20] not only through his social role of resisting the regime's perversions, but also in his existential role as one who achieves apotheosis through the painful shaping of his meaning and his moment out of the neuter waste of time.

[First published as 'The Poet and Citizen in a degraded Community: Martin Carter's *Poems of Affinity (1978-1980)* in *Cultural Resistance and the Guyana State*, First Caribbean Conference of Intellectual Workers, Grenada, November 20-22.1982]

References

1. Carter, M., 'Open Letter to The People of Guyana.' In 'Guyana's National Poet Calls for Resistance', *Caribbean Contact* (Sept., 1979) p.9.
2. Carter. M., 'The Location of the Artist', *Release,* Vols. 8 & 9 (1979) pp 3-4.
3. Carter, M., 'Being Always', *Poems of Affinity* 1978-1980 (Georgetown: Release Publishers, 1980).
4. Carter, M., See *Man and Making: Victim and Vehicle.* The Edgar Mittelholzer Memorial Lectures (Georgetown: National History and Arts Council), October. 1971.
5. Carter, M., compare 'Black Friday 1962' *Poems of Succession* (London: New Beacon, 1977), where a similar crab image is used.
6. Carter, 'Open Letter to the People of Guyana' op.cit..
7. See e.g. the scandals which have surrounded the People's Temple or the House of Israel.
8. See newspapers of November 1973. Also *Man and Making* reference (4) above where, anticipating the regime's action, Carter suggested a bond in charlatanry between politician and obeahman.
9. See *Caribbean Contact* (November 1980).
10. Eliot, T. S., 'The Dry Salvages' in *Four Quartets* (London: Faber 1959).
11. Carter, M., 'Death of a Comrade' *Poems of Resistance* (London: Lawrence & Wishart, 1954).
12. Brathwaite, E.K., 'Martin Carter's Poetry of the Negative Yes', *Caliban,* Vol. IV, No. 1 (Fall/Winter 1981) pp. 30-41.
13. Eliot, T.S., 'Burnt Norton' in *Four Quartets.*

14. Carter. M., 'University of Hunger' in *Poems of Succession* (London: New Beacon Books, 1978). First published 1954.
15. Harris. W., 'The Fabulous Well', *Eternity* to *Season* (London: New Beacon Books, 1978). First published 1954.
16. Wordsworth, William. 'Resolution and Independence'.
17. Carter, M., 'Man and Making' (See reference No.4. op.cit.).
18. *Ibid*., p. 5.
19. Walcott, D., 'Laventille' in *The Castaway and other Poems*; Brathwaite, E., 'Robin', *Bim* Vol. 10. No. 39 (July-Dec 1964) & 'Ogun' *Islands* (London: OUP, 1969). McNeill, A., 'Notes on a September Day', from *Reel from the 'Life' Movie* (Jamaica: Savacou, 1972).
20. Carter, M., *Man and Making, op.cit.*

KAMAU BRATHWAITE

MARTIN CARTER'S POETRY OF THE NEGATIVE YES

I

Each spot on earth has its own psychic signals: man made by his landscape. Old women dream these omens and utter them in what we now call parables and proverbs; men paint them up as signs or slogans on carts or taxicabs or mammy market waggon trucks; make massive art of them on walls. Shape words poets. And of all our english-speaking Caribbean places, the human wrestle with these geo / logical deeps has come most deeply from Guyana: *'I saw him now for the first faceless time as the captain and unnatural soul of heaven's dream; he was myself standing outside of me while I stood inside of him'* [1] or *'The tree rose around me into upward flying limbs when I screwed my eyes to stare from underneath above'* [2] or

> 'I let the grains filter slowly through my fingers like sand falling in a measured drip through the neck of an ancient hourglass. Some of the grains at the bottom of the grave reminded me of that sunless, ashen powder one finds on the floor of abandoned ant heaps. They were mixed now with a darker, heavier, more brittle soil, but when the grave had first been opened, the layer in which I now buried my hands had been dated circa 1250 AD. Within that layer had been found the bones of two Negroid skeletons. / I looked up from the pit, strewn with the irreverent debris of beer and soda cans, at the pure unuttered pool of the Caribbean sky. . . [And] I felt as though the hands through which I now sifted this thirteenth-century dust were branches drawing sap from the grafted tree of my Carib and African ancestors.'[3]

It is this same perceived paradox and link: time space manvironment: that informs Walter Rodney's *How Europe Underdeveloped Africa*,[4] Elsa Goveia's *Historiography,*[5] Edgar Mittelholzer's novels,[6] Gordon Rohlehr's literary criticism,[7] Denis Williams' *Icon and Image,*[8] Aubrey Williams' *Timehri*, [9] A.J. Seymour's sense of God Mammon,[10] Philip Moore's *God Manliness',*[11] Wordsworth MacAndrew's folk and citizen[12], and, I would hazard, much of the politics of that country since the 50s.[13]

But the voice that was always there: essence of the 'modern' period: link, in every sense, between them all from Cameron[14] to Rodney: riddle and clarifier, identity and question; *victim,* as he puts it, and *vehicle'*[15] is Martin Carter[16]

> Now to absorb and be absorbed again
> and in such fashion marry to the world
>
> Sky blue, grass green, glittering noon
> dust white, bones naked, hopes barren – beautiful world!
> No mark, no madness like this sanity[17]

This (Guyanese) dialectical perception of the self and world in Martin Carter has never been properly appreciated, mainly because he has been popularly (and quite rightly) identified with prison protest, struggle: his *Poems of Resistance* (1954) and 'Jail me quickly' (New *World Fortnightly*, Feb. 1966); and that eloquent militant opposition has been supported by an equally eloquent sense of hope which has made us all proud.

> Death must not find us thinking that we die
> ...
> for even now the greener leaf explodes
> sun brightens stone
> and all the river burns[18]

But that protest/hope are part of a whole; the hope not something wished for or aesthetically satisfying; but consequence of the original impulse of objection. The 'greener leaf explodes' is an expression of dialectical synthesis; and I use the Hegel / Marx formulation (though I don't like the term 'antithesis') because it universally describes an observed/experienced process in life: nature: change: relationships. The only factor I would add is that, in considering Carter's expression of this process in his poetry, we should note that his first or thesis stage is also a *material* stage; his second or antithesis stage is or tends to be non-material, implosive, often artistically surreal, if you like; while the third stage of his dialectic involves transformation and vision ('consume', 'absorb', 'explode') and, we should expect, reconciliation; and that each poem and each phase of his poetry also represents a particular aspect of the dialectic; and that Carter now appears to be in his second and most difficult phase. How far the progress, even appearance, of each phase is a matter of will or intellectual / artistic development on a 'Personal' level, and how much a response to the life and death of his times remains to be seen: if such things can ever be said to be separated and / or seen.

II

I have already, to some degree at least, examined Carter's 'material' poetry in 'Resistance poems: the voice of Martin Carter' *(Caribbean Quarterly* 23: 2 & 3:1977: 7-2 3): his poetry from *Hill of Fire* and *To a Dead Slave* (both 1951) through *Poems of Resistance* (1954) (there was perhaps a 1953 edition since the collection or was it individual poems perhaps cyclostyled? was banned in 1953) to *Poems of Succession* (1977): though the last group (the new) poems in *Succession* already indicate the transition to the metaphysical. But the metaphysical, as I've already said, was always there: co-existent although it was, in the first phase, subdominant, and sometimes expressed as a rather wild metaphorical swing away from the physical: a reaction, as in Mittelholzer, for instance, from tree to star, from forest to cerulean cosmos. Only Wilson Harris, at this juncture (1952) had the controlling vision:

The world-creating jungle
travels eternity to season. Not an individual artifice –
this living movement
    this tide
this paradoxical stream and stillness rousing
    reflection...

Branches against the sky smuggle to heaven the extreme
    beauty of the world... [19]

By contrast, Carter, in 'I am no soldier', for example, was writing, 'O wherever you fall comrade I shall arise.' A simple fall/rise syndrome, leading to this almost escapist synthesis:

In the whirling cosmos of my soul there are galaxies
        of happiness

or

O come astronomer of freedom
Come comrade stargazer
Look at the sky I told you I had seen[20]

You might say that this is simply 'bad poetry' and not at all typical of Carter (though 'Look at the sky I told you I had seen' has all his music). But it is poetically 'bad' because in this poem, instead of being 'himself', Carter was trying to write one of those 17th century metaphysical poems dealing with discovery (navigation, astronomy) like Lovelace's 'Gratiana', like John Donne's

Let sea-discoverers to new worlds have gone,
Let Maps to other, worlds on worlds have showne,
Let us possesse one world, each hath one, and is one.

and

Where can we find two better hemispheares
Without sharpe North, without declining West?[21]

In 'I am no soldier', we have the sun vanishing 'into an arctic night', 'the insurgent geography of my life', 'latitude of anguish', 'poles of my frozen agonies, my regions of grief' the image of the 'magnet/electrified by passion emitting sparks of love' and the very Donne-like 'Swinging... me around the burning compass of to-morrow' (in this context *is* Carter and, I would say Caribbean) and 'unhappy Africa'. But 'bad', 'poor', 'unfortunate', 'inexperienced' or whatever we may wish to call it, this pseudo-metaphysical in Carter here nevertheless indicates the need, in Carter, for it: the need to place symbolic cool beside the fire. In other words, the resister: freedom fighter: prisoner of 'I am no soldier', to survive at all, must have within himself the ideology of hope; must 'clutch the iron bars of [his] nocturnal cell/peeping at daylight'.[22] It is just that at this stage, certainly in this poem, Carter has called upon the wrong model for its expression. For Donne and the metaphysicals, starting with a metaphysical thesis, their imaginations could reach out into the still to them 'fabulous', trying to make it 'real'. For Carter in the already all too real prison of the hungry Caribbean, the countertheme cannot be 'fable' (that's 'escape') but *dread.* See Orlando Wong's *Echo* (1977), especially the poem 'Last nite'.[23] Or, to put it in terms of the dialectical 'progression', the antithesis of imprisonment is not *hope* but *no-hope.* It is only with the encounter/acceptance of no-hope (St Omer, Patterson, Naipaul) that the poetry of *dread* begins. [24]

III

Carter's dreadseason started with 'Childhood of a voice'[25] or at least is best recorded there. From the hope of

> ... if only ... rain would fall,
> and ... sky we have not seen so long
> come blue again.

we move quickly to the no-hope of

> Even the round earth is tired of being round
> and spinning round the sun. [26]

to (the even earlier)

> The nausea of a deep sorrow hardens in my bowels
> And the sky's black paint cracks falling into fragments
> cold rain is mist! is air, is all my breath!

which occurs in the same 'I am no soldier'[27] with which we have been concerned. And as his physical cosmos collapses (for the full force of *la nausée* see Jean-Paul Sartre's novel of that name, Paris 1938): the white familiar streets, the comrade ideology, the stars, Carter went silent (c.f. Camus' *L'étranger* (1942)) an dem even said the man was as a poet: finish: so eager some write epitaphs, be neat in everything. But is true. The dreadseason could dead yu; and in a sense it should. But Carter's terrible silence: 1966 to recently: was more terrible than silence: for what was happening we know was a creative cracking inwards: revolution in the cell of self: within the cosmos of the metaphor: aesthetic of the style: implosion: metamorphosis:

> Groaning, in this wilderness of silence
> where voices hardly human shout at me
> I imitate the most obscure of insects
> and burrow in the soil, and hide from light.
>
> Speaking with one on a pavement in the city

I watched the greedy mouth, the cunning eye
I reeled and nearly fell in frantic terror
Seeing a human turn into a dog

Recovering, I studied this illusion
and made a stupid effort to be strong:
I nodded and agreed and listened close
But when I tried to utter words – I barked![28]

In the dark time, my love,[29] Carter was moving from thesis to its opposite: from physical to meta/ physical: the interstanding that 'Our prison of air is worse than one of iron'.[30]

Nor is the image of the prison of the air no isolated image neither. In the late 50s, under the shadow of the dread technology of the Bomb, W.H. Auden gave us 'Ode to Gaea'[31]. And then, in the late 60s, in a poem about the forests of Guyana, in an astonishing prophesification of the Jonestown horror, Derek Walcott wrote

the unheard, omnivorous
jaws of this rain forest
not merely devour all,
but allow nothing vain;
they never rest,
grinding their disavowal
of human pain

and continued:

Long, long before us,
those hot jaws like an oven
steaming, were open
to genocide.

the poem is called 'Air' and ends

There is too much nothing here[32]

The third image: ikons now: is that of those two bowed/unbowed heads: Lamming and Martin Carter: at Walter Rodney's People's Funeral: and the long journey from the University of Hunger through Black Friday 1962 that brought them / brought us to that moment

Even that desperate gaiety is gone.
Empty bottles, no longer trophies
are weapons now. Even the cunning
grumble. 'If is talk you want', she said,
'you wasting time with me. Try the church.'

and

...everywhere
empty and broken bottles gleam like ruin [33]

But even the late poems in *Poems of Succession* (1977) didn't prepare us for *Poems of Affinity* (1980): the quiet, gnomic, utter speech of man as native victim, voice grippen to prison bars of air. Of course the hint was there. At the height and failure (?) of the 'Black Power' Revolution of the late 60s, there appeared

Rain was the cause of roofs.
Birth was the cause of beds.
But life is the question asking
what is the way to die[34]

But the concern here is still with the physical, still with the geopolitical desert and its pessimistic complement (the change from the earlier period is that earlier, the complement would have been optimistic). We hadn't reached dread yet. Jonestown was still unimaginable, Rodney had not happened. 900 had not died in nine months of gunfire in Jamaica: 900 dead within the time it takes to born a baby. The way to die, in Carter's silent 60s, was still perhaps Yeats' beast in the blinded desert/forest slouching towards Georgetown to be born. But the last poems in *Poems of Succession* (the section: pp. 77-117: 'In the When Time') are transitional only; cryptic reports from Halfway Trees of a quite longer journey: towards an alteration of a consciousness, a different way of seeing / saying, a dialectical antithesis:

Accursed, I curse, with
a green lip for a new mouth.
A green and wilder pencil
for a finger. And a freer
and much more dreadful
season for a climate...
[...]
...Often, I repeat, I
have died and dreamed. And
when I see a green tree, I
tremble.[35]

IV

To try to understand where Carter, in this new voice, reaches, we have to return to certain fundamental images of manscape, certain facts of structural experience and take account of how, historically and metaphorically, we've dealt with them. The thesis of our history is plantation: imposed, imported structure/process, slave victims, colonial vehicle: the model out of which our present world proceeds. But there were/are alternatives. We could (like Martin did) protest and perhaps lose our tongues. We could revolt (like Walter did) and lose our lives. Or we could 'runaway' forming, if we could, maroon societies in cockpit, swamp, or forest glimmer, modern city ghetto. But hardest, harshest choice of all: if choice it was and is: is standing liquid, being there/not there, transforming eyes of man into his disguise, *nam;* surrendering the personality into the submerged/surreal; unto survival riddims; almost inanimate, non-imitating, inimical of former/formal models: *the psychological maroon.* 'Don Drummond music have th' effec' of ganja'.[36] See also *Wages Paid,* James Carnegie's existentialist commentary of slavery, Havana 1976. But Carter begins somewhere where *Wages* let us off. What lyric after syphilis; what song from throats red cut; what signals from the blind side of the moon?

Your hair in my hand is a rag
of wonder. I keep searching to find
which one of my many selves has found out
why in my hand your hair is a rag of
wonder.[37]

Here is the poetry of convalescence, of psychic fragility shored up against extremis; not opposition in its 'first' sense now, but *opposis*; the dearly chosen words of someone *who had barked*

Every clear rain drop helps to obscure
the green towers; every grain
of white sand the specks
of bright gold...

It is the same everywhere.
Ants lay waste ants... [38]

The crysallis in this bleak new world is

The world is a cold
wind. It is a glass of sweet water
in a grim place of thirst [39]

and

...Near
a leaf, a rain drop pauses
over a dead land [40]

Never before have we heard this in the Caribbean; is as if, for the first time, we are receiving the poems of Grandee Nanne the Maroon; better, Caliban; and although parts of many of the poems in *Affinity* read awkwardly – the *say* spilling over the how-to-say-it – there is little doubt that we have moved, with this collection, into something new for all of us; just as *Poems of Resistance*, when it came out in 1954 was also new (& knew). In terms of wrote it is the starkness of the ikon jammed up against the hauntness of the riddim makes its subtlety felt because it is not hung on beat, the poet's voice and not his drummer:

...the tide
has gone them bare...

Shrimp is our number. Is so
we stay. Is a way
of counting born we. [41]

The only other poet who is using *language* (nommo: naked word/ikon) is Tony McNeill (see *Credences at the altar of Cloud,* Kingston 1979) and to a lesser degree, but still there, Tony Kellman of Barbados (work largely unpublished but see cyclostyled *The Black Madonna,* B'town 1975). But McNeill and Kellman burn brightly outward: self nerval ends. Carter implodes now: word self under the weight of community's history: transition: crossage: antithesis

A tick on the flank
of a beast is also
a beast; as every answer
creature of a question. In
this world time is a snare
and I am masticated
by its jaws. All I could have
and have done was to borrow
its tongue. With that loan
I have gained a mastery
of the language of our negative yes. [42]

The third significant element in Carter's poetry of antithesis, 'the language of our negative yes', is *time:* hence the title of the book: finite: infinite: *affinity.* In the poetry of the material, time is an old man, a scythe, a swathe that lays waste, a river that rolls on, a ticking calendar that destroys, ravager, estranger, scavenger. In this sense, time is the president of European poetry as it is of European natural science and reason. But there is the antithesis of this (Africa, Asia, Astronomy, Fission) which the Guyana / Amerindian worldview acknowledges and integrates: see Harris, see Denis Williams: in which time creates, becomes an aspect of equilibrium ('timeless moment'), the other half of the calabash of space, clockless pool into which we dream though now not to change the world

The more the men of our time we are
the more our time is [43]

* * * *

In a purple world, I walked
among virgins and trees. Between
the thighs of time, I measured the swing
of a dead clock. [44]

* * * *

Every day is as old
as a new day is. Time
represents itself [45]

* * * *

This morning is new, but the sun
that made it is old.   New and old
is the face of the world's great grief.
                                        ...We
are its measure [46]

Against this continuum, this skyline of accepted time, we sometimes hear that almost fatal tone of fatalism, acceptance of longsuffering, that Mittelholzer recognized (?) and brought us in *Corentyne Thunder* (1941):

> A frog squeaked [?] somewhere behind the mud-house. She looked all about her. No, nothing had changed at all. Surely the savannah must know that Ramgolall was dead and that there were pebbles and pieces of dried mud lying scattered on the floor of the mud-house. It looked so untroubled, so flat and at peace as though nothing at all had happened. And the sky, too, and the wind, the sunshine – all untroubled, the same as if they had been yesterday and all the days before: the sky blue, the wind cool, the sun red because it was low in the west.
>
> Ramgolall was dead, but the whole Corentyne remained just the same. [47]

* * * *

> What is rain for, if not rice
> for an empty pot; and pot for
> in a hungry village? The son
> succeeds his father in a line
> to count as he did, waiting,
> adding the latest to the first
> of his losses; his harvests
> of quick wind padi. For him
> the new moon was dry like the full moon
> that promised. The sea always
> as salt as wet. In his calculation
> his yield was the share that he would reap
> When he cheated, like the moon and the sea. [48]

But the difference is in the rhythm; an excellent example, though they both here share the 'pastorale' or rather the Guyanese version of it, of how much more the poet in the Caribbean can say, when he's really saying it. But beyond that there is the deeper, more fundamental difference of vision: Mittelholzer's material negative no, as compared with Carter's metaphysical negative yes. Shift from padi back to street, and we are ready for the poems of affinity

> On the street, the sun
> rages. The bent back of
> an old woman resurrects
> the brimmed bucket of this world's
> light and insupportable
> agony… [49]

'Light and insupportable' (see similar opposites in Harris) is a reminder, perhaps, that the dialectical effort is still new, still close to the surface, still selfconscious. But the poem lives

> Her back bent, time's bad
> step, and the creeping out
> is ash; is the crushed cloud
> of an incredible want.

The last time I saw her
she was far more truthful
than the damage of the years
carried on her back. The
sky, blue and ever,
imitates her. Bent.[50]

'incredible want' is still awkward; but how truthful 'truthful' falls.

Vile, with exhalations
our time's new wind
terrifies the timid ground
doves, in a swamp of vapours.
They seek refuge
as you and I do, above
that wind. On electric wires
which stretch from nowhere
to somewhere, they perch to perish
with singed feathers. They
fall. *We shall have*
to pick them up. And burn our hands.[51]

'Ground doves', in fact, represents, if my analysis of his dialectic is correct, the beginning third stage (transcendence/synthesis) of Carter's work. The long night journey from prison/protest through the physical and metaphysical consuming fires of implosion, has brought him to this season of ash, where even the doves of God's eye perish. Can we say that we are fortunate to have this testimony? That there was at least one Caribbean artist who walked through the dreadseason of his negative years and sent us back reports upon our ruin? Luckily, Carter has always been conscious of his role as poet; both vehicle (craft) and victim:

Now I have made the point that identity as victim as an active principle presupposes the prior existence of identity as victim as a passive principle. And we have seen how the political leader who once was himself a victim, can become a maker of victims; how the obeahman (as charlatan) who was once himself a victim, can too, become a maker of victims. And how the artist who was once himself victim can be further victimised by the society of which he himself is a part. In the case of the political leader and the obeahman (as charlatan), we can see how the social and psychological history of the society in which they have their being can be self-sufficient and capable. On the other hand, in the case of the artist we can see how this self-sufficient and capable social and psychological history can bring about the alienation of the artist in such a way that the possibility of his disalienation comes to depend upon the sanctions of individuals or institutions who or which do not participate in his original society either as victim or victimisers.

But why is it that of political leaders, obeahmen (charlatans) and artists, only those in the last named category find themselves is this position, that is to say, in a position which requires external sanctions as a necessary recommendation? One of the reasons I would like to suggest, is related to the fact that the artist, whose identity as victim is an active principle, differs

> from the political leader and the obeahman (charlatan) in that, while the political leader or the obeahman (charlatan) victimises others, the artist victimises himself...
>
> He makes a victim of himself in that it is his own consciousness, a function of his power as a human being which he exploits in order to produce. The selection and combination of themes and the sponsorship of certain values in his work reveal the character of his self-victimisation, and furnish for our inspection and enquiry, intimations of the extent of his plumbing of his own identity and intimations of the nature of the freedom he seeks [52]

Well, yes. Perhaps. But Carter bears witness that Caribbean artists, like artists anywhere, can also be the victims not only of themselves, but of their culture. It seems to me that in the poems of this season, Carter is beginning to recognize that. And with that recognition comes that *negative synthesis* which Hegel and Marx could hardly have conceived of: we shall have/to pick them up. And burn our hands?

Notes and References

1. Wilson Harris, *Palace of the Peacock* (London: Faber, 1960), p.23
2. Ibid., p.27
3. Ivan Van Sertima, *They Came Before Columbus: The African presence in Ancient America* (New York: Random House, 1976), pp. 261-62
4. 'Oye is a prime example of that African development which had its roots deep in the past, in the contradiction between man and environment'. Walter Rodney, *How Europe Underdeveloped Africa* (London & Dar es Salaam: Bogle L'Ouverture, 1972), p. 127
5. 'For in history, time supplies the continuum but not the principle of change. To discover that principle, it is still necessary. . . to seek, beyond the narrative of events, a wider understanding of the thoughts, habits, and institutions of a whole society. In the society itself, in its purpose and in its adaptive processes, will be found the true genesis of its history.' Elsa Goveia, *A Study on the Historiography of the British West Indies to the End of the Nineteenth century* (Mexico: Instituto Panamericano de Geografia e Historia, 1956), pp. 176- 177
6. Most critics have noted the intimate connection, in the long series of Edgar Mittelholzer's novels, between man and his environment. A good recent (?) statement is Louis James' Introduction to the Heinemann reprint (London 1970) of Mittelholzer's first novel, *Corentyne Thunder* (1941). See also my 'The Controversial Tree of Time'.
7. For Rohlehr's literary criticism see my 'the love axe/l,' and the fuller treatment, including bibliography, in the book of the same title, Peepal Tree Press, Leeds (forthcoming).
8. 'And how to conceive of style in which there is no agent but ancestral reference stabilised in stereotypes which live in time like some great forest in which a variety of species in ecological balance continually flourish, multiply and decay without disturbing that balance or the forms in which it is expressed? What precise and illuminating term can be found to enclose the concept of forms bound forever in ancestral time by ancestral law, immutable and history-less? In what structure of history can one interpret inherently a historical form, when problems of meaning, function and interpretation are so closely interrelated?' Denis Williams, *Icon and Image: A Study of Sacred and Secular Forms of African*

Classical Art (London: Allen Lane, 1974).

Williams' work has so far been disgracefully neglected by Caribbean critics and his is the one where the space/time man/vironment I'm talking about is, along with Carter and Wilson Harris, most carefully and complexly expressed. See for instance Williams' work on Amerindian art since the 50s, his *Image and Idea in the Arts of Guyana* (1969), and the novels *Other Leopards* (London: New Authors Ltd., 1963) and *Sperm of God* (in progress; see *Transition* 28: Jan 1976): 'Past the coconut coast and the last barefoot-prints and matchboxes and frenchletters is where the land blackens and rises and shoulders the sea and wavelets creep in on their knuckles singing and churning the sand to milk between lunar rockteeth islanded in sand...' (p.9).

9. For Aubrey Williams' *Timehri,* see my article on Williams of that name in *Savacou* 2: (1970).
10. A.J. Seymour's poetry and his invaluable literary criticism over the years, has been imbued with this sense of dialectical paradox, expressed most clearly now, perhaps, in his in-progress autobiography: *I live in Georgetown* (1974), *Growing up in Guyana* (1976), *Pilgrim memories* (1978). See also my comments on his poetry in *Contemporary Poets of the English Language.* (London: St Martins Press, 1970; with new eds *1975 and ?1981) and* 'Kykoveral and the radicals', *New World Quarterly:* Guyana Independence Issue 1966.
11. There is not much written on (or by) the Guyanese sculptor (the Cuffee Memorial) and painter, Philip Moore; but there are some cassette tapes from Carifesta 72 in Georgetown....
12. See McAndrew's poetry and his work on and in Guyanese folk culture.
13. The African/Indian dialectic at the heart of Guyanese politics.
14. Norman Cameron (b. 1903), he who, at the conclusion of Gordon Rohlehr's lecture on aspects of the development of Caribbean literature at Carifesta 72 (at which Carter was, incidentally, an enigmatic commentator) shouted *'And not a word about Norman Cameron...*'; is, as he said then, the father of modern Guyanese literature: *The Evolution of the Negro* (G'town, 2 vols., 1929-1934), *Guianese Poetry: An Anthology 1831–1931* (G'town, 1931), *Interlude,* a collection of his own poems (G'town 1944), *Thoughts on Life and Literature* (G'town 1950), several plays, four Mathematics textbooks (pub. G'town [?] 1942), *An Introduction to Our Social Philosophy* (1965) among many others. In this man's work, too, the 'Guyanese dialectic' is pervasive...
15. See Martin Carter, *Man and Making – Victim and Vehicle:* The Edgar Mittelholzer lectures, October 1971 (Georgetown 1971).
16. Our biographical profile of Martin Carter, like that of most Caribbean writers, lacks clarity. There are, in fact, only two public resources known to me: *Contemporary poets* (successor to and second edition of *Contemporary poets of the English language,* ed. James Vinsen, London 1975) and Donald E. Herdeck (ed), *Caribbean Writers: A Bio-Bibliographical-Critical Encyclopedia* (Washington, D.C.: Three Continents Press, 1979). He does not appear in our third resource volume, Joseph & Johanna Jones, *Authors and Areas of the West Indies* (Austin: Steck Vaughn Co., 1970) but there is supplementary material in A.J. Seymour's *The Making of Guyanese Literature* (G'town, 1978) and a useful and perceptive examination in Stewart Brown's 'Poet in Opposition' (*Index on Censorship* 9:5: October 1980: 32-36) and an invaluable personal memoir from Sydney King (now Eusi Kwayana) which forms the Introduction to the first edition (1954) of *Poems of Resistance.*

Contemporary Poets offers the following information: Martin Wylde Carter,

b. Georgetown, Guyana, 1927; educated Queen's College, G'town; worked as a clerk in the Civil Service for 4 years; forced to resign as result of his political activities. Represented Guyana at the United Nations.

Herdeck: 'Poet, politician, historian. / A gifted and complicated person, Carter has been a revolutionary, information officer for Bookers, Minister of Information Guyana, historian, and direct, moving poet, and excellent reciter of all kinds of poetry including his own. /He was detained for some months in 1953. . . / Carter has done much practical work for Guyana, representing her at the Guyana Constitutional – a Conference in London, 1965; and was a member of Guyana's delegation to the United Nations, 1966-67. / He has been an activist and a dreamer, as well as a respectable Minister of Government.'

What we need is a development analysis of Carter's poetry, as in Stewart Brown's 'Poet in Opposition', q.v.

Carter began in the late 40s as one of Guyana's young cultural nationalists. John La Rose has a photograph which commemorates this: Carter, Harris, Van Sertima and a few others (Sidney King?) dashing and visionary around a bottle of Russian Bear (rum). The poems in *To a dead slave* (1950) come from this period. Quite soon (there was in fact probably no hiatus) Carter was a member of the bi-racial (Jagan/Burnham) anti-colonial, nationalist and Marxist People's Progressive Party (PPP), dedicated to the then colony's independence (see *The hill of fire glows red* (1951), *The kind eagle* (1952), *The hidden man* (1952) and *Returning* (poems reprinted from *Kyk* 17 (1953)). In 1953 came the PPP's electoral victory and the almost simultaneous suspension of the country's constitution by what Gordon Lewis *(The Growth of the Modern West Indies;* 1968) has called 'a characteristic act of Churchillian gunboat diplomacy'. 'On 9 October 1953 the Governor resolved the conflict which had developed between his conception of the way the constitution should be worked and the demand of the leaders of the PPP to run it the way they saw fit. He resolved it by. . . declaring an emergency. . . and by obtaining British troops from the Jamaica garrison to ensure that the news should not provoke disturbances that could not be dealt with.' (R.T. Smith, *British Guiana* (London: OUP, 1962: 175). 'That is why Martin Carter was put in detention camp with a strange hedge of barbed wire and a gate of bayonets. That is why his *Poems of Resistance* (1954): the record and expression of those times were banned in Guiana.' (Sidney King, Foreword to *Poems of Resistance).*

In 1954, the Jagan/Burnham PPP split under pressure. It marks the beginning of the second major phase of Carter's work: a long period of disillusion which is only now perhaps being resolved (?) with the poetry of the negative yes. The Jagan/Burnham split meant the end of effective (bi-racial) nationalism and the having (for Carter) to choose between Jagan's idealistic(?) Marxism and Forbes Burnham's pragmatic anti-colonialism; between Jagan's East Indians and Burnham's African – the class/group from which Carter came and with which, in the new divided climate of Guyana, he was identified. Yet it was not until 1955 that Carter broke with Jagan's PPP. But he did not, at this stage, join Burnham's People's National Congress (PNC). Instead, in 1956, he announced his retirement from formal politricks and joined the oldest enemy of them all, the multinational Bookers as PRO. His own sense of baselessness is expressed at this time in 'Poems of Shape and Motion' which first appeared in *Kyk* 20 (1955) and continues into the early political 60s of anti-Jagan strikes, riots, fire-burning, detentions, intervention of British troops, failure of the Federation of the West Indies, chimera of independence. Out of this Carter gave us *Conversations* , 'Black Friday 1962' and *Jail me Quickly* (1963 published, 1966). By 1964, Carter had joined Burnham's PNC, which had come to power that year and for the next eight years he was Minister of Information and Culture. In 1970 Guyana became a Republic and to mark the occasion, the Government of Guyana invited nearly every active Caribbean writer and artist, both at home and abroad, to help celebrate the event. Andrew Salkey in *Georgetown Journal* (London & Port of Spain 1972) gives us (especially as the years go by) an invaluable personal memoir of this extraordinary moment in Caribbean cultural history: the first time ever that Caribbean seers and sayers were meeting all together in an open, relaxed, generous and stimulating atmosphere, *on Caribbean soil* (Out of this came Carifesta: an even more extraordinary event! Enter Martin:

Martin Carter, the Minister of Information, welcomed us. It was very good seeing Martin again, the most relaxed and simpatico Minister of Government ever to appear in a Cabinet in the Caribbean, and ever to lead a cultural vanguard, anywhere, in the Area.

He stood, there, *chatting* to us and the invited audience of library officials and their guests, and looking for all the world, like a romantic imagist poet, hopped out of the fire and, now, dead center in the flying pan. His words were tellingly chosen; his person, a gentle, tall, big man, a poet who may yet do a very seri.ous injury to the sterile vocabulary and syntax of bureaucracy.

I felt, then, that, if be did succeed in giving something new to the style of his particular ministerial responsibility, not only would it subvert the standard image of the other ministries, for the better, but be would have emerged as the pioneer re-discoverer of the long-lost beating heart in anybody's politics. *Yet, who doesn't know how that ancient art of the possible tends to destroy the revolutionary poet who dares to change its atavistic brutishness into an effective human theory and practice?*

(Andrew Salkey, *Georgetown Journal,* p.102, my emphasis)

This Carter himself acknowledged in 'A mouth is always muzzled' (1969; reprinted as 'Occasion' in *Savacou 3/4: 1970/71).* By 1972 he had resigned from the Burnham government and has been, since then, Poet in Residence at the Universities of Essex and Guyana. From here on, a new firmness begins to appear within the disillusion and the poems that appear in the second part of *Succession* (1977) and all of *Affinity* (1980) have what A.J. Seymour has described as a new gnomic quality; and this is complemented by a new firmer criticism of the country's politics as represented by 'Open Letter to the People of Guyana' *(Caribbean Contact,* Sept. 1979) and his presence at Walter Rodney's funeral in June 1980.

17. 'No madness like this sanity', *The hidden man* (G'town 1952), unnum. p.
18. 'Death of a comrade', *Poems of Resistance* (London 1954), pp. 6,7. There are now three editions of this volume. The London edition with Foreword by Sidney King (Kwayana); a 1964 edition, published by the University of Guyana, with Introduction by Neville Dawes; and a Release edition of 1979, with Foreword by Rayman Mandal. This third edition returns to the text and order of the first issue of 1954, to which references refer unless otherwise stated.
19. Wilson Harris, 'Amazon', *Eternity to Season* (G'town, 1954), p.11.
20. Carter, 'I am no soldier', *Resistance,* p.4.
21. John Donne, 'The Good-Morrow' in *Metaphysical Lyrics & Poems of the Seventeenth Century,* ed. H.J.C. Grierson (Oxford: OUP, 1921), p.1
22. Carter, 'I am no soldier', *Resistance,* p.3.

23. Orlando Wong (now Oku Onuora), *Echo* (Kingston: 1977), p.19.
24. See Gordon Rohlehr, 'West Indian poetry: some problems of assessment', *Tapia,* 29 Aug. 1971.
25. Carter, 'Jail me quickly', *New World Fortnightly* 34 (1966), p.25.
26. Ibid.
27. *Resistance,* p.3.
28. *Poems of Succession,* p.62.
29. *Resistance,* p.14.
30. 'Where are free men', *NWF*, p. 24; *Poems of Succession* (London & Port of Spain: New Beacon, 1977) p. 73.
31. W.H. Auden, *Collected Shorter Poems 1927–1957* (London: Faber, 1966), pp. 251-54.
32. Derek Walcott, *The Gulf and Other Poems* (London: Cape, 1966), pp. 36/37.
33. Carter, 'There is no riot', *Succession,* p.116.
34. 'Occasion', *Savacou* 3/4 (1970/71), p.171; as 'A mouth is always muzzled' in *Succession,* p.85.
35. 'I tremble', *Poems of Affinity* (G'town 1980), p.71.
36. Bongo Jerry speaking on the JBC radio programme, *Requiem for Don Drummond,* produced by Dermott Hussey, Kingston 1969
37. Carter, 'Rag of wonder', *Affinity,* p.57.
38. 'Rain forest', *Affinity,* p.35.
39. 'As new and as old: i', *Affinity,* p.23.
40. 'As well is', *Affinity,* p.51.
41. 'Our number', *Affinity,* p.31.
42. 'With that loan', *Affinity,* p.31.
43. 'Our time', *Affinity,* p.15
44. 'In a world', *Affinity,* p.21
45. 'As new and as old: i,', *Affinity,* p.23.
46. 'As new and as old: ii', *Affinity,* p.25.
47. Edgar Mittelholzer, *Corentyne Thunder* (London 1941; Heinemann reprint London 1970), p.229.
48. Carter, 'Rice', *Affinity,* p.37.
49. 'Bent', *Affinity,* p.41.
50. Ibid.
51. 'Ground doves', *Affinity,* p.43; my italics.
52. *Man and Making – Victim and Vehicle,* pp. 21-22.

First published in *Caliban*, vol. 1, no., 1, Fall/Winter, 1981.

ALAN PERSICO

A NOTE ON MARTIN CARTER'S 'BENT'

Martin Carter, arguably the first major English Caribbean poet of revolution, is perhaps most known for his *Poems of Resistance* (1954), which were described as '...one eloquent refusal to be dehumanised by imperialist bayonets and colonial arms.'[1] And in fact, although much attention has been paid to this distinguished poet, emphasis seems to have been placed mainly on the element of social protest and politics contained in his works rather than on their structural and stylistic features. This paper focuses on the poem 'Bent' in Carter's *Poems of Affinity* (1980). 'Bent' was selected because it seems to be one of Carter's most 'thought' poems, both structurally and stylistically, and because it seems to reflect the themes, the reason for being, the leitmotif of his poetic production as a whole.

It has been argued that critics of Martin Carter's poetry have tended to focus most attention on the message, while not treating sufficiently the formal or the stylistic aspect. Of course, in attempting to focus on style and structure, there is often the danger of being 'drawn into an aestheticism that denies social function altogether.'[2] My purpose is to highlight how the poet creates a fusion of form and content in this poem, and also, to demonstrate to what extent this poem is a true reflection of Carter's work in general. Here is the poem:

On the street, the sun
rages. The bent back of
an old woman resurrects
the brimmed bucket of this world's
light and insupportable
agony. A damage of years.

Her bent back, time's bad
step, and the creeping out
is ash; is the crushed cloud
of an incredible want.

The last time I saw her
she was far more truthful
than the damage of the years
carried on her back. The
sky, blue and ever,
imitates her. Bent.

The theme of the poem is Man's powerlessness against Time and the inevitability of change. Its tone is pessimistic, emphasising change for the worse, change toward destruction.[3] Man is a prisoner of Time, which constantly heaps bundles of pain and agony on the individual.

'Bent' is one of only three poems in the collection that are divided into clearly defined stanzas, and, of the three, it is the only one that is clearly symmetrical, its stanzas being of six lines, four lines, and six lines. The lines of each stanza are noticeably short, between five and eight syllables, suggesting perhaps an idea of directness, intensity, and futility, particularly when taken in the context of what the poem is saying. One cannot help noticing too that there are few verbs, most of which are very carefully chosen and positioned for maximum effect.[4]

The title of the poem repeats itself in each stanza, though in a different way, so that the reader has to remain face to face with the fact of his own destiny: bent, bent back, back... bent. 'Bent' is both the first and the last word! What is striking is that the poet focuses on the old woman's back, on which, in a sense, the whole body hinges. This clearly relates to the idea of the burdens she had to bear, both physically and metaphorically. The poem moves from a concrete, physical reality – the time-worn, bent back of a woman, who ironically should suggest fertility and life, and this serves as a stimulus for reflection on the passing of Time. A contrast is drawn later with the sky that is 'blue and ever', is always there, unchanging, which, unlike the old women, is inanimate. There is a touch of sarcasm in the statement that the sky imitates her, when it was she who came into the world and encountered the sky bent as it is, and when she leaves it will still be bent. The point is that Man is doomed to imitate the sky, but only so far as shape is concerned. He is shaped by Nature, or perhaps his destiny. He is imprisoned in a situation into which he is born, exists, and dies. And that is the tragedy.

The key ideas in the poem then are those of the inevitable change to which Man is subjected, the worsening or the deteriorating of his physical self as well as of his circumstances, and the fact that the direction of the change is pre-established, so that Man is a prisoner, not only in the physical sense, but also in the metaphysical. The bent back of an old woman emphasises in the poet's mind the cruelty, the tragedy of this world in which Man is inevitably at the mercy of Time, that more often than not metes out to him unending and unfair pain and agony. Man's only freedom from such a situation, hopefully, death – 'ash', despite Man's impertinent wish to live forever, his 'incredible want'. Man's brief moments of optimism or hope are snuffed out by his sudden awareness, or his sudden awakening to the truth of his circumstances.

Now in an attempt to show how the message in the poem is also conveyed at the visual, auditory and syntactic levels, I am now going to take a closer look at the poem's language, style and structure.

In stanza one there are many words that show what some linguists and psycholinguists refer to as a deviation from the norm. For example, the sun does not just shine, it 'rages'; the 'bent back' should not normally be so. Note also the negation contained in 'insupportable agony' and in 'damage'.

They connote a movement toward destruction and death, not to life and health. Even in the case where there is a deviation in an apparently positive direction, 'resurrects', 'brimmed bucket', it is of 'light and insupportable agony', which in fact doubles or intensifies the pain and anguish, rather than hoped for relief. This is an example of the movement toward destruction and deterioration mentioned earlier. The last line of this first stanza, conspicuous because of its position, sums up the emotion conjured up by the photo-like description presented in the introduction of the poem: 'agony. A damage of years.' The poem is driving the point home so directly and intensely that the reader cannot escape the reality of it. There seems to be a conflict in the use of 'light' yet 'insupportable' agony. But perhaps precisely because 'agony' is abstract, because it does not have weight in the concrete sense, because it is not necessarily observable to others, it is thus more elusive and uncontrollable, and difficult to eliminate – which reinforces even further the poet's point. Expressions such as 'bent back, brimmed bucket, agony, damage,' are among those that contain harsh sounds that create a sense of heaviness, bitterness, despair and helplessness. But, as was noted, these are precisely the sentiments that are being resurrected.

Stanza two maintains our attention on the bent back, juxtaposed with 'time' and 'bad step'. Time, the central mover, and 'bad' the negative tone, are both associated with 'step'. These three words, that may be seen to form one constituent, linked as they are, capture in telescopic fashion one of the central ideas in the poem. Time is on the move, and the old woman is on the move until, silently and softly, almost imperceptibly, she creeps out to 'ash'. The movement from existence to nonexistence is conveyed on the level of sound also: from the harsh sounds in 'bent back' and 'bad step' there is movement to the soft sound of 'ash'. Man's impertinence in wishing to live forever is abruptly wiped out by his awareness of his harsh reality, communicated here by the sound in the imagery 'crushed cloud'. The idea of suddenness and of brevity is also suggested in the conciseness of the stanza.

The external stimulus of the bent back, which is mainly what is focused on in stanza one, and repeated in stanza two, causes the poet to reflect, in stanza three, on his own relationship to the bent back he is observing, and implies too, from what follows, that he too must be growing old. When he first saw her she was more 'truthful', that is, more authentic, more what she ought to be, in the full bloom of youth perhaps. She is now neither 'ever' nor 'blue', especially where the latter is taken to connote radiance, life, optimism, and strength.

Each of the elements – sun, cloud, and sky, all of which relate to Nature – is very conspicuous in its own stanza. They all assist in maintaining the focus of the poem's central idea, and are used in such a way as to communicate conflict between Man and Nature, a conflict in which Nature is the victor. The sun, often interpreted as a symbol of energy, of a life-giving force, is here, paradoxically, portrayed as cruel and unkind. No wonder the repetition of the idea of the destruction caused by Time. However, in stanza one, it is almost no more than a passing comment on the part of the poet when he observes: 'A damage of years'. In stanza three the observation assumes more importance: 'the damage of the years'. In other words, from being a general observation on the effects of Time, it becomes a direct reference to the effect of Time on this particular, specific old lady. And this leads to a sort of indirect consideration of the poet's own status, within the context of Time, destruction, and destiny.

A close look at the selection of the verbs and the tense in which they are helps us to appreciate the sequence around which the poem was constructed: present – observation and description of an event in progress; present – reflection on the effects of Time; past – reflection on the change that has occurred; present – reflection on a possible relationship between Man and Nature, through the concept of imitation.

'Bent' is one of Martin Carter's most closely knit poems structurally, visually, and conceptually. It is one of his most complete, artistically satisfying poems, pointed and direct, yet reflective and nostalgic. It was stated earlier that this poem is an adequate representative both of Carter's concerns and preoccupations, and of his poetic style: the note of protest and dissatisfaction, the tragic view of life, the identification of self with the Other, the potential agony of existence, whether it be a result of social and political circumstances, or in the course of one's own natural development or process of becoming, the idea that Man is a prisoner of Time and circumstances. In the *Poems of Affinity* the reference is no longer to a prison in the literal sense, but the tenor of the poem still implies a lack of control over oneself, one's movements and one's destiny. Whereas in *Poems of Resistance* he says directly: 'This is what they do with me/Put me in prison, hide me away' ('Letter 1') in 'Bent', he is a prisoner in the world, by Nature itself. Worthy of note in the earlier poems are the references to the natural world. These elements are also present in his later poetry. In one of his best known poems, 'University of Hunger', there is reference to the effects of Time on Man, and again the implication is that it is Man who leaves Nature behind: 'The green tree bends above the long forgotten.' (p. 8) The point is being made that there seems to be an element of continuity in Martin Carter's poetic production.

To conclude, in the poem 'Bent', we note a perfect fusion of form and content, two elements which, although in a sense inseparable, can be isolated for the purpose of illustrating how they support each other as the poet works then to achieve maximum effect on the reader. Reading 'Bent' for meaning in the normal sense, one can understand the poet's views and concerns, but on a purely intellectual level. It is when one perceives in the poem the unique content, that one is truly appreciating not only the poem, but also its creator.

Notes

1. Neville Dawes, Preface to the 2nd Edition of *Poems of Resistance*.
2. Kenneth Ramchand, *The West Indian Novel and Its Background*, (London: Faber & Faber, 1970), p. 14.
3. Carter once noted his admiration for the Chilean poet Pablo Neruda, whose poems also reflect a movement toward destruction and deterioration, and pessimism. *Release*, 1, (1978), p.13.
4. '... because I live in metaphors. Two lines are equal to a book.' Martin Carter, *Release*, 1, (1978), 18.

An edited version of an essay first published in *Kyk-over-Al*, no 37, 1987.

Stephanos Stephanides

THE DISLOCATED IDIOM OF MARTIN CARTER

1. Introduction

This essay on Martin Carter was originally published in *Kyk-over-al* called 'Language and Identity in the Poetry of Martin Carter' (Stephanides, 1988). When asked to contribute that article to this book devoted to the art of Martin Carter, I began to reflect on how and why I first became interested in his work and thought it important to include some of those thoughts in this revised version. I should say that the original article was written in Washington, DC with a feeling of dislocation at having left Guyana. I am now writing this revised version in my native island of Cyprus, to which I repatriated a few years ago, after having emigrated in my early childhood. I experienced this return home as another dislocation rather than relocation. In the words of a contemporary Cypriot poet, Andriana Lerodiaconou, I have translated: 'we know we will never return. Never.' (Stephanides, 1994/95, 807). I also recall Martin Carter's lines 'we have always been somewhere else' (1980, 15). It is in thinking of life as dislocation that this revised essay came about.

When I went to live in Guyana in 1978, my knowledge of the literature of the English-speaking Caribbean (as with most readers of literature outside the region at the time) did not go much beyond the Trinidadian, V.S. Naipaul. Soon after my arrival in Georgetown, and before I had the opportunity to meet Martin Carter or read his work, his name was often mentioned to me as a poet laureate or national poet of Guyana whom I should read. As a migrant I was at first suspicious of the idea of a national poet and did not go out of my way to read him, but it was not long before the various anthologies of his published poems found their way as gifts into my house. As a newly arrived young scholar, I lived alone on Church Street, one of the main boulevards in Georgetown, which made it easy for friends and colleagues to drop in. When they came, they would usually bring something to share with me: drums, guitars, roti and curry, rum, poems. It was on one such occasion that performer and poet Marc Matthews came by to discuss a workshop we were planning together for university students. He pulled out of his bag a volume of Martin's poems and said we should include the poem, 'If it were Given', which he proceeded to read:

> If it were given to me
> I would have had a serious conversation
> with the fertile dial of the clock of the sun.
> But then, I admit, I would have had to change
> the language of the dead. (1977, 90)

The lines struck deep in my imagination and after that I started paying serious attention to his poetry. The lines of this particular poem remained in my mind and became the basis of the essay I wrote on Martin's work years later, after I had left Guyana. In thinking back as to why they had so affected me, it now seems to me that it is because the lines probe the subject's reflexivity of dislocation. As a migrant I had always been aware of my own dislocation, and perhaps it was in seeking a place for my own sense of displacement that took me to the Caribbean to begin with. I don't know. I do know that living in the Caribbean, I became more aware of the potentials afforded me by my own plural and partial identity as a dislocated subject. Martin Carter deeply explores these fertile possibilities of being 'out of place' and 'out of time'. Salman Rushdie, in discussing the question of displacement in *Imaginary Homelands*, has said with reference to the first lines of L.P. Hartley's *The Go-Between* that if it may be argued that 'the past is a foreign country from which we have all emigrated, that its loss is part of our common humanity' (Rushdie, 1991, 12), which is experienced by the migrant in an intensified form. The historical experience of being 'borne across' has shaped the identity of Caribbean culture in all its heterogeneity and the response to this experience has much to offer – even for those, like myself, whose dislocation came about through different circumstances.

2. The Language of the Dead and the Idiom of Dislocation

When I moved from Guyana to Washington, DC in the mid-1980s, I often came across Shiva Naipaul's newly published novel, *A Hot Country* (1984). In this novel Guyana serves as a model for the fictional country Cuyama, a paradigm of a failed postcolonial society. It was a disappointment to find that Martin Carter was completely unknown in the Anglo-American world, whereas Shiva Naipaul's novel was finding an audience. It was in this context that I first wanted to write something about Carter's poetry.

The Caribbean historical experience as defined in Shiva Naipaul's novel is a disappointment from the very beginning, where the arrival of the Europeans is described in a history lesson taught in Cuyamese schools:

> It was told how Sir Walter Raleigh had come to this wilderness. But he had found nothing worth finding – only the overwhelming forest and tribes of miserable aboriginals; men barely progressed beyond the Stone Age... (1984,1)

For Shiva Naipaul, identity is defined by the negative verdict of his history. A little later in the novel a teacher describes the ethnic variety of Cuyamese, and according to the narrative perspective, a varied cultural heritage brings infertility and bewilderment. The conclusion of the novel defines the Cuyamese as having no self, no soul, no creativity:

> But, down deep in their hearts, the mob did not want to create. Creation was not possible for them. (1984, 184)

Carter is in antithesis to the above view, not because he embraces a facile nationalism or social optimism in the face of the negative legacy of the colonial past and with the uncertainty of no straightforward path into the future, but because for him language is a living thing. For Shiva Naipaul, language is a dead thing defining a static reality that has no possibility of change. For Carter, language is a tool to be manipulated in an attempt to wrest the dislocated subject from a language that institutionalizes fragmented subjectivity.

Carter puts language under scrutiny as part of his moral and artistic concern to foster a language that probes the tensions of the dislocated subject, and her/his potential in the community and the world. He resists a language which consolidates a world in conspiracy with time and the negative verdicts of history inimical to the subject's fulfilment. The task of Martin Carter as poet can be likened to the task of the historian whose role, as Walter Benjamin suggests in 'Theses on the Philosophy of History', should be 'to seize hold of a memory as it flashes up at a moment of danger.' 'Only that historian will have the gift of fanning the spark of hope in the past who is firmly convinced that even the dead will not be safe from the enemy if he wins. And this enemy has not ceased to be victorious' (1969, 255).

Language is a valuable tool as it is able to open up the individual's range of choices. But at the same time it is not innocent; its strategies and rhetorics select, arrange, and exclude to create its own mythic figurations to serve its conscious and unconscious purposes. Carter draws attention to this, beginning his anthology, *Poems of Affinity*, with a quote from Heidegger quoting Holderlin, 'language, the most innocent of all occupations, is the most dangerous of all possessions.' [1] In one of the poems in the same anthology he warns:

> As when, as out, and as when as
> in, I walk decidingly about
> disappear. Watch my language. (1980, 75)

His poems use tactics of disruption that open up new spaces. This is evident in the title of the poem 'Proem.' The problematic relationship and dissociation between the speaker/poet and the words/poem signal the poem's relationship to reality. The 'rule breaking' device in the poem/proem difference underscores this and shows poetic language to be endlessly moving from one level of meaning to another as soon as it is established like the displacement of its subject:

> Not, in the saying of you, are you
> said. Baffled and like a root
> stopped by a stone you turn back questioning
> the tree you feed. But what the leaves hear
> is not what the roots ask. [1977, 3]

The art of Carter, and also the art of another brilliant Guyanese writer Wilson Harris as I have discussed in another essay (Stephanides, 1989), embraces the idea that language is a dialogue between two polarities – desire and time, self and history. Implicit in this dialogue is the possibility of transformation through dialogue with itself and others. In the poem, 'In a certain time', this dialogue is portrayed by Martin Carter as the hoot of an owl defying the eye of a toad, an animal that is an instrument of black magic and, therefore, spiritual death. In this context impoverishment of speech comes to signify a breach of faith in one's experience. Carter establishes a link between man's construction of self, his perception of the world, and language:

> So now / how come / the treason/ of the spirit?
> So now / how come / the bafflement of speech?
> 'How Come?' (1977, 94)

An intimate link is suggested here between language and historical memory. Impoverishment of speech is an expression of a sensibility plundered by the negativity of historical legacy. In Carter's, 'Our Time', a muttering at the bottom of trenches expresses man's struggle to blast into 'our time' or the 'time of the now' (Benjamin, 1969, 262). Our perception of world and identity depends on the struggle between time and being which is paradoxically expressed in the following lines where the subject seeks :

> The more the men of our time we are
> the more our time is. But always we
> have been somewhere else. Muttering
> our mouths like holes in the mud
> at the bottom of trenches (1980,15)

The language of the poet in his affinity with the human spirit is a negative/ affirmative dialectic to subvert the jaws of time by a loan of its tongue. In its negation of time, language becomes an affirmation of life, 'the language of our negative yes'. (1980, 31)

Hence the object of the poetic quest is to uncover history's desire and the potential for being. I say potential because it is a desire in language which is in process. This is attested to by the use of the conditional in the title of the poem 'If it were given', cited above.

The death/sun opposition intrinsically links the nature of language with the nature of consciousness and reveals the poetic quest to be a quest for integration and wholeness whose objective is victory over time. The poet is thus potentially a healer for the individual who becomes locked in his journey towards death through experience of loss and defeat. The sun clock is a counterclock to the time of historical duration or conventional time which leads to death. The operative verbs are 'change' and 'haunt,' making the poet's dialogue a counterdialogue subverting the buried past in an attempt to restore man to his original potential. Again to quote Benjamin, the poet is like the historian who 'grasps the constellation which his own era has formed with a definite earlier one. Thus he established a conception of the present as the 'time of the now' which is shot through with chips of Messianic time' (1969, 263) The fertile dial of the clock of the sun, like the Heraclitean flux or the Indian mandala, here becomes a symbol of the wholeness of the inner self which can recreate the fragmented individual or community identity. Carter's is not a poetry of mystical participation, for the ego is not set adrift, but oscillates in its dialogue between polarities – fertile dial, sun clock, life, victory, love versus language of the dead, cemetery, coffins, graveyard, nothing, pain, drought. This tension, often imbued with anguish and torment, is the propelling force behind man's potential to think, feel, and grow. It is the paradox of man's existence that death, which negates life, thus mocking the individual, also gives significance to the act of creation, making life a trophy and victory for man.

'If it were given,' in theme and structure, can serve as a model for understanding the whole span of Carter's work from the '50s to the '80s. While there is an evolution in Carter's poetic form, there is also a continuity in his underlying concern to explore the potential of poetic discourse to challenge or subvert the compelling pressure of Time or the time. This is true whether the oppressor is portrayed as an external agent as in 'This is the Dark Time My Love', or as our own demeaned sensibilities as in 'Our Time':

> Is it only just a misfortune
> to be as we are; bad luck
> carefully chosen? (1980,15)

I am not suggesting that either in Carter's work or in reality there is a clear-cut division between external agent of oppression and demeaned sensibility. Poems may refer to specific political events, the condition of Caribbean man, or the human being's experience of dislocation. Oppressors may be removed, new ones may emerge, and history may continue to plunder our sensibility; but the main concern remains man's capacity to tap a source for the renewal of experience.

In his poem 'They Say I Am,' Carter indicates the source of poems to be in man's cosmogonic yearning; the process of creating true poems means death to the intrusive individual ego:

> Poems are written either for the dying
> or the unborn, no matter what we say.
>
> That does not mean his audience lies remote
> inside a womb or some cold bed of agony.
> It only means that we who want true poems
> must all be born again, and die to do so. (1977, 61)

3. Conclusion.

Carter is often referred to as a 'poet of revolution'. He is that in the broadest sense. In his conception of the wholeness of the human person, Carter's art does not involve a commitment to an unchanging world but explores man's identity as a continuous coming-into-being in the whirlpool between self-destruction and self-creation. In his concern with the paradoxes of language and imagination, he conceives of poetic language as a catalyst capable of raising the dislocated subject's awareness of his place in the universe and his courage to overcome the contradictions of his time.

Note

1. In *Poems of Affinity* page xii, Carter refers to this quotation as being from Heidegger on Holderlin. In effect it is Holderlin's own words quoted by Heidegger in his essay on Holderlin 'Holderlin and the Essence of Poetry.' Furthermore, it is two quotes from Holderlin combined into one. The first, 'language the most innocent of all occupations', is an extract from a letter to his mother of January 1799; the second, that language 'is the most dangerous of all possessions,' is a quote from a study of 1800. See 'Holderlin y la esencia de la poesia' in Martin Heidegger's *Arte y Poesia* (Mexico: Fondo de cultura economica, 1958, p.126, 128, 129).

Works cited

Benjamin, Walter, 'Theses on the Philosophy of History', *Illuminations, Transl.* Harry Zohn, Ed. Hannah Arendt (New York: Schnocken Books, 1969).

Carter, Martin, *Poems of Succession* (London and Port of Spain: New Beacon Books, 1977).

Carter, Martin, *Poems of Affinity 1978-80* (Georgetown: Release Publications, 1980).

Naipaul, Shiva, *A Hot Country* (London: Abacus, 1984).

Rushdie, Salman, *Imaginary Homelands: Essays and Criticism*, 1981-1991 (London: Granta/Penguin, 1991).

Stephanides, Stephanos, 'Language and Identity in the Poetry of Martin Carter', *Kyk-over-al*, 39. Eds. A.J. Seymour and Ian MacDonald, December, 1988.

Stephanides, Stephanos, 'Victory over Time in the Kali Puja and in Wilson Harris's *The Far Journey of Oudin*', in *The Literate Imagination: Essays on Wilson Harris,.* Ed. Gilkes (London: MacMillan, 1989).

Stephanides, Stephanos. 'Three Cypriot Women Poets', Translated from Modern Greek with an introduction. In *Modern Greek Studies Yearbook*, University of Minnesota, Volume 10/11, 1994/1995, pp. 795-835.

AL CREIGHTON

THE POET IS SPEAKING: CARTER'S POLITICS OF COMMUNICATION

The poet is speaking . . .
There is a beak at the back of his throat –
The poem is difficult...
Clap a little
(Dennis Scott, 'Bird of Passage')

The point has been made that to categorise Martin Carter as a political poet is to reduce the range of his preoccupations and devalue his artistic achievements. While that is true, as much a disservice may be committed if the political statement contained in his poems is discounted. The real danger of misreading the poet comes from any attempt to limit or categorise him as being one or the other, as private or public, since that would be a failure to recognise Carter's capacity to communicate his most profound concerns through the use of very specific circumstances as stimuli or vehicle. When *Poems of Succession* (1977) appeared,[1] Brathwaite (1977)[2] described Carter as 'a poet writing so plain, so true... that conventional criticism hesitates ... for lack of models of procedure.' At that time it was true, as Brathwaite observes, that 'so little [had] been written' about him but already too easy conclusions had emerged about perceived patterns in his poetic development. The hesitant critics, it seems, had already found their models of procedure.

Carter earned the (mis)reputation of public/political poet from the overt contents of his first book *Poems of Resistance from British Guiana* (1954)[3] and his known personal involvement in politics in the nineteen fifties. But by the time *Poems of Succession* and *Poems of Affinity* (1980)[4] were published, some sort of consensus was reached that he had changed from political protest poet and, commensurate with a personal withdrawal from public life, he had become contemplative, introspective, and a better poet more concerned about craft and universal issues. This was reflected by A. J. Seymour who recognised a 'shy tenderness' in Carter's later poems and it is implied by Carr (1980)[5] who refers to 'the title and significant political content of... *Poems of Resistance* (1953) (sic)'. Carr has reservations about some of this work which arise from the 'political' quality. He says, 'There are some poems in the 1953 (sic) collection which might cause a reader some moments of uneasiness' but on the other hand, in *Poems of Affinity*, 'The lyrical quality is controlled and tight' and 'the search for words to accurately express meaning and experience has been and is, a strict and disciplined one.'

Carr notes Carter's attention to humanism as well as 'sun, trees, water and clouds ... the roots from which the human condition grows' in *Affinity* in which he finds 'only one explicitly political poem...' He is correct in saying the *Resistance* poems 'achieve the unique effect of speaking to us in a voice which is at the same time public and private' and that in *Affinity*, Carter's tragic experience of Guyanese politics 'has assisted at the forging of his craft and is central to his private life.' Yet he goes on to say the public and private are separate, one being politics, the other art. The assumption, therefore, is that Carter in his later work, free of the unpoetic political and fortified by the integrity guaranteed by the 'private assertion', achieves a fine quality of art which is sometimes lacking in his earlier volume. This attempt to praise the poet by protecting him from the political label is also evident in the impressions of Salkey (1970)[6] who describes Carter as

> The most relaxed and simpatico Minister of Government ever to appear in a Cabinet in the Caribbean and ever to lead a cultural vanguard anywhere in the area.

This is an image of Carter in public life as Minister of Information in the Guyana Government formed from a brief contact when Salkey attended a major conference of artists set up by the administration in Georgetown. It is not an accurate picture but, understandably, Salkey might not have been aware of the much deeper disturbance which is expressed by Carter in the poems of that time and the story behind the poems. The profound connection between the public and the private is very important for a thorough understanding of his work which will resist the kind of neat and convenient separation proposed by Carr. Neither is this issue unique to Carter's poetry as Lloyd Brown (1978)[7] establishes in a discussion of Caribbean poets which suggests that attempts to divide them into public and private camps may be fairly superficial. Brown contends that even so-called private art must deal with pressures within and around the writer to allow him 'to take a stand... carry a social banner'. To do this a 'purely aesthetic self-sufficiency' is not enough. (p. 172)

Among the earliest critical commentary on Carter's poetry is a statement by King (1954)[8] [Eusi Kwayana] which acknowledges the political quality of the work; but this quality is represented as a positive element from which the poet does not need to be protected. According to King,

> ...added significance resides in this poetry because Martin Carter approaches the world from the profound humanist standpoint of a communist. ...This world outlook cannot be non-tendentious, non-party. A world outlook is a most highly partisan thing.

It is accepted here that ideology or political content does not threaten the integrity of the poetry and that a profound humanism and universal vision can coexist with it in the same poem. The confidence with which King makes this comment also resides in the fact that such has been the negative propaganda, that a western reader would be startled to hear that there could be anything profoundly humanist about the standpoint of a communist. However Sidney King, a political radical and pan-Africanist, was a co-conspirator with Carter in the red militant days of the People's Progressive Party in the early fifties and if he is not considered sufficiently impartial to be believed, a look at another independent criticism of the same volume of poetry might be helpful.

It was published by the University of Guyana under the title *Poems of Resistance* (1964) with an Introduction by Jamaican novelist Neville Dawes,[9] who observed that the poems were 'in a line of literary resistance which may be said to begin with Claude McKay'. This 'line' which may also include Una Marson and C.L.R. James in that period from McKay to Carter, still places Carter in that category of public commitment in which many readers of the *Resistance* poems had left him. But what is significant is that, from examining that same volume, Dawes saw, not only 'a new note of militancy in Carter', but a 'universal awareness'. He then went on to suggest, in direct contrast to Carr's position, that 'The universality of the poet's statement has most validity when it is firmly based on his specific experience.' On the one hand, therefore, is a claim that Carter became a universal humanist and a better poet with a concern for craft when he set aside his early militancy while on the other hand is the assertion that the early so-called political poetry already contained a strong universality and humanism; that the poet's social conscience as well as his reliance on specific political experience is a source of strength rather than of weakness for the work.

Although the overriding statement has to be that Carter's poetry is not at all limited to the political and that it far transcends the specific events on which some of it is founded, there is great merit in the second position. Firstly, it is not difficult to find a sensitive concern for craft in the early militant verse and secondly, much of the later work categorised as private introspection, springs from specific issues and articulates some of the poet's most important political statements. A kind of concise, comprehensive evaluation of the work in this context which one can accept, comes from McDonald (1989).[10]

> Long after the politics which prompted a number of his poems have been forgotten, and long after the society which he often so scathingly indicted has been "changed utterly", the poetry will continue to strike a chord among new generations.

That is true. But even in this later criticism there is the implication that for the sake of the lasting integrity of his work, the poet needs to be protected from 'the politics' and the specific situations in 'the society' which 'prompted a number of his poems'. While the later criticism arrives at a better understanding of the totality of the poetry, it is still not free of this tendency to separate and categorise. The practice continues in the blurb by Rupert Roopnaraine on the back cover of *Selected Poems* (1989), quoted by Radzik

(1997),[11] in which he refers to 'The public passion of "Resistance", the private wonder of "Succession", the bright precision of "Affinity".' I am indebted to Radzik for drawing attention to Martin Carter's own comment on this very subject.

> I no longer see politics as overriding. I still have no doubt about the importance of politics. But the personal is needed too – both. The word 'and' is very important in my way of thinking, that is to say, something *and* something, not something and then something else... Not long ago I wrote a poem that I call 'Conjunction'. That is the idea. Things must be joined. There has to be conjunction.
> (Carter, Interview with Frank Birbalsingh, *Kyk-Over-Al*, 46-47, 1995)

What I wish to emphasise is the concept of 'both' and the understanding that 'things must be joined. There has to be a conjunction.' A full understanding of this, which includes what political poetry really means, may be found in McWatt (1985)[12] who focuses on the importance of being and consciousness in Carter's preoccupations, but in the work and in its conquest over time, the 'politics' and the 'personal' as referred to by the poet himself, exist in a symbiotic arrangement.

Nevertheless, Roopnaraine's remark also draws attention to the groups into which the poet himself released the poems over the years. Carter has said that he prefers not to publish single poems, but to release them in groups. This has been his practice since early publications such as *The Hill of Fire Glows Red* (1951) which contain sentiments outside of any political context. The group of poems in the *Resistance* collection represents those that address Guyana's specific political situation in 1953 which the poet felt needed that particular note of urgent militancy. Many of the poems in this group were written in detention. Knowledge of this background is largely responsible for a concentration by some critics on the overtly political in the reading of the poems and a neglect of the craft, the sensitivity and the universal humanist concerns which they also exhibit. In other words, the early poetry contains qualities readily identified in the *Poems of Succession* which according to the criticism, Carter is supposed to have developed in later life.

'I Am No Soldier' is one of the detention poems often badly recited because of a narrow interpretation of its expression of revolutionary solidarity in 'wherever you fall comrade I shall arise' and its heavy use of rhetoric. But as is typical of his work, Carter is able to use his detention as a stimulus for a wider articulation of universal human compassion. The poem reflects the metaphysical quality that underlies most of his work from 1951 to 1993. He makes the sense of suffering and solidarity transcend his own cell in a manner reminiscent of Auden's 'In Memory of W.B. Yeats (1940)' and translates the actual physical location of his prison into a deployment of cosmology reminiscent of Donne (cf 'Hymn to God my God in my Sickness'). In his attempt to 'make one little room an everywhere' Carter allows the agencies of his own discomfort to empathise with wronged humanity across global space and time. He spent three months in a detention camp near Atkinson Airfield (now Timehri, site of the international airport) surrounded by a forested area off the wide Demerara River. ('...the huge noise of night surrounds me.../There is a dark island in a dark river./'). The physical surroundings then become symbols of darkness moving from the 'island' of his personal incarceration to the wider regions of 'forest' and 'channel', extending even further into 'latitudes', 'poles' and 'regions'.

In the insurgent geography of my life
the latitudes of anguish
pass through these poles of my frozen agonies, my regions of grief

Guyana, whose continental space is held in some awe by the much smaller Caribbean islands, is divided into administrative 'regions' which are troubled and for which the poet feels grief. But his regions of grief are personal (his own body) as well as being the far-flung regions of the world. This line of metaphors as well as the kind of geographical space evoked by Guyana's large rivers, lead neatly into 'the whirling cosmos of my soul' to which Carter refers and the range of geographical images as in 'O life's mapmaker chart me now an ocean'.

Following from this are the suggestions of the magnetic pole commensurate with the globe and the frozen latitudes. The discomfort of the coldness pervades the poem in the recurrent references to 'cold gun', 'arctic night', 'latitudes of anguish', 'frozen agonies' and 'cold rain is mist'. But the 'poles' which direct the poem also introduce a management of opposites. There is a distinction between the anti-revolutionary 'soldier with a cold gun' and the warm heart of the revolutionary poet: 'I am my poem, I come to you in particular gladness' in a 'hopeful dawn of earth', 'like sacrifice'. The (assumed warmth of the) sun 'vanishes into an arctic night' but the coldness is repeatedly countered by the warm currents (of river, of ocean) reaching out as in a magnetic field which pulls and attracts ('my heart is a magnet/electrified by passion, emitting sparks of love'), by 'the burning compass'. There are 'galaxies of happiness' and 'the sun's acres of children and of mornings...' to counteract darkness, night and finality. In the crafting of this poem the use of the children to suggest brightness, hope and futurity is as tight as the image of the compass, a cartographer's or navigator's instrument for finding direction, for rescuing one who is lost. The central metaphor grows out of Carter's sense of place and extends geometrically to embrace universal references from a magnetic source which generates warm currents of human compassion.

Another poem in this group, 'This Is the Dark Time My Love', also exhibits the same arrangement of opposites and polarities, although they are tightened into paradoxical phrases and lines resembling the Anglo-Saxon caesura, a style repeated in later works such as 'A Mouth is Always muzzled'. The symbols of warmth also serve for brightness, hope, enlightenment (light) or almost any positive force struggling to counteract the oppressive dark (akin to coldness in 'I Am No Soldier'). Like 'the burning compass' and 'the sun's acres', 'The shining sun' is introduced, 'The shining sun is hidden in the sky./Red flowers bend their heads in awful sorrow.' But in the paradoxical balance of the line in which opposing cosmic forces reflect the unnaturalness of the political anti-humanist situation, it is 'hidden in the sky'; later in the poem, the 'night time' is further qualified by being 'dark'. Positive elements of life and growth are 'slender' and crushed by their opposites, 'whose boot of steel tramps down the slender grass?' Normally festive and celebratory factors such as 'season', 'festival' and 'carnival' become orgies of destruction: 'It is the season of oppression, dark metal, and tears./It is the festival of guns, the carnival of misery.' In this arrangement, 'carnival' assumes the suggestiveness of carnage, the 'metal' which here is an instrument of death, is qualified by 'dark', the symbol repeated in both poems.

In a particularly powerful metaphor, the soldier with the gun (the villain of the piece in both poems) is 'watching you sleep and aiming at your dream'. The dream, an abstract thought process, becomes a tangible victim to be aimed at and felled by a bullet. But further, in Jungian/Freudian (I may even say Harrisian) terms, the dream is the id; the most deep-rooted eternal/immortal soul and subconsciousness of the individual containing the prenatal memory of the past and the future. A dream may also suggest hopes and aspirations, future achievement. To shoot it down is therefore a much more horrific, a much more thorough, devastating and profound assassination. The metaphysical nature of the poem is indivisible from the political as it expresses states of being and consciousness as well as a threat to humanity feared by the poet. All this is in an explicitly anti-colonial poem: a description of Georgetown under British occupation. The military presence is reflected throughout, but in the line 'All round the land, brown beetles crawl about', this presence becomes a plague (of beetles) with biblical resonance, as well as an epidemic, both of which are consistent with the themes of unnaturalness.

In this and other political poems from *Poems of Resistance*, 'the search for words to accurately express meaning and experience has been and is, a strict and disciplined one'. But to quote this constitutes an ironic echo since this is the very description reserved by Carr (1980: xii) for the *Poems of Affinity*. Although not all the work in the Resistance group will stand up so well to the rigour of criticism, it is to be noted that the range of concerns and preoccupations which criticism has confined to *Succession* and *Affinity*, was present in *Resistance*. Moreover, to further confound the stereotyping, some of the most militant statements are to be found, not in the 1954 group, but in the earlier set *The Hill of Fire Glows Red* from 1951. These include 'A Banner for the Revolution', 'Not I With This Torn Shirt' and 'Three Years After This' (about the Enmore Martyrs of 1948), as well as 'You Are Involved" which comes from *The Kind Eagle* (1952) and is most quoted by politicians who must see in it great political utility.

In these same groups and in 'Poems of Shape and Motion' (1955) are preoccupations which are repeated in the later volumes. There is a quest for form, a consciousness of limited self, a sense of the poet as artist/communicator striving after an effective means of creative expression that runs in the collections throughout his career. These themes are often wrestled with when his observation of specific events or issues (very often political) cause painful reminders of frail, transient, sometimes tainted humanity. The landscape in the depressing urban environment that Carter often confronts mirrors this; but there is also the converse, when the poet struggles for empathy with pure, fresh natural elements which persist in the same landscape. This would be as curative or cathartic as the metaphors/images/sublime states of being that the poet labours to find the power to express. He articulates it as a poisonous, corrupting element inside which he finds it difficult to purge. It is the 'O wound wound wound that will not bleed at all!/I lacerate myself! I walk and walk' of a very early poem from *The Hidden Man* (1952). It is also an infection from the outer taint which consumes all within that environment. The 'I taste the bitter world upon my tongue' of this poem, 'I Walk and Walk', is echoed in one of Carter's very latest poems 'Bitter Wood', published in the 1990s. Throughout the volumes of his work, he is troubled by a recurring sense of frustrated communication.

As often as he mourns the tragic or negative eventualities in his native Guyana, he mourns the universal human condition and this may be observed in two similar poems, 'Black Friday' from the group 'Jail Me Quickly' (1964) in *Succession*, and 'Bastille Day' from *Affinity*. They contain echoes of *The Hill of Fire Glows Red* and the 'Poems of Shape and Motion'. The sense of shock, outrage and disbelief which turns into reluctant acceptance in 'Bastille Day – Georgetown'

Not wanting to deny, I
believed it. Not wanting
to believe, I denied
our Bastille Day
[...] With
my own eyes, I saw the fierce
criminal passing for citizen

Is an echo of 'Black Friday's'

I would never have believed it.
I would have made a telling repudiation.
But I saw it myself

The day called 'Black Friday', Feb. 16, 1962 is a date on which Guyana's already simmering political and racial turmoils exploded. Literally. A protest against imposed taxes on 'luxuries' overtook the controls of the political leadership and the law, and Georgetown burnt. The major tragedy that day was the explosion of a bomb on board a ferry boat, *The Sun Chapman*, which was transporting people up the Demerara River to Mackenzie, the mining town 75 miles from Georgetown.

That was one of the battles which also included house-burning in Mackenzie, itself in a virtual civil war between blacks and Indians. The various fires, it is believed, were fanned by covert anti-Jagan CIA activity, and evidence of this was further revealed when several documents containing correspondence between officials of the American and British Governments were declassified. Similar information is provided by Jagan himself in *The West on Trial* (1969).[13] Guyana's working class was used, divided and betrayed.

Carter has been particularly sensitive to such betrayals which he continuously mourns in his verse as a people's tragic betrayal of self. For the poet, situations such as Guyana's racial turmoil are thresholds for one of his preoccupations: he mourns the human tragedy in imagery remarkable for its vividness, detailed eye and pathos. 'Black Friday 1962' contains outstanding examples of this tragic vision.

> Atop the iron roof tops of this city
> I see the vultures practising to wait.
> And…
> always for me the same vision of cemeteries, slow funerals,
> broken tombs and death designing all.

It is a picture of a city (a people, even) doomed to this macabre design by the human vileness also observed later in 'Bastille Day – Georgetown'. Both poems, like others based on specific incidents, transcend those events which serve the poet as stimuli for his articulation of deep concerns which preoccupied him long before the incidents and continued to weigh on his mind long afterwards, often to reappear in later poems. For example, a poem of an entirely different sort, 'On A Child Killed by a Motor Car' (1974), arose from an incident in which Carter's friend, painter Ivan Forrester, reported an accident he had witnessed to the poet. But it allows him to reflect again on temporality, mortality, succession and the future or its destruction, as he does in another short poem 'The Poems Man' (only published in 1997) in which the mature poet meets a young girl crossing a bridge who hails him as 'the poems man': a chance, yet significant meeting of the past, present and future; symbolically in the middle of a bridge.

Carter explains[14] that the preoccupations with death which pervades his work is only the result of a more important preoccupation with life. His poems reflect this in the suggestion that the deathly design of 'Black Friday' and 'Playing Militia' is the inevitable result of a failure to live in decency or dignity; that 'life is the question asking/what is the way to die' as in 'A Mouth is Always Muzzled' and 'Bastille Day'. Inability to live decently, to enjoy an acceptable quality of life is equated with death in 'The Leaves of the Canna Lily'. As he does in verse, there were moments when he illustrated these grave concerns in his actual private life. There was that passing interlude when he often demonstrated his disaffection with the prevailing life in his decadent society and it was feared he was suicidally courting death through excessive drinking which sometimes almost assumed the proportions of a public protest. But his short-lived romance with death and the bottle was perhaps the ironic poetic exhibition of a writer who not only sees us dying, as Dylan Thomas does, but sees life and death as twins (as Harris sometimes shows), and is concerned about a decent way to live. Such was the decadence of the society without, that the poet with his tragic sense of sacrifice, chose this method of demonstrating the resultant taint within.

The vileness native to the human condition is at the centre of 'Bastille Day – Georgetown' (1979). 'I have at last started/to understand the origin/of our vileness, and being/unable to deny it, I suggest/its nativity'. In one reading of these lines Carter associates this vileness with the very origin of man, hinted in the specific lineation of 'our vileness, and being' as if the two go together and this is reinforced in his use of the biblical overtones of 'nativity'. But there is also a sense of shame and guilt since the poet accepts responsibility for the vileness even when it is the commission of others. The guilt of the criminals consumes the whole community of which he is a part. This poem's specific reference is the murder in broad daylight of Father Bernard Darke, a Roman Catholic priest, during a protest march in Georgetown. The massive demonstration was organised by Walter Rodney's Working People's Alliance against government oppression on July 14, 1979, (Bastille Day) and the Priest – who was taking photographs for the radical *Catholic Standard* newspaper – was knifed to death. Carter expresses shock at such an open, daylight murder and how far a thug would go for 'a pot of rice'. The use of lumpenized thugs to break up demonstrations was well known in Guyana and the poet himself had been attacked and beaten by them when he demonstrated outside the parliament buildings in another display of his tragic self-sacrifice.

Carr (1980: viii) saw this as the 'only one explicitly political poem' in the *Poems of Affinity* in which the content is available even to the reader who does not know what is being mourned'. But there are others such as 'Playing Militia' which resists the increasing militarization of the Guyanese society which the ruling party found convenient in the 1970s and '80s. It seems to be directed at the People's Militia, a pseudo-military regiment of civilian PNC supporters which was described as a kind of national reserve, or at the Guyana National Service. As in the poem 'After One Year' where 'Old hanging ground is still green playing field./Smooth cemetery proud garden of tall flowers', even such a 'place of final exile' as the cemetery in 'Playing Militia' is a more vibrant, positive environment than the city.

There is colour, individuality and different flowering trees; 'each leaf is a different green:/Flowers a different kind of red and yellow'. Paradoxically, there is free life as against the anti-life destruction and death in the city.

The city is devoid of life in its 'hatred of trees' and given to destructiveness: 'the phalloid needles of sewing machines/have sown a new drill' which refers both to the uniforms and the military manoeuvres. This new dispensation brings with it a condition of moral decadence manifested in 'the sleeves/of uniforms droop/like wet feathers of a crow's wing/over secret carrion.' In this situation, Carter is concerned for the future of the misguided generation of youths who are initiated into the Militia or the National Service. 'Girls, unbreasted,/wear guns like earrings. Boys ungamed,/grip them like tickets.' But what they might see as a future or as a means to survival, is no more than admission into death for which they need no tickets. 'The spree/is a wake. Admission is free.' Again, Carter is addressing his preoccupation with a quality of life which is so degrading as to be no better than death or which is so sinister that it stifles, frustrates or cuts off the future.

The concurrent problem with catharsis (which the poet finds difficult to achieve) is taken up repeatedly in the poems which treat the symptoms of social or innate human ills as frustrated communication. Ironically, 'A Mouth is Always Muzzled', one of the most important poems that address this theme was not the public political document that it is widely believed to have been. Carter resigned from the PNC Government in November 1970 and it was erroneously believed that the poem 'A Mouth Is Always Muzzled', which appeared in a local newspaper shortly afterwards, was Carter's virtual letter of resignation. But the poem, which is dated as being written in 1969, was not published at the poet's instigation at all, but by journalist Rickey Singh acting quite on his own initiative.

Yet, this 'private' poem, eloquently addresses circumstances relevant to Carter's discomfort with party politics from which he twice resigned. His first departure was from the PPP in 1957 after the split when the united cause of 1953 had been destroyed and racial politics was born, while his second was from Forbes Burnham's PNC cabinet in 1970 when the tyranny that was to follow might well have been germinating. Yet, the poem was not written as a direct consequence of either, but within Carter's continuing quarrel with the factors that frustrate meaningful communication.

> In the premises of the tongue
> dwells the anarchy of the ear;
> in the chaos of the vision
> resolution of the purpose.

Carter's politics of communication, his discomfort when speech cannot be free or when basic necessities of subsistence threaten the integrity and the quality of life, are crafted into this work through its shape, which strives after logic, and its balance of opposites. It borrows the syntax of proverbs in stating truths as in 'rain was the cause of roofs' which Ramchand (1977)[15] identifies as one of the most profound metaphors in West Indian poetry. He accords similar high rating to 'I see the vultures practising to wait' and to the originality in Carter's subtle use of creole syntax in such apparently standard lines as 'was a day that had to come' and 'For is only one way, one path, one road' in 'Black Friday 1962' as well as the famous 'is the university of hunger the wide waste' and 'is they who had no voice'.

The Guyaneseness of the proverbial and the creole syntax, contributes to the stylistic achievements and the originality of Carter, in the same way that his native Guyanese contexts, including place, incident, issue and situation, serve him as sources of strength for his wider concerns. It is largely for this reason that so many of his poems which arise out of specific local stimuli are not limited to or by them, while so much of his work – such as 'A Mouth is Always Muzzled'– can so easily be applied to specific local events such as his resignation from Government, for which they were not written. This is the real nature of the politics of Carter's communication. It is not quite so easy to separate the private and public concerns as much of the criticism would have us believe. His quest for catharsis, for words/expressions/poems which would serve as a purge for social or innate ills finds its most comprehensive coverage in 'Proem'. Here Carter interrogates the varied and complex relationships between poet, poem, subject and audience while he addresses the themes of frustrated communication. 'Proem' is so effective that it seemed very appropriately placed as a sort of preface/prologue to the volume *Poems of Succession*. (While it retained this place in the larger collection, *Selected Poems* (1989), it was removed from that pivotal position and relocated in the 1997 revised reprint).

There is an infinite permutation of relationships expressed in 'Not in the saying of you, are you/said' as the poet explores the properties of art, its subject and the nature of the process of communication.

> Ever yourself, you are always about
> to be yourself in something else ever with me.

The lines seek to understand states of being, change and constancy; the fact that the poem, once released by its author, assumes new dimensions as the property of its audience who may interpret it, sometimes in spite of the writer. It involves a poet speaking for and on behalf of a society and its people; he may be addressing them; they may be his subject. Communication as a circuit which depends on responses is one of the concerns, and Carter continues to deal with its frustration.

> Baffled and like a root
> stopped by a stone you turn back questioning
> the tree you feed. But what the leaves
> hear is not what the roots ask.

These dimensions of change, free expression and communication can have political implications of which the poem might not be innocent. It is an excellent example of Carter's poetry which so profoundly captures mankind's existence (survival, even) within a flawed society, that it is applicable in any political context. The tree, which is 'Proem's' central image, may represent a state in which the natural process of symbiosis between the government (the leaves) and the governed (the roots) is frustrated: the former is alienated.

This poem condenses the concerns of Martin Carter which are evident from his 1951 collection and continue to his latest works of the nineties. Perhaps he felt an urgent need in 1953 for declamatory poetry to address the particular crisis-ridden revolutionary situation of that time. Later, while crises remained, their characters changed and isolating the enemy in the post-colonial society was not as straightforward. Many changes and traits may be attributed to the poet's own growth and his place in society. He might have become more wary, saddened by experience and, commensurate with his personal withdrawal from active political life, more conscious of a revolution that did not fulfil its promise, or one that was betrayed. But it is difficult from the evidence of his work not to see tender, skilful craft in his earlier poems and a political consciousness in his latest ones. Turning to chronology to provide those sought-after divisions in the content and quality of the work is not such a rewarding exercise.

References

1. Martin Carter, *Poems of Succession* (London: New Beacon, 1977).
2. Edward [Kamau] Brathwaite, 'Resistance Poems: The voice of Martin Carter', *Caribbean Quarterly*, vol. 23, nos. 2-3 (June-Sept. 1971).
3. Carter, *Poems of Resistance from British Guiana* (London: Lawrence & Wishart, 1954).
4. Carter, *Poems of Affinity* (Georgetown: Release Publications, 1980).
5. Bill Carr, 'Foreword', Carter, *Poems of Affinity*, p.viii.
6. Andrew Salkey, *Georgetown Journal* (London: New Beacon, 1971).
7. Lloyd Brown, *West Indian Poetry* (Boston: Twayne Publications, 1978), p. 168.
8. Sidney King, introduction to Carter, *Poems of Resistance from British Guiana*.
9. Neville Dawes, introduction to Carter, *Poems of Resistance* (Georgetown: University of Guyana, 1954).
10. Ian McDonald, 'Foreword', *Martin Carter, Selected Poems* (Georgetown: Red Thread Women's Press, 1997) p. 26. Originally published Georgetown: Demerara Publishers, 1989.
11. Vanda Radzik, 'Publisher's Note', Carter, *Selected Poems*, 1997, p. 12.
12. Mark McWatt, 'The Challenge of Space: Being and Consciousness in the Poetry of Martin Carter', J. Allis and J. Jackson, (eds) *West Indian Poetry* (U.S. Virgin Islands: USVI, 1985), p. 143-152.
13. Cheddi Jagan, *The West on Trial* (London: Michael Joseph, 1969).
14. Carter, interviewed by al creighton, 1985; unpublished.
15. Kenneth Ramchand, lecture series at the University of Guyana, 1977; recording, Caribbean Research Library, University of Guyana.

This is an edited version of the essay published in Allis and Jackson, eds., *West Indian Poetry*, op. cit.

MICHAEL GILKES

THE POEMS MAN: LYRICAL HUMANISM IN THE POETRY OF MARTIN CARTER

Look, look, she cried, the poems man,
running across the frail bridge
of her innocence. Into what house will
she go? Into what guilt will
that bridge lead? I
the man she called out at
and she, hardly twelve
meet in the middle, she going
her way; I coming from mine:
the middle where we meet
is not the place to stop.

('The Poems Man', *Selected Poems* 1997 p.229)

The child's cry is ambiguous: is it an awed, but inarticulate recognition of Guyana's famous national poet and widely respected international man of letters, or simply a childish jibe aimed at a familiar, local figure whose eccentric craft is the making of poems? In adopting as the poem's title the girl's description of him, Martin Carter, with characteristic, gently sardonic humour, accepts the implied kinship with other familiar, lumpen urban figures: coconut-man, milkman, garbage-man, obeah-man, cartman, fisherman etc. The gesture is also characteristic of the poetry which consistently underscores the poet's implication in the ordinary life and events of the city; Carter's personal involvement in the human condition about which he writes: 'Those miseries I know you cultivate /are mine as well as yours...' ('After One Year') or 'In a yawning gun world I/ am more a criminal than any /of them.' ('Inventor') This 'affinity' is a natural result of the humanist bent in his work, and has made Carter pre-eminently the poet of ordinary' people: a public poet in the finest sense. Much of his work is also distinguished by its lyrical shape and tone. The poems tend to be short, their language economical (at times almost cryptic) and deceptively simple, the tone and rhythm carefully crafted to this end. In 'The Poems Man', the questions the poet asks himself (it seems particularly unhelpful to speak of a 'persona'. Here, as in most of Carter's work, the 'Poems Man' is also the poems' man): 'Into what house/ will she go? Into what guilt will/ that bridge lead?' illustrate another distinguishing characteristic: concern for the young in a 'degraded' society. [1] He is concerned about the child's welfare, the company she may be keeping, the threat to which her innocence is exposed. But it is also a reflection on his passive role in that prosaic 'crossing of the pair': the 'guilt' seems to include him, the concerned adult whose function as observer/outsider does not allow for practical action. He appears to be entering a poor neighbourhood. The 'frail bridge' suggests the shared, rudimentary' wooden structure which is still a characteristic feature of the poorer Georgetown housing areas. He is returning from, or paying, a visit just as a young girl from the neighbourhood is running off on her own pursuits: 'she going/ her way; I coming from mine'. But the caesura after 'going' and the pause after 'way' place emphasis on 'her way', inviting doubt as to whether her own, childish 'way' (with its echo of the vernacular 'own-way', meaning stubborn) is a healthy direction. Is the house into which she may be going, a decent home, or a den of vice, perhaps a bawdy house?[2] And what does the phrase '...I coming from mine' mean? What 'way' is the poet 'coming from'? Does the phrase refer to his (very different) way of life? The colloquial expression: 'where one is coming from' refers to one's underlying or informing attitude or social background.

Such an interpretation seems justifiable, since there is a hint of vernacular lexical structure in 'she going/ her way; I coming from mine' as well as in 'I/ the man she called out at/ and she, hardly twelve...'). In fact, the subtle use of the vernacular is a notable characteristic of Carter's poetic language, helping to establish a verbal link with the experience of the urban and rural working classes.[3]

The spare, laconic language of 'The Poems Man' is nevertheless meticulously shaped. For example, the lines '...meet in the middle.../ the middle where we meet', with those two 'meets' approaching the two 'middles' from the opposite ends of the lines, enacts the movement of poet and child; the poem ironically coming to a stop with the assertion that 'the middle where we meet / is not the place to stop.' The reader is left, abruptly, to consider the implications of what appears, at first sight, to be obvious. Certainly, the middle is not a true meeting-point, but merely the point where the two cross; an intersection: they are headed in opposite directions. But there is a nagging suggestion in the poem that there ought to be a 'stopping-point', a meeting of poet and 'rude' citizen, of adult and child, of hard-won experience and 'frail' innocence. This idea, the need for social 'conjuncture', appears in another context in the short lyric, 'In a Small City at Dusk':

In a small city at dusk
it is difficult to distinguish
bird from bat...

Stranger to each other they seek
planted by beak or claw or hand
the same tree that grows out of the great soil.
And I know, even before I came to live here,
before the city had so many houses
dusk did the same to bird and bat and does
the same to man.

Though following opposite impulses, both creatures seek the same point of rest at dusk (the 'meeting-point' of two heavenly bodies, the setting sun and the rising moon, moving in 'opposite' directions). There is a strong suggestion of the lack of meaningful communication, perhaps of a genuine meeting-point between Afro and Indo-Guyanese; the two major ethnic groups in Guyana (dusk does 'the same to bird and bat and does/ the same to man') who, though sharing the city, still live in opposed worlds, meeting *en passant*, like the 'poems man' and the young girl.

The lyrical shape and tone of these poems, therefore, contain serious, social and political concerns as well as the veiled warning of tragic consequences:

Whatever we are, let us never forget to wrap
a tender hand upon the all-seeing brow of a child.
The longer we take to do so, the longer will nature divide.
('On a Pavement')

Whatever our political or ethnic affiliations, Carter seems to be saying, our common ground, like our children, needs to be nourished and cultivated. Social responsibility and civic decency, in Carter's poetry, evoke both a lyrical, almost romantic vision, and a bitter acceptance of the reality of 'my strangled city' ('Not Hands Like Mine') and indeed, all cities where:

...Love is stammered, hate is shouted out...
Men murder men, as men must murder men,
to build their shining governments of the damned.
('After one year')

The lyrical and the tragic coexist. As Bill Carr observed in his introduction to *Poems of Affinity*:

[Carter] has accomplished the rare feat of writing tragic lyric poetry. The lyrical quality is controlled and tight... and so one experiences the essence, the nature of the tragedy, but never with any nagging monotony or repetitiousness of tone. (p.xii)

If one adds to this Carter's deeply humane concern with the life of ordinary people, what emerges as a major element in the work as a whole is a lyrical humanism that makes the poetry difficult to categorise as simply 'revolutionary' or 'philosophical' or 'pessimistic' or 'socially aware'. This public poet, with genuine (and therefore disarming) humility, rejects the title of 'People's Poet', aware of the dangers of misunderstanding and of the essentially private anguish involved in the making of 'poet words' in his demanding role as 'poems man':

A poet cannot write for those who ask
hardly himself even, except he lies;
('They Say I Am')

It may be this awareness of the essentially riddling, private nature of his craft:

These poet words have secrets locked in them
like nuggets laden with the younger sun.
('Words')

as well as a deep bitterness at what he saw as the deliberate degrading of a people by a cruel and selfish political regime, that accounts for his sardonic dedication of *Poems of Affinity* to 'all children, flowers and dogs, in that order.'

Carter's humanist stance, his lyrical expression of an essentially tragic human condition, is illustrated with astonishing economy and control in the poem 'On a Child Killed by a Motor Car':

Child, a moment of love ago
you danced in the eye of the woman
who made you. Within another moment
like the innocent wheat that made the loaf
of bread she sent you for
in the field of the heart's ploughed land
you were threshed!

In only 45 words, 38 of them monosyllables, Carter is able to evoke both the ideal of untrammelled innocence (c.f. 'Let every' child run wild' in *Poems of Affinity* p. 69) and its tragic frailty. The natural, almost pastoral, imagery of breadmaking and waving fields of wheat is contrasted and perfectly balanced with the familiar, urban tragedy of young life squandered on the city's roads. There is a finely judged use of anapaestic, 'dancing' feet:

... you danced / in the eye / of the wo/ man who made / you
... like the inn /ocent wheat /...in the field / of the heart's / ploughed land...

The final anapaest ('you were threshed!') coming at the end of a long, breathless sentence, ends the poem with the rushing sound of skidding tyres. The poem captures both the lyrical and the tragic 'moments' of the child's brief life, but its startling economy of style in no way detracts from the feeling of deep compassion. Its lyrical shape and tone mitigates, but does not diminish, the tragedy of the child's death by locating it within the broader context of human mortality[4]: 'the field of the heart's ploughed land.'

Carter's humanism, his rigorous, urban awareness of 'time's disgraceful space' of which 'we are its measure' ('As New And As Old (II)' seems never to have tempted him into the 'magical reality' of the Guyanese interior, the territory' of much of the work of that other great Guyanese-born writer (and Carter's longtime friend) Wilson Harris. If Harris represents the optimistic 'aboriginal vision' of a native tradition of Being, then Carter's is the necessary, balancing, pessimistic 'coastal' view of consciousness. For Harris the rainforest, unlike the crowded city (where 'the language tends to be more declamatory'... 'close to a kind of protest...') allows for, indeed almost demands, an 'interior dialogue': it is a world in which:

> ...one is strange to oneself. One becomes aware of an everlasting stranger within oneself, and that stranger is now able to address one, whereas in more settled areas, that stranger is unwelcome.
>
> (*The Radical Imagination*, Univ. of Liege Belgium 1992, pp.36 and 38)

Carter recognises this 'silent stranger' (see, for instance, 'The Discovery of Companion') within the urban reality, but welcomes him as a 'companion'; even though in doing so, the poet must wear a shirt of flame:

> Yes, to be born again, astonished and made bare
> is awareness of companion...
> And only when a man is clad in flame
> can he be made to know companion.

The urban reality and its effect upon 'that infinitely gentle, infinitely suffering thing', the human mind, is pre-eminently Carter's concern. His territory is the interior 'manscape' of the 'unreal city'. Such a focus is strongly suggested in his 'interior' poems such as 'Not Hands like Mine', 'Cuyuni' and Listening to the Land':

> ...I bent down
> listening to the land...
> On my right hand was the sea behind the wall
> *the sea that has no business in the forest*
> and I bent down
> listening to the land
> and all I heard was tongueless whispering
> as if some buried slave wanted to speak again.
> [My italics.]

Even in the poem entitled 'Rain forest', Carter's focus is on 'the human forest of loss'. In the forest itself he finds that:

> It is the same everywhere.
> Ants lay waste ants.
> Peril lurks ambiguously
> ...The swamps
> are treacherous. The hustling creeks
> of identical water are beautiful
> and still, one cry, one however begun
> human cry, contains all.

It is worth noticing how the word 'same' is made to suggest both a boring consistency ('creeks of identical water') as well as the similarity between 'jungle law' and urban political and civic violence. 'Ants lay waste ants ' as 'men murder men' ('After One Year'). Notice, too, how the word 'still', in the penultimate line, subtly shifts its meaning from 'placid' (describing the surface of the creeks) to 'yet', a conjunction taking the reader back, in one bound, with 'one [human] cry', to the 'urban jungle'.

Carter, like the melancholy Jaques in Shakespeare's *As You Like It* , fixing a somewhat jaundiced eye on Nature, finding no 'tongues in trees, books in the running brooks...' and who, like Jaques may seem deeply pessimistic, learning, from bitter experience (especially in *Poems of Affinity*) only how to gain 'a mastery/ of the language of our negative yes.' ('With That Loan'). Unlike Shakespeare's Jaques, however, Carter is aware of the nature of paradox, of the riddling contradictions of human existence, and of his own implication in 'time's disgraceful space' :

> Accursed, I curse, with
> a green lip for a new mouth.
> ... And
> when I see a green tree, I tremble.
> ('I Tremble')

so that his pessimism is also an affirmation of life itself: 'our negative *yes*'.

From the outset, Carter's approach to poetry is marked by a deep awareness of the responsibilities and dangers that lurk in words, a theme that has 'provoked' (a word he himself uses to describe the urge towards poetic utterance: what he calls 'the task') some of his most beautiful and moving lyrics:

> Orbiting, the sun itself has a sun
> as the moon an earth, a man a mind.
> And life is not a matter of a mother only.
> It is also a question of the probability of the spirit,
> strength of the web of the ever weaving weaver
> I know not how to speak of, caught as I am
> in the great dark of the bright connection of words.
>
> And the linked power of love holds the restless wind
> even though the sky shudders, and life orbits
> around time, around death, it holds the restless wind
> as each might hold each other, as each might hold each other.
> ('The Great Dark')

That is, quite simply, a superb poem. It is at once a deeply philosophical, almost cosmic, vision of the 'web' of Time and language, and a moving love-lyric. The poem's careful, but unobtrusive crafting reflects both the poet's apprehension (in the sense of 'taking hold of' as well as 'fear of') of the whirling worlds of both our outer and inner universes, linked by the alliterative 'webbing' of the lines. The punning conjunction of *sun[son] / moon / man / mind / matter [mater] / mother* also creates a link between the cosmic and human worlds as well as between the world of 'mind' and 'matter'. It is a reminder that we are the product not only of human procreation ('matter'); but also of the invisible and unpredictable world of the mind: 'the probability of the spirit'. Caught up, like the poet, in this webbed language, the reader is then taken on a headlong hurtling ride through time and through the whirling wor(l)ds of the universe of the mind which (like Penelope's garment, the threads of which she continuously weaves and unweaves) is endless. This spinning or falling sensation is arrested in the last four lines by the 'linked power of love', suggested in the movement and balance of: 'And the **l**inked powe**r** of **l**ove ho**l**ds the **r**est**l**ess **w**ind' where the central, 'binding' word in the line is 'love', linking the shared, liquid consonants: *l/w/r*. These four lines are balanced and slowed down by pauses and caesurae, coming to rest in the final repeated line which, with its gently rocking rhythm, seems almost like the embracing of two lovers, or a mother cradling a child in her arms.

'The Great Dark' is a fine illustration of the marrying of form and meaning in an unpretentious, deeply moving, lyrical language. The focus of the poem, in spite of its title, is on love as the uniting and *enlightening* force in the universe. The poem is 'riddled' with light.

It is salutary to remember that Carter has the mastery, not only of 'the grim larynx' of 'our negative yes', but also of poetic utterance of great lyrical beauty and hope : and that he could write this extraordinarily beautiful, singing blank verse during the 'terror and the time' of *Poems of Resistance* (which, he once dryly pointed out, were not ' poems *for resisting with*', but 'of *having resisted*'):

> ...The fisherman will set his tray of hooks
> and ease them one by one into the flood.
> His net of twine will strain the liquid billow
> and take the silver fishes from the deep.
> But my own hand I dare not plunge too far
> lest only sand and shells I bring to air
> lest only bones I resurrect to light...
> ('Till I Collect')

Martin Carter is still most famous for his political poetry, and critical attention to his work has been too much influenced, I think, by that emphasis. The topicality of political poetry, which enhances its power, can, with time, become a liability. The lyrical element in Carter's work is at least as important as its political content, dealing as it does with issues of universally enduring importance such as consciousness and Being, social conscience, the responsibility of power and language as a tool of self-discovery. Carter's poetry can be said to move from revolutionary optimism to despair and bitterness; but its bitterness is in proportion to its greatness of heart. For he remains, above all, the poet of a stubbornly lyrical humanism, which, in refusing to be more than simply human can never be in danger of becoming anything less.

> I walk slowly in the wind
> watching myself in things I did not make:
> [...]
> hearing myself in the loneliness of a child
> in woman's grief which is not understood

in coughing dogs when midnight lingers long
[...]
I walk slowly in the wind
knowing myself in every moving thing...
[...]
I walk slowly in the wind.
I walk because 1 cannot crawl or fly.

('Shape and Motion Three')

Notes:

1. See his 'Open letter to The People of Guyana' in which he writes: 'The PNC's method of ensuring self-perpetuation consists of indulging in a deliberate policy of degrading people... a degraded people are incapable of effective resistance.' (*Caribbean Contact*, September 1979, p.9).
2. C.f. 'I know this city much as well as you do,
   the ways leading to brothels and those dooms
   dwelling in them, as in our lives they dwell...'
   ('After one year', *Poems of Succession*, p.71)
3. In conversation with me in 1989, Martin recounted, with great amusement, a *faux pas* committed by one reader of this poem, who, unaware that the verb 'is' at the beginning of the line represents the vernacular version of 'it is', confidently read the lines as questions, thus emasculating them:

   Is the university of hunger the wide waste?
   Is the pilgrimage of man the long march?...

4. Carter had started working on a collection entitled 'Poems of Mortality', as yet unpublished. (See inside cover of *Poems of Affinity*)

EDWARD BAUGH

LOCATING CARTER

Although Carter is one of the three or four giants of West Indian poetry, his work has not been nearly so widely known or studied as that of the others. Because of its limited circulation and relative inaccessibility until recently, and given the history of its production and its longtime pigeon-holing as protest poetry, and because he himself did not travel the international academic and reading trails all that much, his stature has not been as widely recognised as one might otherwise have expected.

The urgent sociopolitical theme that began to make itself heard in West Indian poetry in the 1940s, most notably in George Campbell's work, found in Carter an even more commanding voice in the 1950s. Whereas Claude McKay had come to the protest mode largely through his experience in the USA, Campbell and Carter, given *their* particular circumstances, found fit occasion for protest on home ground.

Carter renews a defiant elation and faith in the brotherhood of the oppressed, and in the expectation of a new, better society arising out of painful, even sacrificial struggle. He, too, has an initially heady idealism: 'that night there will be thousands of torches / from the hospitals the lame will come / the mad will be sane again / for the revolution' (Carter, *Selected Poems*. Revised edn. [1997], p.43. All subsequent quotations from this edition). Like Campbell and A.J. Seymour, Carter has his 'tomorrow' poem: 'Tomorrow and the world / and the songs of life and all my friends– / Ah yes, tomorrow and the whole world / awake and full of good life' (40). He curses the 'British soldier, man in khaki' (95) and invokes the spirits of freedom-fighting slave ancestors, Accabreh and Quamina. But, if this kind of sentiment and apostrophe to 'the revolution' is not without its ingenuousness, the expression has a refreshing directness and only occasionally becomes somewhat hectic and carried away by itself. Like Campbell, Carter eschews the descriptive, and prefers a symbolic distillation of experience and history: 'The cane field is green, dark green / green with a life of its own / the heart of a slave is red deep red / red with a life of its own' (82). From early in his career, in a poem such as 'Cartman of Dayclean' (50), Carter shows how he can activate a resonant suggestiveness of symbol out of a familiar, home-grown, but distinctive figure alive in the local, popular consciousness.

The symbolic 'red' figures of Carter's early poetry reflect the Marxist colouring of the Guyanese independence struggle. Carter himself was actively involved in the movement and was detained for three months in 1953 when direct British rule was reimposed on the colony. Out of that experience came his *Poems of Resistance from British Guiana*, 1954. Although it was this volume that quickly made him famous within the region, any of his three earlier collections could have appropriately carried that title. For the publication of *Resistance*, he was jailed for another three months. Some of his most memorable poems of these two years were produced out of the crucible of the prison experience. They speak with plain dignity: 'After twenty days and twenty nights in prison / You wake up and you search for birds and sunlight' (89). The biblical echo in 'twenty days and twenty nights' is apposite, recalling Christ's forty days and forty nights in the wilderness. In the 1964 republication of *Resistance*, the phrase 'from British Guiana' was dropped from the book's title, and was replaced in the 1979 edition by 'from Guyana', the country having attained independence from Great Britain in 1966.

A new wave of Guyanese political violence in the early 1960s provoked in Carter a renewed revolutionary celebration and optimism: 'When the sun and streets exploded, / and a city of clerks / turned a city of men' (117). But Guyanese politics was by this time complicated by internal rivalry and betrayal, and the poet's voice takes on a note of bitter disbelief as he cries: 'So jail me quickly, clang the illiterate door / if freedom writes no happier alphabet' (119). We hear him become 'a sadder and a wiser man' as his poetry becomes more baffled, more questioning, and more plaintive: 'And how to leap these sharp entanglements / or skirt this village of the angry streets? / How utter truth when falsehood is the truth? / How welcome dreams, how flee the newest lie?' (120). The later poetry is generally more oblique, and Carter's vatic quality develops in the direction of cryptic conundrum as he contemplates in wonderment the sense of being 'caught ... / in the great dark of the bright connection of words' (153).

By 1980, the Guyanese revolutionary spirit had lost its edge in the sordidness and brutality of post-independence politics. In response, Carter writes poems such as the searingly condemnatory 'Ground Doves,' which uses the image of the gentle, familiar bird, with its symbolism of peace, fragility, and the potentially salvific, to suggest the violence inflicted upon a people: 'Vile, with exhalations / our time's new wind / terrifies the timid ground / doves, in a swamp of vapours. / They seek refuge / as you and I do, above / that wind. On electric wires / which stretch from nowhere / to somewhere, they perch to perish / with singed feathers. They / fall. We shall have / to pick them up. And burn our hands' (189). While speaking to the time and place that produced it, a poem such as this, like Carter's work as a whole, distils the essential human anguish of its particular situation.

But anguish is not the only note of Carter's song. In proportion to the capacity for anguish and anger and defiance, there is the celebration of tenderness and joy. The revolutionary cry is one with the whisper of love: 'My fingertips walk on your face / gently. They tiptoe as a dream does / away from sleep into waking' (148). The poem 'For Angela Davis' invokes 'the blossoming of the / power of love you cherish / which so much overwhelms my tongue' (142). In or under all Carter's work is a passion for the nuanced, childlike, visionary, Blakean lucidity of the lullaby 'For My Son:' 'Who will awaken / One little flower / Sleeping and growing / Hour and hour // Dew is awake / Morning is soon / Mankind is risen / Flowers will bloom' (127).

Of a passionate spirit, finding in life, even in its moments of disillusionment, endless revelation, Carter's poetry, growing naturally out of its Guyanese earth, was never bothered by any need to make difference a theme. Identity is not his issue as it has been in so much West Indian literature. Enough to affirm, elementally, 'Here is where / I am, in a great geometry, between / a raft of ants and the green sight / of the freedom of a tree' (225). Or again: 'Cesar Vallejo. The parrots / call your name, fertile as / rain. My habit of utterance / kneels down at the sound of it. / I, who only wanted to be / and to have a name' (199).

Carter's unpretentious yet magisterial accents and definitive tone, whether simple or complex, were usually content to find appropriate rhythms within or around the reach of the iambic. Yet he was not imprisoned by that metre; he modulated it, almost imperceptibly, into a flatter, freer, less insistent beat, where the meaning, rather than the metrical foot, moves the poem's sound. Compare the more declamatory beat of 'Cartman of Dayclean' – 'The bleeding music of appellant man / starts like a song but fades into a groan' (50) – with the leaner, tougher sound of 'Bent': 'On the street, the sun / rages. / The bent back of an old woman' (188). All in all, Carter is a model of high seriousness and unswerving commitment to craft and quest, despite the constraints of a milieu hardly equal to the needs and capacity of a burning, voracious intellect: 'In a small city at dusk / it is difficult to distinguish / bird from bat' (146).

MARK A. MCWATT

'THE CHALLENGE OF SPACE': BEING AND CONSCIOUSNESS IN THE POETRY OF MARTIN CARTER

This paper attempts to focus on aspects of Martin Carter's poetry other than those of politics and protest, and to do so largely apart from the specific historical period of social and political upheaval in Guyana, in which many critics are at pains to locate the meaning and motivation of Carter's poetry. It would be futile to attempt to deny that Carter is a poet of political protest, of resistance to colonial role – these facts are explicit in several poems – but this paper will argue that the poems claim our attention and appreciation on other grounds as well, indeed that there are motivations and considerations in the poetry that are *prior* to political and anti-colonial concerns.

The continuing interest in Carter's poetry and the undiminished vitality of the poems themselves are evidence of the fact that there is more than social and political protest at the heart of his poetic concerns. If there was nothing more to the poems than protest against injustice within a narrow historical circumstance, then the poems would have disappeared, so to speak, when that circumstance altered. All good poetry of protest or complaint, from Jeremiah to Blake and beyond, has survived because readers of all ages are able to discern in the poems transcendent human values and concerns and qualities of the creative imagination that either lift them out of narrow historical contexts, or, conversely, transforms each context into a paradigm of imaginative experience so that it ceases to be a particular age and becomes instead the one age of man.

If we examine a few critical comments on Carter's early poetry we will find that there is an inevitable emphasis on the 'political' or 'protest' aspects of the poems. Neville Dawes spoke of Carter's 'eloquent refusal to be dehumanized by imperialist bayonets and colonial prisons'[1]; according to A.J. Seymour one can discern in Carter's poetry 'the true history of the troubled period'[2]; and Edward Baugh speculates that Carter's muse 'needed that particular upheaval'[3] of Guyanese politics in the fifties. To be fair to most of these critics, however, they do remind us that there are other qualities altogether in the poetry: which remove it from the prison of a particular age. Baugh points out that 'Carter is a man and a poet first and a politician second'[4]; Eric Roach says that the poems 'are so deeply human, so fine, that their quality transcends the reality and the immediacy of politics'[5], and Edward Brathwaite speaks of Carter as 'a poet writing so plain, so true, so nearly harshly peaceful, that conventional criticism hesitates... for lack of models of procedure.'[6]

These last critical comments do not deny the dimensions of political protest in the poetry, rather they point to something else, something which somehow balances, enriches and bestows a lasting significance on these political dimensions. The critics, however, have not really troubled to investigate in any depth, this 'other' factor. If we look even at Carter's most overtly political collection of poems, *Poems of Resistance from British Guiana*,[7] we find that the simple statement of protest or resistance is always complicated, balanced, or even, it seems at times, attenuated by other images and concerns in the poems. There seem to be two concerns being expressed, one having to do with a narrow social or political focus, the other with a much wider reality that is perhaps the counterpoint or context of the former. In some cases this duality takes the form of an opposition between images of human struggle and images of nature, of the immensity of natural phenomena. This can be seen as an opposition between separate poems: If we compare, say 'On the Fourth Night of a Hunger Strike', with its emphasis on pain, 'courage' and 'struggle', with the poem 'Till I Collect', we find that the latter poem, although its imagery is tainted with 'blood' and 'anguish' is set in an entire universe, rather than a narrow prison, and is uttered or controlled by a different persona, a different and more problematic 'I' from that of 'Hunger Strike'.

In a poem like 'University of Hunger', the dichotomy is internal; we recognise the dimension of protest in the images of the hungry masses in their lifelong futile march for recognition, justice and material comfort:

The plains of life rise up and fall in spasms
The huts of men are fused in misery.

Here are more or less simple statements of the people's misery, but already the people seem unspecific, more remote and more enduring than the purity of protest would seem to require. Later in the poem Carter speaks of the hungry masses passing 'from middle air to middle earth'. He speaks of them 'half-sunken in the land', and 'mingling with dark, heavy waters/ and sea-sounds of the eyeless, flitting bat,' and we begin to discern a widening, as it were, of the poem's context or setting. Carter is grounding his concerns within the immense dimensions of the traditional elements – air, earth and water – in a poetic universe, rather than a specific, real political context. A later stanza reads as follows:

They come like seabirds
flapping in the wake of a boat
is the powder of fire spread like dust in the twilight
is the water melodies of white foam on wrinkled sand.

Here, apart from supplying the heretofore missing element of fire, Carter transposes the concerns of the poem to a different level, it is as though he lifts his eye from a near political focus and gazes into a vast distance (the details of which are certainly identifiable as the littoral landscape of the Guyana coast) – a distance which includes the vastness and authority of traditional poetic symbolism – in order to emphasise a larger, non-physical context for the original human concern, for protest and for resistance.

The duality of concern in evidence here is not the same sort of thing that one observes, for example, in Derek Walcott's 'Ruins of a Great House', where the poet himself provides the logic or mechanism whereby we see the original emotional intensity – the poet's hatred for and protest against slavery and imperial waste – transformed into tranquillity and compassion at the end of the poem. Whereas the movement in Walcott's poem is from the political or social sphere inward, where a personal forgiveness provides the release or solution to the problem, in Carter the movement seems to be from the political sphere outward, to the universal or the cosmic. There is a sense in which the twin foci in Carter's poetry seem more implacably opposed to each other; the very nature of political protest demands that it be narrowly focused and sustained, not relieved by areas of silence and a kind of submergence in the belittling vastness of the universe. Yet it is perhaps the very sensation of vastness that gives the poem its power: the repeatedly emphasised length of the 'march of men' and width of the 'span' give the poem its grandeur, but in the end it is not a political nor a historical grandeur – it is not the grandeur of protest.

One has to look, perhaps, beneath the concern with protest and the concern with grandeur to discover a more fundamental preoccupation underlying the poetry of Martin Carter. As some of his later poems make more clear, Carter seems to be concerned primarily with the nature of consciousness itself. Even the so-called protest poems can be looked at in this light. The political problem, the problem of oppression and the care one experiences for the suffering comrade, are dimensions of a prior, ontological problem: how does one – especially the creative writer – confront and deal with the problem of human presence in the world and with the phenomenon of consciousness.

One might argue that the dualism in Martin Carter's poetry can be traced to the fundamental duality inherent in the operation of consciousness itself; consciousness can be directed outward, to the 'other' and the world, or it can turn inward and seek to discover consciousness of self. This sets up the dualism of self and simultaneous other which one can discern as one of the main dichotomies in Carter's poetry. We find that the 'other' , the object of consciousness, can be neutral and unthreatening, but consciousness turned inward – as self or the 'I' – is frequently associated with fear and anguish. A good illustration of this is the following stanza from 'Till I Collect':

> The fisherman will set his tray of hooks
> and ease them one by one into the flood.
> His net of twine will strain the liquid billow
> and take the silver fishes from the deep.

But my own hand I dare not plunge too far
Lest only sand and shells I bring to air
Lest only bones I resurrect to light.

The first four lines that deal with the fisherman are almost childishly unambiguous statements in which the emotional value is deliberately neutral (the precious, archaic words used to refer to the sea – 'flood' and 'billow' – can be seen as part of the deliberate truncation of emotion); they seem to exist, in fact, principally to highlight the contrast with the last three lines, in which the poet's consciousness turns from object to self/ subject, and is terrified by the perceptions of void and fragment and death that seem to haunt the very process of introspection. There is also the contrast between 'action' (the fisherman's) and 'thought' (the poet's). The necessity to confront both thought and action seems to haunt the poet throughout his career and conforms, perhaps, to the ways in which he deploys words and images in his work. The protest part of his poetic concern is primarily a feature of action, of the world as phenomena, but there is an overlap with the more problematic area of thought, of introspection, of one's own place in that phenomenal world and one's accountability as an artist to something larger than the historical moment and larger than the specific place.

To return to the poem, the 'hand plunged' into the depths of self might recover fragments, bones, terrifying reminders of one's un-wholeness and mortality. Concerning the poet's lack of wholeness, Carter himself has pointed out that the slavery of the West Indian past has meant:

> the disruption of rhythm, the breaking down of the structure of the personality in which integration is lost and action means action, removed from any possibility of being transformed into destiny. [8]

It would seem, then, that the fisherman's doings in the stanza quoted constitute action as action – emphasised by the flat, prosaic quality of the statements; the poet, on the other hand is clearly dissatisfied with action as action and seeks to transform his life's action into 'destiny'. Though the prospect may terrify him, he seeks nothing less then the rediscovery or reconstitution of self:

My course I set, I give my sail the wind
to navigate the islands of the stars
till I collect my scattered skeleton
till I collect...

Note that the setting of this quest for destiny could not be further removed from the 'upheavals of the fifties in Guyana' – 'the islands of the stars' suggests the immensity of this kind of ontological exploration.

Consciousness is painful, therefore when it turns inward upon a self that is someone else's object (the slave) or significantly unwhole or lacking in identity (the ex-slave, the colonial); one recalls Kenneth Ramchand's use of the term 'terrified consciousness' in relation to the racial confrontations (white self/black other) in the West Indies, [9] a term that seems appropriate in this context. There is a philosophical position wherein it is held that consciousness is *of itself* painful and terrifying, involving the kind of vision of nothingness or horror that seems to be suggested in the 'bones' and 'scattered skeleton' of Carter's poem. Although it should be obvious, it is important to stress that such images (and there are numerous similar images in Carter) are not merely evidence of psychic disturbance caused by social or political injustice, but are themselves manifestations of being. The fear does not spring from external causes, but fear here is a dimension of being itself. The terrifying bestial images in 'Groaning in the wilderness' (where humans seem to become dogs – *Succession*, p. 62) or in 'Ground Doves' (where birds are electrocuted and humans burned – *Affinity*, p.43) or 'Our Voice Betrays' (demonic references to time, animals devouring each other and disturbances in the firmament – *Affinity*, p.45) conform to this pattern of meaning. If, turning for a moment to another West Indian poet, we look at Mervyn Morris's *The Pond*, [10] we find that the 'galliwasps and nameless horrors' associated with the pond are discovered in the end to be identified with the self; in other words the image does not spring from nor describe an external source of anxiety, the terror arises from inside and defines not a social but an ontological nightmare.

One finds, therefore, that Carter's particular preoccupation with consciousness balances, in a sense, and extends the strictly political or protest dimension of his work. Some of the poems are, on the one hand, poems of resistance to consciousness itself, with its psychic suffering. In 'Shape and Motion Two', Carter cannot escape the inward tending, reflexive quality of consciousness, which identifies his intimate self with the suffering or fortuity in the people and objects outside the self:

> Watching myself in things I did not make
> [...]
> hearing myself in the loneliness of a child
> [...]
> knowing myself in every moving thing
> [...]
> remembering scorn and naked men in darkness

In 'On a Pavement' he sees the merciful necessity for the obliteration of consciousness altogether:

> Let those minds which are the minds of concrete posts
> blinking out red for stop, amber for slow, green for go
> go mad too and gain a blessed unconsciousness

On the other hand there is the fact, also explored and exploited in Carter's poems, that it is through consciousness that one can liberate the self from some of the terrifying encroachments of the phenomenal world. Where one's sense of space is limited, as it must be not only by physical confinement of any kind, but also by poverty, hunger and squalor; then it is through the resources of consciousness and imagination that one can experience the liberation and extension – that sensation of vastness – that one frequently finds in Carter. Note, for example, how he compensates an image of confinement and physical limitation with images of limitless expansion within a single stanza of the poem 'The Kind Eagle':

Out of tune I carve a monument.
Out of a jagged block of convict years I carve it
The sharp knife of dawn glitters in my hand
but how bare is everything – tall tall tree
infinite air, the unrelaxing tension of the world
and only hope, hope only, the kind eagle soars and wheels in flight.

The stanza is in turn surrounded and summarised by the usage of 'dancing' on the wall of prison. 'This dance of the imagination within the circumstances of physical confinement emphasises the liberating qualities of consciousness, as opposed to some of the confining properties we have been looking at, and that we find as well in 'Who Walks a Pavement' – another poem about imprisonment. In this poem the persona does not evade the prison by means of consciousness:

Iron gate, the terrible hands of a clock,
a calendar with days scratched off and buried,
slant roof of slate black as the floor of tight cell
is not prison, nor a convict shelter.

A prison is go back, go back, go back,
lash of two things shell which is the heart
and heart which is the shell – the hollow tear.
The man of time whose look can stain a sky
who walks a pavement, walks and disappears.

This point is repeated at the end of the poem 'Where are Free Men'

But where are free men, where the endless streets?
Since we were born our wings have had no rest
Our prison of air is worse than one of Iron!

Here imprisonment is obviously not a feature of time, place nor political circumstance, but is rather a feature of consciousness itself.

There is a constant cross-fertilisation, so to speak, of the two opposing tendencies or divisions in consciousness – the liberating tendency and its terrifying, confining opposite. To state it in another way: consciousness of the phenomenal world is always invaded and modified by consciousness of the self and, conversely, consciousness of the self is always tainted by awareness or the world outside. Carter sometimes seems to be playing a game of 'inside-out', examining a situation and his subject consciousness at the same time and in the light of each other, hence there is evinced a concern with the relationship between self and world, and this relationship can be seen ultimately to underlie the dynamic of resistance and protest which dominates a surface dimension of the poems' meaning. In a little poem in *Poems of Affinity* called 'Being Always', Carter elaborates this kind of ontological game of identity for the reader:

> Being, always to arrange
> myself in the world, and the world
> in myself, I try to do both. How
> both are done is difficult. Why,
> I have to ask, do I have to
> arrange anything, when every
> thing is already arranged
> by love's and death's inscrutable
> laws, mortal judiciary, time's
> dollhouse of replaceable heads,
> arms and legs? In another
> house, not time's, time itself arranges
> mine and the world's replacement.

Carter is asking how can one be both passive and active; engaged in both 'action' and 'destiny', true to both the world and the self; and how can one simultaneously inhabit and transcend time? The critic should probably resist the urge to attempt answers to these questions – it is precisely as questions that they maintain their eloquence and imaginative power; as it is likely only in their complex and paradoxical counterpoint of image and symbol, of time and timelessness, that Carter's poems realise their full impact. Carter's poetic imagery achieves what Wilson Harris calls 'a capacity to digest and liberate contrasting spaces'[11] an essential feature of the language of the imagination.

The contrast or juxtaposition of modes of consciousness in Carter's poems seems to ensure that these remain locked in their original paradox; there is no movement towards the kind of emotional accommodation or reconciliation we saw to be evident in Walcott's 'Ruins of a Great House'. Edward Brathwaite is referring to this stubborn core of paradox when he speaks, in the passage quoted earlier, of a poetry 'so nearly harshly peaceful' – the stridency of political struggle and resistance coexists magically with the calm immensities of space, sky and sea, rooted in the coastal plain and foreshore of Carter's Guyana, where

> the pins of the slack pin seine
> irregular the horizon. (*Affinity*, p.29)

Or where

> From the big sweeping ocean of water
> an iron ship rusted and brown anchors itself.
> And the long river runs like a snake
> silent and smooth. (*Succession,* p.57)

The immensity of these spaces suggests and measures the positives, the hope and happiness in Carter's poetry. One of the triumphs of his poetry is surely the impression of space – all the more striking in contrast with other persistent images of confinement and imprisonment of both mind and body. Probably more than any other Caribbean poet, Carter understands what Gaston Bachelard calls 'the poetics of space'.[12] This is not merely the capacity to discover depth and intensity in the ordinary spectacle of the world, as Baudelaire pointed out:

> In certain almost supernatural inner states, the depth of life is entirely revealed in the spectacle, however ordinary, that we have before our eyes, and which becomes the symbol of it. [13]

– although it is obvious in several poems that Carter does precisely this – but Carter also possesses an intuitive understanding of the emotional and psychological value of images of immensity. 'If we could analyse impressions and images of immensity,' Bachelard tells us, 'or what immensity contributes to an image, we should soon enter into a region of the purest sort of phenomenology – a phenomenology without phenomena.'[14] Hence the infinities of air, earth, water and fire in 'University of Hunger', the 'sea' and the 'universe' in 'Till I Collect', the 'tall tall tree' and 'infinite air' of 'The Kind Eagle' – all, in effect, erase the narrow reality of the poet's immediate surroundings and accomplish a sort of liberation of spirit into the purest realms of being and consciousness, where there appears to be a correspondingly infinite peacefulness – the paradoxical 'harsh' peace referred to by Brathwaite. The real product of these images of immensity, Bachelard tells us, is 'consciousness of enlargement'. We feel that we have been promoted to the dignity of the admiring being.'[15] And indeed we derive a sense of the dignity of man and his endeavours on earth from the poems of Martin Carter.

Bachelard's analysis of space and immensity appears so pertinent to the poetry of Carter that one is led to see, as the centre of Carter's poetic works not the poems of resistance, but rather the two 'Poems of Shape and Motion'. These poems emphasise the imaginative centrality of images of space and immensity and ultimately have to do, not with a decline or failure of revolutionary energy, as Gordon Rohlehr suggests[16], but with what Carter himself calls 'the challenge of space in my soul' (*Succession*, p.55) In 'Shape and Motion One' he examines the motion towards the achievement of self – the shape of becoming – through images of the complex organic relationship between 'seed', 'roots', 'swamp' and 'flower', he meditates on the wonder of growth towards fulfilment, not through political action, it is true, but through that sensation of the immensity of the 'space' in his soul that requires to be filled by a corresponding immensity of being. We turn again to Bachelard:

> Immensity is within ourselves. It is attached to a sort of expansion of being that life curbs and caution arrests, but which starts again when we are alone. [17]

At the end of the companion poem, 'Shape and Motion Two', Carter arrives at a simple and powerful statement of the middle shapes or size of man's reality – man is seen as occupying the 'middle earth' between immensity and immediacy, between the contingencies of time and space and the vastness of consciousness. Man is a kind of amphibious creature, caught between the discursive forays of the mind and the grandiose powers of the spirit. Carter locates him on the Guyanese foreshore, between sky and earth, the waves breaking at his feet; he is tormented by the sufferings of his fellows, perhaps, but also gazing at the limitless sky:

I walk slowly in the wind.
I walk because I cannot crawl nor fly. (*Succession,* p.57)

Notes

1. Neville Dawes, Preface to second edition of Martin Carter's *Poems of Resistance* (Georgetown: University of Guyana, 1966).
2. A.J. Seymour, 'The Arts of Guyana' In *Kyk-Over-Al*, 27 (1960)
3. Edward Baugh, *West Indian Poetry 1900-1970* (Jamaica: Savacou, no date), p.13.
4. Baugh, p.13.
5. Eric Roach, article in *Trinidad Guardian*, 9th December, 1971.
6. Edward Brathwaite, 'Resistance Poems: The Voice of Martin Carter' in *Caribbean Quarterly*, Vol.23, Nos. 2 & 3, (June - September, 1977) p.20.
7. The poems of this collection are included in Martin Carter, *Poems of Succession* (London: New Beacon, 1977). All quotes from this edition.
8. Ivan Van Sertima, in *CAM Newsletter*, No.11 (Jul-Nov, 1969).
9. Kenneth Ramchand, *The West Indian Novel and its Background* (London: Faber, 1970, p.223.
10. Mervyn Morris, *The Pond* (London: New Beacon, 1977, (p.42)
11. Wilson Harris, 'A Talk on the Subjective Imagination' in *Explorations*, (Aarhus, Denmark: Dangaroo Press, 1981), p.57.
12. Title of a provocative and enlightening work on aesthetic theory by the French philosopher Gaston Bachelard. *The Poetics of Space* (Boston: Beacon Press, 1969). Translated Maria Jolas.
13. Charles Baudelaire, *Journaux Intimes*, quoted in Bachelard, p.192.
14. Bachelard, p.184.
15. Ibid.
16. Gordon Rohlehr, 'The Creative Writer and West Indian Society', *Kaie* No. 11 (August, 1973), pp.48-77.
17. Bachelard, p.184.

First published in *West Indian Poetry*, eds. Jennifer Jackson and Jeanette B. Allis, Proceedings of the Fifth Annual Conference of West Indian Literature, US Virgin Islands, 1985.

STANLEY GREAVES

A VISION OF LAND AND LANDSCAPE IN THE POEMS OF MARTIN CARTER

Over many years of conversation with Martin Carter references to landscape painting surfaced from time to time. There were moments when he would comment specifically on traditional Chinese painting while relating episodes in the life of the poet Li Po whom he admired as man and poet. On one occasion he described the kind of painting he would like to own. It was to be done Chinese style featuring a mountain and a tiny human figure sitting at the base of it. Carter always felt that representations of the human figure should not be the major focus in landscape painting. They were just another element in the presentation and people need to know their place. Arrogance had no place in true landscape.

In Carter's study is a small colour print of the painting 'The Tempest' by the 15th century Venetian artist Giorgione. This work is often considered as marking the inception of true landscape painting in Europe. It went against the established practice of the time whereby landscape was used merely as a backdrop to human presence. It was an expression of man in-and-of nature as opposed to man and nature, a distinction that appealed to Carter.

By no means can the poems of Carter be categorised as nature poems. By the same token however there exists in his work many references to natural phenomena which he has used to make statements of a metaphysical nature about the human condition. It is the imagery contained in some memorable lines that contrasted strongly with the work of Guyanese artists in the field of landscape painting that caused me to look closely at Carter's work from this perspective. There was a perception that he had dealt with notions of land and landscape that had escaped the attention of some painters of landscape.

Among the first generation pioneer artists of the 1930s, Edward Burrowes was a lover of the English and Dutch Schools of topographical landscape and Hubert Moshett followed the path of Impressionism. Most landscape artists worked between these polarities. Ron Savory in the 1960s dealt with expressionistic presentations of the hinterland – trees, rocks and water whose forms were modified by colour and light. Bernadette Persaud in the 1980s created work of a heightened romantic nature on the theme of mortality. George Simon at the late 80s and early 90s was making forays into the metaphysical. These are the painters whose work to some extent paralleled what Carter was proposing. There is the important distinction, however, that while notions of landscape presentation was central to the work of the artists, allusions to landscape were used by Carter to support the major themes of his poems. Exceptions to this were poems like 'Rain Forest' and 'Cuyuni'.

The words LAND and LANDSCAPE embody two different perceptions. There is an element of the exploitation of natural resources in the former and an attempt to recognise spiritual links to the land in the latter. LAND takes us into the realm of commercial exploitation, feats of civil engineering, travel and trade. A totally different mind set existed in most traditional communities based on hunting and farming that recognised the inherent spirituality of the land. LANDSCAPE takes us into the realm of cosmology, spirituality – the creation and worship of goddesses and a sense of being part of something that transcends mere material existence. One of the essential characteristics of any high culture is the manner in which the two concepts LAND and LANDSCAPE are inextricably linked or merged into a single construct that supports the existence of the people of that culture.

One definition of Mankind could be – creatures who feel/believe that there is a spiritual reality behind the material aspect of things. This belief when applied to LAND produces LANDSCAPE. In focusing on the concept of LANDSCAPE in Carter's poems we are engaged in examining work which has been produced by personal effort unsupported by relevant concepts of any kind subscribed to by our creole culture. Dealing with LANDSCAPE brings us into the realm that fuses philosophy, religion and art. The only civilisation to have achieved this to an astonishing degree is that of China where artists have been able to resource propositions and concepts in art, religion and philosophy in the pursuit of landscape painting. A thing recognised and admired by Carter.

There is no Guyanese system of the meditative or contemplative life, save perhaps that of the Amerindian shaman whose culture is not accessible to the majority of the creole and 'cosmopolitan' population. The term 'cosmopolitan' has a very specific meaning in Guyana, rooted in the social history of the country. 'Cosmopolitan' is a purely descriptive term meaning a person, and by extension, a people of mixed racial descent. Given the non-existence of an indigenous philosophical system, we therefore have to assume a policy of appropriating what we need from divers sources with apologies to no one. A form of eclecticism would develop that carries its own dangers. Wilson Harris, longtime friend of Carter, views the use of significant appropriations from wherever, as a potential source of strength. The *caveat* of misinterpretation and misapplication, however, still applies.

> Synchronicity implies a gestation of variable yet interconnected motifs and imageries in all cultures, which assist us to salvage meaning in an apparently meaningless world.

Carter, on the other hand, has often said that 'Salvation lies under your feet, you don't have to look elsewhere.' This is not the place to examine either proposition adequately, but they do set the polarities of the discussion on the relationship of LAND/LANDSCAPE. It will be enough then to say that it is the role of symbolic thought expressed through the personal aesthetics of Carter's poetry that is of concern here as regards the proposed theme.

Coming to terms with Carter's propositions will pose problems of understanding and relevance to the reader whose own relationship to both LAND and LANDSCAPE will have to be scrutinised. In the context of our society, instead of both poet and reader sharing the same culture based concerns in philosophy and aesthetics, it is the poet Carter who is being placed in the position of leader/shaman to provoke such concerns. In this, a role which has been conferred on him not without protestation on his part, he presents values that relate to the spiritual and material development of the community or nation, to be ignored at their peril. One feature of Carter's use of landscape is the link he creates with the complex social history of Guyana. The complexity can be seen in the ways Carter makes reference to topography, social and political history and personal development through illustrations of landscape.

In, 'Not I With This Torn Shirt', the very opening lines establish the parameters of our history: 'They call here/ – Magnificent Province!/ Province of mud!/Province of flood!/ Plantation – feudal coast!'. 'Magnificent Province' – a land of wealth in the eyes of the coloniser, provokes the poet's ironic response seen through the eyes of the oppressed. The first reference is geographic/climatic referring to the coastal plain, fertile but prone to seasonal flooding. While not the imagery of traditional landscape painting it could perhaps be used in a symbolic sense as Burrowes did in a small ochreous monochrome painting entitled 'The Retired Civil-servant' – a piece of driftwood, a couple of coconut shells lying on mud near to muddy water. The other reality is of social history, the plantation system of sugarcane cultivation based on slave labour. The sustained irony of the poet as slave poses another question:

Who are the magnificent here?
Not I with this torn shirt
but they, in their white mansions
by the trench of blood!

Shirts torn, and by implication un-torn, become the symbol of status for both slave and slave-master. The colour white in 'white mansions' refers to both house and implied shirt as symbols of a corrupt system that has created trenches of blood. The major theme here is of a feudal slave-based society, questioning the identities of both slave and slave-master that rest on the sub-theme of LAND. The concept is further illustrated in 'Like the Blood of Quamina':

Across the night face of the river
whenever cane is ripe

there is deep red flame –
flame like a smouldering hill of fire

The 'night face' being black belongs both to river and slave. Fields of ripe canes were set on fire to burn off the razor sharp dried leaves and chase away snakes and other vermin. An extended wish/meaning here would include the slave-masters as well. Smouldering fire represents the emotions of the slaves that led to the kind of revolution of which Quamina was a leader. A man who, though against the use of excessive force by the slaves, ironically died through such excesses applied by British troops, his blood, 'flowing through the green forest'. Here, the very landscape becomes a symbolic participant in the very human drama that is creating history. The image has strong visual connotations for the artist. There are hills on fire, the black face of river and slave, Quamina's blood becoming river. Green and red – the strongest of contrasting colours being the colours of life, of forest and man respectively. And yet such a landscape, possibly of epic proportions, has escaped the mind-eye of the landscape artists. There is another small painting by Burrowes of a creek in the jungle, both enveloped in flames, that could be possibly be interpreted as being of a similar nature to Carter's vision. What is missing, however, is a sense of scale.

'Death Of A Slave', makes the same proposition linking social history with landscape. It is obvious that the whole drama has the land as some kind of impartial stage. Treated in this manner it becomes LAND in the eyes of poet or artist. By transforming land to LANDSCAPE, the land becomes a text rather than stage. As a text it remains available to be read by subsequent generations giving them a sense of their own *locus* in space and time. According to Harris it is a text:

> In which they can read themselves in a different way and read the world around them in a different way, the landscape around them, the living text of the landscape around them.

These words, embodying a sense of catharsis, substantiate Carter's own proposition in other poems, but 'Death Of A Slave' sees the entire land and inhabitants becoming transformed by the shroud of slavery that touches everything:

Above green cane arrow
is blue sky
Beneath green arrow
is brown earth
Dark is the shroud of slavery
over the river
over the forest
over the field.

Further in the poem we are given an image that has frightening implications.

The land so far has been producing sugarcane crops, but under the shroud of slavery: 'time plants the seeds of anger'. Such seeds of anger can produce plants that carry the fatal fruits of armed clash in which 'all are involved/ all are consumed!' as he puts it in 'You Are Involved'. This was witnessed in the death of Quamina, among the deaths of countless others, slave and master alike, who have now become part of the spirit of the LANDSCAPE.

Moving from the insistent theme of slavery Carter moves into the realm of *pathetic fallacy* in 'Death Of A Comrade', to make the very land mourn the fallen one. Man is placed in the centre of creation. Nature itself, of which death is a part, does not regard the demise of the Comrade as part of the divine or natural plan. His death becomes an outrage. In a sense we are asked to witness the land under another form of slavery, the system of colonial political domination that refuses to enfranchise a people. And so the earth mourns in splendour with an anticipation of hope: 'for even now the greener leaf explodes/ sun brightens stone / and all the river burns'. These are all images of strong visual content. We are not enveloped in metaphysical presentations of a kind impossible to relate to in purely visual terms, the kind of encounters experienced in much of Carter's later work.

In the later poem 'Rain Forest', from *Poems of Affinity*, nature itself becomes the first focus of attention to be replaced in the end by man:

> ...The hustling creeks
> of identical water are beautiful
> and still, one cry, one however begun
> human cry, contains all.

There is a swift transition from an aesthetic perception of the creek in the first lines to a focus of attention on mankind. We sense that while the land was created by Nature it is the presence and the affirmation of man by man that transforms LAND into LANDSCAPE through 'one however begun human cry'. A cry that puts man in the centre of the universe. This is of course a very limited application of what Carter believes 'contains all', but which serves the purpose of this essay.

'Not Hands Like Mine' addresses the issue created by the colonial occupation, one can almost say colonial creation of what is now called GUYANA. This is the creation of a complex society involving the original inhabitants, the (misnamed) Amerindian peoples, the Europeans and the procession of enslaved and indentured peoples removed from their own cultures, 'Not hands/ like mine/ these Carib altars knew;/ nameless and quite forgotten are the gods'. The hands are those of the new arrivals in the land of the Caribs. The colonisers in their arrogance have destroyed the altars, but not the memories of ancient gods of the Caribs, but have been quite successful with the slave population. Altars actual and symbolic have to exist in the concept of LANDSCAPE which the colonisers in their minds have transformed to LAND. The following lines convey a message of despair, but if we have read Harris correctly, the 'language of imagination' contains the power to recreate LANDSCAPE. Carter has a slightly divergent view I feel in this expression, 'A thing is intimated, it cannot be recalled, you let intuition work for you... you cannot control nature.' We can indulge ourselves by attempting to reconcile the two positions by linking RECREATE to RECALL, and IMAGINATION to INTUITION. Put together in this way they give a somewhat more extended meaning to the specific course of action of replacing, in a metaphorical sense, the altars of the ancient gods thus re-establishing LANDSCAPE in the consciousness of man. In the cultural mix that is Guyana, a case can perhaps be made that while such optimism might be considered misplaced and even impossible at the collective or national level, it may well work at the individual level. This I feel is the message of George Simon's metaphysical landscape paintings that reaffirm 'these Carib altars' even though:

Now still
are the fields
covered by the floods;
and those rivers roll
over altars gone;

Throughout conversations with Carter over the years he has always employed a device which I called 'couplets', perhaps 'philosophical couplets', though 'high sounding' might be a more accurate description. He would take two words to create a discourse that illustrated a philosophical principle which he would then apply to specific situations. One such couplet is 'THIS not THAT' establishing the concept of specificity which I in turn would now apply to LANDSCAPE as being THIS (the desired condition) and not THAT – meaning LAND. Another such couplet is FORCE and FORM. These were identified as '...working together as presentation'. In this particular conversation, I offered the illustration based on ceramics where FORCE became the application of an idea to create FORM in clay towards the PRESENTATION of a vessel. The life of the FORM is expressed in the tension or dialogue existing within the perceived characteristics of the FORM. An application of this concept makes the Cuyuni River the PRESENTATION in the poem 'Cuyuni'. In the sense that Nature/FORCE produces LANDSCAPE/FORM of which the Cuyuni River becomes the PRESENTATION.

The most awesome visage of Nature as LANDSCAPE is presented in 'Cuyuni' where the river becomes Nature personified and is transformed into a lens to focus its power. In the face of this, hubris – human arrogance – is put into its proper place:

So then if perhaps in some stupid fit of arrogance
I said something any fool can understand

and this river heard me, and decided on vengeance,
where is one who could give me
weapons I shall be able to use?

In a shift of position it is nature now through LANDSCAPE that defines man. Man in turn recognising this immanence has to apply it to LAND (a misapplied perception at most) reaffirming its original condition of LANDSCAPE which was never really lost. It is an attempt to reverse a kind of rape, a most confounding thought, but an attempt nonetheless that has to be approached through the all encompassing power of the LOVE that transforms everything.

and still, one cry, one however begun
human cry, contains all.

The painting 'The Tempest' says it all. LANDSCAPE becomes the theme of the work. The three figures including a mother and child are in-and-of the LANDSCAPE which at the same time also includes man's monuments to himself as exemplified by the buildings, bridge and broken column. We have then a total PRESENTATION of LAND/LANDSCAPE existing in harmony with proper relationships being observed.

The opening lines of 'Cuyuni' provide the image of the poet-as-man contained in a matrix of rock/water. The poet/man therefore is to the LANDSCAPE of the river as it itself is to the original LANDSCAPE of Nature/FORCE. This proposition states that the spirit of the land existed *ab initio,* but man needed to recognise this as something that cannot be conferred. We have moved now to LANDSCAPE that was never LAND. It is no longer a question of the transformation of land by man but rather the transformation of man by the ORIGINAL LANDSCAPE.

If any of you can I shall be willing to take the risk.
But I must warn you if good advices
prove as useless as a paddle in the falls
you will be happy to be transformed as much as I will have to
by the side of this menacing, sullen river...

This essay has addressed the materiality and spirituality of land through the mechanisms of LAND and LANDSCAPE. I have not attempted to deal with the landscape of the spirit which is contiguous and has to be dealt with on some other occasion. In restricting the reading of Carter to the issues of LAND and LANDSCAPE, the main themes of the poems used have been put to one side. This inevitably creates a limited reading of each poem, a condition I hope that will be accepted for the intended purpose of the essay. My contention is that unless we address the issue head-on we will continue to be strangers to the LANDSCAPE just as were the antecedents of so many of us. National aspirations of all kinds become affected. Instead of a nation that produces acceptable FORMS as a result of our endeavours we are in danger instead of producing monstrous entities.

The final word is to the landscape painters of Guyana to exercise greater rigour in the development and application of artistic intellect and imagination to their creations in the manner of Ron Savory, Bernadette Persaud and George Simon at home, and Aubrey Williams and Frank Bowling abroad. Furthermore, great or significant paintings in this genre cannot be produced if LANDSCAPE is not lived.

August 1997

KWAME DAWES

A COMMENTARY ON MARTIN CARTER'S DISCUSSION OF HIS POETICS

Reading Carter talk about poetry reminds you that his fascination with the poetic process is almost an obsession. His interest is classic in the sense that he approaches the language of defining poetry through Western discourse and notions of prosody. His constant reference to the etymology of words – the Greek of words – reveals something about the careful classicism that is inherent in his work. The other fascinating truth about Carter is the manner in which he seems determined to avoid the label of nationalist poet. There is an easily understood tendency to read Carter as the 'people's' poet – as the voice of contemporary post-colonial Guyana. But Carter himself seems reticent about this title and seeks to explain it away. In a talk with Fred D'Aguiar, Carter reveals this important quality of caution:

> FD: As a poet, you're seen as a national poet in the sense that in Guyana when people think of poetry, your name comes up immediately as the poet who appears to have captured in this half of the century what it is that Guyana had been through... This could be a trap, an obligation, it could also be something that may follow you. How much of a sense do you have of that, especially given the Guyanese context and so on?
>
> MC: First of all, I think the word national is a misnomer. It is totally irrelevant to what you're doing. And if any adjective be put to it, Guyanese would be the only adjective that is permissible. But to say that a man's a national poet is making a conjunction of incompatible things. So I would not acknowledge that term national in the first place. The second point that you are making – that people may repeat, and then may write or say that something that has been written represents something else – comes back to craft, really, to a great extent. You get a sound occurring, let us say, very early in a given line, and another sound occurring way down in a following line. And those two sounds connect the two lines. So one line may seem to be of a different direction than the other line, yet they are connected by an element in both lines. What I think they mean when they say it stands for this and it stands for that is that it somehow reminds them of their own speech. It reminds them of tones, tones that they themselves have not been able to describe or express. But somehow you get, what is the best word for it, reverberations, I think that is the best word for what I think they call different things. And they use other names because those names are available, easily available. People may understand what they say, but they don't mean that really. As I said in the first case, applying words like nationalism and so on doesn't really help anyone to understand.

D'Aguiar cannot be blamed for his question because he is putting to Carter what has been said repeatedly of his work. Carter responds by shifting the issue from the politics of his verse to the poetics of his verse and the way that poetry is apprehended by the reader. There is almost an unwillingness to become typed as a 'political poet' as against a poet fascinated by questions of form, craft and the basic principles of poetry as a complete vocation in itself. Carter does not offer polemic notions of the poem as servant to society, he resists those ideas, and yet one recognises a contradiction in the very fire and engagement of his early poetry. This is part of the fundamental progression of the poet from a writer of political fire to a writer who seems increasingly drawn into the self, into the poetics of the artist as an isolated figure generating the poem through the 'muse' of discovery. When D'Aguiar attempts again to credit the poet with a socio-political role, a role that has come to be used to understand poets like Kamau Brathwaite, Derek Walcott and Lorna Goodison, Carter shifts the discussion again – somehow avoiding the role that D'Aguiar seems to want to draw him into. It is the business of naming, of giving voice to experience that is regarded as central to the anti-colonial or post-colonial agenda of writers like Walcott and Brathwaite. Carter does not embrace this notion. He, instead, suggests that the discovery of meaning belongs to the 'people', the ones who read the work. He somehow manages to withdraw the poet from the equation:

> FD: So you don't think you can have a poet who might coincide in his writing with a movement that would cover a fixed geographical space? For example the evolution of Guyanese thinking as a geographical reality as distinct from British Guiana. Now a poet coming out of that might be seen to spearhead the articulation of those sentiments where in the populace they can't quite put the words in it, but they recognise the sentiment when they see a combination of words in a particular order called a poem written by you. And they take this poem and say, 'This is what we mean by us as distinct from you.' When that happens, the poem has taken on a communal kind of life, it appears that you've tapped into something much bigger than anything you could have been thinking about consciously as you put the poem together. How much do you subscribe to that notion of the poet as a kind of medium?
>
> MC: In a poem I wrote, which puts it as I would like to put it, these lines occur: 'If these are riddles, then riddles write themselves.' By that I mean... that there is a stage in the production of a poem where you don't know what you have written, and it's not until you are finished that to some extent, you realise what you have done. Now even that is limited, because there have been many cases in which, by accident, or by someone calling my attention to it, that I've gone back and looked at a poem, and I have discovered things which I am quite sure I did not have in my mind at that time. So what you are saying is correct in that it is possible to pick up and to say things which are present to you without you yourself being consciously aware of them. Now I think that happens with the readers, too. For instance, I'll give you an example, a very simple example, but it makes the point. There's a poem in which I had a line ending in 'want.' Something-something 'where it wants.' 'Where it wants.' Now read at a certain level, 'it wants' would leave the word 'to' understood. But someone could come to you and say 'where it wants' meaning 'where it needs,' instead of 'where it wants to,' which is an intention. So we have a need substituted for an intention. Well, and yet when that comes to you years after the poem has been written, you go back and read it and you are corrected by that response from someone who is not in the slightest bit interested in that level of the poem. So that an unlearned person, a person

> without experience in these things can come up with something which is very enlightening...

Carter will not lay claim to the role of 'spearheader' of a movement, or voice of a nation. He suspects that label. I do not think that this is merely an act of coyness, for there is in Carter, a sophisticated manner of treating the question of nationalism in poetry that seems to be immensely modernist. His articulations, outside of the poem, tend to argue for a notion of the poem as an end in itself. There is the element of discovery in the construction of a poem, the sense that a poet does not 'set out' to write a poem about a given theme or idea; that the poem simply happens. There is something strangely irreconcilable about Carter, the commentator on his poetry, and Carter the poet. But what is more likely the case is that we are looking at two different poets: Carter of a younger and more engaged period, and Carter, a mature man and poet increasingly fascinated by the vocation of poetry and the dynamics of the poetic experience as a mystery-filled experience. This curious contention emerges when Carter speaks about dialect in his poetry. In his book *Come Back to Me My Language*, Ted Chamberlin, had seen in the poem 'University of Hunger' a language form that is 'unmistakably Guyanese.' (p.95) Chamberlin's read is a sophisticated one, making these distinctions in his discussion of Carter's use of dialect:

> Or rather they are unmistakable, and it is precisely this uncertainty that is of particular interest. The opening phrase of Carter's poem reads: 'is the university of hunger the wide waste./ is the pilgrimage of man the long march.' What appears as an interrogative in standard English is in fact an assertion in Guyanese dialect (and well beyond, in fact, for dropping the pronoun before the verb is very common in West Indian speech...) The ambivalence created by these lines depends upon the allegiances of its language both to the authenticity of West Indian speech and to the authority of a lyrical tradition of English literature that goes back at least to the fourteenth century. (p.95)

D'Aguiar picks up on this read and puts the question of language to Carter suggesting that this use of 'dialect' represents a distinct use of an idiom. Carter is quick to make a distinction between the discussion of idiom, which he sees as a linguistic question related to the question of dialect, and the discussion of poetics which is quite a different thing for him. It is an important distinction that Carter is making here for it tells us a great deal about his own position on the business of poetics and language:

> Then you move into poetics, you're giving it another order. And my contention is that while it may have traces of its origin, we are not to allow ourselves to fall into the genetic fallacy of confusing the result with the source. So while the source may be the dialect in linguistics, as a linguistic category, the result is a poem in the poetic category... I would like to suggest that when we move from linguistics and move into poetics we are dealing with things that I call emergences, which no poet, I think, really sets out to do. But all that happens is the poem is

> a result... In other words, the poet himself discovers that he's written a poem only at the end. (*Talk Yuh Talk*)

Carter, then, will not concur that he is exploring an idiom that is related to nationalism. Carter is playing on an idiom, but using that idiom largely in a standard English context. It is the break from standard English that gives the opening lines of 'University of Hunger' their weight and importance. His norm, then, is the standard form. And in many ways, this is the norm of the West Indian poet. Those who are more inclined to explore dialect forms do so, not with the purpose of juxtaposing the dialect with the standard form as read from the standard perspective, but seek to create a dualism of vision, a double-headedness that allows both languages to dialogue with each other. This is not Carter's agenda, and it is in this that we begin to see Carter as a figure whose approach to poetic discourse in the West Indies is deeply traditional and rooted in Western models of poetic discourse.

There is a perceivable progression in Martin Carter's poetry that begs for some explanation. His *Selected Poems* chart in one place the scope and breadth of his work, from the direct language of 'Shines the Beauty of My Darling' in which the poet articulates his commitment to the poem as a political tool, to the dense riddles that he offers in some of his most recent poetry. Carter has progressed and one is tempted to see the pattern as a movement from the public to the private. If this is a simplistic read, it is one that Carter encourages us to embrace, for Carter's life does make that progression associated with ageing. And there is much in his writing that suggests that he is really constantly writing about the purpose of poetry, its use, its relevance both for society and for the artist – the poet – himself.

> If I wanted
> I could make pictures of night
> the map of stars above the mass of water
> the mass of water underneath the stars
> the beauty of my beloved
> like a flower bringing dawn light into dark
>
> Yes, if I wanted
> I could close my eyes right now
> and bring these things like life into my brain. (*Selected Poems*, p. 37)

There is an explicit tension that he offers here between what he perceives to be 'life' and what he considers the function of the imagination. The act of closing the eyes becomes, then, an act of escape, a journey into the 'unreal' world of romanticism. Carter suggests that he could do these things, but something else forces him from the lyrical, the personal – something forces him to open his eyes because of the 'newness' of these times:

> but new are these times
> and no matter where I turn

the fierce revolt goes with me
like a kiss– (*Selected Poems*, p. 37)

Carter's romantic reality is a fierce one that is rooted in the political realities facing the people who are oppressed all over the world. The earnestness of his expression here could border on the trite cliché – the easy type. But Carter's playful irony, his ability to transform a love poem into a lyric justifying political articulation is testament to his wit and the distinction of his particular imagination:

and like the whole world dancing
for liberation from the slave maker
shines the beauty of my darling in her laughing eyes. (*ibid*)

For Carter in the early fifties, the muse was no longer the 'white goddess' who would haunt a poet like Derek Walcott, but 'the fight for freedom' – the inclination toward political action. This poem becomes one of his many articulations of his *raison d'etre* as a poet. There is a terrible passion that consumes this grand conceit:

No!
I will not still my voice!
I have
too much to claim –
if you see me
looking at books
or coming to your house
or walking in the sun
know that I look for fire! ('Looking at your Hands', p.39)

The poet enacts his quest for fire in books by alluding to a Shakespearean 'pseudo-rebel' whose times of sleep are an escape, a kind of defeat in the face of the power of colonialism. It is Caliban, in Shakespeare's *Tempest* who wakes to dream again. But Carter unsettles this image of defeat and offers his own version, one that offers the weight of his commitment to writing about struggle and change: 'I do not sleep to dream, but dream to change the world.'

There is much about this that is youthful and exuberant, and it is inevitable that the poet who will emerge some fifty years later will be far more reflexive, a great deal more subdued in his passion. There is a significant movement from the livid passions of these early poems to the complex language and lyricism of his later poems. Indeed, Carter charts the movement. His poetry reflects on the uses of poetry and one senses in the later poems a disillusionment with the poetics of revolution. Irony becomes far greater and one senses also that the very language that Carter employs is seen to have different uses. The work is not as accessible, not as direct. The poet is no longer shouting.

GEMMA ROBINSON

MARTIN CARTER'S POETIC ESSAYS IN COMMUNITY

In his address to the Eighth Convocation Ceremony at the University of Guyana, Martin Carter said 'nationally and internationally, we want to mutter "All gone", acutely aware of our victim role in a ruthless world.'[1] Carter's speech offers an implicit critique of the Guyanese government, and the 'free community of valid persons' that he argues for was the utopian opposite of the political situation facing Guyana in the 1970s. This moment of assemblage at the University paradoxically underlines both the bringing together of people and a profound sense of cultural confusion. It is such an aspiration for cohesion and a continuing recognition of the conflictive nature of society that I think begins to define Carter's discourse on community, and his address reveals a writer concerned to rethink radically the scope and scale of the term. The collective 'want to mutter "All gone"' which Carter identifies – emphasising the breakdown of society – is expressed as a blank statement, the two words providing a nihilistic ballast for each other. Yet the address is not one of defeat: the utterance "All gone" is a wish rather than a statement of fact, and Carter is careful to make the distinction that if there are 'victims' in his 'ruthless world' this is a 'role' – a part played and therefore open to change, rather than an inherent identity. Similarly, Carter's poetic essays in community can perhaps be seen as *essais*, scriptive *attempts* to create a poetic space within which varying concepts of community can be reassessed and reconstructed.[2]

In response to Carter's societal concerns, Wilson Harris's 'The Place of the Poet in Modern Society: A Glance at Two Guyanese Poets',[3] focuses on *Poems of Resistance*, arguing that the poet should be seen as 'an agent of conscience – rather than facile consensus – within a colonial complex in which the legacies of the past held out no straightforward path into the future'.[4] This review rejects Sidney King's revolutionary enthusiasm for Carter's work: 'when the people began to display their youthful vigour, Carter turned his attention to nurturing the forces of the radiant future'.[5] While Harris is perceptive in identifying how Carter would later be classified as a political poet, his attempt to broaden the criticism of Carter's work involves a further classification – that of the 'visionary poet'.[6] Harris concludes his essay with the suggestion that Carter's work is more accurately associated with prophetic apoliticism. However, the idea that Carter is a poet *sui generis* betrays a different, but as equally ideological an interpretation of Carter as that written by King. For as King asserts Carter's immersion in 'the forces of the radiant future', Harris writes him as the lone seer of the future.

Other reviews have asserted the political engagement of Carter's poetry. Edward Kamau Brathwaite in 'Resistance Poems: The Voice of Martin

Carter' critically identifies Carter's early poetry as that of a self-styled 'people's revolutionary poet; their cultured street preacher'.[7] His review of Carter looks beyond the poetry of the 1950s to *Poems of Succession* (1977), suggesting that Carter's poetic voice changed according to the contemporary political climate in Guyana – the 1950s 'street preacher' became a 'voice' reticently articulating a 'post-1962 disillusionment consciousness'.[8] This summary treatment appears to me overly categorical and, as I hope to show, the progression of Carter's work does not yield such easy designations. In 'The Poet and Citizen in a Degraded Community: Martin Carter's *Poems of Affinity* (1978-1980)' Gordon Rohlehr attends to the simultaneous implications of disillusionment and resistance in Carter's work, but perhaps fails to emphasise fully the subtleties within the poet's understanding of community.[9] While it is reductive to deny the political urgency of Carter's collections, it is also reductive finally to trace out a specious development from youthfully optimistic poetry of political protest to a poetry that marks Carter's withdrawal from, and disillusionment with, the political sphere. Sidney King's collective poet clashes with Harris's visionary. Brathwaite marks the juvenile public poet's transformation into a jaded private poet. This essay is an attempt to destabilize these chronological and interpretive divisions: the embracing framework of 'community' will, I hope, reveal the broad span of Carter's poetic concerns without limiting his identity to that of a political poet. As Carter writes: 'for political activity is not an end in itself, but only a means to an end, the end of social change'.[10]

Carter's 1974 address continues this dynamic of social change: his discussion is not posed as a debate on a given set of social relations, but as a transformation: 'from what we function as – an aggregation of begging, tricking, bluffing, cheating subsistence seekers and assorted hustlers – into a free community of valid persons'.[11] The pantomimic 'hustlers' are a motley assemblage of people united, it seems, only to provide a network of mutual exploitation. Aggregation here becomes the opposite of community. Indeed the finely timed description of this aggregation – with its repetition of present participial endings and the alliterative 'subsistence seekers and assorted hustlers' – seems purposefully over-declamatory, as if to emphasise the uncluttered, utopian option of 'a free community of valid persons'. What is perhaps abstruse about Carter's discussion is his refusal to intimate to his audience the concrete ways in which this community can be created. Yet I would argue that such a criticism fails to engage with the core premise of the argument: Carter consistently implies that the creation of a free community of valid persons is a collective endeavour, not the following out of a singularly authored manifesto. He condemns the government's divisive tactics of rule as a bid to describe some one or other individual or section of the community as anti-Guyanese, as though indeed there is some holy text somewhere which spells out what being pro-Guyanese is. But the truth is that every society is made of conflicting interests: the interests of the rulers and the interests of the ruled; competition within the ranks of the rulers and competition within the ranks of the ruled; and it is from the creative encounter of these interests, from the clash of all these forces that a valid hierarchy of values emerges to challenge the very premises that sponsored them. Nor can this encounter be abolished.[12]

Carter carefully undermines any thought that he is preaching a gospel of Guyanese identity, refusing to accept even the possibility of such a 'holy text'. But this refusal does not seek to close down debate. Profoundly aware of the conflicting pressures that accompany any grouping of people, Carter makes the uncompromising assertion that this conflict can never be abolished. Yet the options left to such a group are boldly configured as positive: 'from the clash of all these forces [...] a valid hierarchy of values emerges to challenge the very premises that sponsored them'. Carter's concern for cultural difference and the complexity of shifting social relations is part of a suggestion that diversity creates new possibilities for coexistence as much as it can cause societal friction. A 'free community of valid persons', it seems, is not a sterile assembly of people; rather Carter picks up the energetic productivity of his 'subsistence seekers and assorted hustlers' and suggests that the creative energy of conflict can be channelled as a productive force as opposed to a network of exploitation. The 'validity' of a hierarchy of values emerges then not as a 'given', but as a communally achieved system.

The address should not be read as a piece of social planning – Carter does not speak as a man with answers. Thus when he requests 'respect of the riskers who go forward boldly to participate in the building of a free community of valid persons', it is a demand for collective self-respect and a demand for collective participation. The 'riskers', he implies, need not only be those making speeches and formulating academic arguments, but the risks of community building should be taken by those in the audience, should be shouldered by all.[13] Responding to Carter's democratic hope, I first consider several figures among those taking the 'risk' of community building in Guyana and, progressing from these parallels, reveal the success of Carter's poetic essays in community. A. J. Seymour, Wilson Harris and Walter Rodney – three men spanning three generations – each create a different sense of community as they discuss, derive and promote strategies for coexistence. Together, Seymour, Harris and Rodney address the need to redraw the boundaries of 'community', and that each approaches this differently demonstrates that these boundaries are far from settled.

A. J. Seymour's involvement in the construction of Guianese cultural identity lies in the formation of *Kyk-over-al*. The first editorial in December 1945 summarises the heuristic outlook of the magazine:

> What are our aims? *Kyk-over-al* we hope will be an instrument to help forge a Guianese people, to make them conscious of their intellectual and spiritual

> possibilities. There's so much we can do as a people if we can get together more, and with this magazine as an outlet, the unified cultural organizations can certainly build, we believe, some achievement of common pride in the literary world.[14]

As indicated by the name, *Kyk-over-al* (a Dutch word meaning 'watch over all', and the name of the first European trading post established in Guiana in the sixteenth century), Seymour's Guiana is a site of both colonial inheritance and emergent nationalism. The disparate congregation of immigrants, yoked together over three hundred years of imperial domination, Seymour hopes, will grow conscious of its unity which, once forced, can be refigured as cooperative. Forging a Guianese people becomes a twofold endeavour that involves first, the acceptance of the colonial formation of Guiana, and second, a commitment to uniting the people joined by such a legacy. And Seymour's editorial and poetic work consistently demonstrates this twofold endeavour. The special issues of *Kyk-over-al* devoted to anthologies of West Indian poetry and Seymour's own collection of poems, *The Guiana Book* (1948) represent his most direct attempts to foster 'the achievement of common pride in the literary world'.[15] Poems such as 'Raleigh comes', 'Kykoveral', 'Slaves' and 'For Christopher Columbus' stress the sweeping historical vista of *The Guiana Book*, and mark an implicit emphasis upon the creation of an overarching framework of national unity. Seymour's notion of a Guianese people, then is reliant upon an idea of community that privileges the collective, rather than the individual. As such, his poetry can be read as an ambassadorial promotion of this potential community.

Wilson Harris, in a considered but critical review of *The Guiana Book*, argues that Seymour's poetry 'is to be associated with the contemporary artifice of a closed union, a finished work, a collective unity', but Harris also admits that 'Seymour's genius lies in the spirit and exploration of the name, the epic tradition, the historical monument'.[16] These two seemingly contradictory evaluations of Seymour identify both the failure and the success of his editorial and poetic work. Consider, for instance, this extract from 'Kykoveral':

> Kykoveral
> Strange name for stones, a heap of stones
> But a strong name to take imagination
> And tie it to a peak in Time.[17]

The sweeping expanse of the lines supports Harris's assessment of Seymour as an explorer, even creator, of Guiana's historical monuments. However, in Seymour's symbols of collectivity the poet's adoption of a specious notion of shared history can also be read. Harris writes that *The Guiana Book* aspires to be 'a finished work' representing 'a collective unity', and such an aspiration for neat closure points up the forced nature of Seymour's poetry. In 'Kykoveral' Seymour articulates the monumental significance of tying 'strong names' 'to a peak in Time', but the lines typify the simplicity of the poet's historical project. In his concern to argue that Guiana has the cultural resources for nationhood, Seymour elides the 'strangeness' of Kykoveral; glossing over the incongruity that Guiana's national monuments may also be symbols of imperial conquest, the poem begins to petrify rather than commemorate Guianese history.

Harris's other critical essays form a small but dense discussion of writers' position in society, a discussion which complicates Seymour's simplified view of the relationship between literature and the formation of nationhood. In 'The Writer and Society' Harris discusses the writer as someone who imaginatively pieces together the 'consciousness' of a community, and he recalls the liminal character of Tiresias as his symbol of the writer's role:

> What one finds in this drama of consciousness is that Tiresias is the embodiment of death as well as life, masculine as well as feminine, because it is through him that the writer lays bare a fiction corresponding to a community whose wholeness in reality cannot exist except by confessing its own insubstantial limits, thereby invoking not only the horror of disorientation but an implosive compass of freedom as well within such insubstantial limits overlooked by prejudice from the microcosm of society and rejected equally by prejudice from the macrocosm of inanimate nature. A fiction of implosion indeed we can never completely grasp in the way we appear to grasp a documentary realism of the surfaces of life whose object after all is to maintain the *status quo* of a given one-sided assumption.[18]

The androgyny of Tiresias is certainly an appealing symbol for Harris – unlimited by gender boundaries, freed from the conventional states of life and death, this character can also embody an extended notion of community as the sum of all people, living and dead, male and female. Harris is partially reiterating the almost proverbial claim that fictions reveal society to itself, but he is also concerned to extend and elaborate the reach of this argument. 'The writer lays bare a fiction corresponding to a community whose wholeness in reality cannot exist except by confessing its own insubstantial limits'. While Harris's syntactical arrangement allows the third clause to refer to either 'a fiction' or 'a community', it is most revealing when read as a statement on community. Claiming the insubstantiality and limitlessness of fiction is not an innovative suggestion, but when such qualities are carried across to describe the limits of community, the innovation becomes apparent. Harris does not go so far as to say that fictions invent community, but he strives to clarify their reciprocal relationship, suggesting that a community can achieve a Tiresian wholeness only through rejecting the notion of wholeness as synonymous with substantial limits. Community for Harris is an abstract notion – literally an entity of 'insubstantial limits' – and rather than attempting to bring a concept of community into focus, he insists that the very opposite is required. The 'horror of disorientation' and 'an implosive compass of freedom' are Harris's terms for the potential and painful liberty a community can reach, terms which provide an insight into the tensions between freedom and stability that are encountered in a post-colonial community.

There is, of course, an alternative argument. Harris's holistic, even Jungian community can be as unsatisfactory a model as any attempt to portray the concrete links between people that occur on the 'surfaces of life'. He suggests that the writer 'both transcends and undermines (or deepens if you will) the mode of society since the truth of community which he pursues is not a self-evident fact: it is neither purely circumscribed by nor purely produced by economic circumstance'.[19] Certainly a community defined only in relation to economics is rightly seen by Harris as overly narrow, but I would also argue that his own statements have a similar narrowness. 'Community' is a fluid, insubstantially limited entity, but 'truth' it seems is not. The 'truth of community' may not be described as a 'self-evident fact', yet Harris still articulates it as 'the truth' – a singular finite noun, something which can be pursued, and possibly delimited and captured. Harris's vision of community and the writer may be less actively creative than it at first seems, at odds with Carter's sense of 'the creative encounter' between clashing interests. According to Harris, a writer '*lays bare* a fiction'[20] – a curious verb which suggests that the author uncovers a pre-existing fiction, as well as suggesting the self-conscious fictionality of Harris's writing. The 'wholeness' of community, then, might be best understood not as the breaking of limits, but also as the breaking of surface limitations in order to allow the real limits of community to be perceived. In this light, *Palace of the Peacock* (1960) offers Harris's utopian glimpse into the potential of fiction and community: 'Each of us now held at last in his arms what he had been for ever seeking and what he had eternally possessed'.[21]

If Wilson Harris aspires to construct fictively a unified community, and to tap into a unified community that exists immemorially, his notions of collective coexistence may appear to be the antithesis of the work completed by the activist Marxist historian Walter Rodney, work which incites political action, rooted in a discipline which interprets the economic determination of communities. In *A History of the Guyanese Working People 1880-1905* Rodney discusses the punishing construction of Guiana's coastal plantation region:

> The Venn Sugar Commission of 1948 estimated that each square mile of canal cultivation involved the provision of forty-nine miles of drainage canals and ditches and sixteen miles of the higher level of waterways used for transportation and irrigation. The Commissioners noted that the original construction of these waterways must have entailed the moving of at least 100 million tons of soil. This means that slaves moved 100 million tons of heavy, waterlogged clay with shovel in hand, while enduring conditions of perpetual mud and water.[22]

Here, statistics are invested with a hidden narrative about the social production of the narrow strip of empoldered coastland. Whereas the Venn Sugar Commission has evidently attempted to retain an objective empiricism about the canal construction, Rodney's discussion of Guyana can be read as an ambivalent response to a question provocatively posed by Harris:

> Are there moments in history when energies flow out from broken traditional patterns into a phenomenon of ironic achievement as exploiter and exploited are driven to reify their inner traditional values again by seizing on a material project?[23]

Certainly the building of canals, even the coastal community of Guyana itself can be seen as an 'ironic achievement', but Rodney seeks to explain the nature of such an achievement. His discussion of 'moments in history' is not satisfactorily conceived within Harris's esoteric model of human behaviour within the world as an abstracted structure of flowing energies. While both Harris and Rodney seek to reconceptualise the relationship of 'the exploiter' and 'the exploited' through their association in completing material projects, Rodney implies that it is not enough to write that people 'are driven' to certain actions, as if part of an unfolding and preordained drama. The history of community building in Guyana is, as Rodney confirms, a history of literally humanising the landscape. Community is described very clearly not as one given locality and set of people within it, but as a perpetually embattled site of conflict and cohesion.

George Lamming has written that Rodney 'believed that history was a way of ordering knowledge which could become an active part of the consciousness of an uncertified mass of ordinary people and which could be used by all as a medium of change.'[24] This interpretation of Rodney as an altruistic provider of the building blocks of community – as a man who considered the discipline of history to be a democratic process which enabled people to transform the way they lived together – is appealing. It also displays, I think, a similarity with Carter's hope for a free community of valid persons: both Carter and Rodney write and speak not wishing to lay down their own laws, but in order to create a fertile atmosphere of educated exchange. In perhaps less abstruse terms than Carter and Harris, and in more radical terms than Seymour, Rodney offers practical ways in which people can begin to create their standpoint as a free community of valid persons. These words are from the final speech he delivered:

> You need to try and get hold of this document [Rodney refers to the fraudulent constitution Burnham imposed]. You have to struggle to understand the kind of language it has, but it is promising you slavery and therefore you have to try and understand so that you are in a better position to resist that slavery.[25]

The 'struggle' emphasised is one against a narrow constitution which places all political power in Burnham's hands, and also one committed to an idea of political freedom which actively encourages the terms in which political power is couched to be continually argued, if not communally agreed. 'Struggling to understand' language – how language can be used to create, coerce and reform political ideals of community – is thus recognised as fundamental to the creation, coercion or reformation of the way in which people live together.

Carter's poetic contribution to the 'building of a free community of valid persons' can be viewed as a continuous struggle to understand, create and question linguistic strategies for the construction of communities. In his early poetry Carter does not weave together a constellation of co-operative social relations, but rather shouts an angered and antagonistic list of alternative definitions of Guiana. The interactions of copresence need not suggest harmony or unity, for if Carter's poetry is to be successfully conceptualised within a notion of community, the sense of friction – the clashing physical and linguistic encounters – in the term must be addressed. 'Not I With This Torn Shirt', the opening poem of *The Hill of Fire Glows Red* (1951), marks how contentious the notion of a community can be:

– Magnificent Province!
Province of Mud!
Province of flood!
Plantation – feudal coast!

Who are the magnificent here?
Not I with this torn shirt
but they, in their white mansions
by the trench of blood! [...][26]

It is a fervently exclamatory opening to the poem and the collection, and as such carves out a sense of the clashing encounters that have helped construct Guiana. In the poem Carter concentrates the balance of colonial domination into a series of epithetic variations on the name of the country, highlighting the pronounced dichotomy between differing perceptions of the region: 'They call here,/ – Magnificent Province!'. The uneasy ballast of the dash and the exclamation mark at the end of the second line acts as ironic 'scare marks' for such an epithet, intimating both a blithe image of a conquered territory, and the poet's bitterness at such a construction. His brusque rhymes, and the gloweringly brief descriptions of a province of mud and flood, of a 'Plantation' and a 'feudal coast' are a blunt riposte to the grandiloquent posturing that Carter identifies in the colonial commentators of Guiana. In the first lines, Guiana appears to owe its magnificence to its very status as a province (etymologically, a conquered territory): the glory belongs to the conquerors. But like Walter Rodney, who argues for an understanding of the human cost of creating and sustaining a 'Magnificent Province' of the British Empire, Carter's poetic persona demands that his presence, however torn, be woven back into the narratives of Guiana.

Carter's *Poems of Resistance from British Guiana* (1954) express the dramatic pitch that Guianese politics of independence reached in the postwar period. Certainly, Carter's detention as a political prisoner between 1953 and 1954 during the suspension of the constitution suggests that his political career meets his poetic career. Brathwaite writes, 'Carter's prison experience gave him not only new rhythms [...] but a whole new formal shape of poem: 'You are involved' and 'Death of a slave': which correlate in line and language, with the barred, controlled, formal cell and structure in which he found or imagined himself'.[27] Yet the poems Brathwaite cites here had appeared in print *before* Carter's 'prison experience', and to me this reveals the dubiety of depending on biographical detail for a reading of Carter's poetry. While the events of 1953 certainly inform his work, I think it is important not to assume that these poems were determined by them. Poems such as 'This Is The Dark Time My Love' and 'I Come From The Nigger Yard' dismantle the specious confines of a poetry defined by Carter's actual imprisonment, and it is in these works that Brathwaite's perceived 'new shape of poem' begins to take form. My reading of *Poems of Resistance* then considers not only the 'cells' in which Carter 'imagined' himself, but also the diverse constructions of resistance that Carter explores.

Seven of the eighteen poems had appeared either in a different structural form, with a different title, or independently before *Poems of Resistance* was published, and such a composite formation suggests the wide reference of the collection. Carter juxtaposes old and newly written poems, contemporary and historical contexts, and in doing so builds up a variegated text of resistance. In 'This is the Dark Time My Love' the aborted sonnet form of the poem reveals Carter critically experimenting with literary convention:

> This is the dark time, my love.
> All round the land brown beetles crawl about.
> The shining sun is hidden in the sky.
> Red flowers bend their heads in awful sorrow.
>
> This is the dark time, my love.
> It is the season of oppression, dark metal, and tears.
> It is the festival of guns, the carnival of misery.
> Everywhere the faces of men are strained and anxious.
>
> Who comes walking in the dark night time?
> Whose boot of steel tramps down the slender grass?
> It is the man of death, my love, the strange invader
> watching you sleep and aiming at your dream.[28]

Initially 'This is the dark time, my love' is suggestive of the promise of dark for lovers, and the heavily weighted caesura seems charged with sexual anticipation. Yet the ensuing three lines unpack the alternative meanings of dark – the poetic persona imagines, not a peaceful sleeping world, but a landscape of hidden creeping industry and a sky of hidden light.[29] The staple iambic pentameter movement of the three lines is broken, and thus it is on 'awful sorrow' that the stanza stumbles and stops. Such a symbolically cowed landscape perhaps reveals Carter's debt to the poetry of William Blake, and the ensuing verses betray the difficulty in constructing alternative models of community, both poetic and social.

Carter abandons all inference of the iambic pentameter in the second stanza, and restating 'This is the dark time, my love', the incremental repetition no longer suggests the proposal of a lover. The following lines now reveal the subversions of nature only hinted at in the first verse: 'It is the season of oppression, dark metal, and tears/ It is the festival of guns, the carnival of misery'. In contrast with the exuberant anatomization of liberty expressed in the earlier poem, 'Shines the Beauty of My Darling' ('and like the whole world dancing/ for liberation from the slave maker/ shines the beauty of my darling in her laughing eyes'[30]), the almost overdramatic emphasis in 'This is the Dark Time My Love' is placed on external oppression. Celebration, whether festival, carnival or the change of season, is marked not by a collective willing observance of rites and rituals, but by a dictated militarism. The sense of communality exists only in the ubiquitously strained 'faces of men'; the overriding perspective is that of a besieged couple, and by symbolic association, a besieged community. When the poet asks 'Who comes walking in the dark night time?/' the final beat of the pentameter is held in the question mark: a heavy pause which emphasises the atmosphere of siege. The final two lines – 'It is the man of death, my love, the strange invader/ watching you sleep and aiming at your dream' – can conclude the poem as a bluntly conceived political vehicle, but they can also reveal the poem as a brutalized *menage à trois*. The deliberate enclosure of the words 'my love' – separated by commas, and immured by the 'man of death' and 'the strange invader' – reveals the implosive relationship between poet, 'love' and 'invader'. And rather than explicitly state the symbolic significance of the poem for a Guianese people besieged by British troops, Carter allows the sense of imprisonment to reverberate out beyond his textually imprisoned 'love'.[31]

If Carter demonstrates in 'This is the Dark Time My Love' that his revolution aspires to be poetic as well as social, in 'I Come From The Nigger Yard' the poet expands and reaffirms this stance:

> I come from the nigger yard of yesterday
> leaping from the oppressors' hate
> and scorn of myself;
> from the agony of the dark hut in the shadow
> and the hurt of things;
> from the long days of cruelty and the long nights of pain
> down to the wide streets of to-morrow, of the next day
> leaping I come, who cannot see will hear.[32]

Here Carter provocatively creates a poetic persona who narrates his autobiography as comparable to the birth of a nation, and it is a remorseless autobiography. Coming out of the shadows, the poetic persona's dramatic entrance, and equally the miasmal landscape and the desperate nonspecificity of 'the hurt of things' gradually come into focus – a past becomes slowly reconciled with the present. The doleful bravura of Carter's elegy for the dispossessed in 'University of Hunger' – 'The green tree bends above the long forgotten./ The plains of life rise up and fall in spasms./ The huts of men are fused in misery' – is transformed in 'I Come From The Nigger Yard' into an expression of the bravado needed to create the elusive 'to-morrow'.[33] And it becomes clear that the initial claim of origins is a claim won and expressed at great cost: 'In the nigger yard I was naked like the new born/ naked like a stone or a star./ It was a cradle of blind days rocking in time.' The repetition of 'was' throughout the poem, however, hints at the transformation awaiting the poetic persona and his nation. But rebirth alone is not enough to herald the new 'to-morrow': Carter emphasises that *where* you are reborn is crucial: 'So I was born again stillborn and fierce', but the ensuing line smarts with cruel bathos, 'screaming in a slum'.[34] Plantation nigger yard is swapped for urban slum and Carter does not shrink from the grotesquerie of such a changed birthplace and progeny – 'and me, like a dog tangled in rags/ spotted with sores powdered with dust/ screaming with hunger, angry with life and men'.[35] The image of a swaddled, talcumed, fed and sleeping baby is ironically impugned.

The poem can be compared to Harris's complex sense of the relationship between fiction and community (rather than Seymour's straightforward hope for the cultural concretion of a Guianese people): Carter provocatively, and pertinently invokes the 'horror of disorientation' in this series of rebirths. However, a third birthplace is offered – 'Where men make hammers things that cannot break/ and anvils heavy hard and cold like ice'.[36] The communist imagery is bold, offering an almost magical promise of social transformation. But the final two verses, if not undermining this desired 'happy ending', certainly question the poet's inheritance of a stable and static arcadian world. The future community is composed in metamorphic terms:

> when the land changes and the world's all convulsed
> when different voices join to say the same
> and different hearts beat out in unison
> where on the aching floor of where I live
> the shifting earth is twisting into shape
> I take again my nigger life, my scorn[37]

There is no ideal community into which the poetic persona can be born. Rather, Carter's almost geologically layered poem demonstrates that his sense of 'to-morrow' is formed by the diverse forces of time ('when the land changes'), space (a world 'twisting' away from such places as nigger yard and slum) and, most importantly, people (the 'different voices' of social change). 'To-morrow' is not a synonym for nation, revolution, or even Guyana: it is a term of perpetually conflicting interpretation, a 'triple dialectic of space, time and social being', or in the words of the poet: 'it is me the nigger boy turning to manhood/ linking my fingers, welding my flesh to freedom.'[38]

A collection titled, *Poems of Affinity*, might suggest Carter's later achievement of the perfect concept of community – the achievement of a poetry that articulates the ties between people and place in terms of ideal social unity – but Carter makes no such claim. Nor, however, is disillusion the dominant tone; rather, an ambivalent sense of irony and empathy pervades the collection. One way to read *Poems of Affinity* is as the desperate posing of unanswered and unanswerable questions: questions which range from social confusion – 'Is it only just a misfortune/ to be as we are; bad luck/ carefully chosen?' – to the esoteric – 'If/ trees die, what happens to/ caterpillars?'.[39] The questions articulate a hope for affinity in a world that the poet writes as arbitrary, and as fragile as it is random. Carter, discussing the collection has said, 'Everything borders with something else. When you speak to me about something, I usually see it one way, then in another in one flat second. And that is what I'm trying to do – to deal with two things simultaneously, not separately'.[40] This interest in the permeability of borders seems close to Wilson Harris's discussion of the relationship between fiction and community: his hope for a 'fiction of implosion' which goes beyond the 'surfaces of life' to reveal the insubstantiality of a community's boundaries. However, Carter never claims to be able to uncover 'the truth of community'.[41] Rather, Carter's unanswered and unanswerable questions are, I think, part of an attempt to deal with the 'borders' and 'boundaries' that may be seen to delimit communities. Equally, it is a mistake to locate a sequence of question and then answer within Carter's poetry, and thus from the lack of proposed solution to conclude his pessimistic desperation. Such a sequence is denied by Carter's very attempt 'to deal with two things simultaneously', to explore 'borders' – the place where 'everything' meets 'something else'.

The enigmatic opening to 'Our Time' is typical of this 'attempt': 'The more the men of our time we are/ the more our time is'.[42] The rest of the poem acts as an unravelling of the implications of this proverbial statement, but to requote the sentence in context reveals that the ensuing lines do not provide a sequential exposition:

> The more the men of our time we are
> the more our time is. But always
> we have been somewhere else. Muttering
> our mouths like holes in the mud
> at the bottom of trenches. Looking
> for what is not anywhere, or certain.[43]

Carter's initial circular promise of a heroic era for mankind quickly fragments to reveal the irony of the mutuality between generic 'men' and 'time'. The simultaneity expressed in this poem is not a process of mutual and perpetual social growth – indeed the demand for the production of 'men of our time' soon reads as a hollow rhetorical utterance – simultaneity is detected in expressions of displacement, inarticulacy, and uncertainty. 'But always we have been somewhere else. Muttering/ [...] Looking': it is an ironic variation on affinity, and on Carter's assertion that 'everything borders with something else', for the borders, if they exist, are here obscured. Unpacking the phrase of the title in order to suggest the hope of common belonging to, association with, or possession of a particular historical moment is a powerful, but overly palliative endeavour.[44] The homogeneous imperative of 'our time' is rearticulated as a cruel homogeneity:

> [...] Badly abused
> we fail to curse. Our fury pleads.
> Yet fury should be fire; if not light.
> And what is the mother of fury
> if not ours.[45]

Communality is negatively achieved: passively abused, the only action the 'we' of the poem perform is to 'fail to curse'. Indeed Carter's language imitates this failure. His staccato sentences and lines seem truncated, the instigators of 'abuse' remain unnamed and the two intransitive verbs, 'curse' and 'pleads' are denied the objects of their transitive variants. At whom 'we' curse, and with whom 'our fury pleads' is not provided.

The performative power of language is questioned – cursing and pleading are foreshortened by full stops, and even more forcefully, the poet queries the register of 'fury'. Words do not constitute or effect positive acts, they do not even refer to an assumed meaning: 'Our fury pleads./ Yet fury should be fire; if not light'. The fury that Carter's early poems, such as 'Not I With This Torn Shirt' and 'I Come From The Nigger Yard' articulate, is here contemplated rather than enacted within the poem. But such contemplation can be performative: in 'Bastille Day – Georgetown' the poet states:

> I have at last started
> to understand the origin
> of our vileness, and being
> unable to deny it, I suggest
> its nativity.
> In the shame of knowledge
> of our vileness, we shall fight.[46]

The mention of 'Nativity' and 'origin/ of our vileness' does not act as an introduction to further incontestable information about the murder of the Guyanese priest, Father Darke.[47] Carter's poem is one of inceptive apprehension – 'I have at last started/ to understand [...]' – and the performative speech act of the poetic persona is tentatively stated – 'unable to deny it, I suggest its nativity'. There are no claims to solutions, only a suggestion, but the empty space left after the full stop following 'nativity' seems to deny even that. However, perhaps Carter's empty line is part of a conscious poetic provocation: this void can be seen to fulfil paradoxically the role of a suggestion, marking out a semantic space to be filled not only by Carter, but also by those who read his poems.

'Bastille day', the marker of revolutionary nativity, becomes an ironic metaphor of a 'vile' collective insurgence. The contiguities and contrasts between Carter's revolutionary poetics can be pointed up in these parallel quotations:

> those who are eager to be men
> will be glad
> for the revolution
> I myself shall be so fiercely happy
> that I will make my shirt
> a banner
> for the revolution,[48]

> In the shame of knowledge
> of our vileness, we shall fight.[49]

The possibility of a collective social movement articulated in the sanguine tones of 'A Banner For The Revolution' is implicitly denied in 'Bastille Day – Georgetown'. But it is the mode of articulation that is rejected rather than the possibility as such. In the former poem the futurity of 'the revolution' is stressed, and the text brims with figures eager to become 'men' of that future. 'Bastille Day – Georgetown' shares this insistence on the future, but the sequence of revolution is not so clearly anticipated, nor are the emotions that provoke, and are provoked by, revolution necessarily positive. The joyous tone of the first quotation is countered in the second by the 'shame' that forces the poet and his unspecified companions to 'fight'. Clothed, not in makeshift banners, but 'in the shame of knowledge/ of our vileness', the poetic persona's revolutionary outfit marks a collective ignominy, and also reveals the impetus to fight. Yet the poem's close reads ambiguously: 'we shall fight' can be a determined call-to-arms – the monosyllables beating out the collective obligation to engage with and overcome their shame. An alternative reading, however, draws on the inconclusiveness of the collective action that follows 'our Bastille day'. 'We shall fight' may share the ironic obligation Carter describes in 'After One Year' – 'Men murder men, as men must murder men'[50] – and thus 'fight' may not refer to collective opposition to the vileness of 'Bastille day', but to a portentous prediction of perpetual internecine conflict. However, giving precedence to one reading would be to interpret a fixed conclusion to the poem, and this, I think, is finally denied by Carter's emphasis upon 'we' and 'our'. These personal and possessive pronouns are all-inclusive, stretching to the inhabitants of Georgetown (as the title suggests) and beyond this city boundary. Carter carefully constructs a statement of collective shame, and in his sparse words – 'we shall fight' – I read his attempt to leave the resolution of that 'shame' open to contest.

The two complementary poems, 'As New And As Old (I)' and 'As New And As Old (II)' repeat in form the ambiguous resolutions offered by Carter in 'Bastille Day – Georgetown'. Their almost identical titles suggest a basic congruence of theme, and in the poems Carter invents clashing and fluid affinities between the binary opposites of new and old. The first poem opens:

> Every day is as old
> as a new day is. Time
> represents itself. Night fakes
> the rule of stars; as we fake
> light's good pencil. A child's
> chalk ridden black board. Alphabet
> of hope in a season of insects. Crawl
> of the beast in a season of days. I
> unapologetic, remember why every
> day was once a new day. As new
> and as old as my childhood roaming
> among grass [...][51]

Affinity – the bordering of everything onto something else – proliferates almost incongruously within the poem. While 'Time/ represents itself', other 're-presentations' are arranged on the page. Writing is 'faking' here, but the multifarious simulacra it produces are more compelling to me than the imperious autonomy of self-representing 'Time'. Images of material scribblings and an 'alphabet of hope' are juxtaposed; the words do not form sentences, but rather create incongruous fragments of affinity. Whether the child's chalk writing formulates an alphabet of hope, or whether the provisionality of chalk suggests a further provisionality of an alphabet of hope is not resolved. What remains on the page, however, are the 'unapologetic' words of the poetic persona, 'unapologetic' for he flouts adherence to sentential form, and instead asserts language's 'inner principle of proliferation'.[52] Such proliferation creates internal contradictions within the poem: the 'world is a cold/ wind. It is a glass of sweet water/ in a grim place of thirst.'[53] The ambivalent meaning of 'world' is stressed by the juxtaposition of 'coldness' and sweetness', and by the layout of the poem: sentences begin mid-line, but the tempo of the lines overrides the finality of the full-stops that divide them. Carter's 'world' is simultaneously 'cold' and 'sweet', and responding to this, I suggest that the second poem should be read within this framework of simultaneity.

'As New And As Old (II)' is not necessarily a sequential response to the first poem, nor need it be prioritised as a refutation of the first; rather the two poems play with and against each other, picking up identical and contrasting words and images. In the second of the paired poems Carter writes:

> [...] New and old
> is the face of the world's great grief,
> a kind of music we listen to and hear
> when the toil of silence builds
> our house of language in this wind's
> throat, the grim larynx.[54]

Prompted by Carter's suggestion that the world's great grief creates 'a kind of music', I read the two poems as forming a musical counterpoint – a simultaneous sounding of two melodies. 'As New And As Old (II)' acts as a dense intertwining tune, and repeating the words, 'world', 'wind', 'grim', 'new' and 'old', the poet constructs the pair of poems as locked in reciprocal reference. The long sentence quoted above may not yield straightforward glossing, but a consideration of the internal counterpoints perhaps offers one route through its labyrinthine imagery. In the internal half-rhymes of 'face', 'silence' and 'house' a link can be traced out between the world's anthropomorphic grief, the 'silence' that this precipitates, and the makeshift dwelling place of 'language' that is built by such a 'face' and 'silence'. Although 'language' is cast as subordinated to the inarticulate and immovable silence and grief, it is language that also forms the fulcrum of the poem. Remembering that in 'As New And As Old (I)' Carter writes, 'the world is a cold wind', the phrases – 'the world's great grief' and 'this wind's/ throat, the grim larynx' – read as a vertical counterpoint. The matched possessive construction and the alliteration of 'great grief' and 'grim' reveals Carter patterning language to reinforce the correspondence between 'world' and 'wind', and their mutual possession of 'the grim larynx'. While the 'house of language' is constrained in this metaphorical organ, paradoxically the only physiological purpose of the larynx is the production of voice – of language. When Carter writes, 'our time's disgraceful space. We/ are its measure'[55] he deploys the ambiguous constraint and freedom of language, offering at least two readings of the lines. The confession, 'we/ are its measure' may be the pessimistic admission that people embody their society's disgrace. However, in the poet's acceptance of collective culpability there can also read an intimation of the possibility of collective atonement. This need not be religious; 'measure' is a poetic term, denoting rhythm, and while I do not think that Carter explicitly offers poetry as the only true medium of atonement, his lines enact the critical power of cadence. To provide the measure of 'time's disgraceful space' could be an attempt to assuage that disgrace. If 'we/ are its measure' then 'we' –

the stressed endword, open to possibility – could make that measure once again 'graceful'.

Poems of Affinity, being Carter's latest collection, forms in some ways an end point to his work.[56] But if it is an end point, it is one which paradoxically asserts that this is not a definitively conclusive end. The final poem, 'Is why', closes with the non-sentence – 'About time to' – and I suggest that the full stop after 'to' makes sense only within Carter's open-ended framework of affinities.[57] '"About time to" do what?' is the implicit question prompted by these words, but Carter's ironically precipitant and abortive punctuation enacts the absurdity of end points. Twenty-five years earlier Carter had written 'I take again my nigger life, my scorn'[58]: the poet's perpetually repeated action marks out the congruency of Carter's earlier and later poetic essays in community. The hope for a free community of valid persons permeates his poetry, and while a complete definition of this free community is impossible, Carter's poetry suggests that what is possible, or perhaps even necessary, is its constant rewriting and re-evaluation.

Notes

1. Martin Carter, *Address to the Eighth Convocation Ceremony at the University of Guyana* (Georgetown: University of Guyana, 1974), p. 2. This address also appears as 'A Free Community of Valid Persons' in *Kyk-over-al: A Martin Carter Prose Sampler*, 44 (1993), pp. 30-32. The quote is edited there as 'our victim's role in a ruthless world', but I think that the use of 'victim' as an emphatic adjective is as persuasive. See p. 31.
2. Note that Carter's *attempts* in the Address argue specifically for a reform of 'Guyanese national community', but they need not be limited in this way.
3. This essay first appeared in *The Graphic Independence Souvenir* (May 26, 1966). The bibliography in *Selected Poems* (Georgetown: Red Thread Women's Press, 1997) records Harris's as the earliest review. There are of course the Forewords written by Sidney King (now Eusi Kwayana) to *Poems of Resistance from British Guiana* (London: Lawrence and Wishart, 1954) and by Neville Dawes to *Poems of Resistance* (Georgetown: University of Guyana, 1966).
4. Wilson Harris, 'A Glance at Two Guyanese Poets' in *Explorations: A Selection of Talks and Articles 1966-1981* ed. Hena Maes-Jelinek (Mundelstrup: Dangeroo Press, 1981), pp. 5-9 (pp. 7-9).
5. King, Foreword [no pagination].
6. Harris, 'A Glance', p. 9.
7. Edward Kamau Brathwaite, 'Resistance Poems: The Voice of Martin Carter' in *Caribbean Quarterly*, 23 (1977), 7-23 (p. 9).
8. *Ibid.*, p. 18.
9. Note that Rohlehr changed the title to '"Assassins of the voice": Martin Carter's *Poems of Affinity*'.
10. Martin Carter, 'Politics and the Individual' in *Kyk-over-al: A Martin Carter Prose Sampler*, 48-49 (p. 48). [First published in *Thunder*, vol. 5 no. 42 (January 1955)]
11 Carter, *Address*, pp. 1-2.
12. *Ibid.*, p. 3. Forbes Burnham's presidency of Guyana is a potent example of the danger of the singularly authored political manifesto. By December 1980

the Burnham government was propped up with almost dictatorial powers, and persistent election rigging kept him in power until his death. See *Guyana: Fraudulent Revolution* (London: Latin America Bureau, 1984).

13. *Ibid*., p. 3.
14. A. J. Seymour, 'Editorial Notes' in *Kyk-over-al*, vol. 1 no 1 (December 1945), p. 7.
15. Seymour compiled and edited *Kyk-over-al Special Issue: An Anthology of West Indian Poetry*, vol. 4 no. 14 (mid year 1952), and *Kyk-over-al Special Issue: An Anthology of Guianese Poetry* vol. 6 no. 19 (Year-end 1954).
16. Wilson Harris, 'The Guiana Book' in *Kyk-over-al* (December 1948), 37-38 (p. 37, p. 38).
17. A. J. Seymour, *The Guiana Book* (Georgetown: Author, 1948), p. 17.
18. Wilson Harris, 'The Writer and Society' in *Tradition, the Writer and Society: Critical Essays* (London and Trinidad: New Beacon, 1967), pp. 48-64, p. 49.
19. *Ibid*., p. 60.
20. *Ibid*., p. 49.
21. Wilson Harris, *Palace of the Peacock* (London: Faber and Faber, 1960), p. 117.
22. Walter Rodney, *A History of the Guyanese Working People* (London: Heinemann, 1981), pp. 2-3.
23. Wilson Harris, 'A Talk on the Subjective Imagination' in *Explorations: A Selection of Talks and Articles 1966-1981* ed. Hena Maes-Jelinek (Mundelstrup: Dangeroo Press, 1981), pp. 57-67 (p. 64).
24. See the foreword in Rodney, *A History*, p. xvii.
25. A transcript of this speech, delivered on June 6 1980, Bourda Mall, Georgetown, appears as an appendix in *Walter Rodney: Revolutionary and Scholar: A Tribute* ed. Edward A. Alpers and Pierre Michel Fontaine (Los Angeles: Center for Afro-American Studies and African Studies Center, University of California. 1982), pp. 161-74.
26. Martin Carter, *Selected Poems* (Georgetown: Red Thread Women's Press, 1997), p. 33. Ian McDonald in the Foreword writes: 'Many of Martin Carter's poems [...] have appeared in past collections, magazines and anthologies with numerous errors and even with whole stanzas inadvertently omitted. The author has meticulously checked the text of each of these selected poems and they now appear as originally composed' (p. 21). Throughout the essay I refer to the latest edition of *Selected Poems*, while bearing in mind any textual variations that appear in other editions of Carter's poetry.
27. Brathwaite, 'Resistance Poems', pp. 13-14.
28. *Ibid*., p. 94.
29. In the first and third editions of *Poems of Resistance* the first stanza reads as two sentences of two lines each – the first word of the second line, 'All' is not capitalised, as if to reinforce further the line's status as a running sentence. However, I have followed the version from *Selected Poems*. The finality of each capitalised and endstopped line augments my sense of a progressively dismantled love poem.
30. Carter, from *The Hidden Man* in *Selected Poems*, p. 37.
31. For a possible source of the insistently personal perspective that Carter pursues in 'This is the Dark Time My Love' see Vercor's French Resistance novel, *Le Silence de la Mer* (Paris: Les editions de minuit, 1942). Carter's line – 'Whose boot of steel tramps down the slender grass?' – and the ominous arrival of the 'strange invader' reads as an overly fervent allusion to the novel's ironic opening.

32. *Ibid.*, pp. 96-98 (p. 96).
33. Carter, *Selected Poems*, p. 77. Note that in the texts of 'University of Hunger' that appear in *Kyk-over-al*, vol. 5 no. 17 (1953) and the first and third edition of *Poems of Resistance* the word 'roofs' is used in place of 'huts'. The version from *Selected Poems* may indicate Carter's revision in order to pick up the line from 'I Come From The Nigger Yard' – 'from the agony of the dark hut in the shadow'.
34. Carter, *Selected Poems*, p. 97.
35. *Ibid.*
36. *Ibid.*
37. *Ibid.*, p. 98.
38. The first quotation is from Edward W. Soja's *Postmodern Geographies: The Reassertion of Space in Critical Social Theory* (London: Verso, 1989), p. 12. For the second quotation, see Carter, *Selected Poems*, p. 98.
39. Carter, 'Our Time' and 'Too Much Waiting' in *Selected Poems*, p. 175, p. 192.
40. See Frank Birbalsingh, 'Interview with Martin Carter' in *Kyk-over-al*, 46/47 (1995), 218-34 (p. 228).
41. See Harris, 'The Writer and Society'.
42. Carter, *Selected Poems*, p. 175.
43. *Ibid.*
44. Compare Seymour's capitalised use of 'Time' in 'Kykoveral' for such a palliative endeavour. Note also that in the first edition of *Poems of Affinity* (Georgetown: Release, 1980) 'time' in the title of the poem is pointedly lower case.
45. Carter, *Selected Poems*, p. 175.
46. *Ibid.*, p. 201.
47. On the contents page of the first edition of *Poems of Affinity* the poem is titled, 'Bastille Day – Georgetown (On the occasion of the murder of Father Darke)', but the parenthetical information does not appear with the text of the poem as if to encourage it to be read stretched beyond the boundaries of a narrow occasional poem. See *Poems of Affinity*, p. iv, pp. 66-67.
48. Carter, 'A Banner For The Revolution' in *Selected Poems*, p. 43.
49. Carter, 'Bastille Day – Georgetown' in *Selected Poems*, p. 201.
50. Carter, *Selected Poems*, p. 119.
51. Carter, *Selected Poems*, p. 179.
52. Michel Foucault, *The Order of Things: An Archaeology of the Human Sciences* (London and New York: Routledge, 1970; reprinted 1994), p. 40.
53. Carter, *Selected Poems*, p. 179.
54. *Ibid.*, p. 180.
55. *Ibid.*
56. In an interview with Martin Carter in December 1995, he suggested to me that he was no longer writing poetry. *Poems of Affinity* may be seen as Carter's final collection, although the reprinted *Selected Poems* publishes poetry written in the 1980s.
57. Carter, *Selected Poems*, p. 209.
58. Carter, 'I Come From The Nigger Yard', p. 97.

NIGEL WESTMAAS

MARTIN CARTER'S PROSE: AN APPRECIATION

Guyana's most celebrated poet, Martin Carter, has subjected the society in which he lives to deep, varied and often unnoticed contemplation over the years. At times, his examination has taken the form of public prose. In recent years, tempered some say, by an inner censorship, Carter has not offered new public work. What has remained consistent in the moments of active, public prose, has been an unyielding seriousness of approach to whatever subject he turns his attention.

From what might be his very first composition of public prose – a piece written in the school magazine when he was President of the Queen's College Bee-keeping society, to more recent times – Carter's prose has encompassed not only a generation but has been firmly connected to his personal concerns as student, as political activist, and later as a poet of distinction living in Guyana. Consequently, his prose works vary from the political insights in the organ of the Peoples Progressive Party, *Thunder*, in the 1950s, to reflections on the state of art and literature, science, and even, as in at least one case, his interpretation of the impact of television technology The depth and variety of work has surprised many of his countrymen and friends, since Carter is largely recognised as a poet and that Muse has brought forth a few volumes of great poetry.

Reviews, short stories, speeches, interviews, articles and editorials are all included in Carter's prose repertoire over a period of fifty years. Over one hundred and ten different pieces have been uncovered so far. No doubt, there are many more in hiding – in a library here, an old timer's home, the newspapers, and more than likely many in the poet's collection, published and unpublished!

Martin Carter's method and style of analysis of political issues, to which he turns time and again in prose, speech and interview, appears no different from the way he handles art and literature in prose. All fall under a humanist truncheon and are spelt out with extraordinary craft of language. His language is characterised by such economy, rhythm and finesse of argument that one risks considering it poetry in prose form. This passage, written in the 1950s is typical:

> subsisting on a diet of Hollywood films, true detective magazines and other such trash; bounded on one side by the sugar estates, and on the other by the waterfront, the people of the city are like creatures in a cage, pressed down into the mud under the weight of a hopeless sky, the people live like ants in an ants nest, biting at each other because there is nothing else for them to bite at. And when a voice emerges out of all this muck all the little lap dogs bark in furious excitement, defending the master, who from time to time will administer a well aimed kick for remembrance.

Carter's prose presentations can appear complex and over-laden with *meaning* to audiences, who are at times unsure of his drift and intent. But he can also be incisive, direct, often cruel, witty, and uncompromising in word or speech, and equally devastating in repartee or interview. Many an interviewer has fallen victim to the 'Carterite response' and been left strewn, bemused, with the strange feeling that they had ventured a foolish question. The following is standard diet:

Q: When did you become a poet?
MC: One does not become a poet, one finds oneself a poet.

After his memorable address at the University of Guyana 1974 Convocation ceremony – entitled 'A Free Community of Valid Persons', Carter was asked about his reference to AXOLOTL [a lake creature found in Mexico] in the speech. The questioner enquired whether he was speaking as a scientist. His reply was devastating, but typical: 'You know one day my eldest son came home and said that his friends had asked, 'Is your father a poet or biologist?' I asked him, 'Would they know the difference?'

And there is an interesting story he tells of the impact of an article he wrote for *Thunder* in 1955 entitled 'WANTED: A GREAT OBEAH MAN'. An executive member of the PPP at the time, Carter was defending his party from attacks from hither and thither – some calling for great leaders to emerge to the satisfaction of all and sundry – a leader, in addition, required to perform completely opposite requests at the same time. His article, in a fit of brilliant irony, requested a faith healer to help the authorities create the 'miracles' apparently desired. Unfortunately for Carter, the spirit of the article was taken at its literal extreme, and soon after its publication, a man approached him at headquarters and introduced himself with great assurance, 'I is the man yuh want!'

Carter, like other literary giants, has reflected over and over on the state of the arts and literary creation in Guyana and the Caribbean. He has been tough and unyielding against those who treat mediocrity with sympathy. And what about encouragement for young writers or poets? Again Carter is unyielding:

> 'Encourage young composers or novelists? I am always worried by the word – 'encourage'. Too often it means that with the best intentions we praise what is third rate and omit to point out that art requires talent – real talent and not mere literacy in any medium. I see no substitute for passion, internally generated, and hard work.'

In his treatment of the race question, an issue central to the modern political history and society of Guyana, and a theme to which he turns again and again, Carter's prose betrays deep concern that wounds of the psyche – born in part of Guyana's peculiar history and struggle – persist in varied forms and hinder free development of the personality. Throughout his varied examination of race, its deformations and consequences, the corresponding logic and humanism prevails. Are his countrymen, for example, merely an 'aggregation of subsistence seekers?'

This following statement, written in 1964, just two years before Guyana gained independence, is characteristic of the deep concern, or what some say is deep despair, he has exhibited in prose over the years.

> Life in a country as materialistic and philistine as British Guiana soon blunts the edge of the mind. The almost fanatical preoccupation with hollow issues, the gossip mongering which passes for conversation, and the inevitable political hysteria, leave little time for the serious examination of ideas.
>
> I know the psychological squalor of everyday life is exhausting. I know that the urgent practical problem of making a living comes first. What I do not know is why so few revolt, either by word or deed, against such acute spiritual discomfort.

Is there one statement that can personify this poet and master in the field of language? The back cover of the first edition of Martin Carter's *Selected Poems* comes close: 'a truth-teller of rare grace of wind where thought is sensuous and lyrical.'

RECOLLECTIONS BY MARTIN CARTER'S CONTEMPORARIES

WILSON HARRIS

MEMOIR

Martin Carter was a rather close friend of mine in the late 1940s into the 1950s and up to my departure from Guyana (then British Guiana) at the end of the decade. But we rarely corresponded after 1959 when I left the Colony. We shared a deep interest in the integrity and life of the imagination. Integrity is a hard word. I have lost friends I genuinely cared for because of something I had said which appeared to them to disparage their work though my intention was to illumine a quest for meaning through and beyond a particular frame or convention. This is not the case with Martin of whose work I have written or said little even as I admire his craft and dedication.

Paradoxically the division between us is wrought I would imagine from the complex background we share. 'Guyana' stems from an Amerindian root word which means 'land of waters'.

Martin's home has remained in Georgetown in consistency with a homing instinct within the wilderness of the Guianas. With my first expedition deep into the interior or heartland I had embarked on voyages – little though I knew it – that would take me across other hazardous oceans rich and dangerous as the rainforest. The voyaging archetype is as native to Guyana as the homing instinct.

Stewart Brown has invited me to write something for a book he is editing on Martin's achievement as a poet. I also gather from his letter that he has assembled – or is assembling – an impressive body of writers fully attuned to Martin's work which they greatly admire.

I have no doubt in re-reading Stewart Brown's letter – in which he consolidates a body of critical opinion on Martin's poetry – that my best contribution to his book lies in a memoir, a looking back across an ocean of time, it seems, to Martin's home in Georgetown. He lives now but a stone's throw from Anira Street where a group used to meet from around 1950 I think, when Martin's *Hill Of Fire Glows Red* appeared in a series edited by A. J. Seymour called *Miniature Poets.* It was a pocket series launched by Seymour in difficult economic circumstances.

The group which assembled at Martin's house discussed everything under the sun (politics, art, literature, philosophy...) A serious group but not without its black humour.

Members of that group pop randomly into my mind like subterranean fireworks in the cave of memory. There is a darkness to the landscape of memory – whether cave or corridor or labyrinth – but this heightens the womb of space and gives spatial hindsight and lightning recall to features and image and event.

Rory Westmaas came on occasion. He was a stern advocate of socialism at the time but possessed of a ribald and fiery sense of humour. (Martin and he were later to be involved in a hunger fast when the British Guiana constitution was suspended.) Rory sometimes cast himself in the role of a people's judge. Jackson – another member of the group – idolised Rory but was terrified of him. He was sentenced to hang on a Monday morning should he backslide. What a way to start the week! Indeed Rory's joke was a reflection on the lot of labour – condemned to strangulation wages – in a plantation economy. Jackson saw the moral in the metaphoric sentence passed on him but was uneasy nevertheless.

One of Martin's celebrated poems 'University of Hunger' – and another I recall which begins with the line 'I Walk Slowly In The Wind' – appeared in the 1950s decade. A curious reflection now crosses my mind. Jackson's pillory or gallows of subsistence on a cruel plantation Monday morning is suspended invisibly in the body of those poems.

I hasten to add that this shadow of memory is devoid of critical gravity. It springs entirely from the random ferment which imbues this memoir.

In that context it is not my intention to address all the persons who participated in the Anira Group. But Keith Carter, Martin's elder brother, comes strongly into mind. Keith studied law at Oxford and returned to Georgetown from the United Kingdom around 1950 I would think. His was a fascinating presence in the group. His lean glance and features combined return to me now. They flare with suppressed passion yet are unmarked by sentiment. His was a dry and devastating wit. He had no illusions in my judgement, about the future of politics. He was an intellectual marxist and a great admirer of the existentialist pathos and lyrical fatalism in A.E. Housman's poetry.

It is impossible to say whether Keith's *fin-de-siècle* humour influenced Martin's sensibility. It seemed to me that Keith admired Martin's gifts, he admired an immediacy of sensation like a razor's glance in a shaving mirror: 'a spark seed in the destiny of gloom' ('I Come from the Nigger Yard').

Martin was under house arrest in 1956 when George Lamming visited the Colony and organised a series of readings. Martin was prohibited from reading his poems at the Carnegie Library in Main Street. I volunteered to do so and read *Shape and Motion* and a few other poems of his. The Anira group was then in the process of disintegration.

Influential friends may have affected the lifting of Martin's house arrest and I recall his attending a party at the home of Dr Frank Williams, a medical practitioner who took a strong interest in cultural affairs. This may well have been in 1956 not long after the Carnegie event.

The Governor of the Colony Sir Alfred Savage was also a guest. Martin and he chatted amiably about the work of the Irish Poet William Butler Yeats. Martin quoted a line which runs roughly as follows in my memory across the years – 'What if the mob at the door is the state'. The Governor had not seen or read this poem. Neither had I. I have scouted libraries in England since then and have been unable to obtain it. I know it exists for Martin possessed the text in an unexpurgated volume of Yeats's *Collected Works*.

I have, on occasion, in a dream, written to the apparently vanished members of the Anira group. Such letters are stamped *unread or unclaimed* even before they leave my hand. A curious coincidence occurred within the very week I received Stewart Brown's request to write something for his book. I could scarcely believe it. Another letter arrived. Stamped UNCLAIMED. I had written it in 1996 to one Sidney Singh who gave his address as Marshall Falls, Mazaruni River. I had replied immediately to a letter he sent to me in which he enclosed an interesting map and some pictures. I wrote and thanked him for the material and offered to send some books. He admired St. John Perse, F. Scott Fitzgerald, Hart Crane, and books on ancient Mexican sculpture and on the sculpture of Henry Moore. I was sure I would hear from him again. But instead, after almost a year or more, my letter was returned by the Bartica post office, unopened, unread.

Bartica is a mining town or gateway into the Mazaruni River, the Cuyuni River, and the Upper Essequibo River. I knew it well on my survey expeditions. But it was a foreign land for the bulk of the population on the coastlands. It provided me with one of the roots of a composite field of consciousness within the language of fiction...

Sidney had been a member of the Anira group. He never failed, when he was in Georgetown, to visit Martin when others shied away in fear of the authorities and the constraint or duress they could inflict.

He left Guyana in the 1960s and wrote to me from time to time, letters with foreign stamps, Mexico, Venezuela, Honduras, Bermuda, the Bahamas.

I mention him now because the unclaimed letter he never lifted from the Bartica post office sets the last vestige of a seal on the Anira Street group. It had really disintegrated long before but some measure of numinous soil encircling many dimensions of imagination remains. Grave, Cradle.

The last time I visited Georgetown was 1987. I spent a week. By an incredible twist of fate Martin's mother died in that very week. I was asked to read the eulogy. She was, in spirit, a member of the Anira group. Her wonderful tolerance and good humour made everyone welcome. So too did Phyllis, Martin's wife, who has written a foreword to an early booklet of his poems.

I met Martin after this in London in 1991. We were giving readings for the Arts Council in various parts of England and were able to spend a brief time picking up the threads of old acquaintance.

Martin was appointed Minister of Culture when Independence came. A well-deserved honour, it seems to me, for a remarkable poet.

(8th September, 1997)

Jan Carew

TRIBUTE TO MARTIN CARTER

Requiem for Martin

Martin, the exit of death
led you down Streets of Eternity, softly
like the falling tide
that leaves Guyana's foreshore burnished with sunlight
jewelled with crabs, curlews, pikers
and sea gulls married to the wind,
but the tide will rise again
in restless rhythms of awakening
And those who *'bend down listening to the land'*
will forever hear you singing,
'I come to you with a particular gladness...
I come naked as a stone, or a star...'

Prologue

I met Martin Carter at the Jagan's home in Kitty in the 1949. It was during a dry, summer season when Trade Winds cooled the Georgetown nights and dray carts with lanterns swinging like lazy pendulums plodded along the sea wall road on their way to the city markets. I had returned home to Guyana for the first time in nearly six years after studying in the United States. On that historic night I met Cheddi and Janet Jagan, Martin Carter and Sidney King (Eusi Kwayana). Martin was tall, brown as a seasoned mora nut, his hair wild and curling, and he had large Diego Rivera eyes that seemed specially designed to scan far horizons, and long elegant limbs that were at ease with themselves. And when he spoke, it was as though his tongue softened syllables in chosen words before he uttered them. There was an easy camaraderie born of shared convictions and pristine dreams of Guyana's liberation from colonial rule, binding this group together. The nickname of 'Show-boy' that youths in Accra had given Nkrumah would have fitted Cheddi Jagan equally as well, because Cheddi was dark, handsome with flashing eyes and thick patent leather hair curling at its outer extremities. He and his wife, Janet, had just returned from street corner meetings in Georgetown that night, and once he was at home, his restless energies were reigned in. But those eyes of his, looking at you, summed you up, even in moments of repose, and left you in no doubt that he was a born leader, that the passion for justice burning deep inside his fierce heart would never be extinguished. Sidney (Eusi), tall ascetic, speaking so softly, you had to lean forward to hear what he was saying, looked like a black Jesus and carried an aura of gentleness around with him, but you sensed that there was an implacable resolution at the core of that gentleness. Janet, dwarfed when she was standing beside Martin and Sidney (Eusi), had a beauty and a passionate sense of commitment that set her apart from the rather plain and quiescent females that the colonial proconsuls more often than not chose as wives. It did not take me long to discover that this group had brought something new to Guyanese politics – a new and ineluctable dedication to the cause of colonial freedom, an innate modesty, and a profound respect for the people. Our conversation that night centred on the Political Action Committee bulletin, and how it could be improved. That was half a century ago – a blink of an eye in historical time. Marx once said that history always repeats itself, the first time is tragedy, and the next farce. Today, there are those who seem to be making every effort to prove Marx right.

'In the cold earth, in the cold, dark earth, time plants seeds of anger...' Martin sang out in his 'Death of a Slave' and in dignifying the martyrdom of an anonymous slave, he was also according a new kind of dignity to countless unsung Guyanese heroes and heroines down the centuries – the forgotten ones who had come from all walks of life and from far corners of the earth. They had come and mingled with the people of the First Nation – the Amerindians – and linked up with them in order to affirm their human dignity.

The Jamaican poet and novelist, Andrew Salkey, said that writers, artists and musicians make sense of our unique and complex Caribbean experience of life, and shed new light on our society. Martin Carter's poetry, therefore, is like the sheet lightning that illuminates dark Guyanese skies at the beginning of the rainy season. This analogy is very apt, because great poetry IS like lightning, and lightning is never timid. It flashes and sheds light in the midst of darkness and great turmoil in the heavens. Martin Carter is, in a very profound sense, the poet of Guyana's awakening, a Guyana that was rousing itself from the cruel torpor of colonialism, slavery and the imposition of indentured labour.

His poetic voice spoke to us across the real and imagined divisions of race, class, caste and religion, and it spoke with an amazing tonal range and resonance. There were his pamphleteering *Poems of Resistance* and his *Poems of Shape and Motion*. There were also what I call his 'poems of reflection.' And here are two very revealing excerpts from his poems of reflection. The first is from his poem 'Cuyuni' and the second from 'If It Were Given'.

> ...far from the noise of language
> where gods still live and brood on thrones of rock
> [...]
> If it were given to me
> I would have had a serious conversation
> with the fertile dial of the clock of the sun.
> But then, I admit, I would have had to change *the language of the dead.*

Jules Michelet, the greatest of French historians, tells us that at certain moments in history people throw up leaders who can articulate for them their innermost longings, their hopes and aspirations, and Guyana produced more than its fair share of these voices. But during that heady period when the British colonialists were playing their old game of divide and conquer, they were also busily seeding animosities and contumely between classes, races, castes, between city dwellers and folks in the countryside, encouraging Indian nationalism in Guyana, while jailing and persecuting Indian nationalists in India.

It was in the midst of this social, political and psychological confusion that Martin Carter's poetic vision emerged, at this historical nexus that Martin sang out in his poem 'University of Hunger':

> I come to you with a particular gladness

But he also told us in another poem:

> I come to the world with scars on my soul
> wounds on my body, fury in my hands
> I turn to the histories of men and the lives of peoples....

He took the title 'University of Hunger' from Maxim Gorky's *My Universities*, a series of autobiographical sketches of this Russian writer's wanderings across vast stretches of his country before he finally settled down to write. What is significant about this poem, which begins with cadences akin to music,

> is the university of hunger the wide waste
> is the pilgrimage of man the long march...

is that in order to find an authentic Guyanese voice, Martin Carter, like some of the finest intellectuals of his generation, had to go through a period of de-schooling. The intellectuals of Martin Carter's generation, searching for new Guyanese identity, began re-examining the roots of their own culture, and at the same time they went on journeys of exploration into the world of ideas, and particularly those ideas that the colonial rulers tried to suppress with their all encompassing laws against 'sedition'. These intellectuals turned to neglected reservoirs of our culture and began seeing the Amerindian culture, the transplanted African, Hindu, Muslim and European cultures through new eyes. They read works of history, philosophy, political economy, and this included works by Marx, Engels, Hegel, Rilke, Caudwell, James (C.L.R.), Spengler, and Martin Buber. And, they also read modern American, Russian, French and Latin American literature. And yet, Martin Carter was, in a very real sense, a home grown poet. Apart from brief sojourns abroad, he lived in Guyana most of his life. Shelley tells us that poets hold up gigantic mirrors in which a society can see creative reflections of itself, and Martin Carter, in the five decades of his adult life, held up a mirror in which Guyanese society saw unique images of itself. The light and shadows in the mirror of his words heightened the images of what we are as a people. He took words from our everyday speech, our oral tradition, mixed them in the crucible of his imagination, and when he gave them back to us, they were touched with magic. His creative alchemy made those words etch themselves on the palimpsest of our minds indelibly.

> I do not sleep to dream but dream to change the world.

Martin Carter's political awakening marked the second stage in the evolution of his poetic vision, and he became our first important revolutionary poet, and what he did as a revolutionary poet was this: he used words, images, incendiary ideas like etching knives to tear across minds caught up in a dreaming torpor.

> I take again my nigger life, my scorn
> and fling it in the face of those who hate me

He crafts words, images, symbols, ideas and throws them back at us:

> jumping shadows...
> the combustion of my days...
> morning locked against the sun...
> houses tight with sickness...
> oceans of memory sinking in the sand...
> the prostrate coughing hour...

What fantastic images these random lines from his poems conjure up! Quite inadvertently, he was creating a new language, one with words that we could speak aloud and listen to inside the mind's ear at the same time – incendiary words, tender words, words opening like sleep-and-wake flowers! And this takes us to the third stage in the evolution of Martin Carter's poetic vision, when he abandoned rigid ideologies during a tempestuous period in which Guyanese society was acting like a scorpion trying to sting itself to death. It was a time when the pristine dream of independence from colonial rule and freedom for all, had turned into a nightmare of internecine strife and repression, when the posturings and grotesqueries of a neo-colonial dictatorship had become the order of the day.

'This I have learned,' Martin Carter had cried out with a prophetic voice,

> today a speck
> tomorrow a hero
> hero or monster
> you are consumed...

For decades Martin Carter, instead of leaving Guyana as so many others had done, remained, and protected himself behind a shield of cynicism. But in the midst of social and political strife, and a dictatorship that used murder as an instrument of policy for the first time since the epoch of slavery, his poetic voice rang out like bells of the Angelus, and he sang for us in his 'Poems of Shape and Motion',

I was wandering if I could make myself
nothing but fire, pure and incorruptible...

I was wondering if I could find myself
all that I am in all that I could be...

Great poets have a mighty fire inside them that can take words as brittle as charcoal, and calcine them into diamond, and this is exactly what Martin Carter did, and in doing this, he left us a fitting obituary, for one of the great revolutionary poets of his generation,

Death must not find us thinking that we die...

As our foremost revolutionary poet, Martin Carter's peers are Hikmet, Neruda, Mistral, Vallejo, Roger Mais, Andrew Salkey – the list is open-ended – we must not allow his legacy to perish because of our indifference. He led us down paths of hope and despair but his profound humanity, his courage, his passion for truth, the sheer power of his talent dimmed the despair and brightened the hope.

May, 1998

ERIC HUNTLEY

NO ILLUSIONS

The year is 1953. Brown beetles on two legs and in army jeeps are swarming all over the place. Never before in living memory were British soldiers deployed along the coastal belt. Prior to this occurrence The West Indian Regiment would have been sent. Their presence was, ostensibly, to prevent a 'communist takeover' and to 'maintain law and order' after the suspension of the constitution by the British government. The arrival of British troops numbed and shocked the budding nationalist movement, throwing the general public as well as political activists into confusion. Nothing in the text books we had imbibed had prepared us for anything of this nature. Along with arrests, random searches, books and publications banned, the detention of Martin Carter, among others, helped to still one of the vital consciences of the nationalist movement. The Peoples Progressive Party, unprepared to operate clandestinely, was put to the test.

Among the many items smuggled out of prison was a copy of Martin's *Poems of Resistance*. Having succeeded in getting them out of prison the problem was how to get them printed. With the main printery for the party, owned by Mr Cyril Shaw under police guard, this had to be ruled out. To the rescue came a small printery owned by the government at the Mental Hospital in New Amsterdam and managed by a supporter of the party. Cheddi Jagan, at this time not yet arrested but whose movements were restricted to Georgetown, sent the manuscript to me for delivery to the printer. One of the poems in the collection, 'I will not still my voice' had an instant impact among the activists who dared the emergency regulations and sold copies on the streets and in homes. For many, these poems were to restore the fighting spirit so badly bruised by the recent events.

Fortunately, we had known better times, particularly during the early fifties when hope was like a banner at full mast. It was a time of tremendous camaraderie. For those of us like Martin who were former government employees and were now unemployed it was a time of sharing. With 'mauby money' in our pockets, the occasional drink and cigarettes for Martin and other smokers, we managed to keep our collective dreams alive.

Martin was of course a father to Keith and husband to Phyllis. With the dismissal from office of the PPP and a future of unemployment, Martin was the first father I knew who took care of his baby son while his wife went to work. Changing of nappies, bottle feeding were not always a convivial atmosphere to conduct political discussions, but we managed.

Martin, of course, was not only a poet but also a political activist and member of the executive council of the PPP. However he was never one to follow the party-line unquestioningly. As members of the left wing of the party we met occasionally and agreed on a general position. However, during the course of final discussion in the full council, Martin would ask questions to draw out from speakers all the possibilities for a resolution of the issue. If as a result of the ensuing discussion more light was shed on the issue which convinced him otherwise, he would follow his own mind, regardless of what was decided on previously. Aggravating as this was, this quest for the truth was much more important for him than party political loyalty. Little did I know at the time that his habit of asking questions helped not only himself but the listener as well, who became part of the process with Martin acting as the catalyst or midwife.

The decision to select Martin as a candidate for the New Amsterdam constituency in the 1953 election was in itself an anomaly. As a member of the left wing of the party we had sufficient support to place him in a safe seat. Indeed, if the party as a whole felt that it was important to have someone of Martin's calibre in Parliament, then it was up to us to find him a safe seat. This was however not done and as everyone knew, his chances of winning against W.O.R. Kendall were low, if not impossible. However, I do not believe this mattered to Martin, for once selected he decided to use the campaigning, as Eric Williams of Trinidad did much later, as a people's university. Meetings held at the corner of Pitt and Main Street in New Amsterdam became a forum at which issues such as the World Movement for Peace between East and West, the liberation struggles for an end to colonialism, the history of the West Indies, the philosophies of ancient Greeks and Chinese and much more were discussed. Never once did Martin ask for the vote of his listeners, choosing instead to share with his countrymen and women his vast knowledge and insights of world history and religions. Of course, Martin could not have done all this alone; and by his side were Rory Westmaas, Herbert Thomas, Neville Annibourne, Jessica Huntley, Cheddi Jagan, Harry Lall, and others. New Amsterdamers had never before or since seen or heard anything like it.

It was an election campaign in which the party's supporters' hopes were without bounds. In April 1953, when the PPP won, it found itself inundated with demands for solutions to many pent-up demands and grievances from the electorate. It soon became evident that the party could not satisfy the mountains of requests and it was Martin's editorial in the party's paper *Thunder*, under the caption 'We Harbour no Illusions', which recognised and let the electorate know that the party might be 'in office' but they were not 'in power'.

Martin's wealth of storytelling did not diminished with age and on my last visit to Guyana in 1992 he related the following story told to him by Bally Latchmansingh (now deceased) a fellow detainee from West Berbice.

A member of his family went to roundup some cattle in the savannah on the Berbice coast. For several days nothing was heard from him and a search party was sent out. He was finally found, exhausted and near to death, he had lost his way. His family, so glad to have him back and shocked at his poor health, fed him continually in the hope that this would restore him. Having survived the ordeal of starvation he died soon after from overeating. Even love can end in tragedy.

JANET JAGAN

GLIMPSES OF MARTIN CARTER IN HIS EARLY YEARS

I have not seen very much printed about Martin Carter's life. What we have are several editions of his poetry, from the pages of early *Kyk-over-Al* publications in the forties and fifties and a series of prints of local poets known as the Miniature Poets, which included Martin Carter's *The Hill of Fire Glows Red*. I remember this edition very well because those seeking to print the series solicited donations at several quarters and I made my contribution. At one time I had all of the entire collection of the small, about 5 inches long, very neat books of poetry. This edition of 1951 contained some of his most magnificent poems and, I am certain, were inspired by his political involvement at that time.

Look again at his 'Three Years After This', his poem to the Enmore Martyrs.

> Three years after this
> I walked behind a memory of flowers
> a memory of flowers red and white
> and yet, and yet my city had no shame
> my city with a prison for a heart...

He was describing our annual commemoration at the graves of the five Enmore workers who were killed in 1948 – 'three years after this'.

'No! I will not still my voice'; 'This is my hand for the revolution'; 'Oh/wake and give to me the flames, the red flames!... Oh/wake and give to me the flames, the red flames!' and his inspiring 'And so/If you see me/looking at your hands/listening when you speak/marching in your ranks/ you must know/I do not sleep to dream, but dream to change the world'. These are the poems of a young, passionate revolutionary, inspired to rid the world and his own Guyana, of repression and exploitation.

Martin Carter was, in the early fifties, a civil servant and thus could not take active part in political life. But he was strongly involved in the radical politics of the time and was, secretly, a member of the People's Progressive Party led by Dr Cheddi Jagan. I was at that time General Secretary and editor of the Party monthly journal *Thunder*. We worked out an arrangement whereby Martin would write for *Thunder*, using the name 'M. Black', to protect him from violating the civil service restrictions on being involved in political life. His first recorded publication in *Thunder* was a poem 'The Indian Woman' appearing in September 1950. It was a compassionate poem about the sufferings of plantation life:

> He, dead beat with day's murderous toil;
> She wearied out with weeding come
> To their dim hovel and the rags –
> Those rags called bed of poverty.

His next contribution was in October 1950 when he wrote about 'The children of Israel' in which he discussed the bitter life on sugar estates, comparing it to the persecution by the Pharaohs of the children of Israel. He referred to the Rev. John Smith who had written: 'The rigours of Negro slavery, I believe, can never be mitigated. The system must be abolished' written in 1823. M. Black observed that for believing such things, Smith died in jail 1824.

In *Thunder* of July 1951 M. Black addressed young people, calling on them to destroy evil conditions. He referred to the slums of Georgetown and reminded his readers that the country was under a colonial administration which served the interests of those 'who have made this country into a glorious plantation with dim villages and weary townships'.

During this period, we lived at 97 Laluni Street, Queenstown, Georgetown. Martin lived in Anira Street, which was one block north of Laluni and about a half block down from the cross street. Thus, we were a mere one and one half blocks apart. Meetings of the Executive Committee of the PPP were kept at our house and Martin attended as a secret member. Many times he and Wilson Harris, Guyanese writer and poet, came over to our house in the evenings and read to us their latest poems. Those were unforgettable evenings.

Martin attended many political meetings, although he was not allowed to speak. This poem he gave me after a meeting at Vreed-en-Hoop in November 1951 – 'Last night your voice was ringing/like a horse-shoe on a cloud/ringing to me as though you were my lover. Last night/I could not see your face above the crowd/but your voice rang for the revolution/ like my own heart ringing/my own heart ringing/for fire in a world too cold for life. Last night your voice was ringing/like a bell for the revolution!/ a clear bell for the revolution!'.

In 1953, the PPP contested the first elections under universal adult suffrage. Martin Carter, who by that time had quit the civil service, was a candidate for the New Amsterdam seat. His was one of the few losses, as the PPP won an outstanding victory at the polls. The heady days of our 133 days in office ended on October 9th with the British government suspending the constitution and the arrival of British troops to occupy the country.

Martin and others were detained at the airport (then under US military) known as Atkinson Field. He was heavily involved all during this time and his magnificent *Poems of Resistance* 1954 were inspired by this period of resistance. I remember, along with his wife Phyllis, being involved in the publication of these poems.

All through the years since that time, and despite, at times, very serious political differences, we remained friends. Nothing could wash away those times we all spent together in the struggle to liberate Guyana. In the most recent edition of his selected poems, Martin dedicated the collection 'To the Memory of Dr Cheddi Jagan and the Spirit of Guyana's Independence Movement'. His love and regard for Cheddi withstood time and events over some 47 years.

November 1997

DAVID DE CAIRES

A MEASURE OF HIS HOPE

I met Martin Carter in the early sixties. No longer the young, revolutionary dreaming to change the world Martin was bitterly cynical. We used to meet quite frequently on Sundays at his mother's house in Anira Street, Queenstown, where his elder brother Keith also lived. Keith had, like Martin, been a member of the People's Progressive Party in the fifties. On those Sundays large quantities of rum were consumed. Yeats was Martin's favourite poet and he would frequently recite passages from his work, in particular from 'Easter 1916', the part near the end that begins 'And what if excess of love bewildered them till they died' as well as excerpts from 'The Second Coming'. Keith's favourite party piece as the day progressed and the alcoholic content increased was Pericles funeral oration. Rory Westmaas, another mate from the fifties, would sometimes be there. Rory delighted in singing a song from the Spanish civil war.

Throughout the day there would be loud declamations against a variety of institutions and people. At first I was quite concerned about how the neighbours would take all of this. I later recognised that they had become quite used to it and had either written Keith and Martin off as incurably eccentric or were too overawed to do anything. I understood that what was going on was essentially a *cri de coeur* against the colonial condition, accentuated, I believe, by their own internal contradictions.

Keith and Martin were both exceptionally intelligent men, steeped in European culture but with deep seated radical impulses. Typical of the mixed middle class in some ways, but not in others, they exemplified some of the contradictions in the West Indian intelligentsia. They were both lapsed communists and indeed one of the first questions they would ask a new acquaintance with left wing credentials, real or imagined, was 'have you thawed out yet?' Keith was the more radical, Martin the poet and thinker.

When the *New World Fortnightly* magazine was started in October 1964 Martin wrote us a letter of welcome which was published in our first issue. In it, among other things, he said:

> Life in a country as materialistic and philistine as B.G. soon blunts the edge of the mind. The almost fanatical preoccupation with hollow issues, the gossip-mongering which passes for conversation, and the inevitable political hysteria, leave little time for the serious examination of ideas. I know that the psychological squalor of everyday life is exhausting. I know that the urgent practical problem of making a living comes first. What I do not know is why only so few revolt, either by word or by deed against such acute spiritual discomfort.

At the end of 1964 Martin gave us five poems under the title 'Jail me quickly'. They were published in our second, third and fourth issues and created a considerable impression. They were republished in issue No.34 on 18th February, 1996. The poems were 'Black Friday 1962', 'After one year', 'What can a man do more', 'Where are free men' and 'Childhood of a voice'. They have always been among my favourites. *New World Fortnightly* was published on a shoestring budget and I regret to say no fee was paid. We were deeply touched by Martin's generosity and support in allowing us first publication.

In 1966 we invited Martin Carter and George Lamming to be the joint editors of the *Guyana Independence Issue* of *New World*. In addition to his work as editor Martin contributed 'A question of self contempt' with its wonderful vignettes on Mr Bovell and Mr Singh. I believe this should be a part of any anthology of Martin's work. It contains the following passage: 'And I looked at Bovell's skull and saw a bump. I wondered whether an owner had turned homuncule and taken up residence. My own head I rubbed. He was wondering why. Incapable of explanation, I remained silent'.

George and Martin did an excellent job but unfortunately we ended up heavily in debt. We printed too many copies, largely due to George's enthusiasm on the possibility of overseas sales. Regrettably we were never paid by our distributors in London, New York and elsewhere and *New World Fortnightly* ceased publication shortly thereafter.

Martin has been a director of Guyana Publications Limited, the company that publishes the newspaper *Stabroek News* of which I am chairman, since its inception in 1986, the year after President Forbes Burnham died.

For the past ten years Martin, Lloyd Searwar, Miles Fitzpatrick, Ian McDonald and myself have had dinner once a month at each other's homes to share our news.

Martin Carter is a large man in every sense of that word. With his strong, brooding presence and his eternal, bitter hope he has always represented for many of us a challenge to keep going and to do what we can and a proof of the enormous potential and possibilities in our Caribbean region. His bitterness and despair have been a measure of his hope. In his various undertakings, his trials and tribulations, his long depression he has retained a quality of spiritual integrity without which we would all have been much poorer.

August, 1997

Milton Williams

FOR MARTIN CARTER

Dear friend and brother, today I sit
in my bedsitter and think of our negritude;
and about the history of our wounds;
our separation from our pristine hamlet
in some African village or city,
or that beside the river Ganges.
And I know we are cursed by our adoption,
by our transplantation and subsequent mutilation
in the rice and canefields of the New World
of Guyana, where especially we emerged.
And I understand now more than in nineteen
fifty-three, when our constitution was superseded,
and you were placed behind barbed-wire fences,
how you vanguarded our rehabilitation.
For there I was, an inscrutable English,
and was nonplussed by the words, Imperialists and Colonials;
by the necessity of seeing everything as black and white.
Yet now, after twelve unhappy years in England,
where I have felt the strangeness of being black
and a colonial most lividly, I see you
as smitten by the mail of integrity
and I concur. Never think this as being too late.
I am a singer. I want to be a very great singer.
Though suspended four thousand miles away
I must embrace my roots or die unfilled.

DEREK WALCOTT

'...HIS IMPULSE IS ALWAYS LYRICAL'

in conversation with David Dabydeen

DABYDEEN: I have a feeling reading Carter that there is something 'unfinished' about this work and I don't think it's to do with rum drinking – that is, not doing enough work – and I was wondering if it had to do with the politics of the region, the lack of support for the arts, that dictatorship, that grinding despair that afflicted writers. Do you think that is why it is 'unfinished'?

WALCOTT: No, I don't think I would call it unfinished, I don't think you mean technically but I know what you mean. I think you mean there is some kind of conclusion which is not necessarily a personal or moral conclusion. I think Martin never stopped being responsible for his society. The danger of responsibility is that it can be too generic. In that sense, I think you may feel that about his work and I perfectly understand it. The thing about Marxist poetry or any poetry of ideology is obviously that a lot of it sustains its belief in the ideology, really believes in the possibility of the ideology – and that kind of poetry is going to have to come up with optimism. Optimism leads to social prophecy and so what one has to respect is that devotion Carter had to the idea of responsibility – it can lead to another kind of generic feeling in which the poet subdues personal feeling for something larger which may be a vision: and words like vision and prophecy and dream become common words in that kind of vocabulary which draws its source and power from an idea of the people, of the country, an idea of equality – all of them fair and just.

In fact what I'm saying would be the antithesis of what a writer like Carter might believe and that is my personal interpretation of what the human condition may be. In that case I would agree with the very accurate kind of question which you may ask of certain kinds of political poets. There were certain poets like Yevtushenko or Mayakovsky who were a strong influence on Martin Carter. Because nothing is finished the work of man is unfinished. But the poem does need a conclusion and perhaps that conclusion is private and by that sense treacherous because it is private. If he is saying 'I grew up in a nigger yard yesterday or I did this or I did that' that 'I' is not only him, that is an absent 'I', that is a statement for the race. So there is another edge – I think I know what you feel is that edge is missing a kind of a conclusion, a sort of harmony or symmetry or what Yeats called a closed box of a poem. Martin's sense of being responsible for the society is a very,

very noble thing but it may lead to oversimplification of a condition. But don't forget there are also many personal poems of Martin's.

DABYDEEN: He moves away from the early political Marxist optimistic poetry and he enters into a deep individualistic, metaphysical brooding. There's a density about his later work, the language almost moves to abstraction away from the concrete realities of Guyana. Do you think that his movement towards abstraction has to do with the landscape of Guyana?

WALCOTT: I've only made the one trip to Guyana. By the way, Martin was a terrifying person in many ways. Martin was a bad drunk, he was very abusive, he was very angry, he was angry because he was surrounded by people he might have called idiots. Guyana was a very strong Protestant base and he tried to build a revolution out of that Protestant thing – but revolution is more easily Catholic. Revolution is close to blasphemy and there is nothing to blaspheme against in Protestant Guyana. Apart from the direct social-economic challenge posed by the condition of cane-workers and labourers, the heredity of cruelty that is in the Caribbean. I thought the Guyanese, as a middle-class, were very elegant and also very self-contained, very self-assured and in a way, irritatingly self-assured, very smug in many ways and I can see easily why Martin would have been infuriated. I can see why you could get Marxist poetry out of that kind of supercilious, self-centred character that existed in Guyana. What Guyana has produced is a very rebellious kind of artist, so that all the terrific actors, painters and writers who have come from Guyana, have come against an exasperation of a system that settled in itself.

What I felt in Guyana was that, behind my back, there was such overwhelming sense of space, size – I couldn't take it. I come from a small island and I haven't travelled that much and I thought – behind my back there is infinity and I carried the weight of that infinity in terms of horizon, the savannahs of Guyana, and I felt that sense of width would tend to make a writer, like Carter, as it does other writers. And that sense of space was pretty close to the idea of a Russia – in other words the same expanse in the concept of Russia, including the concept of rebelling against, in Guyana's case, Bookers. That was a sociopolitical addition to the space. And then there was this ignoring of the presence of an Amerindian mythology. So writers like Martin and Wilson Harris show that there is another part of Guyana which may be the real part of Guyana, not the world of recent arrivals, including the Africans.

DABYDEEN: Coming back to the idea of being unfinished, there's a beautiful line in *Texaco:* when Marie dies Chamoiseau talks about 'the Cathedral that death has broken.' There is really a deep religious impulse, a metaphysical intensity, in Carter's poetry. But I remember the cathedral in Guyana, it always strikes me as being unfinished because of the tropical weather, the way that the sun bleaches the cathedral, the way that the wood is eaten away and sometimes I wonder if that is the kind of image of Carter himself, a cathedral broken by death but already broken?

WALCOTT: I remember in the early days when I met Martin, I would sit on the veranda with him – I had a couple of guys and a cousin, Slade Hopkinson, all these guys on reflection they were brilliant, they were good conversationalists, they had humour. I'm not talking about misunderstood geniuses but I'm saying that what I felt in Guyana was this intelligence. But there was also this drinking which was frightening, really scary and I drank but it became something more than just drinking – it became a sort of release but almost a punishment, a heaviness, and fatal in some respects. The role that Martin played used to irritate me sometimes because it was too conspicuous a role – it was, 'I am a poet and I'm gonna write poetry and you guys are this or that.' He had to fight to that degree to insist on it. I don't know how he could fight that much to insist on the difference between him and the Guyanese society. The predictable contrast between poet versus philistine. Of course the profounder thing was, it was political – it wasn't just purely the misunderstood genius, it was the two things combined.

But it was only later I began to see that behind him there was a *phenomenal* sweetness of nature – *phenomenal* because I thought, this is not Martin Carter, this is not the bullying drunk that I had heard so much about, admiring his poetry but deciding very often not to get into some kind of argument, certainly, or some kind of position about this or that because I would have been wiped out by the abuse. I could have responded in a very coarse kind of West Indian manner but sometimes the abuse was so devastating that it was terrifying the way he conducted it, he was a conduit of it. That was there a lot. Then I began to see other things about him that redeemed it, the gentleness that was there even in body, in gesture and in voice was extremely moving and extremely sweet and if we are talking about his poetry and the man, I think there is that in him in contrast and balance to the vehemence and the belligerence.

The other thing is this. It is so Guyanese where Martin is and he is so rooted in Guyana, so profoundly responsible for the place, that his voice hasn't attracted foreign publishers. The sound of his voice may have been too rhetorical for a European publisher, though probably not for a Russian publisher. Certain kinds of rhetorical poetry, however passionate, becomes special to its origin which is Guyana. When you see Carter sliding into something very emblematic, and very powerful, then here's what happens for me. You get very close to something that is a very powerful, reinforced cliché in a way; it is using that because it is addressing people, being on a platform or public square to some degree and still bringing into the situation a personal poignancy. 'I see the vultures practising to wait' – it's a terrific line because they aren't actually waiting, but practising to wait, that is, the shifting of their bodies and the weight of their bodies – 'practising' is like grating on galvanize, chalk on board, and actually the effect becomes acid and irritating. Technically it's a superb line and there are many lines like that that happen. But, in a sense it is still a rhetorical sound, it still has an echo of the past, like an echo-chamber sound. I don't know the latest stuff too well. The whole question – and this will include you as a Guyanese writer – is that there is a challenge for me, and the bewilderment... you see here, where you are now, you can step outside and you are in the presence of a particular thing, a hell of a view, strong sunshine, sea, a beautiful view, right. And there is something that continues to cleanse, there is a sense of continual cleansing that happens in the wind and the sea, a refreshing cleansing that happens. I didn't feel like that in Guyana – huge as it was, I felt that in some ways there was a feeling of terrifying entrapment and that the writer had to break through that and the way to break through it could not be the conventional 1, 2, 3 sequence of either novel or poem. This is what Wilson virtually says and what Martin in his own way was saying later, and the painters as well. That is a permissible mythology, very permissible. The bafflement and the mystery that happens in terms of space and the terror of those infinite spaces which made the city with all the external paraphernalia of a city, basically a settlement on the edge of a river.

Anyway, back to Martin, his impulse was always lyrical, he was a great reciter, he had a great voice, he had a great joy in the sound of the poem. In terms of assessment, I would say the example of his work was phenomenal and the sweetness was – in the end I finally felt extremely close to him when we last read together – I felt a tenderness that was extremely moving. He was so softly spoken and so gentle. I've seen the other side of him. This morning I looked at myself and I took some stuff out and I began to look at West Indian writing – you know, I have a collection. And I said to myself, why have you segregated these people, why are they on a shelf over there and all the other guys – no, it's just that I have a West Indian shelf. I began to take books out – I took out Garth St. Omer and I looked at the prose and I thought this is good. I looked at John Hearne's book, I looked at the prose, I said this is good. I looked at Jamaica Kincaid's book, I thought this is damn good and so it went. And so as I went from book to book, just checking I thought – West Indian literature even in English is totally underestimated, *totally*. The literature is astonishing, the quality is astonishingly high. And Martin's position in all of this is special.

Saint Lucia, January 1999

GEORGE LAMMING

MARTIN CARTER: A POET OF THE AMERICAS

(in conversation with Stewart Brown)

BROWN: Do you recall what your reaction was to Martin Carter's poems when you first encountered them?

LAMMING: Only that it was a very authentic voice, and all the more so because it was linked to the events taking place in Guiana. Guiana in the 1950s and especially around 1952, '53, a little before the suspension of the constitution, was in fact, I would say, politically the most advanced in consciousness of all the Caribbean territories and it was the one that was targeted as the most dangerous because of this definition – self-definition sometimes – of the PPP as Marxist or Leninist or so on, so that Guiana was always in the news and voices coming out of Guiana had a special significance.

What I think was unusual and very striking was that the English speaking Caribbean was not used to having poets who were so directly involved with active political movements, as Carter was, or who put poetry in the service of such a movement. I am not aware of any precedent within the English speaking Caribbean. That kind of engagement was more a feature of Hispanic writing within the region, so he stood out for that reason. And then his work had this remarkable sweep. There was something about Carter's early poems that had an echo of Whitman, that sweep, that freedom of line, so one tended to think of him as a poet of the Americas rather than of the islands.

BROWN: Do you remember when you first met Martin?

LAMMING: Yes, very vividly. I met him on my return visit to the Caribbean and what was my first visit to Guiana, in 1955. I had been in the United States as a Guggenheim Fellow and then I had an assignment to do an article for *Holiday* on the Caribbean which took me through all the territories, and I ended up in Guiana. I found a Guiana that was still in a State of Emergency, after the suspension of the constitution and the imprisonment of the Ministers. Carter had been in prison and when I met him he was still under a kind of house arrest really, he could not go beyond a radius of about half a mile from the house and there were regulations restricting the number of people who could visit the house at any one time. This had been going on for some time. He was very drawn but amazingly cheerful, he had a way of describing horror as though there were some sort of comic element in it. He was, on the surface, without any sign of bitterness, although I am reasonably sure that there was a lot of pain and hurt and resentment going on inside him. Resentment at the notion that a little Governor – as I think he would have imagined the Governor to be – could in fact come into what he regarded as his land, Carter's land, and dictate where he could go and where he could not go. I think he felt a kind of humiliation, personal and collective, about that predicament. I remember that very well, I was very moved by that.

I recall a remarkable party held just before I left Guiana. I was producing some radio programmes – presenting the literature of the region through radio, and we discovered that the Governor, a man called Renison,[1] listened to these programmes regularly. So when, at the end of the series, I asked a friend of mine to let us have a party in his house for all the people involved in the programmes, somebody suggested we send an invitation to Rennison. So we did, and Rennison sent back, saying that yes he would come. Now that was a big secret, not letting anyone know that he was coming, because we had already invited Cheddi Jagan who had been involved in the programmes. So Jagan was there with his wife, and then Rennison came and people were astonished. I mention that because I remember that I introduced Rennison to Carter and they got to talking. But Rennison wasn't fully aware of whom he was talking to – in the sense of the total circumstances of Carter's situation – and he was telling Martin about the quality of the light on the skyline when he drove around a certain area of the city in the early evening and he asks Carter 'had he been around there recently?' and of course Martin said 'No, it wouldn't be legal for me to do that,' and Rennison just stopped immediately, realising that he had entered territory for which he hadn't fully prepared himself. But Carter didn't pursue that any further.

BROWN: You worked with Carter in 1965, co-editing the Guyana Independence issue of *New World Quarterly*.

LAMMING: *New World* was a very fine quarterly. They had the idea that they would do a special issue to celebrate the independence of Guyana and they brought me out, I was living in London then, to edit the issue and Carter would assist me. Martin, who is very good at reading and editing and so on is not so good at any kind of organised activity and I had some difficulty because most of the time I couldn't find him. I didn't know where he was and nobody knew where he was at that time. I think that was a very bad time for him because after moving from that revolutionary, anti-imperialist, anti-capitalist period he was unemployed for some time until he was rescued, in an odd kind of way, by Bookers – the company that most obviously represented the continuation of that old social order. He edited some kind of in-house paper for the company and I think that he was rather burdened by his predicament of having to do such things in order to support his family.

However I remember that he was extremely good in a particular situation we had to resolve. We wanted the Independence issue of the journal to cut across all the party lines but that was very difficult because we had asked Burnham – who was then in power – if he would help in facilitating an order for the journal. We didn't want any money from him directly but we knew that the journal would be of a quality that it should be circulated among the schools – it was to be a sale and a purchase, not a subsidy. Well Burnham said 'yes' automatically, because Burnham liked the idea of being associated with that kind of product and especially with the names of the people at a regional level who were associated with it. But we also wanted Jagan. However, the polarisation of the parties in Guiana at that time was so intense that the very mention of Burnham to Jagan, or visa versa would normally put an end to any further conversation. So getting the two of them to agree to appear in the same issue of the journal would be a real scoop.

I particularly wanted Jagan because I had got hold of the first chapter – though it wasn't published yet – of what became his autobiography, *The West On Trial*. And that's the best chapter in the whole book, it's the chapter in which he speaks about growing up in the Corentyne, as a boy without shoes until he came into Georgetown. It's a very very moving chapter. I asked Martin to join me and we went to see Cheddi early in the morning, to ask him whether we could open the journal with his chapter. We didn't tell him about the government purchase but what we told him was that since the journal was a celebration of independence, as a matter of courtesy we were going to ask Burnham to just write a preface for the issue. Eventually, after a long discussion, after I had described in detail what would be in it, like the famous essay by C. L. R. James on Kanhai etc, marvellous stuff, Cheddi agreed. I think the success of that mission to persuade Cheddi to let us use his work really had to do with the lingering affection that Jagan had for Carter, and that the feeling was mutual. Although he had broken with Jagan – he had broken with all of them in a way – at a party level, he had never broken at the level of personal friendships. It was very extraordinary, although the break was so decisive, and caused so much bitterness, one had a sense of Carter being deeply valued, respected and loved, at a personal level and as a citizen, by Jagan.

BROWN: Did you keep in touch with Carter after that period?

LAMMING: Yes, we met at intervals because I then became very attached to Guyana and made several visits to Guyana when I was in the Caribbean. And Carter then came once to Barbados, he had a daughter who was married there. And then we met in Havana on various occasions, so it was that kind of friendship, when ever we were in the same country somehow or other we made a point of meeting up.

BROWN: Do you have favourite poems of Carter's?

LAMMING: I always return to 'University of Hunger', a wonderfully sustained kind of ballad, and I find 'I Come from the Nigger Yard' a very very fine poem, which used to blow peoples minds at one time but the more I read it I come to understand that there is much more in that poem than just protest noise. This is the interesting thing about Carter, when you re-read the early Carter, the poems that are in appearance political poems have a dimension that is not usually inherent in ordinary political poems. You see that 'I Come from the Nigger Yard' and 'University of Hunger' and other poems from *Poems of Resistance* secrete or conceal a particular vision of a society that is threatened by abortion. Carter is always having that vision. You see it then when you move away from the overtly political poems in the 'Poems of Shape and Motion', that attempt to describe a coming into being, a wanting to be other than what is. And so I don't really see a break in Carter at all, I see a change in tone and modalities of expression but I think there is a continuity of vision right through to the very hermetic *Poems of Affinity*. And even in those later poems when there is an occasion which 'triggers' him – a poem like 'Assassins of the Voice' which I use a lot in speaking of the fear and cowardice of that new plantation bourgeoisie – you see again, one may say the old Carter but it's the same, the same Carter vision. And always with a great concern for craft. Carter is much more concerned than people normally understand, about the shape and texture of the poem. Whatever he may be writing about, 'craft' is very high on his list of requirements for the poem. That is not a quality that one normally associates with writers of political protest poetry.

BROWN: No, and he was an intellectual too, in ways that don't fit with that stereotype of the emotional poet of protest, both very interested in and very knowledgeable about current issues in critical theory and philosophy.

LAMMING: Yes, well, unlike many Caribbean writers of my acquaintance, Carter was also a great reader, a voluminous reader, and he read under the compulsion of what I would call a very philosophic turn of mind. Carter thinks very much in the way that the philosopher would think, and he brings that philosophic turn of mind to all details, however minimal, of the society. So that he has a way sometimes, even in normal conversation, of talking in metaphors about very ordinary things that had not really struck him as all that ordinary at all.

BROWN: Would you locate Carter's work alongside your own in any way?

LAMMING: I think there would be parallels. I think we would share a view that it wasn't just a question of being anti-colonial, because behind what appears to be the anti-colonial statement there is an appeal for the creation of an alternative society. It's not a question of just getting rid of people – foreigners, white rule and so on, though that is there and has to be stated, but inside that appeal there is also the critique – which runs through my work – the critique of that delinquent, emergent middle class that is just waiting to take over and who really represent nothing different from the people they are trying to replace. It's really an attempt to call into being an order of society and a state of social relations which we imagine to be potential in the society and to be capable of realisation.

BROWN: Carter was unusual in that he moved from expressing his views about social injustice to actually becoming a practising politician at one point in his career, a move which drew various kinds of comment – some of it negative – at the time. I wonder how you felt about what he had done?

LAMMING: I didn't pay too much attention to it, though I may have talked to him about it at times. I don't think anyone ever doubted Carter's integrity. Whatever he entered, whatever the strains were, he could offer a moral and valid reason for doing it, even if there were things he took no pleasure in doing. I am absolutely sure he took no pleasure in being a member of the government. He wasn't the kind of person to whom that had much appeal – that 'status' would not appeal to him as something – in itself – worth having. He wasn't that type at all. Why then would you get committed in that way? I think the reason that he might offer, not even verbally but to himself, was that he saw himself as being used in a positive way. He represented something that could not be found in other members of the government. And therefore he was there on behalf of Guyana, he was not there on behalf of Burnham, if you see what I mean, he was not intervening on behalf of Burnham, rather he was intervening on behalf of whatever is decent in Guyana. And that is why he never held these positions for very long.

BROWN: You've said that you don't really see that division that others have noticed, stylistically, between his early and his later work

LAMMING: No, its the continuity of vision that I see, but there is a difference in the style, certainly. The rhetorical resonance of '...Nigger Yard' and 'University of Hunger' for example, a lot of that is reduced, almost weeded out in the later work. But it happens in stages really, the 'Poems of Shape and Motion' sequence seems to act a kind of bridge between the early poems and the later. You get to 'Shape and Motion' and he's moving deeper and deeper inside himself as distinct from articulating the external world. Going inside. Then I think he reaches the point in the *Poems of Affinity*, which are autobiographically very exact, that there was a tragedy at work in Guyana that went beyond utterance, you had to stumble or speak in syllables. He senses a monster, a demon, something which could no longer just be reported on or analysed, you had to stammer when you approached it. And there is that sense, in the later poems of cutting language down, very bare, very spare. And I think that what he is looking at in *Poems of Affinity* is also what he is fearing might happen in the earlier poems, but that vision of potential – in the Angela Davis poem for example – is still there, but there is a tension in him between that and an increasing pessimism, really, about the possibility of his ever seeing it fulfilled.

BROWN: Both as a man and as a poet Carter seems to have been almost universally revered within Guyana and across the Caribbean. Why do you think that was?

LAMMING: Carter has a stature in the collective consciousness of Guyana that is quite unique among writers in the English speaking Caribbean. I mean in Guyana the name Martin Carter had a resonance as something authentically Guyanese, as one of the Guyanese institutions, one of the institutions of which they are most proud. I was very struck by that. It is very much like the way people respond to the name Nicholas Guillen in Cuba, 'Nicholas' can only be one Nicholas, its Guillen. I think that has a lot to do with the marriage of the poet and the activist in struggle in the early 1950s, that he is remembered in that way. And at that time Carter's speeches would quite often take the form of the reading of those poems. A number of those poems in *Poems of Resistance* would be read at those political meetings and those memories of the poet inside that kind of struggle, and of that kind of struggle taken to another level by the poet, those memories went very deep in the consciousness of a generation. And they got transmitted to succeeding generations. He once told me a very interesting story... much later when he was in the deeps... that one of the things which gave him the most solace was that he was once walking somewhere and there was a little girl, who must have been maybe six years old or something like that, who saw him and called out to her mother, 'Mummy Mummy look, that look like the poems man there.' And that business of being identified by a six year old as 'the poems man' gave him a joy that went beyond any critical analysis.

BROWN: And do you think the fact that he stayed in Guyana more or less throughout his life contributed to that sense of identification the Guyanese people felt with him and his work?

LAMMING: I'm not too sure that that is so. He is unlike all the other Caribbean writers who have become known beyond the Caribbean who have had their reputations made outside the region. We would not have been known or accepted in that way, had we not been accepted outside. Carter is one of the few, if not the only one, whose reputation was made inside the region and validated inside it, that did not require external validation. For most of the other writers their constituencies, in terms of their readers, required the validation as to whether it was a great book from the *Observer* or the *Statesman* or the *Times* or the New York whatever. That validation was necessary in terms of putting the seal of approval, 'yes this is worthwhile, ours…' on the work. And he never had that external validation, in a way it came from within and that is very unusual.

About the remaining home, I've never been quite clear why that happened. Whether it was early marriage or whatever I'm not sure. I'm inclined to think, sometimes, that it was a pity he didn't get a break from Guyana because I think that his staying put in Guyana did great damage to him and forced him to do great damage to himself in a variety of ways. He might have experienced some kind of relief if there was a certain distance for a while, I mean away. Whenever he went out it was for very brief spells.

BROWN: Do you think there is anything in the notion of his work being *too* deeply rooted in the Guyanese experience to easily transcend its time and place? And if not, how explain his relative obscurity when other, less accomplished Caribbean poets seem to have impressed international publishers?

LAMMING: I don't know… I would have thought that his quality as a poet is so good, I mean in my view he is one of the best, much better than some of the more prominent poets who are the most promoted. But if he is that good a poet and is that authentic to the Caribbean, he really ought to have some kind of appeal outside, because the two things go together. I don't think the one goes without the other although it is quite true that the relation to the Caribbean may help in the promotion of certain writers rather than others.

One reason is partly that he has been (sometimes literally) locked inside the Caribbean, he's not been out much, he's not been a man given to conferencing and being engaged in the kind of networking that takes place, you know, in these kind of gatherings. And I've always felt, with Martin, whether it was about poetry or anything else, that he has no gifts at all for self promotion. Anything that is going to happen, in a positive way for Martin, somebody else is going to have to organise that. Carter is wholly and totally without that instinct for self promotion and I have a feeling that that may explain, not the neglect really but the overlooking of his work, he just doesn't engage at all in any kind of self promotion… and my impression of him always has been that he is without any sense of competing with others, you know he has a very firm sense of his value and what it is he set out to do and he feels no need of arguing whether he is better than or not as good as anyone, he's not disturbed in the slightest.

BROWN: Finally, looking back over the last 50 years and the emergence of Caribbean writing as a significant body of literature, where would you put Carter's work in that story?

LAMMING: Well I think that if you are looking at the literature he will remain among the greatest of the writers of that period. I think if we explore what is there we have a very major statement about the region. I think it's a pity that we didn't have more of his prose, for he wrote with a remarkable lucidity when he's trying to get that vision across in prose, like his piece on the role of the artist that we published in that Independence edition of *New World*. But I think that his place as such is very secure and I think that with time, when they are looking to see what kinds of utterance came from the corners of these Americas then Carter will stand in the very first ranks of the writers of the Americas.

Sheffield, May, 1999.

1. Wilson Harris, in his account of the party (see p. 293) says that the Governor was Sir Alfred Savage.

Syl Lowhar

TO MARTIN CARTER

Your voice and tongue are wind and wave
Breaking the dykes of Europe's power;
Your heart's a Shango drum
Waking the spirit of your ancestor
From the damp shadow of his leafy grave
Deep in the Canje Creek. If he could speak
Lips would spill an epitaph in blood,
Vengeance secrete from his bare bone,
Priming the dung-rich stalks to bloom with fire.
But he is cold and silent as a stone
That the torrential stream has pushed aside.
If you could dream of nightmares in the wood
With dogs nosing those footprints in the swamp;
Of his encounter
With cutlass, whip, his own black brother,
You'd curse your colour and your race forever
On the Groyne where the wet wind groans
The hair of the drowned is washed like weed;
Rafts rock in the waves, foam spits on our dead
Whose seed and runners spread throughout the land.
If only Massacooraman would come
To avenge our murdered fathers
And break these powered liners
Arriving again for gold.

        Listen!
There is a stirring in the leaves;
A movement on the banks of three great rivers.
Birds panic from trees into the sky
Shrieking, shedding feathers.
The drum beats louder, louder
The echo deep inside grows clearer, clearer,
I see a creature rising from the water,
Whose eyes are torches of fire.

First published in the Guyana Independence Edition of *New World Quarterly*, 1966.

JOHN LA ROSE

MARTIN CARTER 1927-1997: A PERSONAL MEMOIR

The name Martin Carter came out of nowhere, out of the blue. In conversation. From the lips of Janet Jagan. She came from Guyana, still then British Guiana, to visit us, to establish closer links between us. With us she was welcome; very welcome, but not at all welcome with the British colonial authorities, not with the Governor and not with Renison, then Colonial Secretary of Trinidad and Tobago. They banned her from the country and deported her back to Guyana. This ban in 1952 was the new beginning of the bans of pro-independence leaders from countries all over the region by the British colonial power.

We were the Workers Freedom Movement in process of becoming the West Indian Independence Party. All the key trade unions and their leaders adhered to the WIIP. Lennox Pierre, a leading progressive lawyer, poet and steelband expert and musical innovator, became Chairman; and I became the General Secretary. Like Lennox my interests and involvement were also with literature, kaiso, carnival, steelband, music, radio broadcasting, and the study of language.

Our closest Caribbean relationship was with the PPP and our links grew closer over the years. The links extended beyond politics. Janet Jagan was the General Secretary and Martin Carter, a public cultural and social figure, was a member of the PPP executive. For us, especially for Lennox Pierre and myself and the many other serious cultural figures in our movement, *Kyk-over-al* from Guyana and *Bim* from Barbados were a continuation of the halcyon *Beacon* period with its short stories, music and social critique.

Janet Jagan knew that we, I in particular, had already met and spent many long hours in discussion with Linden Burnham, another major leader of the PPP. Odo, as we also called him, had come to Trinidad for his marriage to Sheila Latasse an optician whose family was Trinidadian and lived in St Clair. He had made a good impression on us and we made plans for future interchange.

During her visit, we became aware, from information she provided, of the internal rivalries and leadership difficulties within the PPP. She spoke highly of Martin Carter and Sydney King. Both were members of what she regarded as the progressive section of the PPP. In *Thunder*, the organ of the PPP, which we received as they were published, we avidly read articles by these two and discussed their range, erudition, and literary style, as well as their ideological, political and social direction. These were movements travelling in the same direction towards Federation, Independence and Socialism. They were not ideological monoliths. They were coalitions, confections of various ideological, social and ethnic strands like all trade unions and popular movements.

What followed in later years, when the splits in the PPP occurred, possessed the novelistic quality of historical vagary, of epic effort and tragic journey as in C.L.R. James's *The Black Jacobins.*

The first publication of Martin Carter's poetry, that we saw, was *The Hill of Fire Glows Red,* in the series published by A J Seymour. It confirmed for us the judgement that Janet Jagan had made of Martin's work. Here was a special poetic voice which inflamed the burning angst that fed the fires of our passion for change.

The opening lines of the poem 'Do Not Stare At Me' read like thunder before the storm:

> Do not stare at me from your window, lady,
> do not stare and wonder where I came from...

His poem 'Looking at Your Hands' still moves me whenever I read it, even several decades later:

> And so
> if you see me
> looking at your hands
> listening when you speak
> marching in your ranks
> you must know
> I do not sleep to dream, but dream to change the world.

The last stanza was like an anthem of our hope and aspiration for a world in postwar convulsion. In the dream, in the imagination is the beginning. We dreamt to change the world.

Martin Carter, and the rest of us, were voracious and voluminous readers, probing nuances and testing crosswinds in the urge to forge a new world from the phoenix of failure and folly, heroic striving and fragile success. Guyana in the 1950s was a crucible of change, challenging an oppressive BG, or as some called it, Bookers Guiana. And Martin Carter was at the centre of this maelstrom. The PPP won their stunning victory, winning 18 out of 24 seats in 1953. After only '133 Days to Freedom' their government was forcibly overthrown with an invasion from the Black Watch regiment. Prominent leaders were detained on what was called 'a concentration camp' on the Mazaruni River. Martin Carter was among the detained. In the aftermath came dislocation and ethnic division, which disrupted the earlier vision of multicultural and multi-ethnic accommodation, economic progress and social justice.

Martin Carter's poetry collections: *The Hill of Fire Glows Red* (1951), *The Kind Eagle* (1952), *Returning* (1954) had established his status in Guyana. But it was *Poems of Resistance* (1954) which established his Caribbean and international reputation as a poet in the tradition of Walt Whitman, Pablo

Neruda, Nicolas Guillen and Mayakovsky. All this enduring creativity seems to have emerged like a full-blown butterfly from a very special chrysalis: a literary and cultural matrix in tandem with Wilson Harris, the original imaginative thinker, poet, critic and novelist, and in the overarching presence of A J Seymour poet and editor of *Kyk-over-al*.

I have a photograph of Wilson Harris from that period, concentrating intensely while reading from his first novel. He is sitting surrounded by equally intense listeners, all standing, who included Martin Carter, Ivan Van Sertima, Sidney Singh and Milton Williams. Some appeared to be looking at the writing on the page while he read in what appeared to be a moment of palpable excitement. They were inside the excitement and dilemma of the time.

I met Martin Carter in Trinidad in 1953. He, with two of his comrades, was on the way to a World Festival of Youth. Two of our delegates to the same festival joined them and they travelled away together. The day we met was like a congress into the night: laughter, discussion, information exchange and analysis, argument and challenge, the exuberant meeting of literary, political and philosophical minds. When they returned Martin Carter, Rory Westmaas and another comrade were banned from entering Trinidad. In spite of our legal challenge, they were all deported back to Guyana as Janet Jagan had been months before.

The overthrow of the PPP government aroused an explosion of instant solidarity: open air meetings, demonstrations, meetings in trade union halls, other confrontations. I read, we all read, from *Poems of Resistance* in open air meetings, in almost every solidarity event. Some lines possessed such beautiful resonance and power. Poems like 'University of Hunger' and 'I Come from the Nigger Yard' rallied audiences while the tragic mood and melancholy, the dark foreboding of the moment were encapsulated for us in 'This is the Dark Time My Love'. The opening stanza was like the perpetual anguish of a Goya painting from the Black Goya period, the period of resistance to the Napoleonic invasion:

> This is the dark time, my love.
> All around the land brown beetles crawl about.
> The shining sun is hidden in the sky.
> Red flowers bend their heads in awful sorrow.

His poems 'Letter 1', 'Letter 2' and 'Letter 3' and 'Death of a Comrade' were reminders of the price of suffering and separation, the worth and integrity of defiance, that 'Death must not find us thinking that we die'. But the poem we read most, which bound us together across the seas, that poem was 'I Clench My Fist'. The peroration, in the last stanza, spoke of an unalterable commitment:

> Although you come in thousands from the sea
> Although you walk like locusts in the street

Although you point your guns straight at my heart
I clench my fist above my head; I sing my song of FREEDOM!

But from then, from those times, never such bright morning again.

The pristine hope and assurance, now dented, slowly vanished. Absolute confidence in the future was replaced by growing racial distrust, recrimination and ideological dissatisfaction. Racial symbolisms, which had previously encouraged hope, were now undermined. The all-encompassing progressive future for all was severely punctured. The fault lines of racial rivalries and generally racial voting, exacerbated by determined foreign interventions against Cheddi Jagan's PPP, led, over time, to a deadly explosion of racial riots at the beginning of the 1960s.

I scarcely heard about Martin Carter in those years, only titbits of information from mutual friends. Then, at the height of the gloom of racial violence came his haunting poems of 'Jail Me Quickly':

were some who ran one way
were some who ran another way.
were some who did not run at all.
were some who will not run again.
And I was with them all
when the sun and the streets exploded.

The inventive hiatus in the sentence construction, the heart tug of the words rang out like the opening bars of a funeral march. He was in the turmoil, an integral part of it.

I did not see Martin Carter again for many years, not until I went to Guyana for the celebration of the Co-operative Socialist Republic in February 1970. Andrew Salkey's *Georgetown Journal* (1971) is a record of that event. My most distinct memory of Martin at that time was his always singing 'Where Are All The Flowers Gone'. It was during the visit to Guyana that Martin expressed his hope that New Beacon Books would publish a book of poems and I agreed. Eventually the poems for the book came by hand through Aubrey Williams. Martin's first title for the book was Poems 1970-1950 but, after some time, he changed the title to *Poems of Succession*. And that is how it was published in 1977.

The decision to hold the first Carifesta was taken while we were in Guyana, and soon after we returned Andrew Salkey and I met in London with Martin and A J Seymour. They were on their way to a UNESCO conference in Italy. We met at Andrew Salkey's home. We insisted once again, in keeping with the perspective we had embraced in the Caribbean Artists Movement, that the Carifesta should be truly Caribbean, not simply English speaking areas, especially Martinique, Guadeloupe and Suriname. I had most connections and addresses and we provided them. Carifesta has been till now pan Caribbean.

Martin Carter and I scarcely saw each other after that, but I always heard about him from Aubrey Williams who paid frequent visits to Guyana. We often spoke about Martin and the intriguing succession of difficulty and transcendence in his life. Aubrey seemed to have spent time with Martin whenever he visited Guyana.

I saw Martin Carter later while he was at Essex University and when he came to the conference of Caribbean writers at the Commonwealth Institute. We met at my home. The conversation and discussion was always wide ranging and personal. We had both lived voluminous lives. His last request to us, when we last met, was to obtain a book for him about the philosophy of Leibnitz and send it down to Guyana for him. We did.

In this personal and incomplete memoir I end with a quotation from the 'Poems of Shape and Motion' which I have always read whenever I have given small intimate readings of the poetry that most moved me from the work of Boris Pasternak, Edward Kamau Brathwaite, Wilson Harris, Nicolas Guillen, Rabindranath Tagore, Aime Cesaire, from my own work and from Martin Carter.

From 'Shape and Motion One':

> I was wondering if I could shape this passion
> just as I wanted in solid fire.
> I was wondering if the strange combustion of my days
> the tension of the world inside me
> and the strength of my heart were enough.

and then the almost impossible

> I was wondering if I could make myself
> nothing but fire, pure and incorruptible.

and pondering the agony and the angst:

> I was wondering if the agony of years
> could be traced to the seed of an hour.
> If the roots that spread out in the swamp
> ran too deep for the issuing flower.

and as the wondering comes to its inevitable end:

> I was wondering if I could find myself
> all that I am in all I could be.
> If all the population of stars
> would be less than the things I could utter
> And the challenge of space in my soul
> be filled by the shape I become.

The year was only 1955. Almost at the beginning of his wandering and meandering.

Rest in peace, dear Martin.

October 1998

JOHN FIGUEROA

MARTIN CARTER

In 1971, or was it '73, I was on exchange to the University of Indiana in Burlington, Indiana. As I was far from the Caribbean I was glad to receive an invitation to a Carifesta to be held in Georgetown. It was a special kind of Carifesta, because it was also to celebrate Guyanese independence.

Many things worth recalling happened at the Carifesta: there was a large Rasta band blowing enormous horns, Miriam Makeba paraded her wonderful self in a leathern outfit which included leathern shorts, Dr. Williams, special friend to Mr. Burnham, held a wonderful day-party under a very green mango-tree in his country home. To half-quote some poet or other, it was heavenly then to dance with Makeba.

There were some what one might call itches. For one thing, a number of West Indian poets boycotted the occasion, among these was Andrew Salkey. There was an undercurrent of feeling against Burnham and that kept some of our better writers away. Some of the arrangements were odd – we were all invited to a reading on Saturday morning. It was supposed to last for three hours, and all of us scribblers took a lot of poems to read. Imagine our surprise when an hour and a half had passed, none of the visitors had been called upon. The Chairman, Arthur Seymour, explained to us that on that occasion only local Guyanese were being allowed to read.

The Celebration Ball was wonderful, the music was exciting, and as could be expected, the drink flowed in rivers. But what I most recall about the Carifesta was my meeting with my old friend, Martin Carter. We had been given enormous houses, which seemed to be built of mahogany. I was alone in one such house, and at about ten on Sunday morning, Martin called on me. He stretched his long self out on a couch in the drawing-room, and after we exchanged greetings and news, he said, 'John, I know that you like the poetry of St. John of the Cross, and have translated some of it.' He then closed his eyes, and spouted – that is the right word – line after line of St. John in Spanish:

> Dejando mi cuidado
> Entre las azucenas olvidado.

It was a most moving, indeed almost shaking, experience. It illustrated a point that needed to be made at Carifesta, which tended to be exclusivist, that wonderful poetry like that of St. John of the Cross belonged to all of us, even to a revolutionary poet, Martin Carter.

Our discussion was interrupted by a telephone call and Martin was soon defending himself in loud and hurt tones against an accusing voice. It turned out that the Sunday morning papers had levelled some serious criticisms against the Carifesta and against the Right Honourable Forbes Burnham. The honourable and high gentleman was clearly lambasting Martin Carter and accusing him of having been behind the criticism. Martin was at that time Minister of Information in Burnham's government, and some hot words were spoken. Martin rushed out, we had no chance to delve deeper into St. John.

The next time that I saw him at this Carifesta was not so auspicious. There was a long and boring session led by Kenneth Ramchand on 'Education in the West Indies'. During question time, the Guyanese author, Mr. Cameron, almost in tears, protested that his long work and research into Caribbean education had been totally ignored by Kenneth Ramchand. Things were about to get heated and unpleasant, when Martin and two other characters, who had drank not wisely but too well, trooped through the hall shouting 'Nonsense! Stop this stupidness.'

It was unfortunately the last time that I saw my old friend Martin Carter, and we never got a chance to continue our exploration of St. John of the Cross.

> Upon a gloomy night,
> With all my cares to loving ardours flushed,
> (O venture of delight)
> With nobody in sight
> I went abroad when all my house was hushed.

1st October, 1998.

ROY HEATH

A GIMLET EYE...

So many writers and critics have spoken and written about Martin Carter's remarkable work that any further stone I might add to the edifice of praise would almost certainly appear superfluous. Besides, not being a critic myself, an attempt at analysis of his poems would not stand comparison with the contributions of those better equipped than myself.

What I can speak about, however, is the Martin Carter of the period before he sought publication, but when he had already written much poetry: the years 1947 and 1948. This was, for him, the period of fermentation, of search for form and subject; and, like all great artists, he appeared to be driven by an inner compulsion to create. It is this time, these two years – when Martin and I met frequently – which have left an indelible impression on me.

One afternoon he showed me a new batch of poems he had written. When I expressed my admiration for one, 'The Indian Woman', he seemed surprised. What I, as a secretly aspiring writer, found astonishing, was the choice of an everyday subject, so familiar it needed a gimlet eye to be noticed. A woman at work in a field was not a romantic subject, and both he and I were, in those days, mesmerised by the work of John Keats. This awareness of the world of our immediate surroundings, range yard, streets, people, was for me something new in Caribbean poetry. And, in my view, this is one aspect of Martin Carter's originality, and one which has had a profound influence on my own work. Which recalls an incident that occurred some time later. Benny Bishop the photographer, who was teaching me the rudiments of his craft, sent me out with a camera with instructions to use up all the film. I came back several hours later, having taken a single picture. Irritated by my excuse that I had found no suitable subject matter while away, he took the camera from me, walked to the street corner and back, during which time he used up the remainder of the film roll. Two of the seven photographs he had taken he was able to exhibit later at a show: one depicted a dray cart with its shafts pointing upwards and the other a small boy unself-consciously smoking a cigarette. I had learned my lesson. If Martin had demonstrated that the familiar could be the starting point of high art, my photographic experience served to confirm this. My fiction is preoccupied with the evocation of the familiar.

I have never considered Martin Carter a political poet. If he was imprisoned in 1953 for political reasons, *Poems of Resistance*, a product of his prison experience, is a very personal testament. Carter was clearly overwhelmed by the terrible political events of the fifties and sixties, which, in turn, stimulated his creativity. But a distinction must be made between the stimulus and the result. The 'poetic' difference between 'The Indian Woman' and 'The Nigger Yard' lies in the intense emotion generated by the latter as against the pale beauty of the former. Neither is a 'political' poem. Both evoke the common cultural experience of Guyanese. Political poems there are, but they also belong to our familiar world and are of no greater or lesser significance than the offerings in 'Conversations'.

I do not miss an opportunity to disclose my early association with this founder of the modern movement in Guyanese art. Once more I proudly declare that his poetry and passion for art have been an influence on my work I readily acknowledge.

July 1997

ANNE WALMSLEY

ENCOUNTERS WITH MARTIN CARTER

A SHORT CHRONOLOGY

Invited to take part in this book about the work of Martin Carter, I first said 'no'. What could I add of interest or relevance to what others will say, or have said so very much better? But something of Carter's work in words has been known to me since I first began to read widely in the literature of the Caribbean, in the early '60s. Encounters with his work have been significant landmarks for me, through ever keener awareness of its quality and depth, of its wide resonance. The listing below is my small tribute to this 'poems man' extraordinary.

1961 Read 'Death of a Slave', 'Voices', 'Words', 'University of Hunger' by 'Martin Carter (B.G.)' in *Kyk-over-al* no.22, 1957, *Anthology of West Indian Poetry*, edited by A J Seymour, who gave it to me on my first visit to Guyana, from Jamaica, April 1961.

1967 Met Martin and Phyllis Carter, with Frank Pilgrim, in Georgetown, February 1967, at a dinner given by Jim (EJB) and Pam Rose, also visiting Guyana. Martin Carter's astonishment when, introduced, I instantly said 'University of Hunger'. Told him of my school anthology, in preparation, and my wish to include one of his poems. Bought *Poems of Resistance* in Georgetown (65 cents), in the University of Guyana 1964 reprint edition. My first choice for the anthology, 'Words', rejected by Longmans' advisor, who found the imagery too complex for a readership of 12-15 year olds. Then selected 'This is the dark time, my love'; my own fears that this poem also might be found inappropriate were allayed when, on a visit to a Georgetown school for Longmans, I saw it printed large on a poster or blackboard. No reply from Martin Carter to my request that, to accompany this poem in my anthology, *The Sun's Eye*, he write on himself in the 'Notes about the writers'; Andrew Salkey kindly wrote on Carter's behalf.

1978/9 Intensive re-encounter with the poetry of Martin Carter through Stewart Brown, fellow student on the MA course in African Studies at Sussex University, and already an informed, passionate admirer of Carter's work.

c1982 Heard Ngugi wa Thiong'o give a talk at the Africa Centre, London, in which he quoted Martin Carter:
'I do not sleep to dream, but dream to change the world'.

1986 Interviewing Andrew Salkey in Amherst, Mass., heard how, when invited to read in the USA, he always included poems by Martin Carter.

1990 Lent *Selected Poems of Martin Carter* (Demerara Publishers, 1989) to Accabre Huntley, daughter of Jessica and Eric. She and Maridowa Williams, daughter of Aubrey, chose two poems – 'I do not yet know' and 'Rain Forest' – to be read by Accabre at the Aubrey Williams Celebration, Commonwealth Institute, 12 June 1990. These lines especially resonant:

> 'I do not yet know the name men have given
> that fluttering yellow and ubiquitous butterfly
> whose life is not long but whose beauty is so startling'.

1992 Heard (and recorded) Martin Carter talking with Fred D'Aguiar and Grace Nichols on BBC Radio 3, 11 February 1992, during their Arts Council tour – with Wilson Harris – of the South-West. Carter read 'University of Hunger'. After Nichols' reading of her poem 'Blackout', written on a return visit to Guyana in 1990, D'Aguiar commented: 'If it wasn't for the articulacy of the writing, it would be a picture that is utterly depressing.' Carter memorably said: 'Of course. It [the poem] has to liberate her from precisely what she's saying, so that she knows it better for having written it and therefore she has acquired some psychological distance from the raw, empirical fact. In so doing, of course, there are two gains, I think. One is for Grace as a person, and also for people who will read it and who would come to realise that it is possible to know it and not be defeated by it. So there is a possibility of triumph through a work of art; that art should not only be communication – the word that everybody talks about – but also be a triumph of the spirit.'

1993 Revisiting Guyana and Barbados to look at work by visual artists, learnt how central is Carter's poetry to many of them: Bernadette Persaud, Ron Savory and, especially, Stanley Greaves. Re-met Martin and Phyllis Carter at the home of Ian and Mary McDonald, in Georgetown, and then at their own home. Gave Carter a copy of my *Caribbean Artists Movement* book, and shared with him the many references to himself and his work, and a photo of him standing, listening, between Wilson Harris and Donald Locke, in February 1970.

1995 In Guyana again, and at Castellani House – the National Gallery of Art – for a meeting with its Board of Management, held in its 'bottom house'. These words by Carter were on the wall behind us: 'Because a poet cannot truly speak to himself, save in his own country.'

1997 Saturday evening, 14 December, Jessica Huntley rang with news that Martin Carter had died that morning, in Georgetown. Joined more than twenty British-based friends and admirers in a letter written by Jessica and faxed to Phyllis Carter the following day. It ended:

> 'We hope you will take comfort from the fact that Martin was much loved, honoured and respected. His work has always been an inspiration and will continue to reverberate the world over. He will be sadly missed.'

My own thankfulness for such a life in words, and such words, alive, always.

MARTIN CARTER'S IMPACT AND INFLUENCE ON YOUNGER WRITERS

John Agard

NEWS BACK HOME
(for Martin Carter)

In an alien city I heard them tell
of a poet's beating back home
where the sun is taken for granted

Rumour bridged the miles with a groan
only this time rumour was flesh and blood
realer than the pranks of summer

How piece together this scarecrow puzzle
of picket in a wilderness
of voice trampled by insane fist
of broken ribs of images gone mad?

WITHOUT RHYME OR REASON IF PROTEST HE MUST
MAN MEK HE EAT HE POEMS IN DE DUST

And Martin on the verge of a foreign summer
I remember your line – 'a mouth is always muzzled
by the food it eats to live...'

Meanwhile the sound we hear now is only
the people lining up for a poet's blood

It was an attack on Martin Carter that prompted me to write the above poem, which appeared in an issue of *Caribbean Contact*, either in the late seventies or early eighties. And that beating of a cherished poet crystallises for me the callousness that characterised the political climate, which was to witness the killings, amongst others of photographer Father Bernard Darke, a former Maths teacher of mine, and historian Walter Rodney, who was seeking to bridge the racial divide – another of our great minds gone.

I mention the attack on Martin in the context of this chain of politically fostered thuggery and desperation, because he was a poet whose very being became iconic of our political history – just as his imprisonment and *Poems Of Resistance* epitomised the early nationalist movement in Guyana and the British imposition of direct rule. Here again Martin's vulnerability was speaking to us.

When he became Minister of Public Information in the post-independence euphoria, the cynical view expressed was that Martin 'like he join the establishment'. But he was responding to the mood of the time and meant well. I remember going to his office with Brian Chan, Janice Lo Shinebourne, Terrence Roberts, Charles Barrow, John Rickford, Victor Davson, Keith Khan, all in our early twenties, dreaming in our ways of the artistic life, whether via word or paint or music, and all involved in the literary magazine, *Expression*. Martin was approachable and interested in what we had to say. We felt we were in the presence, not of a government minister, but an elder of the tribe, an esteemed poet who wanted to hear what younger voices had to say.

And when suddenly the news broke that Martin had resigned from the government, here again his action took on iconic import. He resigned with a poem – published in the local press and with the lines 'A mouth is always muzzled/by the food it eats to live' sounding a prophetic note. But Martin was not to be silenced by a comfortable ministerial position. Through the combined act of resignation and poem, his voice became a national reminder of the sovereignty of conscience, steering us back to a course of integrity, assuring us that as flawed human beings, even visionaries, we have a right to a change of heart.

Heart is the key word. For while at the heart of politics, Martin voiced the politics of the heart. As apocalyptic fires raged over Georgetown, the mystic fires of passion rage in the human heart, and Martin's work engages sacramentally with both.

> I was wondering if I could make myself
> nothing but fire, pure and incorruptible.

Through an almost Buddhist identification with the transmuting baptism of fire, which figures strongly in his work, Martin becomes 'this poem; like a sacrifice' – a hovering voice of conscience when treason of the spirit threatens all.

MERLE COLLINS

THE COMPLETE PERFORMANCE

The fierce beauty of Martin Carter's poetry speaks to me in ways I rarely attempt to explain. Perhaps it was in England, towards the end of the 1980s, that I came best to know and feel the power of Martin Carter's poetic expression. A fellow-student from Guyana gave me two small volumes – *Poems of Resistance* and *Poems of Affinity*. In the former volume my student-friend had written his own caption, obviously influenced by the political fervour of Carter's voice: '...today's freedom song is whiplash for tomorrow's Revolution.'

At that time, when, in the aftermath of political events in Grenada, I discussed Caribbean politics and history with hesitation, I read Martin Carter's poems quietly, drawing from them a sense of continuing prophecy, marvelling that he could so beautifully express the awful timelessness of desolation and of hope. His poetry was for me an integrated expression of art, history and politics, voicing painful Guyanese (and Caribbean) political realities in impossibly beautiful language. I describe it like this in retrospect. Usually I just read the poems because they expressed the darkness of disappointment and fed some indefinable wish for something deeper.

> This is the dark time, my love.
> All round the land brown beetles crawl about...

Recently, I remembered those days and went to the collection again, when one of my students (Guyanese) at the University of Maryland, captioned an essay with a quote from Martin Carter's 'I Come from the Nigger Yard':

> I turn to the histories of men and the lives of the peoples
> I examine the shower of sparks the wealth of the dreams
> I am pleased with the glories and sad with the sorrows
> rich with the riches, poor with the loss...

Martin Carter's spirit, as expressed through his poetry, has had on me (and, my experience would suggest, will continue to have on generations of students of the Caribbean experience) the kind of influence one rarely feels during the guarded incommunicativeness of 'actual' encounters.

His *Poems of Affinity* hold for me a concern with 'a recurring despair', awe about the cyclical nature of time and of human existence. I have a fascination with Caribbean poetry in print and performance. Where Martin Carter's work is concerned, the poems on the page speak to me in ways that create their own haunting echoes, are, strangely, their own complete performance.

> In another
> house, not time's, time itself arranges
> mine and the world's replacement.

DAVID DABYDEEN

ON NOT KNOWING MARTIN CARTER

Cheddi Jagan used to speak of a lost generation of Guyanese, those who fled, or were taken, overseas, to avoid the ravages of Burnhamite Guyana. I was one of the lost generation in that I left in the late 1960s, a boy not knowing the name of Martin Carter, much less his writings. I suppose the next fifteen years were spent surviving England, which meant struggling with the language of its culture (which at least was joyous compared to other immigrant challenges). Apart from V.S. Naipaul's *Miguel Street* I never encountered a Caribbean novel or poem between the years 1969 and 1984, settling instead in the Wessex of Thomas Hardy, the taverns of William Hogarth or the passionate landscapes of D.H. Lawrence.

Then suddenly, as a result of the Brixton riots of the 1980s, the Black British History Conference of 1981, the publication of James Berry's *News from Babylon* in 1984, another kind of literature was tabled, and I read for the first time Jean Rhys, Roger Mais, Merle Hodge and Sam Selvon. Having grown up in pure ignorance of Caribbean literature, I was able to read the writings with neither contempt inculcated into the colonial mind, nor with indiscriminate awe that comes from a craving for identity. I have to confess that the excitement of discovering the region through its literature was Colombian in proportion; I must also confess that nowadays I scarcely read 'native' English writings. Fifteen years was enough.

At present Martin Carter's work engages our attention at the University of Warwick, since we are overseeing a Spanish translation of his selected poems, for a UNESCO-sponsored publication. Ironically I was introduced to his writings through a young English student who was doing a Ph.D. on his work. I acted as supervisor, which meant having to read Carter's poems carefully. I had gone to them expecting political protest, perhaps dated, belonging to the world of colonial agitation. I came away marvelling at the metaphysical density of his lines, the complex interplay of ideas, the lyrical gift, the seriousness and integrity of his art. And, above all, the sense of a poet who shunned rhetoric and cliché because he believed that the role of the poet was to give voice to felt truths. There are no lies in Martin Carter's poems, which is a marvellous and monumental achievement, given that in Burnhamite Guyana the word had become soiled or stillborn. The truthfulness of Martin Carter's words survived the tyranny of Guyana which fostered deceit and equivocation.

When I eventually met Carter in the 1990s, to seek his permission for the Spanish edition of his poems, he had more or less lost his power of speech, because of illness. I sat in his presence not knowing what to say, for I was in genuine awe of his talent and his role in the making of Guyanese history. Now that he is dead I wish I had said more than mumbled my admiration for his work. Now I memorise some of his lines, as a way of keeping faith with the courage of poetry.

March, 1998

FRED D'AGUIAR

IN MEMORY OF MARTIN CARTER

-i-

Word, image, breath, body, help me say now
What moonlight scribbling on the bay puts down

And the bay shakes off or scrambles into something new.
Moon, water, cloud, sky, don't let my spirits get low.

As land frames this bay or bay wraps land, so I want
To understand, Martin, the poet, and fellow countryman;

How a life can come and go no matter what you hope
Or do; how skin as delicate as cloud or smoke

Breaks down to dust; how breezes scatter the dust.
We have his words. We lean on them. They bolster us.

We carry on. Our time soon come. Like Martin's came.
His heart stopped, his chest fell and failed to fill again.

His eyes settled back in their sockets, his jaws slackened.
He no longer answers to his name, its ring widens

Beyond him. Poems with his name make him
Live again. He walks a line with a creole rhythm.

There's a bounce to his step, just short of a hop
And a drop. And rhyme and reason. They don't stop.

Martin rhymed. Martin reasoned. His words chime;
A bell everybody tries to ignore at closing time.

The bell at the start of Mass; that marks the hour.
Now its tongue is wrapped in cloth or ripped out;

His body, empty, tongueless. But not his words.
His poems make so much noise. I hear them above

Low-flying jets, sirens, carpets of parakeets,
Children playing with building blocks in streets;

Over drill sergeants at local army barracks;
Their tropical downpour; their wet mouth of fog

On a window; Lake Erie snow over buffalo;
Hard and hot as nails on a track flattened by a train.

Martin's poems model their sting on marabuntas;
Their sweetness understudies sapodillas;

With Stabroek market on Saturday for onomatopoeia.
Between road and yard sits trench for enjambment

The continent balks at all prospects of definition.
A tangled vine ensnares his work and refuses translation.

Martin's poetry arches its back and takes the lean
Of continental drift. The rain forest runs off into his poems.

Georgetown's streets arrange themselves like stanzas.
600 feet below sea level the land rears up and gazes

With muddy head at Martin's poems lined up offshore,
Full of seaweed, crustaceans, Harmattan dust, crude oil.

-ii-

When a man you love dies,
Even if you have loved him
As a flower must surely love a bee
Fearing its sting and craving its visitations,
Loving the bee and not its sting,
Seeing all that pollen gathered from
Roving the world, dripping off its feet,
Wingtip, beard and wanting to be a part of it,
How do you commemorate him?

A full moon sails across the sky
Or clouds coast by,
A cobalt sky, a luscious moon.
One band of moonlight crosses the bay
In shivers, climbs the balcony and falls
On me with the weight of moonlight:
Cool, dull, weak as a shadow,
Silent and printless.
Martin Carter
Your memory is this light, this bay,
This sky that will soon
Be too bright and then vacant.

The first bee crawls up the hibiscus
Stamen and the dew not even gone,
Petals still folded in a fist.
No one told that bee.
It simply wants to make honey.

Faint moonlight, mixed with dawn
Is enough for it to see in.
It would tell you it could find
That flower with its eyes shut

And one translucent wing
Tied on its back.

The sky drops the moon,
Clouds flock by. A bangle of moonlight
Is barely discernible now as the day
Intrudes and either the moon
Expands into a sun or it shrinks
From sight. Traffic begins –
One giant bee. The morning, a rose,
Opens; Martin in everything.

A PATH CLEARED...

I met Martin Carter in February 1992 on a two-week Guyanese Writers Tour organised by the Arts Council. On the tour with us were Grace Nichols and Wilson Harris. Martin Carter is a tall, thin, elegant, softly spoken man, scant with his words and exact when he locks eyes with you through the thick lenses of his dark-framed glasses. His body exudes calmness. His mouth is set in a smile. This is the man I had to square with those combative poems from the anti-British agitation of 1950's Georgetown. This zen-like composed body gave birth to poems many have aligned with the birth of a nation, of a post-colonial consciousness, of a democracy of the soul as it shapes and is shaped by social and political forces that are essential to its well-being. And therefore it is a communal soul that belongs to Martin Carter, a socialist soul if you like in negotiation with the private contemplative self for those precious acts of utterance that poems are.

I grew up in Guyana. In school, had there been a poet laureate for Guyana, Martin Carter would have occupied the chair. His 'University Of Hunger' is the staple diet of every Guyanese child. In addition to the poetry is the life of the poet, his persona, the sense of other poems residing in that body or in the process of being made, his composure, stature, public self, poetic about his body, poetic in society, a model of what poets are and how they continue to be long after the situation that catapults them into the public eye has come and gone. Martin Carter represented this trope of hope to Guyanese at home and abroad.

Strangely, at the same time, I was also in the company of the only other

Guyanese writer who has managed to protect this artistic sensibility, namely, Wilson Harris. Martin Carter stayed in Guyana while Wilson Harris continued his continental obsessions from England. Martin Carter is characterised as an urban poet, a poet concerned with the city and how people share that space and make sense of each other in such risky proximity. Wilson Harris has always maintained that nature, in this case the Guyanese hinterland and rainforest interior, its sparsely populated spaces, is a library for humanity, if only we paid attention to it. Every insight, every bit of self-improving knowledge resides in this geographic encyclopaedia that nature, with its rocks, rivers, trees, light, and composites of all these, represents.

At first glance, Martin Carter's social and historical frameworks seem antithetical to Wilson Harris's nature-based metaphysics: one is social or group-centred, the other, private and individual; one political, the other, philosophical; one historical, the other mythical. No doubt each writer begins with these idiosyncratic particularities but my reading of both would argue that each heads towards the other immediately. A careful reader of Carter's poetry finds urban, social and political markers to begin with, but rapidly discovers that the poems widen into other constituencies to do with the benefits of nature, the instruction of landscape, with the specificity of Guyana's position on a continent as opposed to an island.

Wilson Harris, fine-tuning his discoveries over the course of a magnificent 50-year career, seems quintessentially solitary in his pursuit of an individual taking repeated readings from nature. But Harris, too, has often demonstrated his concern with community, with those who have perished and need to be recovered through fiction in order to instruct the living. And he has also been concerned with those most in need of forging links with the very elements of nature from which they have become separated, namely, the urban and city dweller.

Martin Carter's poetry testifies to his belief that a poem is a song, a speech act and an organic thing. Each poem strikes a contemplative pose. Each poem is heard as a rule of composition. Silence is necessary for the poem to come into being, as opposed to clamour, but it is the voice and thought that are unified in the field of the poem. When Carter reads, this contemplation is re-enacted. His presentations are largely monotones with the spikes of a rising pitch occasionally thrown in.

This view of the poem matches that from antiquity. Poets are born not made. Their special status comes from the single disposition that poetry chose them, not them it. Poetry is therefore not a career – though it may be a life-long engagement – it is a calling. The imagination of the poet is ultimately moral, founded on principles of right and wrong and geared towards the improving of humanity as a responsible species. Since politics is the primary test site where people fail or triumph as people it figures that Martin Carter, the poet, would feel his talent best tested in the political arena and efficaciously deployed at ameliorating conditions for the least powerful and most poor of the people trapped in it.

Martin Carter talked to me about a tradition of poetry he hoped to contract into with his own output, a canon, yes, widened from Europe to include Sanskrit, Inuit, Native American and Far East as well as Middle East and African oral traditions. In effect a world canon of poetry of all time from every culture, sharing elements of craft and composition, to do with a global and therefore universal and shared characteristics of humanity. He subscribes to a theory of universality, of a common humanity that outweighs regional and racial differences. These voices, despite their particularities, share more facets in common than they hold differences. This puts him at odds with much thinking to do with the sacrosanct nature of tribes, races and regions.

There does appear to be a shift from the more public persona of his younger days to the sobriety and coveted isolation of seniority; a movement from public poet to private thinker. But his poetry always displayed elements of thought forged in the peculiar laboratory of the isolated poet-persona even as his articulations sought to connect with the wider public sphere. One marked difference between the earlier poems and the later ones is the sense of the writer of the later poems erasing all the tracks. Elements that show the likely origin and intended audience of a poem, such as the poem's starting point and frames of reference that form a part of the earlier poems, are removed for something more pared down and less moored to a known social situation or public predicament.

Does this amount to a retreat from the public into the defeat of the private? Not at all. It's a process of maturation and of the poet changing his territory, making his art work in new and unpredictable ways. Take, for example, Martin Carter's move from the longer more discursive poems of his earlier books to the brief, recognisably minimalist art of more recent years. Less is more. Each poem is an act of distillation and condensation. And as if in confirmation of the universal, there is a purity of diction and weightlessness to the poems more attributable to Zen Buddhism than to a Guyanese sensibility forged in the political arena of a British colony. But then Martin Carter is Wilson Harris's contemporary. Town meets country in both of these distinct bodies.

The canvas of heritage for any poet following Martin Carter is wide and unfinished as legacies go. I take from Martin Carter's poetry a permission to write the politics of the self in society as much as the privacies of the inarticulate soul striving towards meaning in the language of poems. In the single fragile body of the man is the multiple and mutually inter-dependent worlds of the bustling metropolis from which we derive the flaws of human history and the isolation of the natural landscape where myth and knowledge reside. To represent each as dual and opposite is wrong since each is multi-faceted, with elements present in both of the social or group loyalties and the private or isolated individual. The variable is in the movement of that figure from the social/political to the more private/natural sphere. Martin Carter's life and poems represent a path cleared in the thick undergrowth of politics and poetry, a path for me to take or measure my own progress by when I take a diversion; either way he's ineradicably there.

December 1997.

Kendel Hippolyte

ALL OF A MAN

> All of a man is heart is hope
> All of a man can fly like a bird.
> *Martin Carter*

Memory, of course, plays tricks, but the picture it yields to me now of my first experience of Martin Carter's work is: a translucent afternoon of quietly strong light; a class full of young boys, faces upturned, still open to everything; myself just out of sixth form and reading from that wonderful anthology, *The Sun's Eye*...

> This is the dark time, my love.
> All round the land brown beetles crawl about.

Unexpectedly, for me and for many of them, I think, the poem cast a spreading shadow that separated us from the light of the mild school afternoon, taking us into its world of dream-threatened dark:

> Who comes walking in the dark night time?
> Whose boot of steel tramps down the slender grass?

And yet what could those eleven and twelve year olds and I at eighteen have really understood about the horrendous realities below that poem? In one sense, socio-politically, virtually nothing. But it seized our imaginations, entering and occupying territory that was normally invaded only by novels of war and plague in other lands and times. It somehow brought the prosaic modern Caribbean into the realm of legend, of mythic worlds where archetypal forces, clothed temporarily in the persons of the era, fought the eternal war of good and evil:

> It is the man of death, my love, the strange invader
> watching you sleep and aiming at your dream.

My vision of the ideal poet began to be formed when I was in lower sixth and encountered the poetry of William Blake. Nearly thirty years later, Blake remains for me the archetype of the poet – a political radical whose politics began and ended in the person, a prophetic visionary with a mystic's seventh sense of other worlds, a poet whose language spans poems which can be understood by ten-year olds to works so dense that scholars have devoted lifetimes and only partially elucidated them.

For me, Carter is the poet in the English-speaking Caribbean who most closely approximates the ideal inspired by Blake, whose work most completely embodies all aspects of what I believe should be a poet's relationship to society, self and the language. And as with Blake, I read him least for his language, his craft – not because I see less value there, but because the lessons I can learn there are indirect; absorbed, if at all, through osmosis.

Carter's increasingly dense compression of image, his utterly natural tendency to gnomic utterance, his at times almost extreme concision of syntax and vocabulary are not – perhaps for now – word-ways that I feel drawn to walk on. Reading other poets, like Walcott or C.K. Williams, one sometimes comes across lines which draw out a sudden, involuntary gasp of admiration, simultaneously shot through with a shrewd appreciation/assessment of the technique at work there. Not so for me with Carter poems. I must read him for the sense of being which rises off the page into my life. When I think of the being of a poet, the quality of personhood I aspire to and the way in which poetry and person interact to create a certain desired state of being, a quality of inner life, it is Martin Carter who rises quietly in the mind, like grace.

I have often wondered how it is that, as one of the three acknowledged greats of Caribbean poetry in English – Walcott, Brathwaite, Carter – there is so little critical material on him. Somehow the flurrying debates over the meanings of Caribbean history, the acrid quarrels over Caribbean identity which flared up in the academic papers and journals of the 1970s paid comparatively little attention to Carter's work. I am still not sure why, but in a strange – and not so strange – way, his marginality in the groves of Academe makes sense. Compared to Walcott or Brathwaite, there is less evident wordplay, less overt manipulation of poetic devices, seemingly less preoccupation with technique. Carter always comes across as a man talking from the heart, sometimes to others, sometimes to himself but unmediated by poetic shaping or by a self-aware public stance on issues. There seems to be nothing split, no fragmented consciousness, no controlled artistic schizophrenia from which literary criticism can spin yet another web of theory.

There is a sense of unarguable truth, of lived experience spoken of directly, in the poems. Again, compared to Walcott and Brathwaite, there seems to be virtually no use of the standard device of personae, of masks. The I in a Carter poem, early or late, seems to be always the poet, no one else. And the poet, early or late, seems to be always the man, no one else. The overwhelming impression is of a voice speaking nakedly from experience. The poems, even when they have the rhetorical flourish of 'University of Hunger' or 'I Come From The Nigger Yard', seem no more than a true account, a testimony from personal experience to which no tint of writer's ego has been added. With Carter, it seems, the poem is the poet is the man.

Of course, one knows nothing is so simple. Even just slightly closer examination reveals the conscious craft that must have gone into chipping down the poems into these hard, glittering gems like 'You Are Involved'. One knows too that the integration of person we feel in the work does not come from a linear simplicity of self-regard, but from seeing all too clearly the opposed elements of the self. And indeed, there is evidence in plenty of the internal struggles which hold that self together – but implied, only grudgingly yielded. Carter's is a case where a personal, watchful reticence about the inner life and a poet's natal watchfulness about the efficacy of words make a guarded, testing acquaintance. In the later work especially, the poems which manage to emerge from that meeting, like 'Four Poems' and 'Demerara Nigger', have a hard texture of irreducible truth.

It is occurring to me that I am making claims for his poetry without the slightest attempt to substantiate them by reference and explication, by quoting chapter and verse. A time must come for that too, of course. As a time must come to untangle the threads of thought snarled in among the strands and knots of always true feeling and sensual perception, so that we can see, as whole as possible, the philosophy, the vision of being from which the poems have grown. A time will come for that kind of analysis. Which can be, at times, its own kind of tribute.

But I feel no compulsion to the vivisection that entails. What I feel now is what I felt when I was asked to contribute to this book: gratitude. For all these years, my slowly deepening acquaintance with the poetry of Martin Carter has nourished my own sense of the shape of poetic vocation. Relationship to his poetry has been, to use one of his memorable phrases, the discovery of companion. The work, the man, their inseparability, have been a rare grace. I wish now that I had his gift for aphorism, for the simple, apt, telling phrase that continues to resonate in the nerves. Because I would like to say thanks in my own words. But perhaps it is not amiss, in a tribute so woefully short of quotation, of the taste and feel of his poetry, to borrow his own words (from 'Whence Come They') and let them tell of my gratitude to the man and his poems:

> I hardly know
> how to say thanks. But I am grateful
> to be so glad they never went away.

LINTON KWESI JOHNSON

GIVE THANKS

About twenty years ago, I had the honour of sharing a stage with Martin Carter. I 'warmed-up' the audience for him at a lunchtime reading at the Soho Poly Theatre in London. I recall being reasonably well-received by the predominantly white literary-type audience, but just being asked to open for Martin Carter was in itself an enormous boost to my ego as a budding poet. Looking back, that reading must have provided the audience with quite a contrast – the rhythmic rage of the young Black British apprentice and the quiet eloquence of the Caribbean revolutionary master.

I had been familiar with some of Martin Carter's poetry from the early seventies. I have the late Jamaican poet and novelist, Andrew Salkey, to thank for that. Andrew had the habit of using every opportunity he had to promote other people's poetry. One of the poets whose work he took great delight in exposing was Martin Carter. It was on one of those occasions, a reading at the Keskidee Centre, that I heard Andrew reading Carter's 'On the Fourth Night of a Hunger Strike', 'This Is The Dark Time My Love' and the immortal 'Death Of A Comrade' amongst others. That recital, hearing those poems, had a profound impact on me.

In the early seventies I was a young political and cultural activist armed with unlimited idealism and total commitment to the Black liberation struggle. I had not long discovered Black literature and was already harbouring ambitions of being a poet. It was through my political engagement that I discovered poetry and I was drawn towards political verse. When I heard Andrew Salkey recite those poems by Martin Carter, I was at once inspired because they epitomised for me what I thought committed revolutionary poetry ought to be like. A few years later, when the Trinidadian publisher/activist John La Rose gave me a mint copy of the paperback edition of *Poems Of Succession* in 1977 I realised that there was much more to the poetry of Martin Carter than the 'political' dimension. His 'Poems Of Shape And Motion' (1 and 2) remain all-time favourites of mine as do 'Death Of A Comrade' and 'A Mouth is Always Muzzled'.

On the one and only occasion that I met him, Martin Carter was just as I had imagined him to be. He was tall, quietly-spoken and dignified, with an aura about him. Needless to say, after that encounter I was in even greater awe of him. I still have that copy of *Poems Of Succession*. It is now in a tattered state. I go back to it from time to time and I am rewarded every visit. Martin Carter is one of those poets to whom I feel indebted. As a way of acknowledging my indebtedness I have recorded a rendition of his 'Poems Of Shape And Motion' on my new album, *More Time*. I give thanks for the inspiration and the example.

Mo Bay, Jamaica, 12 December 1997

KAREN KING-ARIBISALA

A MEMORY OF MARTIN CARTER

I met Martin Carter just once. I wonder if he remembers? I was a teenager. Our family had returned to Guyana after living in Africa and Europe. His nephew, who lived with him, held a birthday party at Martin Carter's house and we young people had a great, rather noisy time together. Afterwards, I phoned to thank the family and Martin Carter then phoned my father to express his appreciation of my 'bothering to say thank you'. My father was delighted. He had trained his daughter well in the manners department. But for me, this seemingly insignificant act of Carter's became a kind of symbol of Martin Carter the man. A man capable of caring in a personalised way on an individual level but also one who, from my reading of his poetry, I found tenacious in his holding on to principles of freedom and justice in a Guyana which was, at the time of his writings, violent with soldiers and 'warships terrible with death.'

He was detained in prison in the year of my birth, involved in a struggle, fighting for the likes of my generation, and I don't mean only in Guyana. His poetry, his words, his urgent compassion transcends country and place. One of his most resonant lines to me is 'I do not sleep to dream but dream to change the world.' By his poetry, and also by a seemingly simple phone call of thanks, he has done that and much more.

Lagos, Nigeria. November 1997

ROI KWABENA

IN TRIBUTE TO MARTIN CARTER

I was first exposed to the poetry of Martin Carter at primary school level in Trinidad. It was 1968, two years before the Black Power disturbances, and seeds of discord had already sprouted. Local debate at the time addressed issues of National Identity, Race, Class and Employment. The Caribbean was adjusting to the perils of Political Independence.

At the core of the issue of National Identity, was Language and this affected our lives as students most of all. We were expected not to write the way we spoke and as a consequence many students were disheartened. So at teenage years when Caribbean literature was introduced on our syllabus, we felt especially justified. Among the books was the classic *The Sun's Eye,* an anthology of Caribbean writers compiled by Anne Walmsley.

For us *Sun's Eye* was our own manual for dissension, with Carter's contribution therein a scaring psalm. This book was our saving grace. We no longer needed to be threatened nor punished by the guava, sweet-lime, tamarind or poui whip to recite by heart the poetry of Europeans. *Sun's Eye* gave us an opportunity to see ourselves in the mirror of works by Wilson Harris, Martin Carter, Andrew Salkey, Kamau Brathwaite, Derek Walcott, and others. It was a welcome relief to be rid of antiquated tales of buccaneers, English weather, Dover hills of chalk and poverty in Victorian London.

I can distinctly remember the joy on the faces of my fellow students under the almond trees in the school-yard as we delved into this treasure-trove; understanding the testimony of F.A. Collymore's 'Hymn to the Sea' and laughing as we imitated ourselves reciting the 'Song of the Banana Man' by Evan Jones.

However nothing can replace the satisfaction of reading the assuring but 'subversive' lines of Martin Carter's poem 'This is the Dark Time My Love'. I remember our teacher proudly taking the pains to explain the context in which this work was created. Now, here our teacher was not discussing the tides on the east coast of England nor the burial of Sir Henry Morgan. This was about us, our then present and the future.

It was with pride that we accepted the serious contemplation of Carter and willingly memorised this poem. It provided us with an understanding of life under political oppression with the attendant effects on interpersonal relationships and the society as a whole. Several of my fellow students from those heady days still write poetry, some became bankers, lawyers, economists, politicians, calypsonians and even trade unionists. I am sure like me, they would remember the pride with which we recited before the entire school these hallowed lines:

It is the man of death, my love, the strange invader
watching you sleep and aiming at your dream.

Further reading of Carter's poetry ensured that I was led to works by C.L.R. James, George Lamming, Walter Rodney, Marcus Garvey, Angela Davis, Franz Fanon, Aime Cesaire, Robin Dobru, Amiri Baraka, Sonia Sanchez and so many other progressive writers.

I wish to acknowledge how much my own work has been influenced by Martin Carter. Particularly so, in my reaction to regional historic events like the detention of Black Power advocates and the failed mutiny by members of the T&T Regiment in 1970; the murder of fellow unemployed graduates-cum guerrillas of the National Union of Freedom Fighters; periods of industrial unrest throughout the decades; the brutal killing of Dr. Walter Rodney; the murder of Maurice Bishop and the invasion of Grenada in 1983; political violence in Jamaica and the attempted coup by the Muslimeen in 1990 in Trinidad.

In tribute allow me to humbly attempt to echo the aspirations he always advocated as a pioneer of Caribbean literature:

can our leaders
the scribes – forsake
honest dedications...
in this bitter tide of despots / traitors
with masks deceiving – false shallow smiles
defiling the aspirations, muted violently...
forked tongues uttering words of honey...

'fearless scribes' from *seasons of exile* (1986)

Birmingham 1998

ABDUL MALIK

THE LIGHT

I met Martin for the first time in the late 70s in Trinidad (of Trinidad and Tobago)... a cultural occasion marking our encounter... of a kindred kind... for we were... both... politically... poetically... driven... twice committed to the same cause... of humanity... and in that ultimate creative quest... there is no end... no end to his... mine... yours... our... humanity... our communal spirit... our... spiritual bond... no end... to this poetically correct line... that his communal spirit will live on... will live... in... this... light of a spiritual kind... a light that transcends borders... of flesh and blood... time and space... the unseen... the unknown... in life... as well as... in death... a light... that had encompassed... spiritually... his 50's commitment... had encompassed... spiritually... in that very same time... and space... my own growth... and becoming... had encompassed... spiritually the unseen... If my boyhood... daze... between Islands... between Grenada... and Trinidad... had encompassed... spiritually... the unknown... of my moulded commitment... THE WEST INDIES MUST BE WEST INDIAN... in the 50s... of growth... and becoming... the 50s of his time... and space... the 50s... of Third... World... corners... being... overtaken... being... overturned... the 50s... when BG was B-I-G... a clouded... cornerscape... a distant thundersound... of rivers... of forests... of borders between... Iron... and Stone age... borders between... corporate capitalist... and primate communalist... borders between... genocide... slavery... indentureship... borders between... darkness... and light... the 50s... when BG was B-I-G... when mind setters trailed... godlike... from the ethereal mists... to teach and dwell in Grenada... one Desmond Hoyte among them... the 50s... when the light of a Guyana dawn was R-E-D... primal... historic... united... forbidden... when the towerscape... of a new West Indian beginning... was cast... asunder...

I met Martin for the second and final occasion at Carifesta 1995 in Trinidad... we were both invited... participants... travellers... stationed... at the same inn... there was much more to ponder... for he had collaborated... with me... and other writers... on Taino-Covering- Columbus... a collection of poems and short stories published in 1992... commemorating the alternate view of Columbus... which I had edited... much more to ponder... now... in this spiritual light... of Amerindian... peace... in the 90s... for I did see the inner glow of his optimism... know... within... myself... the centuries of his sound stillness... truly hear... in his voice... Our... humanity... Our... communal spirit... Our... spiritual bond... echoing... re-echoing... in... this... dark... dark... time...

E.A. MARKHAM

FOR THE ENVIRONMENT

for Andrew Salkey (1928-1995)
& Martin Carter (1927-1997)

It is cold this Christmas
I have no idea what it costs
to heat me: *God have mercy.*

The corner shop in Crouch End
selling knick-knacks
is now something else. The brothers
with children to educate

have gone back to Ireland.
Here, in Sheffield two bookshops
which made us welcome, have gone
taking the space for browsing.

So we must live within our means
like aged parents
in new surroundings

(And who will respond to the old
jokes: it's the buttons, man,
the buttons rattling
in the new jacket, nothing more).

And I think of Andrew and Martin gone,
that generosity of spirit buried,
Andrew and Martin gone
their literary grandchildren
hustlers below stairs
full of frenzy, full of noise
desperate to inherit the house.

And I think of island and family gone,
and the heritage of remembering
respecting those spaces
new filled with rubbish.

And I am here, standing in
committing such things to memory
while memory lasts.

MARC MATTHEWS

WITH NUFF RESPECT FOR MARTIN CARTER

1.
14 December 1997... Pauline the shape shifter was the messenger
'Lightning fastman' she said, 'had gone,' could no longer wait for them
to learn, left he for all to read a diary of directions circumventing illusions,
left he sorcerer's prescriptions for unveiling the world that is a dream/
revealing betrayal of the dream that is the world/
illuminating life blossom/brilliant in garden of night/dawn
gathered to garland the dial oracle of the sun

2.
No I will not mourn
wear no black bandaged
biceps, but a bright bandanna
reflecting dream colours of sun

No I will not hang my head
my face stretched in sorrow
nor slow march, stand solemn
at grave side, rather head high
face cragged with smiles, step
light wedding stride, rejoicing
at sight of life the breath of
your words resurrected from
death, gave meaning where
was meaningless.
No dirge with choir will I
chant of loss, anguish,
grief, but Anthems of spirit
and praise songs asserting
your freedom now from
petty platitudes, free at
long last for what has
been given to join those
gone youngmen fire petals
of passionate sun.

Martin Carter's lyrics are astounding, penetrating, awakening. The stifled voice, by articulating that which the suppressed spirit knows, blazes trails through the dense growth of material illusion to the clearing, where earth, mirror smooth, reflects not only experience but its narrative of meaning. Who does not bear witness to the truth he sings… 'a mouth is always muzzled/ by the food it eats to live'.

Martin, mathematician, biologist, shaman, how my heart raced in exhilaration when I read his verse in grey oppressive London thirty-three years ago.

I count myself fortunate to be among those warmly welcomed by this humble genius of a man, this man who, and I quote… 'dream to change the world'; who recognised that 'rain was the cause of roofs'. Where can be found a greater declaration of truth that we all know to be true than his 'I come from the niggeryard of yesterday'. He has not been awarded Nobel or Booker prize, because he is best described by the Grenadian poet Abdul Malik '…don't want no recognition all I want is revolution'. Martin sings from a human heart songs the human heart passionately sings. Have we not all experienced being barked at by dogs, surprised to hear ourselves barking among the swine pretending to be human, (I paraphrase his verse). Who among us can deny that 'love is stammered, hate is shouted out'… which of us is blind to the 'shining governments of the damned'? Where have not graveyards turned into playing fields? To read Martin Carter is to be brought in touch with yourself and the validity of your being, to release silence from prison, to make your life richer, and humble enough to pronounce your truth.

My spirit is strengthened by his revelations. His being. On reflection it will take another century for one like him to come along. I end with hand on heart, say: RESPECT TO THE MAN who reminds how men should swear '…with a hand upon a groin'.

MARK MCWATT

THE WARSHIP, THE POET AND DANGEROUS WORDS

It is dawn one morning on the island of Leguan in 1953. A six-year-old boy is awakened by his father.

'Come, I want to show you something'.

The boy, in striped pyjamas and rubbing sleep from his eyes, is led out onto the long verandah overlooking the wide Essequibo. There is a faint mist on the river and the distant east bank cannot be seen, but somewhere in midstream a large grey shape studded with a few faint lights can be discerned.

'That's a British Warship', the father says, and the boy feels a thrill of excitement.

'The British sent warships with soldiers to take over the government.'

The grey shape and the words of his father seemed magical to the boy, he'd always known that there was a big strange world beyond the things he knew, and now it seemed closer connected to his river-island world. It seemed a little frightening, for it occurred to him to wonder whether the ship had guns that could destroy the verandah on which he stood.

'Why?'

'Why what?'

'Why the British taking over the government?'

'Oh, they say that those in the government are bad, they are trying to fool the people with funny ideas that they read in dangerous books.'

A deep silence. 'Dangerous books', this was a new idea for the small boy. A sinister new ship in the river, a sinister new idea about books. He had never seen anything in books besides pictures and words.

'How they take over the government?'

'Arrest them, put them in jail. They put plenty people in jail because they say they are dangerous, can stir up the people if they allow them to talk or write in the papers.'

It must be words that are dangerous, the boy decided, as he continued to look at the warship; he looked at it while he ate breakfast on the verandah and he looked at it most of that morning, when the sun had come out and cleared away the mist. He looked at it long enough for it to become an enduring image, etched in his memory, vivid still many decades later. But equally haunting was the thrill of excitement at the idea of 'dangerous books' and of individuals with strange powers who had to be jailed or they would 'stir up' the people.

It was a decade later, at high school in the sixties that I learned to associate the name of Martin Carter with these early memories. By then there had been other political disturbances, riots and more British soldiers sent to restore order. We came to know the names of those involved in the struggle, those imprisoned because of the danger of their words. When I discovered that Martin Carter was one of those put in jail in 1953 I decided that it was to him especially that my father had referred, and from then, the image of the warship and the notion of 'dangerous words' has always brought to mind as well the image of Guyana's foremost poet, writing his dangerous words even in the prison of the enemy.

By this time I knew about Carter's poetry – 'about' because I think I'd actually read as yet very few of the poems (I remember 'Cartman of Dayclean', 'University of Hunger' and 'I Come From the Nigger Yard' – although I find superimposed on my earliest memories of these images from Rupert Roopnaraine's superb film *The Terror and the Time*) although these few were enough to fill me with a sense of awe at the man and at the power of his words. I read and enjoyed lots of English and American poetry in school but did not think that it had much to do with myself or with Guyana; however my slender acquaintance with Carter's work, and with a few poems of Seymour, was sufficient to convince me that the kind of power I sensed there was the only kind of power that I would ever be interested in achieving – the power to make a place and a people come alive in the mind of anyone who can read. What I found there was a kind of recognition, or self-recognition: my life, my thoughts, my surroundings, the home of my spirit, lived powerfully and purposefully in the poems of Seymour and Carter – men who lived in my city, walked its streets every day, who knew their parents' past and wanted to shape their own future. I felt that I must feel as they did.

I was certainly 'stirred up' by these men's words, and knew then what my father had meant all those years ago, but whereas he was unsympathetic, or at most neutral (as I suppose was the norm for a colonial civil servant at that time), I identified strongly with the expressions of protest and indignation. I strove to magnify, if possible, my own sense of the injustice of the system – I thought I was ready to fight and write and be imprisoned to help free my country; but these were a teenager's fantasies and I did nothing beyond luxuriate in the faint, innocuous whiffs of tear-gas that caused us to be evacuated from our classrooms the times when there were disturbances outside the nearby legislative building. Subversive writing indeed, but it was a subversive time, a time that was redeemed for me because its heroes were not only the politicians (of whom my father had taught me to be suspicious), but people like Martin Carter: teachers, writers, journalists, poets – poets most of all.

When, in the early 1970s, I began to take my own poetry seriously, despite (or perhaps because of) letters of rejection from metropolitan publishers, it was thoughts of Carter and Seymour and Mittelholzer and Wilson Harris that focused my wavering resolve and kept me writing. But Martin Carter especially grew in stature and in influence for me each time a collection of his work was published or republished. I came to feel that the political struggle and the protest were not the most important things in his poems; with a fascination I can still feel, I began to encounter in the poems a quality of mind – of thought and perception – that struck me as being recognisably, unmistakably Guyanese, even as it both mocked and encouraged my own feeble efforts. For me, Carter's poetry had expanded narrow protest, first to the vast reality of the Guyana coastland – sky, river and sea then to the whole universe of human experience and of the symbolic codes that poets use to evoke it.

My course is set, I give my sail the wind
to navigate the islands of the stars
till I collect my scattered skeleton
till I collect... ('Till I Collect'; *Selected Poems,* p.45)

In the end the larger vision became more relevant for me and for the directions of my own imagination, than the poetry of resistance; indeed I discovered that there was a lot more to the *Poems of Resistance* themselves than I'd originally thought/seen. Carter had the great gift of simultaneously defining and transcending the political moment – seeing its true dimensions and significance within the vast context of time and space; it is a kind of imaginative clairvoyance that few writers achieve, and it still excites me that this talent was born and nurtured in an environment that is familiar and ordinary to me – ordinary, and yet extraordinary when it is submitted to the intense gaze of the creative imagination and transformed through poetic language and symbol into another life that will never fade.

Although I cannot claim to have known him very well, Martin Carter's death just before last Christmas (after I'd started to write this) was a great blow. I'd got it in my head that I'd known him since that day in 1953 when my father and an old warship brought the news that they were jailing men who were dangerous because of their words. And now the flow of words was stopped by death; the very mortality that he had promised to write about in his next collection had overtaken both that project and the poet himself, and there was for me a debilitating sense of loss... Until I picked up a copy of the recently reissued *Selected Poems* and encountered again that inexhaustible life and spirit and breath. The first poem that I read then said all that was necessary for the occasion, and can serve as epitaph and conclusion to these inadequate words:

Being, always to arrange
myself in the world, and the world
in myself, I try to do both. How
both are done is difficult. Why,
I have to ask, do I have to
arrange anything when every
thing is already arranged
by love's and death's inscrutable

laws, mortal judiciary, time's
doll house of replaceable heads,
arms and legs? In another
house, not time's, time itself arranges
mine and the world's replacement.
('Being Always': *Selected Poems*, p.191)

Cave Hill. Barbados – February, 1998.

PAULINE MELVILLE

THE POET

The reading took place in a rather bleak room in London's Institute of Contemporary Arts. The room was well lit. The audience consisted of some fifty people, Guyanese who had settled in England and British people with an interest in Caribbean artists with the addition of possibly one or two who had just come out of curiosity or to shelter from the dark winter outside. There was the usual polite but restrained bustle as people took their seats.

And then the poet stood up. He was a tall, well-built man, dark-complexioned with a soft, squarish face. He wore a smart light tweed jacket, well-cut, but underneath this was an old, slightly frayed, square-necked, white cable-stitched pullover. It was difficult to see whether the book he carried in his hand trembled or whether that was an optical illusion. Most of us knew that many years earlier he had been jailed for his beliefs during the struggle for Guyana's independence.

He began to read:

'I walk slowly in the wind...'

Around the voice I could hear the sound of the waves breaking against the sea-wall in Georgetown.

And then something happened to the audience. A sort of tremor went through them. It was as if they had woken from a trance, as if they were turning to each other and saying 'Oh yes. This is what a real poet is. This is how it is supposed to be. We had forgotten. We must have been asleep.' An ancient voice seemed to speak through the centuries to us. Immediately, we all knew that poetry is a serious matter. All sorts of wisdom moved around and through the sound of the words. The audience understood that, for him, poetry was the gravest of passions.

If it is possible for a country to speak through a man, Guyana should be proud to have such a voice, stained with its history. Tears came into the eyes of more than one listener.

I had known him for many years, his intelligence fast and broad, innocent and searing, assessing a remark, foreseeing the outcome of the conversation and choosing not to reply with more than a brief, sardonic comment. Here was Guyana standing among us.

The poet, of course, was Martin Carter.

MICHAEL MITCHELL

HAVING SPEECH

for Martin Carter

To my own advantage
the lane   a lazy beam of light
the seascape
a drowned thing   for which no price could be obtained
an opportunity to speak
appropriately like a cabinet of treasures
with the great man
where he sat
Mr Carter   I said it slowly   the man had had a stroke
in all your life you never tried to run
corrupt regimes   oppression   the physicality of lust
two figures plunging through the bushes opposite
no thank you for your poem first
I never ran
before I learned to talk

and now   if stillness counts
the other will reply and keep the time
her own   unmasked by fantasy
the coming storms
or jealous disposition of the night

Dorsten, Germany, 2.12.97

MERVYN MORRIS

FAREWELL FUNCTION

he basked in admiration
dreaming
paradise

until
his metamorphosis

into a morbid
out of body witness
at the operation

like a patient etherized
returning
from the edge

& catching an obituary
draught

Grace Nichols

FOR MARTIN CARTER

Walking slowly in the wind
like your cartmen of dayclean,
pushing one one
against the stars and scars
of a city whose altars
knew hands like yours.

Pushing against the misery huts
the city flames
and ocean floods

Berating the shining Governments
of the damned –

Your words, Georgetownman,

Priestman, marrying images,
Canna lilies and canals,
drinking from the anguished chalice,
yet placing a hopeful sacrament –
star, seed, flower,
upon our tongues.

How you kept your ear
to the ground, Martin,
your heart to our city's pulse.

SASENARINE PERSAUD

WATCH MY LANGUAGE: FROM CHEDDI JAGAN TO MARTIN CARTER

'All of a man is heart is hope'
Martin Carter

At a certain time when I was growing up, it seemed that there were always references to a person who wrote and recited his poetry publicly. I say seemed because at a certain age one is never certain of some things but has snatches of impressions. One knew that it was an important and momentous time – that there were upheavals, tension and great sweet victories. And then things, some things, got clearer. Out of that stabilising centre of home, family and relatives, pujas and kathas and the recitals from the great poetic epics of India in mandirs came a calm and an euphoria. And then those disturbances one never forgets, no matter how long one lives: the roving gangs of black men on bicycles, and the men, the Indian men in our little cul-de-sac street of all Indians, on the edge of Kitty bordering Campbellville where we lived with my great-grandmother, keeping an armed, around-the-clock, vigil. If these roving packs of black men, who pounced on and beat up solitary Indian men trying to go about their daily chores in the city, should decide that our enclave of Indians was easy picking, then let them come.

Things were never quite the same again though all of that ended and things seemed to revert to normal. And it was left to 'the Babulall', as Rohan Kanhai was known to Indians, and his batting genius, to take up where Jagan left off, let us down. Every ball Kanhai lashed, every run, every boundary was a salvaging of lost Indian pride – of defiance. We moved and I changed schools. I remember a huge celebration, and waving of flags, the learning of songs, an anthem and an exhortation in school that we must be happy, should be happy. Something like independence. We, the people of this young country were free at last – but at school, but only at school – not at home.

Through all of this I knew that this person who once wrote great poems, and read them, was fashionable again; that that devious black man who now ruled, the enemy of Indians, quoted this man who wrote these quotable verses. And this quotable man had sold out to this quoting man – so he too was no good. I didn't know then that Carter was Minister of Information in Burnham's government. Much later, I would ask that same vexing question; how could Carter have been taken in by that man? And much later still be as frustrated and unsatisfied as I first was with the answer. Race and human emotions are complex things.

So too that osmosis of opinions and hang-ups one sucks in while growing up. Those things, like the great race divide, which seeps into one's consciousness without one fully comprehending them. I grew into a greater consciousness hearing teachers at school fawn over Carter, and those black leaders, the enemy, at every turn spouting, 'I come from the nigger yard of yesterday/leaping from the oppressors' hate/and scorn of myself...'.

I was no 'nigger'. And I hated the word, as I hated being lumped together with people of African descent as 'we black people' – involved in the struggle of black peoples the world over. I felt, like my relatives, that I was being made invisible. In my boy's mind I rebelled and resented that I should be expected to celebrate a blackness which wasn't mine. But if my relatives resented this celebration of blackness which made then invisible, they also resented and blamed Jagan for his sitting back, for his non-violent stance and our predicament as second class citizens. Why did he hold us back? If the blacks wanted a fight let us fight, carve up the country, set up our own state – they would only respect us in strength!

Race is a thing which nobody in our time and space could escape and labelling is often the most convenient tool in the strategy of dismissal. The Euro-American pushed aura of Gandhi's PASSIVE-resistance was the stereotype expected of Indians and the Jagan non-violent approach strengthened the stereotype.

But I was learning from Martin Carter. If Carter could affirm and celebrate and find strength and acceptance in his 'niggerness' in his poetry and do the same for black people, why couldn't I do the same thing in poetry with my Hinduness for myself and my community? I still get critics, including Indian ones, who are leery of my outspoken Indian-groundedness – a positioning from Carter's – but who can sing and celebrate his, 'I Come From the Nigger Yard'. But I am racing ahead.

I came late to Jagan and then to Carter. Their lives intertwined in our history of a certain time and place: Carter served the Kabaka, and Jagan kept us down, did not let us carve out a state for ourselves when we had the guns and the arms and the anger and the will. Later, directly exposed to the machinations of Burnham and the PNC, and the attendant racism, I would rebel and resist Carter – and Jagan – much more consciously and independently of my parents and relatives. I throw in Jagan because in many ways my revision of my appraisal of Carter was dependent on my reappraisal of Cheddi Jagan – and visa versa.

In the sixth form at Queens College, I was lucky in having the late N.A. Robinson as my literature teacher: write all that poetry if you must, Sase – but also read all the fine poetry around too – Carter, Walcott... Well after exams, he would urge. But reasoning-thinking-analysing is a slower process than the reflexive emotional. We were in the late seventies and switching from the London G.C.E. to the CXC examinations and Carter's poetry was in one of the books on the soon-to-be-introduced syllabus...

But I have jumped ahead again. I was teaching at the Central High School and the CXC History syllabus was being phased in first and Jagan's classic *The West on Trial* was on the syllabus. George Moore, the acting deputy principal who was teaching history, in an extraordinary act of courage for those tenuous times did not hide his copy of *The West on Trial*, with which he walked to classes and back openly – like a badge of honour. George Moore, a man of African ancestry, was one of the nicest, most agreeable persons on our staff, a respected but approachable elder, and we had never seen him angry until that day we good-naturedly teased him, as we had done so many times before: what was this 'Jagan history' he was teaching the kids in class? He slammed down *The West On Trial* on a table in the staff room and glared at us, a young largely Indian staff: What do you really know of Cheddi Jagan? What do you really know of Dr. Cheddi Bharat Jagan that is not propaganda? Have you read his classic? Why don't you read this book of this extraordinary Guyanese first before passing half-scalded judgement? Or words close to those boomed across the room like a cannon. There was a long silence. It was one of those extraordinary and rare moments in one's life. George Moore put his book in his locker and quietly left the room.

I hunted down that copy of *The West on Trial* I had bought at the GNTC Bookstore – subsequently destroyed by fire – a book which I had breezed through before and read it again, carefully, slowly – if one can read such a fascinating book slowly. That, now battered, copy has the date scrawled across the title page: 86.09.29. It turned out to be a most extraordinary book – a book, which alone, I knew would guarantee Jagan a place in the history of Guyana, as one of its most outstanding writers and historians.

This was a watershed moment in my life. How could my relatives be so wrong about this man? And what of Carter? Many of the things I had imbibed from my society I was finally ready to re-examine, and throw out if need be. And so it was that I could finally go to Carter, and let the work and one's subjective reason speak. Yes, subjective reasoning. Objectivity is a myth. Carter again, 'Watch my Language'.

This was at a time when I was awash in poetry. I wrote, read, slept, dreamt, poetry. A throwback to high school and especially my time at Queens College and the prescribed poetry. I had found Tagore at Queens too. An odd a place? Not really. Remember Marvell's, '...Thou by the Indian Ganges side/Should'st Rubies find...' And there was the Hindu Society and the deliberate immersion in the Indian world; The Hindu Society and the voluntary immersion in celebrating things Indian were, in many ways, our tools in defying the Burnham regime and the racism of that time.

So there I was, teaching and politicking and poetrying. I lived for poetry, writing a poem a day for almost a year before slacking off into a poem every four days or so for another few years, and reading as much as I could from both sides of the Atlantic and further afield. From the Public Free Library as it was then – Burnham's National Library! came later – there were the contemporary British, and occasional European poets in *Encounter*, *London Magazine*, *Poetry Review* and other journals while from the John F. Kennedy Library, a greater slew of contemporary magazines and a rich poetry book section. I must have made an unconscious effort not to have a favourite poet because while there were many great poems in the lot, I could never remember names of poets.

Into all of this now came Carter. I was immediately spellbound by Carter's poetry, and I felt then that he was unquestionably the greatest poet in the English Language this half of the twentieth century. Here was a poet whose lyricism effortlessly bridged that gap between the written and spoken, academic and non-academic in a way done more consistently in this century only by Rabindranath Tagore. Afterwards I would go on to read Walcott and Brathwaite and other West Indian poets. But their work only served to confirm and strengthen my original assessment of Carter. Only at their best they came close to what Carter had accomplished in all his poetry, well all his poetry which I had read at the time.

Of course, there was that gap where Carter left them all behind – those poems of resistance and defiance and mourning and sadness, poems like; 'Weroon Weroon', 'University of Hunger', 'Death of a Comrade', 'Letter 1', 'Letter 2', 'This is the Dark Time My Love' – which aptly described the time again before our eyes. Only this time the foreign invaders were the Guyana Defence Force soldiers marching through all those Indian villages, intending to cower the Indians; particularly that village I knew on the West Demerara in the aftermath of the baldfaced, brutally rigged 1973 elections. And then there was the People's Militia and The Guyana National Service putting on all those military parades on every least excuse of a 'National' occasion around Georgetown.

Perhaps Walter Rodney and the WPA, and Carter's somewhat redeeming association with them, his turning against the regime – the 'roughing-up' he received from the regime's thugs – helped. It was not a time for lollipop poetry. And I think the students knew that. I would read a Carter poem once, and then analyse it, go over the history and the politics – show how the poem was relevant to the time it was born of and to our own time and the students would want to hear the poem read again and again. There would be a hush and full silence, and then questions and comments. And when the bell went for the end of a period everyone would want to stay longer and do more poetry. That was what Carter's poetry did in a time when students tended to shy away from poetry.

Close encounters with Carter were few. Once or twice I visited his house on Lamaha Street to drop off copies of poetry collections by friends – P.D. Sharma's *The New Caribbean Man*, for instance, which Sharma had just published in Los Angeles and wanted me to take to Carter. Very brief meetings. I would pass Carter on my bicycle or on my motorcycle on Vlissengen Road as we both headed for the seawall – his long, brisk striding walk unmistakeable – for the calm and rage of the Atlantic, and the sea breeze, that seemingly endless expanse of water.

Another day it was at Bill Carr's house, a roaring discussion and drinking party in session, I was dropping off another copy of Sharma's book and, as Carr had suggested, one of my first poetry manuscripts for a Carr demolition. I had earlier had the privilege of listening to Carr present a brilliant paper at the University of Guyana titled, 'Stewards of their Excellence' on the work of Carter, Walcott and Brathwaite, and that presentation had impressed me.

I had heard and seen Carter on other occasions. But the indirect encounter which stuck with me was that time we drank rum in the same rum shop. He with his few friends and I with mine. It was a rumshop in Alberttown, at the corner of Fifth and Light Streets. There was cricket on and we were off work early, headed for Bourda. I can't remember if there might have been rain, or the match being over earlier than expected, or simply that good old Guyana excuse – the existence of a convenient rum shop – but we were stopped off there for a drink. It was the first time in my life that I got really plastered, and it was my last.

What I also recalled thinking before I ceased recalling anything else on that afternoon was this: here was a great poet who walked about his city, lived in it, drank in it without putting on any great airs – and he was neglected for it and for his truth seeking which did not always coincide with other people's. I also recalled feeling sorry for him, wondering if in his disillusionment with the rampant corruption of the Burnham regime and the near total breakdown of morality in our society, he wasn't simply drinking himself out and wasting this great gift of his – conscious of the gap in the publication of his poetry. I felt that if I continued on this way that could happen to me too, and I didn't want that to happen to me. Perhaps this may have had something to do with my own resolve the next day to give up drinking.

There are gaps. I left Guyana in 1988. To be sure Carter came to Canada – at least in his work. In a paper 'The Indian Presence as a Caribbean Reality' presented at York University during the conference celebrating 150 years since the arrival of Indians to the West Indies, George Lamming would read from another of Carter's masterpieces, 'Looking at Your Hands' and posit that the political dynamism and racial unity of the Indians and Africans of Guyana of the early 1950s – for which Cheddi Jagan more than any other person was responsible – was the fertile soil for the early genius of Carter (and for Jan Carew and Wilson Harris) – and that Carter was never to write like that again. This was an intriguing opinion with which a few writers present agreed.

And then that next year (1989) Demerara Publishers would bring out

Carter's *Selected Poems*. Nothing of its calibre had been published from within the region before – nor since – and it was a pleasure to receive a copy from Ian McDonald. I walked around Toronto with my copy in my bag, reading in my lunch breaks at work, on the early morning subway, in the quiet of night.

Then it dawned on me why I admired Carter's poems so much – particularly his early poems up to 1966 – it was the seeming simplicity and directness of language, which I had found and loved in Tagore. And going back to Tagore and reading them side by side, the parallels were uncanny. I am browsing though my copy of *Selected Poems* now and seeing all those poems of Carter's, alongside which I had written in Devnagri script – Tagore: 'Shines The Beauty of My Darling' (*The Hill of Fire Glows Red*, 1951), 'I Stretch my Hand' (*The Hidden Man*, 1952), 'Let Freedom Wake Him' (*Poems of Resistance*, 1954) – and even in such later poems as "Rain Falls Upwards' (1966), 'Before the Question' (1973), 'In a Certain Time', 'With That Loan' (from *Poems of Affinity*, 1980) and 'One' (1984).

I couldn't help asking myself if there was a Tagore/Upanishadic/Indian influence; recalling mention of the British Guiana Dramatic Society's performances of Tagore's plays and work in the thirties and forties in Georgetown. Tagore was, has always been, a presence in Guyana – even in the naming of the Tagore Memorial High school on the Corentyne Coast. Was Carter aware of all this – some kind of osmosis. Tagore's famous verse 35 from the Gitanjali was/is a prayer used in the Guyana parliament. Who was responsible for that? And could Carter the politician and parliamentarian be unaware of it and its power and lyricism, of the personification of the poet as supplicant and prophet – and that personification of god much noted in Hinduism and a distinctive mark in Tagore's work, and in his own?

Carter read widely, including of the Latin American poets, who themselves had greater contact with Indian thought and poetry through Tagore. On his well publicised South American tour Tagore had spent a few months in Argentina, reading and lecturing, and after falling sick, recuperating – guest of the well known Argentine writer, Victoria Ocampo. And Tagore came and brought all that was expected of the spirit of India. In the Guyanese fight for independence from Britain Carter was The poet, The literary presence in that struggle, not unlike Tagore who was The literary presence during the fight for Indian independence – at least in the eyes of the west. Was Carter conscious of this?

And did all this matter? Influences are extraordinarily quirky things. I had stopped making those 'Tagore' notations alongside Carter's poems. In any event, which intellectual living his life in Guyana, or Trinidad, could not be aware of Indians and Indian culture and literature? Not even Walcott whose association with Trinidad, and its smaller percentage of Indians, was relatively short – and this comes out in his Nobel address.

Martin Carter not only deserved the Guyana Prize – which he won – but surely should have won the Nobel Prize for literature. I was amazed, but not really surprised, that other writers from Guyana in North America felt this, that as one of them put it, 'Walcott could not even kiss the dust of Carter's feet'. Interestingly, almost all of those who feel this way are Indians – a throwback to ancestral aesthetics, to Tagore, to the Upanishads? What is objective and not clouded by race? Not the Nobel Prize, not anything. Certainly not Brathwaite's African-leaning 'nation language' or even my yogic realism – but then I have never claimed that my yogic realism is the aesthetic of ALL West Indians.

Guyana is different, distinct from the rest of the West Indies and that difference has not only to do with the landscape but with the Indian population and its culture, and speech patterns and literature.

It was good to see Carter note the distinctiveness of Guyana from the Caribbean in his interview with Frank Birbalsingh in *Kyk-over-al*, and also the positive quirkiness which sets the writings apart. And Birbalsingh couldn't trip him up as he clinically took on Brathwaite's 'nation language'. The proponents of 'creole' – including Birbalsingh himself – must have cringed. Martin Carter had lost none of his sharpness and clarity and eloquence – not even in an interview. Carter continues to be as important a voice, for a certain community, as he was in the 1950s and early 1960s. And he is right. Language is indeed a personal thing and those of us who write largely in a standard English do so because it is the form of expression we are most comfortable in. And we are original and universal in it. We are direct in it. We achieve clarity in it. We communicate effectively in it, and as evidenced by Carter's own poetry, produce works of genius in it.

Martin Carter is unquestionably Guyana's first world class poet, and if one includes Guyana in the English Speaking West Indies, he is also the first and foremost world class poet from that region – nobody had achieved the sustainable poetic excellence and genius he achieved in the early 1950s – not even Walcott. And, perhaps, he is the only genuine poet – no playwright-poet, or historian-poet or novelist-poet or even academic-lecturer-poet – we have. No confusion of form. Yes, there has been dabbling here and there – and who doesn't dabble here and there? But finally this is what I need to say:

forgive me, if ever I came
to stand before you
in your own worn boots
thinking I brought myself.

Today I come unshoed
and lotus my legs
and wait to watch your language.

JANICE LO SHINEBOURNE

MARTIN CARTER – BEACON

Neville Dawes, in his introduction to *Poems of Resistance* said,

> Martin Carter was in his early twenties when he wrote *Poems of Resistance.* The present generation of new Guyana youth will need the inspiration of these poems in a time of crisis. (p.iii)

I was in my youth when Neville Dawes wrote that. For me, it has never ceased to be a time of crisis for Guyana. *Poems of Resistance* created a powerful enduring political iconography of Guyanese history from slavery, indentureship, painful and harsh political struggle for survival against nature, poverty and the capitalist and militaristic forces of destabilisation. Its images and passionate rhetoric still express our current dilemmas. I think in particular of 'University of Hunger', 'Death of a Comrade' and 'Not Hands Like Mine', a history summed up by the lines in 'Death of a Slave':

> In the dark earth
> in the cold dark earth
> time plants the seed of anger.

Poems of Resistance also commemorates his commitment to a public role as a nationalist poet. It meant he had to live without the boundaries between the public and private man, between political involvement and family life. One poem in particular, 'I am no Soldier', reveals the anguish this caused him, and captures it in his experience of imprisonment:

> I will come to each and to every comrade led by my heart
> Led by the magnet of freedom which draws me far and wide
> over the sun's acres of children and of mornings

From his early period my favourite poems are, 'You are involved', 'Weroon Weroon' and 'This is the dark time my love'. They succeed in integrating and balancing finely a passion for political service with the need to hone his craft – a poetic language and voice. In my opinion this balance was always important for the survival and happiness of the man. He gave exemplary political service and he evolved a poetic language that will always move us and deepen our lives.

The early political poems find the young poet assuming heroic postures but they capture the passion of the time. Without him we would have no record of what the anti-colonial struggle really meant to Guyanese in the fifties, and to me this is priceless for no one has captured the integrity of those struggles better than Martin Carter. In a sense it does not matter that political passions were exaggerated. In another sense it matters that a young man who was also a poet dedicated himself to voicing them so recklessly. The price that he paid is evident in the later poems when the dreams of political liberation seem to have become the rubbish of history and reduced the poet to a beggar of dreams:

> Proudful and barefoot I stride the street
> who wants my shirt can have it.
> Only the giver gets. The unwanted
> unwants the world. The bruised heel of his foot
> kicks like a meteor. And the dim dark behind
> the blue illusion stands like an altar in a temple
> in a forsaken land. Having failed to learn
> how to die, they all perish ungracefully.
> Laocoön, for all the snakes, struggled well.
> ('For a Man who Walked Sideways', 1974)

Martin Carter has struggled more than 'well'. When I was a young writer in Guyana he was the most accessible of older established writers. I remember my first contact with him. I used to take my turn to stand on the street corner in Water Street, Georgetown, selling a small literary magazine produced by young writers. He bought a magazine off me and invited me to join a group discussion at his house in Lamaha Street. I was supposed to ask him to support the magazine so I did. He invited me to his office nearby and promptly wrote a cheque for a generous sum. After that I visited his home several times in the company of other young writers for those famous seminars that he held there. He initiated me into having a sense of writing as a public service but he also taught me that writing was an act of conscience, not propaganda. He taught me that the quality and honesty of the writing defined the effectiveness of that public service, not what people wanted to hear, and that to do the job well you had to have your ear to the ground of politics as intensely as you worked at the craft of your writing.

He shunned being identified entirely with a liberal literary and arts tradition which would have embraced and elevated him, had he gone into exile in London or the United States. He did not go into exile, he was not tempted by the personal fame and aggrandisement that it would certainly have brought him. He remained in Guyana where he is closest to the roots of a public tradition of writing that all his life he never ceased to work hard to define and articulate at any cost. In this sense he succeeded entirely in his early desire to be a poet for Guyana. His life and art is a model of public service combined closely with artistic achievement and it has been a beacon of inspiration that shone across the distance to me here in London, and always will. His poetry speaks for my parent's generation and my own generation's memory. For our desires and dreams, our pain and disappointment.

OBITUARIES

EUSI KWAYANA

A FRIENDLY, DREAM-FUL, DANGEROUS MAN: MARTIN WYLDE CARTER, OR, 1927-1997

(First published in the *Guyana Review*, Jan. 1998)

His brain must have been the last part of him to die. I would have thought it would be his very human heart. Perhaps it is his heart which will never die. But an hour after Martin Carter expelled the air from his chest for the last time, when his Chosen One, Phyllis Howard Carter, and a few of us stood at his bedside, he seemed still deep in thought. I say to myself, 'He is in a new mode now. His thoughts will no longer come to us through his fingers, now cold. His poems from now on will be trained to the cosmos in a new script, a new font, unlike any writing that we know or have known. Those who meditate and dream will tap the ideas from the eternal fountain of universal thought.'

For the last 40 years and more, Martin Carter has been recognised as a poet and writer. From time to time, his membership of the People's Progressive Party and its leading organ, *Thunder,* has been mentioned. His detention and imprisonment have been public knowledge. His political and cultural activity, his real struggle and its consequences and his poetry which so effectively gives us, in our own name, a personality and presence in the world, are real, but not the whole of his reality.

Left out of this narrow profile of Carter are his familyhood, his friendships and conversations and his rich and fruitful intellect. Even what is written here will not be a complete measure of his range and depth. At least it will point to other facets of his universe which are often neglected by some writers, who can only see greatness in terms of prestige. This is a failing even among those who have known Carter for the greater part of his adult life, ever since the 'Miniature Poets', the [Arthur] Seymour Series which published his *Hill of Fire Glows Red* with its reference to Phyllis in 'Shines the Beauty of My Darling'. This amorous reference bore poetic fruit in *Poems of Resistance* in the lines, 'Tell me, the young one – is he creeping now – And is he well and mischievous as ever?' This first offspring of the marriage was named Keith, after Martin's elder brother whom he loved and regarded as an oracle. For years after marriage, Martin and Phyllis lived with his widowed mother, and one sister, Joan and brothers Pat and Ben. No doubt, this was an economic need, but it was an example of sharing territory in a civilised way. Phyllis's brother was always a visiting member of the household.

The children grew up seeing their parents involved in genuine friendships with people of all possible shades and origins who were always welcome in their homes. This included workers, people of no particular standing, and anyone who felt like having a chat with someone who was important and human. Lloyd Payne was one of the close friends I often met there in the accommodating gallery, complete with rocking chair, in Anira Street in the days before and after 1953. Lloyd was the one who took him to church for his marriage. It was there I met Douglas Armstrong, then a budding boxer, writer and thinker. The place was a living shrine. Sugar workers, town people, all felt free at any time to visit Martin for a chat. During the days when we were all restricted by the Governor's order; people from the village [Buxton] and Lusignan, or Bachelor's Adventure, going on missions to the Party office, would come back to me and say, 'I dropped in to see Martin and have a talk.' They usually left, feeling more human than before.

There was a small school of ideas which met in a room in Norton Street, every Friday night after the PPP public meeting. Those often present, according to my memory, were Sidney Singh and Wilson Harris, friends of Martin Carter. My drinking days had come to an end after five years, at 20, in 1945. They were drinkers, but on these occasions they smoked rather than drank and I did not know the dangers for me. We sat and talked for hours, week after week, probing all the problems of society and of thinking and being. This was only one of the many occasions he sought for conversations with friends.

He visited bars and talked, talked to men and women hanging out, making all the acquaintance with the misery he wrote about, never trusting appearances, never writing people off, regardless of their status in life or their education, listening even to those dismissed as insane. His very theory of self-contempt came from one of these encounters. At the same time, he was not uncritical of the masses and had hard words for them when they seemed to submit to abuse. Many would-be writers and poets came to him for criticism. He would often tell them what form of writing to try and whether their verse was poetic or not. I, for example, always say, when asked, that I write verse, not poetry, since he long discounted me as a poet and advised me to stick to drama.

The Carters, though urban people, seemed wedded to the idea of the extended family and my impression is that younger members of the original family of the brood lived in the maternal home or kept in daily touch with it. There are, of course, many other families like them and that is what makes them special. They were famous, but not special, not carried away with it, not aloof or remote from people.

Every time I see an article written about Martin Carter, mentioning his friends as though he lived in charmed circle, I want to reach for my less elegant pen and write the truth. I tried this notion out on eldest son, Keith, soon after the funeral and described a slightly built man I have met only there and met talking with Martin at any hour, three times out of five, on my rare visits. Keith sparkled. He said. 'Yes, Ivan Forrester. They call him Farro. I heard he was at the funeral but I'm sorry I didn't see him.' Farro is not middle class and doesn't look it either yet all the family regards him as one of them. Farro is an artist of special gifts and industry.

Moreover, Keith knew all his father's drinking friends and spoke of them with affection. They were mostly good people of no special standing in society. They valued one another. And I venture the opinion that this kind of company was an important source of Martin's remarkable wisdom. [Rupert] Roopnaraine has written about him as uniquely a poet of the city, referring to many of his richest lines. No doubt among these lines was the one about 'the man who walks a pavement, walks and disappears.' He also writes of him as a walking poet, 'a man living among my people.'

In my review of *A Children's Story of Guyana's Freedom Heroes,* by Janet Jagan I expressed concern at her omission of Martin Carter as the tallest tree among them in a deeply cultural and intellectual sense. Happily, this omission was made good in her tribute to him, read by Ian McDonald at the poet's funeral. She then deemed him a hero. Martin's probings into the 'histories of men and the lives of the peoples' was deep and rewarding. He made a close study of all Guyana's cultures and was well-informed on the ethos as well as the artefacts and the work and other life styles of the indigenous peoples. At a political meeting at Buxton on 14 December, Ashton Simon, one of their sons, read him a poem to the Moon Stone, written for him after his passing.

Many critics of Carter's poem shrank at his some of his lines like, 'I clench my fist above my head – I sing my song of freedom.' What, they ask, has poetry to do with that. They have read that somewhere. Eliot used to be, at least in Guyana, a point of reference for this kind of posture. Yet I can think of few pamphlets more thoroughly political than Eliot's *Murder in the Cathedral* with its deep understanding of political attitudes, not yet fathomed by many political scientists of the present day. Unfortunately for them, Carter was not a mere poet. He was a multi-talented person. Critics who come to him expecting to find, either in him or in his work, a one-track outlook, would have to make him over. To sum up what I have in mind, his poetry was not a political instrument, but his politics were an expression of his poetry.

I was going on to say at some point that Martin Carter was a philosopher who was constantly reflecting on ideas and existence and the meaning of every thing. He was up to date with the world, sometimes ahead of it. One of his findings about us as Guyanese was our 'self-contempt', which he learned from an old woman who told him in confidence, after a public meeting in the city, that the reason why she supported that party was that 'the white woman is there.' His findings about us were thus not always flattering. My friends, the critics, will have to take him as he is, 'nothing extenuate, nor set down aught in ignorance.' He was a poet who was more a than a poet.

He took pride, I believe, in being at least abreast of the world intellectually from his place in Guyana, never wanting to emigrate. In his words, what Janette Forte calls the 'desired addresses' in England and North America were 'good to go to, plant rice and come back.'

He brought his 'bad' habit of conversation into his political activity. This, along with his gift of penetrating thought, made him a friendly, dream-ful, dangerous man.

IAN MCDONALD

MARTIN

(First published in the *Sunday Stabroek*, Georgetown, December 21st 1997)

After Martin Carter suffered a stroke three years ago he would still accept invitations to some public occasions though on such occasions he did not want to speak. He sat and listened to the proceedings and talked privately to friends in the audience afterwards. On one such occasion I was in the audience. Martin was on the platform. My eyes kept turning in his direction and anyone could sense that the attention of the audience was more on the big man contemplating a universe of his own than on the others up there doing the talking. When the proceedings ended and people were getting up to go I heard a man, a few chairs away from me, as he moved to leave, say to nobody in particular, perhaps simply to himself, 'That man have aura!' One didn't need to guess what man he meant. There is a gleam of some outstanding thing, a hallowing of the air around, an unmistakable ambience, an aura indeed, which surrounds a very few and which can be sensed and it is with them all their lives signalling their greatness. If we are lucky we meet and get to know one or two such men or women in our lives.

Quite soon after I arrived in Guyana in 1955 I met Martin so I have known him most of my life. I was privileged. If Martin was even a small part of your life you knew you were greatly privileged. When Martin died I spoke to many people who had known him well and all expressed in one way or another a desolation as if an important part of their own lives was lost forever.

Marc Matthews rang me from London and he was grieving and could hardly speak. He told me that people, now living in England, who had known Martin had been telephoning each other for hours that day, talking through their grief and loss, comforting each other as if every one had lost someone very close and could hardly bear it.

Could it have been that it was simply (simply indeed!) the great poet in Martin which gave him this aura, which made countless people feel when he died that part of them had died and that their world was bereft? After all, he was indeed a very great poet – the greatest poet Guyana has produced, one of the outstanding creative writers of the English-speaking Caribbean, a peerless examiner of the human heart, a poet sure to be measured with the great poets of the Americas and the world as time slowly but surely dissolves the dross and leaves the granite standing. Who am I to define Martin's essence better than Wordsworth who answered his own question, 'What is a Poet?' with a grandeur hard to match:

> The rock of defence of human nature; an upholder and preserver, carrying everywhere with him relationship and love. In spite of difference of soil and climate, of language and manners, of laws and customs, in spite of things silently gone out of mind and things violently destroyed, the Poet binds together by passion and knowledge the vast empire of human society, as it is spread over the whole earth, and over all time. The objects of the Poet's thoughts are everywhere; though the eyes and senses of man are, it is true, his favourite guides, yet he will follow wheresoever he can find an atmosphere of sensation in which to move his wings. Poetry is the first and last of all knowledge – it is as immortal as the heart of man.

That is an affirmation in which I and so many others recognise the everlasting value and significance of Martin's poetry. Yet the great poet in him does not wholly explain the effect he had on each one of us, the indefinable aura, the unique presence. Well, I say to myself, the aura was indefinable so why try to define it? Still I have this need to try. I know I will not do it well – such efforts are really undoable – but I want to get something out of my heart to say for Martin, to Martin, for all he contributed and added to my life.

It was not just the poet in the man. There was an unique *seriousness* in Martin which captured one's attention and love. It was a deep seriousness about his task in life, about life itself, about life's meaning, that went beyond anything I have felt in anyone else I have known. The task of the poet is sacred, one's integrity is sacred, the loyalties of love and friendship are sacred, the rights of men are sacred and are too often abused, the wonder of the world is sacred and why is it that most men seem not to know it, life's potential is sacred and why is it that it is so often neglected?

A counter-aspect of his abiding seriousness about such things was the bitterness and despair he felt and often expressed about the brutishness of men, the extraordinary superficiality and hollowness of public affairs, the spiritual desolation that seems to have entrenched itself everywhere, the plunge of the world into hatred and ignorance. All this I write may make him seem a very heavy and humourless man. Far from it. He could laugh and carouse with the very, very best of the laughers and carousers. But there was that core of seriousness about the sacred, the sacredness of the word, the sacredness of the works of man in the world, that never left him and that I will never forget.

Through the years I sent Martin notes of things I had noticed and thought he might like to see. Once I found something Yeats had written in an obscure journal and sent it to Martin. Yeats, at his best, was one of the few poets who survived Martin's severe appraisal of what is good in poetry. Here he was writing something I felt about Martin's own poetry; 'A feeling for the form of life, for the graciousness of life, for the dignity of life, for the moving limbs of life, for the nobleness of life, for all that cannot be written in codes, has always been greatest among the gifts of literature to mankind.'

Martin greatly loved the Chinese poet Li Po who after a gloriously disreputable life drowned in a river when he fell in the shining water trying to put his arms around the reflection of the moon. Martin used to tell me that it was written about Li Po that 'writing hates the successful life'.

Another time I sent him a biography of Coleridge, whose work he also admired, and he returned it later with scribbles of delight and awe and questioning in the margins. Never was such defacement so welcomed! The book is now perhaps the most treasured possession in my library.

And another time I sent him a number of extracts from the notebooks of the American scholar-poet Theodore Roethke brought together in a book entitled *Straw For The Fire*. There were a large number of extracts I sent to Martin. When I met him soon afterwards he thanked me as he always did for what I had thought of sending to him. Then he gripped my arm – and it was painful because he was a strong man and grew forgetfully intense at such times – and he quoted two of the extracts from Roethke I had sent. I don't have to look up my diaries to remember the words: 'Remind yourself once more of the absolute holiness of your task.' And 'To write poetry; you have to be prepared to die.'

I salute Martin's wife, Phyllis, friend of his friends always, incomparable wife-companion, brave for Martin throughout his great life, generous-hearted to a fault. He would have been less without her, who can doubt it. She and their children were as precious to him as the poems he loved and that is saying a lot.

MERVYN MORRIS

MARTIN CARTER: MORE THAN AN EXCELLENT POET

(First published in *The Sunday Observer*, Jamaica, Jan. 4th 1998)

Martin Carter, who was born in Georgetown, Guyana, on June 7, 1927, died there three weeks ago. One of the leading poets in the English-speaking Caribbean, he is perhaps best known as the author of *Poems of Resistance* (first published in 1954) which includes some pieces written in prison.

After the British government suspended the British Guiana constitution in 1953, Carter was one of a number of activists locked up (in 1954) for disobeying emergency regulations. 'This Is the Dark Time My Love', one of the famous poems in that collection, notes the intrusion of British soldiers ('brown beetles crawl about'), and it ends:

> Who comes walking in the dark night time?
> Whose boot of steel tramps down the slender grass?
> It is the man of death, my love, the strange invader
> watching you sleep and aiming at your dream.

Part of Carter's importance is that, though he never ran for office, he was – unusually in the English-speaking Caribbean – one writer whose political commitment took him well beyond words. In 1953, he gave up his civil service job because he had felt obliged to protest publicly in support of a friend locked up for marching in a banned political procession.

In 1966, he took part in the talks in London on Guyana's Independence. Between 1967 and 1970 he was a member of Guyana's annual delegation to the United Nations. He was appointed to the Cabinet in 1967, as minister of information and culture. In 1970, he resigned from the Cabinet and the Government.

His political experience and consequent changes in his perception are reflected in his poetry. If the persona in one poem declares 'I do not sleep to dream, but dream to change the world', in another (later) poem we are reminded that 'All, all who are human fail' and, in another (not long before Carter resigned from the Cabinet), that 'a mouth is always muzzled/ by the food it eats to live.'

One strand of development in Carter's poetry moves from eloquent optimism towards reticence and disillusion, increasing acknowledgement of 'the treason/ of the spirit' of 'the unfortunate air/ which stifles' and that 'Everything blindfolds.' The poet-persona shares the suffering and corruption he identifies. In 'Bent' an old woman 'resurrects/ the brimmed bucket of this world's/light and insupportable/ agony.' A poem grieving the death of Walter Rodney arraigns 'Assassins of conversation'. Another, occasioned by the murder of a Catholic priest (Father Darke, who had published newspaper criticisms of the Burnham regime) ends in bitterly ironic reference to the 'nativity' of evil, recognition of original sin.

> I have at last started
> to understand the origin
> of our vileness, and being
> unable to deny it, I suggest
> its nativity.
> In the shame of knowledge
> of our vileness, we shall fight.

The 'we shall fight' is teasingly ambiguous: suggesting that we fight because of our vileness, and/or that we shall fight against the evil inherent in ourselves.

Though Carter is often (rightly) identified as a poet deeply involved in politics, he also has other – sometimes intertwining – concerns: such as history – 'In the cold dark earth/ time plants the seeds of anger', the legacy of ancestors – their 'tongueless whispering', and love – of wife and family, especially, as in 'Letter 2', 'For My Son' and 'My Hand in Yours'.

Among his recurrent preoccupations are the role and nature of the poet – 'we who want true poems/ must all be born again, and die to do so' and the mysterious power of language – 'Not in the saying of you are you/ said.'

One of Carter's skills, not always mentioned in commentary on his work, is the unobtrusive incorporation of creole. When, for example, he begins a poem 'is the university of hunger the wide waste' this is not a question but an assertion in creole: [*it*] is the university of hunger [*which is*] the wide waste. Similarly, in a poem called 'Four', a standard English sentence is immediately followed by a laconic creole construction: 'All had been hanged already./ Hangman gone home.'

Carter's poetry, as a significant body of work, is available again. In May last year, Red Thread Women's Press of Georgetown Guyana, published a revised edition of his *Selected Poems* (first published by Demerara Publishers Ltd in 1989). Ian McDonald notes in the Foreword that the major collections of Carter's poems – *Poems of Resistance*, *Poems of Succession*, *Poems of Affinity* – are out of print, that the smaller selections are rarely to be found even in libraries and that 'Many of Martin Carter's poems – even poems as celebrated as 'I Come from the Nigger Yard' and 'Poems of Shape and Motion' – have appeared in past collections, magazines and anthologies with numerous errors and even with whole stanzas inadvertently omitted.' Though this publication is not without errors itself – several in the Bibliography and at least one in a poem, 'Bent' (page 188) – the Red Thread *Selected Poems* is clearly the collection to have.

Carter was not only an excellent poet but also a compelling reader. A sonorous baritone, well over six foot tall, he was never casual and did not overdramatise. He intoned each poem musically, with loving attention to rhythm.

As a person he seemed to me gentle, modest and witty. He had a philosophical turn of mind which, the few times I was in his company, was always trying to be precise about consciousness and the paradoxical operations of language. His poem, 'Proem', (dated 1974) fairly represents, I think, that aspect of the man.

Not, in the saying of you, are you
said. Baffled and like a root
stopped by a stone you turn back questioning
the tree you feed. But what the leaves hear
is not what the roots ask. Inexhaustibly,
being at one time what was to be said
and at another time what has been said
the saying of you remains the living of you
never to be said. But, enduring,
you change with the change that changes
and yet are not of the changing of any of you.
Ever yourself, you are always about
to be yourself in something else ever with me.

In an interview with Peter Trevis, Carter remarked: 'one does not choose to be difficult or complex. The material you deal with requires a certain way of doing it and that is not a choice'.

VANDA RADZIK

ONE DREAM IS ENOUGH: A TRIBUTE TO MARTIN CARTER

(This article was carried in the *Sunday Stabroek*, Georgetown, on December 21, 1997. It was edited by Andaiye and published in her *Sunday Stabroek* 'Woman's Eye View' column on behalf of Red Thread Press.)

Martin Wylde Carter, his very name is a poem. His life's work a proem. 'Not in the saying of you, are you said...'

Martin Carter's public life is a book that writes this nation's history. His private life brimful with family, friends, events, conversations. His poetic life shaped by his trade, craft, fired by his great, good intelligence, tempered by love and loss, presented in the form of his poems and prose that will ever be, in the words of Wilson Harris, an 'eternity to season'.

Martin Carter loved the poetry of fellow South American poet, Cesar Vallejo and wrote poems in his honour. This was one of his own that he once said he was 'satisfied' with. It is quoted here – a toast to Martin himself in his own inimitable words:

> Brother, let us now break
> our bread together. My
> plate is a small world. My
> world a small plate. From
> a place in which plates
> and worlds are utensils
> we have reconstructed our
> selves, with a power of difference...

The title of his brilliant address to the University of Guyana students in 1974 – 'A free society of valid persons' – was Martin Carter's dream for Guyana. It was never to be realised in his lifetime – 'not even close', he used to say, finger pointing skyward, philosophical grin or grimace spread-eagled over his familiar face. And this pronouncement would usually be followed by an appropriate quotation of his own ... 'So jail me quickly, clang the illiterate door/if freedom writes no happier alphabet.' ... 'Men murder men, as men must murder men,/ to build their shining governments of the damned.'

Martin Carter came to loathe the psyche of a Guyana largely bereft of moral dignity and integrity, burdened by political deadlock. He frequently fretted over his poems being quoted ad nauseam by those politicians and others whom he used to say could only really bark and bite. And he increasingly wrote in a style not easily lent to the easy, empty rhetoric of the platform. He wished to codify his poems more; I don't think he could bear to have his alchemy turn to lead. The results were the brilliant gems of *Affinity* and the smaller later collections. Hard, chiselled, faceted with years of work, emerging as what is surely, some of the best and truest poetry of all time. Rupert Roopnaraine has written a brilliant essay 'Re-reading Martin Carter', taking the most often quoted poem 'All Are Involved' and watering and cleansing its roots, so that we could read it again ourselves, revisit its significance word for word, restore its significance, revise its context.

Martin Carter's recent personal grief was the discomfort he felt in reading and writing, cruel legacies of the stroke he suffered late in life. His frustration at the loss or diminishment of his ease with words was his worst pain in spite of the fact that his self consciousness in this regard far outweighed the occasional stammer or lapse in syntax on his part. But it was a disease he felt sharply and keenly and which he bore stoically and graciously during some of his last public events: one international – the Gabriela Mistral gold medal award from Chile, land of Neruda, in December 1996 ; the second – national, the launching of the reprint of his *Selected Poems* by Red Thread Press in May 1997 (the original Demerara Publishers edition was winner of the 1989 Guyana Prize); the third – private, the celebration of his 70th birthday on June 7 of this year, beautifully arranged by his wife, Phyllis, and his children and shared by his close friends and family.

The most recent joy in his life was his granddaughter, Sahalia. The two shared a very interesting and very special connection with each other. And it is not without significance that Martin dedicated his *Poems of Affinity* (1980) to children, flowers and dogs.

Women are celebrated in some of Martin's best poems – his prison letters and *Resistance* poems are dedicated to Phyllis, his wife, a constant source of strength and his anchor throughout his sometimes tumultuous life, and perhaps best summed up in the poem: 'Shines the Beauty of my Darling' from his first published collection *The Hill of Fire Glows Red* (1951)

> Like guardian at my side
> is the fight for freedom –
> and like the whole world dancing
> for liberation from the slave maker
> shines the beauty of my darling in her laughing eyes.

Without a doubt, amongst the finest and most fastidious examples of his craft are his love poems: in 'Under A Near Sky':

> The beat of water on the faraway sand
> comes, bringing me all your woman figure
> dress blown away, and hair alive as foam

And, from 'No Easy Thing':

> Do not be late, needed and wanted love
> What's withheld blights both love itself and us:
> As well as blame your hair for blowing wind
> As me for breathing, living, loving you.

Eusi Kwayana, one of his political companions of the earliest years, once wrote a beautiful essay on Carter entitled *Politics and The Human Heart.* It is a right and fitting thing to join the two in speaking of this poet.

Politics were part and parcel of the making of Martin Carter, man and poet. Guyana's finest hour, our National struggle for Independence, has been defined and immortalised by the poetry of Martin Carter's *Poems of Resistance.* The squalor of the succeeding eras, the splitting of nationhood into the two race-based political parties and the subsequent demise of the dream as internal tyranny and madness set in during the 70s and 80s, are etched into our consciousness in the collections of *Succession* and *Affinity,* culminating in those most telling poems, the two that mourned the assassinations of two very different freedom fighters – 'Bastille Day – Georgetown' dedicated to Jesuit priest Fr. Bernard Darke, and the poem entitled 'For Walter Rodney', the first line of which reads 'Assassins of conversation...' and which ends '...Risker, risk./I intend to turn a sky/ of tears for you.'

And what of the timing of his own death – to quote a line of his own making – 'bad luck, carefully chosen'? In a lifetime measured by symbol and marked by metaphor, his dying in the midst of Guyana's most recent 'combat of ants' (his words, often repeated, on Saturday afternoons or similar times) is signal. Little wonder he closed his eyes and turned his face to the wall for the occasion.

Suddenly, air is very much colder...
In a certain time, I have lingered.
But as an owl hoots
to startle the vile eye of a toad
and initiate its own defiance of dark:
I also speak. Having despised
all fangs, I neither have nor want
a time to bite...
('In A Certain Time').

In one of his last public interviews he referred again and again to the last poem he published, 'Conjunction', and the need for things to be conjoined. For the word 'and' to be made deed. For us to conjoin, to make the connections he dreamed of, would be the most eloquent tribute, by far the best remembrance we as a people could give to the man we call our national poet.

Martin Wylde Carter – 1927-1997.

For any man
and for any time, one dream
is enough.
This is true.

KEN RAMCHAND

THE VOICE OF ONE CRYING...

Trinidad Guardian, Dec. 17th 1997

In 1953, the People's Progressive Party (PPP), a multiracial party led by a young dentist with an American wife and a lawyer recently returned from England, won 18 out of the 24 seats in the British Guiana general elections. One hundred and thirty three days later, on October 9, the first day of the inter-colonial match between Trinidad and British Guiana, this elected Government was overthrown: 'Her Majesty's Government has decided that the Constitution of British Guiana must be suspended to prevent Communist subversion of the Government and a dangerous crisis both in public order and in economic affairs'. The elected government had thought it was the government.

At Bourda cricket ground, Trinidad scored 391 and 297 for 4 wickets declared, with the captain Gerry Gomes scoring a century in each innings. British Guiana made 424 and were 62 for 3 at the end of the fifth day. British troops had been brought in from the Jamaica garrison on the night of October 8 and were most present, patrolling with guns at the ready, when the announcement of the suspension was broadcast. There hadn't really been a crisis. The suspension of the Constitution was the crisis.

Before all this, in the collections of the early 1950s, *The Hill of Fire Glows Red* (1951) and *The Kind Eagle* (1952) Martin Carter wrote proactive and hopeful political poems about the situation of his country, listening to the land, carrying a banner for the revolution, dancing on the walls of his prison. These poems did not fail to register that the whole world was a prison too, and their tone suggested a temperament or a philosophical outlook larger than the particular time and season. But they were songs of freedom, full of fire and fury and hope:

This world's hope is a blade of fury
and we, who are sweepers of an ancient sky,
discoverers of new planets – sudden stars
we are the world's hope –
and so therefore, I rise again, I rise again.
Freedom is a white road with green grass like love.

Carter was a partisan in the nationalist movement headed by Dr. Jagan and an enthusiastic practitioner of the radical politics of the period. In 'Do Not Stare At Me' (1951), a middle-class woman is upbraided for seeming to be unsympathetic to the class struggle. But the allegorising poet sees the function of poet, labourer and nursing mother as aspects of the same human endeavour:

Stare at the slums in the south of the city!
Stare hard and reason lady, where I came from
and where I go.

My hand is full of lines
like your breast with veins, lady,
and one must rear, while one must suckle life

In response to the British occupation ('the festival of guns, the carnival of misery'), Martin Carter wrote the more historically located and politically directed *Poems of Resistance* (1954) including the magnificent 'University of Hunger', 'I Come from the Nigger Yard', 'Death of a Comrade' and 'This is the Dark Time My Love'.

The British jailed him for his politics. In 'Letter 1', the first of the three poems from prison, Carter is 'proud as the tree the axeman cannot tumble' and confident that a day will come like a tide from the heart of things when freedom will descend blazing from on high:

It will come to this land and every land
and when it comes I'll come alive again
and laugh again and walk out of this prison

But by the beginning of 1955, the multiracial PPP had divided into a Burnham faction and a Jagan faction. In October 1957 the Burnham faction changed its name to the People's National Congress. Politically instigated racial violence would become standard. The country would bleed for many years. The scars would remain.

There were riots in the city. Carter wrote 'Black Friday 1962' about the killings and burnings in Georgetown, and about how the crowd start to scatter:

were some who ran one way.
were some who ran another way.
were some who did not run at all.
were some who will not run again.
And I was with them all,
when the sun and the streets exploded,
and a city of clerks
turned a city of men!

The poem seems to celebrate energy and movement and the traces of a possible new order in chaos. But it laments, and is ultimately bitter about, the carrion time and the emergence of arrogant king crab:

And I have seen some creatures rise from holes
and claw a triumph like a citizen
and reign until the tide!

Atop the iron roof tops of this city
I see the vultures practising to wait.

In this post-resistance phase, his voice becomes the voice of one crying in the wilderness. He laments defeat and quiescence in 'There is No Riot' (1975); and the universal discarding of dreams in 'We Walk the Streets' (1974). His poems on the death of fellow-poet Eric Roach and on the psychic breakdown of the poet Milton Williams show that he is well aware of the dispensability of poet, poem 'map, ring, letter or man.' His agonisings over the power or powerlessness of words, the unpredictability of communication, and the near-impossibility of effective and honest political action tend to dominate the later poems, and to drive him into poetic inquiries into or musings about fundamental and evasive causes. The introspective and sometimes gnomic quality of these precise and abrupt later poems have prompted some commentators to be inclined to see the later poems as diminished, as a falling off.

But there is no falling off, and there is no break between early Carter and late Carter. He was concerned equally with social and metaphysical issues. He was moved to contemplate and collect the dark history of his own country and the lost steps of all mankind, 'the grave of pride/ the sudden flight/ the terror and the time/'. His monument and the work that contains the essential and necessary Carter is the epic 'University of Hunger' our finest dialect poem and perhaps still the greatest single poem by a West Indian.

BIBLIOGRAPHY

BIBLIOGRAPHY

This bibliography incorporates and builds on the work of Joan Swamy who compiled the bibliography included in the 1997 edition of Martin Carter's *Selected Poems* and the work on Carter's prose by Nigel Westmaas, which has been updated by him for this bibliography.

COLLECTIONS OF POEMS

The Hill of Fire Glows Red, Miniature Poet Series (Georgetown, British Guiana: Master Printery, 1951).

The Kind Eagle: [*Poems of prison*] (British Guiana: 1952).

The Hidden Man: [*Other poems of prison*] (British Guiana: 1952).

Poems of Resistance from British Guiana (London: Lawrence and Wishart, 1954, with a foreword by Sidney King).

— Published as *Poems of Resistance* (Georgetown: University of Guiana, 1964, with a preface by Neville Dawes).

— Published as *Poems of Resistance from Guyana* (Georgetown, Guyana: Release Publications, 1979).

Jail me Quickly: five poems (British Guiana: 1966, with an introduction by Ian McDonald).

— Reprinted in *New World Fortnightly*, Vol.1 No. 34, 1966. pp. 19-25.

Poems of Succession (London: New Beacon Books, 1977).

Poems of Affinity 1978-1980 (Georgetown, Guyana: Release Publications, 1980, introduced by Bill Carr with an appreciation by Stanley Greaves).

Selected Poems Georgetown: Demerara Publishers, 1989).

Selected Poems [Revised 2nd edition] (Georgetown: Red Thread Womens Press, 1997).

Poesías Escogidas /Selected Poems (Leeds: Peepal Tree Press, 1999). (Dual English/Spanish edition, edited David Dabydeen, translated by Salvador Ortiz-Carboneres, with an introduction by Gemma Robinson).

ANTHOLOGIES

Aftermath: an anthology of poems in English from Africa, Asia and the Caribbean, edited by Roger Weaver and Joseph Bruchac (Greenfield Review Press) p. 215.

An Anthology of African and Caribbean Writing in English, edited by John Figueroa, (Oxford: Open University/Heinemann, 1982), p. 233/268.

Breaklight: an anthology of Caribbean poetry, chosen, edited and introduced by Andrew Salkey (London: Hamish Hamilton, 1978). Various pagings.

Caribanthology 2: On Justice-Human Rights, edited by Arthur Drayton, Bridgetown, Cedar Press, Barbados, 1989, p.15.

Caribbean Anthology, edited by Lorna Cocking and Joan Goody, London, ILEA Learning Materials Service, 1987, pp. 48-50.

Caribbean Poetry Now, edited by Stewart Brown (Sevenoaks: Hodder and Stoughton, 1985), p. 6, 27, 65.

Caribbean Poetry Now [Revised, 2nd edition], edited by Stewart Brown (London: Edward Arnold, 1992), p. 6, 28, 88.

Caribbean Rhythms: the emerging English Literature of the West Indies, edited and with an introduction by James T. Livingstone (New York: Washington Square Press, 1974), pp. 201-207.

Caribbean Verse: an anthology, edited and introduced by O.R. Dathorne (London: Heinemann Educational Books, 1967), p. 23.

Caribbean Voices: an anthology of West Indian poetry, Vol. 1 – Dreams and Visions, selected by John Figueroa (London: Evans Brothers, 1966), p. 102.
— *Vol.2 – The Blue Horizons*, selected by John Figueroa (London: Evans Brothers, 1970). Various pagings.
The Co-operative Republic – Guyana 1970: a study of aspects of our way of life, edited by L. Searwar (Georgetown: Master Printery), p. 53.
The Heinemann Book of Caribbean Poetry, edited by Stewart Brown and Ian McDonald (Oxford: Heinemann, 1992), pp. 43-46.
Hinterland, edited by E.A. Markham (Newcastle: Bloodaxe Books, 1989), pp. 72-86.
Merrywhang, edited by Ron Heapy and Anne Garside (Oxford: Oxford University Press, 1978), p. 49.
My Lovely Native Land, compiled by Arthur and Elma Seymour (Trinidad, London: Longman Caribbean, 1971). Various pagings.
The Penguin Book of Caribbean Verse, edited by Paula Burnett (Harmondsworth: Penguin, 1986), pp. 214-219.
The Routledge Reader in Caribbean Literature, edited by Alison Donnell and Sarah Lawson-Welsh (London: Routledge, 1996), pp. 222-227.
The Sun's Eye: West Indian writing for young readers, compiled by Anne Walmsley (London: Longmans, 1968), p. 46.
The Sun's Eye (Revised, 2nd edition), edited by Anne Walmsley (Harlow: Longman, 1989), p. 58
Talk of the Tamarinds: an anthology of poetry for secondary schools, edited by A,N. Forde, (Trinidad: Columbus Publishers, 1971). Various pagings.
Themes of song: an anthology of Guyanese poetry, edited by A,J. Seymour (Georgetown: printed by B.G. Lithographic, 1961). Various pagings.
A Treasury of Guyanese poetry, edited by A.J. Seymour (Georgetown: printed by Guyana National Lithographic, 1980). Various pagings.
Voices of Guyana: an anthology, edited by Donald Trotman, with a foreword by A.J. Seymour (Georgetown: Guyana Centre Publication, 1968), p.6.
West Indian Poetry: an anthology for schools, edited by Kenneth Ramchand and Cecil Gray (Trinidad and Jamaica: Longmans Caribbean, 1971). Various pagings.
Voiceprint: oral and related poetry from the Caribbean, edited by Stewart Brown, Mervyn Morris, and Gordon Rohlehr (Harlow: Longman, 1989). Various pagings.
Walter Rodney: Poetic Tributes (London: Bogle L'Overture Publications, 1985), p. 51.
West Indian Poetry (Revised, 2nd edition), edited by Kenneth Ramchand and Cecil Gray (Harlow: Longman, 1989). Various pagings.
A World of Poetry for CXC, edited by Mark McWatt and Hazel Simmonds-McDonald, (Oxford: CXC/Heinemann, 1994), p. 3, 122.
You Better Believe It: Black verse in English, edited by Paul Bremen (Harmondsworth: Penguin, 1973), pp. 215-216.

POEMS IN PERIODICALS, NEWSPAPERS ETC.

'After one year', *New World*, Vol. 1, No. 2, 1964, p.7. also *New World Fortnightly*, No. 34, February 1966, p. 22 (as part of *Jail Me Quickly* – see below).
'All of a man', *Kyk-Over-Al*, No. 15, 1952, p. 29 (as part of *Poems of Prison* – see below).
'Anonymous', *New World*, Vol. 8, February 1965, p. 24, also *New World*, Vol. 2, No. 3, 1966, *Independence Issue*, pp. 66-67.
'Bare night without comfort', *Kyk-Over-Al*, No. 15, 1952, p. 27 (as part of *The*

Kind Eagle: (Poems of Prison.)).
'Black Friday, 1962', *New World*, Vol. 1 (?), No. 2, 1964, pp. 5-6; also *New World*, Vol. 2, No.3, 1966, *Independence Issue*, p. 66.
'Cartman of Dayclean', *Kaie*, No.1, October 1965, p. 14 also *Poet*, January 1972, pp. 7-8.
'Conversation I', *Poet*, January 1972, p. 8 also *Kaie* No.1, October 1965, p. 15.
'Conversations', *Kyk-Over-Al*, No. 28, December 1961, pp. 154-155 (7 poems).
'Childhood of a voice', *New World*, Vol.1 (?), No. 4, December 1964, p. 35; also *New World Fortnightly*, No. 34, February 1966, p. 25 (as part of *Jail Me Quickly*).
'Death of a Comrade', Published as 'For a Dead Comrade' in *Thunder*, Vol. 3, No. 5, May, 1952 p. 7 also in *New Nation*, No. 58, October 24, 1976.
'Death of a Slave', *Kyk-Over-Al*, No. 14, 1952, pp. 53-54; also *Kyk-Over-Al*, No. 22, 1957, p. 11; also *Kaie*, No. 4, 1967, p. 70.
'Demerara Nigger', *Kyk-Over-Al*, No. 30, December 1984, pp. 8-9.
'Discovery of Companion' *Kyk-Over-Al*, Vol. 5, No. 15, 1952, pp. 30-31 (as part of *The Kind Eagle (Poems of Prison)*).
'Ever with me' *Gisra*, Vol. 5, No. 4, 1974, p. 64.
'For My Son', *Kyk-Over-Al*, Vol. 6, No. 19, 1954, (Poem No. 99 - no pagination).
'Four Poems and Demerara Nigger', *Kyk-Over-Al*, No. 30, December 1984, p.7-9.
'Fragment of Memory', *Kyk-Over-Al*, Vol. 6, No.19, 1954, (Poem No.5 – no pagination).
'Human Guide', – see 'O human guide'.
'I come from the nigger-yard', *New World Quarterly*, No. 3, 1963, p. 11.
'Immortal like the earth', *Thunder*, Vol. 5, No. 41, December 18, 1954, p. 6.
'In the shadow of a soldier', *Thunder*, Vol. 6, No. 66, July 9, 1955, p. 2.
'Jail me Quickly: five poems', *New World Fortnightly*, No. 34, February 1966. Includes: 'Black Friday 1962'/'After one year'/ 'What can a man do more'/ 'Where are free men'/ 'Childhood of a voice', pp. 21-25.
'New Day', *Kyk-Over-Al*, Vol.6, No.19, 1954, (poem No.3 – no pagination).
'Listening to the Land', *Kyk-Over-Al*, Vo1. 6, No. 19, 1954, p. 66.
'Looking at your hands', *Kyk-Over-Al*, Vol. 4, No. 14, 1952, p. 52.
'O human guide', *Kyk-Over-Al*, No. 15, 1952, p. 30 (as part of 'Poems of Prison' – see below).
'O where to hide', Kyk-Over-Al, No. 15, 1952, p. 27; (as part of 'Poems of Prison' – see below).
'Occasion', *Savacou*, Vol. 3, No. 4, 1970-1971, p. 171.
'Ode to midnight', *Kyk-Qver-Al*, Vol. 22 No. 6, 1948, p. 5.
'On the fourth night of a hunger strike', *New World*, Vol. 2, No. 3, 1966, *Independence Issue*, p. 65.
'One' in *Poetry Review*, (London) vol.80.no.4, Winter 1990/91, p.13.
'Our time', *Kaie*, No. 18, November, 1985, pp. 87-88.
'Poem', (First line: 'Someone, somewhere shall know one day'), *New World Fortnightly*, No. 39, 1966, p. 2.
'Poem' (First Line: 'Strong Memory, bright pressure of a hand'), *New World*, No. 19, 1965, p. 2.
'Poems of Prison', (Also published as *The Kind Eagle*: (*Poems of Prison*), 1951), *Kyk-Over-Al*, No. 15, 1952, pp. 27-31. Contents: 'Bare night without comfort'/ 'Who walks a pavement'/ 'You are involved'/ 'O Where to hide'/ 'The kind eagle'/ 'All of a man'/ 'O human guide'.
'Show me a little freedom', *Kaie*, No. 16, July 1979, p. 86.

'Three poems of shape and motion: a sequence' – see 'Shape and Motion One'/ 'Shape and Motion Two' / 'Shape and Motion Three'.
'Shape and Motion One', *Kyk-Over-Al*, Vol. 6, No. 20, 1955, p. 141.
'Shape and Motion Two', *Kyk-Over-Al*, Vol. 6, No. 20, 1955. pp. 141-142.
'Shape and Motion Three', *Kyk-Over-Al*, Vol. 6, No. 22, 1955, pp. 142-143.

BIBLIOGRAPHY OF MARTIN CARTER'S PROSE

'The Queens College Apiary in 1943', *The Queens College School Magazine:* May 1943 - 1944 -Spring.
'A Serial Imperialism', *Thunder,* June 1953, Vol. 4, No. 7, p. 3, 10.
Editorial: 'Non-Cooperation', *Thunder,* May 1, 1954, Vol. 5, No. 5.
'Which Side Are You On?' *Thunder,* May 15, 1954, Vol. 5, No. 7.
'The Civil Service and National Liberation', *Thunder,* May 29, 1954, Vol. 5, No. 9, p. 4.
Editorial: 'Raving and Reaction', *Thunder,* June 1954, Vol. 5, No. 11.
'The Power to Change', *Thunder,* July 24, 1954, Vol. 5, p. 2.
Editorial: 'The Lesson of August', *Thunder,* July 31, 1954, Vol. 5.
'Yankee Eye Wash', *Thunder,* August 7, 1954, Vol. 5, No. 19.
'An American Oracle', *Thunder,* August 28, 1954, Vol. 5, p. 4.
'Disarm or Perish', *Thunder*, September 11, 1954.
'Freedom Not Charity', *Thunder,* January 8, 1955, Vol. 5, No. 42, p. 1, 5.
'Pablo Neruda', *Thunder,* January 15, 1955, Vol. 5, No. 42.
Editorial: 'Time of Crisis', *Thunder*, January 15, 1955, Vol. 5, No. 42.
'Politics and the Individual', *Thunder,* February 12, 1955, Vol. 5. No. 42, p. 4.
Editorial: 'Surrender or Fight', *Thunder,* February 26, 1955, Vol. 6, No. 48.
Editorial: 'No Separate Salvation', *Thunder,* March 5, 1955, Vol. 6, No. 48.
'What is a Politician', *Thunder,* March 12, 1955, Vol. 6, No. 48.
Editorial: 'The Bevan Explosion', *Thunder,* March 26, 1955, Vol. 6, No. 52.
Editorial: 'Portrait of Churchill', *Thunder,* April 16, 1955, Vol. 6, No. 55.
'A Dark Foundation', *Thunder,* April 16, 1955, Vol. 6, No. 55, p. 5.
Editorial: 'Easing World Tension', *Thunder,* May 21, 1955, Vol. 6, No. 59.
Editorial: 'From Babylonian to British', *Thunder,* May 21, 1955, Vol. 6, No. 60.
Symposium: 'Is There a West Indian Way of Life?' *Kyk-Over-Al,* Mid 1955.
'A Progressive demand from UDP', *Thunder*, June 11, 1955.
Editorial: 'Bribes for What?', *Thunder,* July 2, 1955, Vol. 6, No. 65.
Editorial: 'Our Newspapers and What they Stand For', *Thunder,* July 16, 1955, Vol. 6, No. 67.
Editorial: 'Dr. Williams and the Caribbean Commission', *Thunder,* July 23, 1955, Vol. 6, No. 69.
Editorial: 'On Swaraj', *Thunder*, July 30, 1955, Vol. 6, No. 70.
'Hamlet', *Thunder,* August 20, 1955, Vol. 6.
Editorial: 'West Indian Regiment', *Thunder* August 27, 1955, Vol. 6, No. 74.
'This Race Business', *Thunder,* September 10, 1955, Vol. 6, No. 75, p. 4.
Editorial: 'But Where is Mr. Burnham?' *Thunder,* September 10, 1955, Vol. 6, No. 76.
'The Racists Among Us', *Thunder,* September 24, 1955, Vol. 6, No. 75.
'Freedom from Imperialism... Freedom to Evolve', *Thunder,* October 8. 1955, Vol. 7, No. 79.
'Wanted: A Great Obeah Man', *Thunder,* October 22, 1955. Vol. 7, No. 79.
Editorial: 'Of Governor and Governed', *Thunder,* October 29, 1955, Vol. 10, No. 83.

'Penal Reform or Economic Measure', *Thunder*, November 12, 1955.
'Where are the Heroes?', *Thunder*, November 26, 1955.
'Dogs will bark but to no Avail', *Thunder*, December 17, 1955.
'Sensibility and the Search', *Sunday Argosy*, January 26, 1958.
Letter: 'Artist as Artist', *Kyk-Over-Al,* May 1958, Vol. 8, No. 8, No. 23; See 'Greatness and Bitterness': Response to A.J. Seymour's open letter on the theme 'greatness and bitterness' based on Yeat's poem 'Meditations in Time of Civil War' (1923), pp. 19-20.
'Out, Out the Fire', (Short Story), *Kyk-Over-Al,,* May 1958, Vol. 8, No. 23.
'A Note on Vic Reid's *New Day', Kyk-Over-Al,* December 1958, Vol. 8, No. 24, p. 81.
'A New Life', short story, unpublished, circa 1960s.
'Maccabee at Sea', short story, unpublished, circa 1960s.
Letter: 'Meaning of the Arts in the Caribbean', *Kyk-Over-Al,* December 1960.
'Martin Carter Says: Recent Events Spring From Deeper Social Undercurrents', *Chronicle*, Friday, March 23, 1962.
Untitled article in *New World Quarterly,* 30th October, 1964.
'The Race Crisis – British Guiana', (Speech) Puerto Rico, circa 1964.
'Power, Race & Trouble', circa 1965.
Editorial: 'Unemployment', *Booker News*, January 8, 1965.*
Editorial: 'Safety Competitions', *Booker News*, January 29, 1965.
Editorial: 'Adventure in Reading', *Booker News*, February 19, 1965.
'On Being a Guyanese', *Booker News*, March 5,1965.
'Catering for Changing Taste', *Booker News*, March 19, 1965.
'Decolonisation', *Booker News*, April 9, 1965.
'Return to Competition', *Booker News*, April 30, 1965.
Editorial: 'The Chairman's Statement', *Booker News*, June 11, 1965.
Editorial: 'Guianese Society'. *Booker News*, July 2, 1965.
Editorial: 'The Story on Page One', *Booker News*, 23 July, 1965.
Editorial: 'A Need for Discussion', *Booker News*, August 13, 1965.
Editorial: 'Challenge and Change', *Booker News*, September 3, 1965.
Editorial:, 'Running Their Own Show', *Booker News*, September, 24, 1965.
'Sambo at Large', 1965. (Essay on Experiences of Cardiff Conference).
Review, *New World Quarterly,* Parts 1 & 2, October 29, 1965.
Editorial: 'The Case for Research', *Booker News*, October 15, 1965.
'Why Guiana Needs Independence', *New Statesman*, November 5, 1965.
Editorial: 'Accord in Athletics', *Booker News*, November, 1965.
Editorial: 'Playing our Part', *Booker News*, November 26, 1965.
Editorial 'Learning for Life', *Booker News*, December 17, 1965.
'A Natural Fish-Pond', *Journal of the British Guiana Museum & Zoo*, July-December, 1965.
'Short Notes on the Luga-Luga', *Journal of the British Guiana Museum & Zoo*, July-December, 1965.
Editorial: 'A Wider View', Editorial, *Booker News*, January 7, 1966.
Editorial: 'Colonialism? What Do You Mean?', *Booker News*, January28, 1966.
Editorial: 'Viewpoint on Adult Education', *Booker News*, March 4, 1966.
Editorial: 'Of Books and Citizens', *Booker News*, March 25, 1966.
Editorial: 'Our Part in Technical Training', *Booker News*, April 15, 1966.
'A Question of Self-Contempt', *New World Quarterly* (Guyana Independence Issue), 1966, pp. 10-12.
Editorial: 'Science in Service', *Booker News*, May 6,1966.

Radio Interview: 'A Guyanese Poet in Cardiff', *Kaie-Independence*, May, 1966.
Editorial: 'Two Worlds', *Booker News*, June 10, 1966.
'Question of Fiji', Speech at the General Assembly, United Nations, New York, 1968.
Broadcast Statement by the Minister of Information, (M.C.), Friday, August 1, 1969.
Foreword to *Guyana Police Force Magazine*, 1970.
Edgar Mittelholzer Lecture Series: Man and Making – Victim & Vehicle (National History and Arts Council, Ministry of Information, 1971).
'What is a Guyanese: Striking Similarity to a Gru-Gru Worm', *Sunday Graphic*, December. 19, 1971.
'Why are we so Mealy-Mouthed?' *Sunday Graphic*, July 9, 1972.
'The Crab's Way', *Sunday Graphic*, October 8, 1972.
'If a Man Lies to Himself, the World will Lie to Him', *Guyana Graphic*, April 1973. (Broadcast on Radio Demerara, April 1973).
'Apart from Both', *Gisra*, December, 1974, Vol. 5, No. 4, pp. 45-46.
'A Free Community of Valid Persons', Speech at the University of Guyana, *Caricom Perspective,* 1974.
'About Poetry', in *Kaie*, no. 14, July, 1976, p. 83.
'Six Poems of Milton Williams' (Selected and Introduced by Martin Carter), *Release*, vol. 2, 1978.
Foreword to Stanley Greaves' Exhibition Catalogue, 1978.
'In Contradiction', Bill Carr Raps with Martin Carter, *Release*, 1978.
'A Religious Interpretation of Guyanese Proverbs', *Release*, Vols. 3 & 4,1978.
'The Poetry of Michael Aarons', Review by Martin Carter, *Release*, Vols. 3 & 4, 1978.
Interview in *Caribbean Contact,* February, 1979.
'The Poetry of Christopher Aird', *Release*, 1979, p. 21.
'Poems by Rayman Mandal: introduced by Martin Carter', *Release,* Vol. 6 & 7. 1979.
'Resist brute fact of human degradation', *Catholic Standard*, No. 33, September 2, 1979, p. 5, 7.
'The Location of the Artist', *Release*, Vol. 8 & 9, 1979.
'Open Letter to the People of Guyana', *Dayclean Special*, 1979.
'The Reality of Independence', *Caricom Perspective*, April-June, 1986.
'A Note on Jagan', *Stabroek News,* December 11, 1987.
'The Freedom to Choose', *Stabroek News,* November 12, 1988.
Interview by Rovin Deodat, *Kyk-Over-Al*, No. 40, 1989.
Interview by Peter Trevis, *Hinterland Caribbean Collection* (Newcastle: Bloodaxe Books, 1989).
'A Chat with Martin Carter, Guyana's National Poet' by Manuel Abrizo, *El Universal,* January 6, 1990.
Note on Bernadette Persaud's Exhibition, May 29, 1991.
'The Changing Context of Arts and Artists in Guyana Today'. Text of Presentation made at Burrowes School of Art, October 4, 1991.
'Interview with Frank Birbalsingh', *Kyk-over-al*, 46/47, December 1995.

* *Martin Carter was editor of Booker News from January 1965 to June 1966.*

CRITICAL RESPONSES

Asein, Samuel O. 'The "Protest" Tradition in West Indian Poetry: from George Campbell to Martin Carter', in *Jamaica Journal*, Vol. 6, No. 2, June 1972, pp. 40-45.

Baugh, Edward, *West Indian poetry, 1900-1970: A study in Cultural Decolonisation*, (Kingston, Jamaica: Savacou Publications, Pamphlet No. 1, 1972).

Brathwaite, Edward, 'Kyk-over-al and the Radicals' in *New World Quarterly*: *Guyana Independence Issue*, 1966, p.55-57.

Brathwaite, Edward, 'Martin Carter', entry in on Martin Carter in E.R. Murphy, ed., *Poets of the English Language*, (London: St Martins Press, 1970).

Brathwaite, Edward Kamau, 'Resistance Poems: The Voice of Martin Carter', in *Caribbean Quarterly,* vol. 23. Nos. 2 & 3, June-September 1971, pp. 7-20.

Brathwaite, E.K., 'Martin Carter's Poetry of the Negative Yes', *Caliban,* Vol. IV, No. 1 Fall/Winter, 1981, pp. 30-41.

Breiner, Laurence A., *An Introduction to West Indian Poetry* (Cambridge: Cambridge University Press, 1998). (Carter refs. p.78-81, 133, 163-4, 171, 184).

Breiner, Laurence A, 'Is There Still a West Indian Literature?' in *World Literature in English*, vol. 26. no. 1., Spring, 1986 pp. 140-150 (Carter refs. p.143/4).

Breiner, Laurence A., 'The Eighties' in Bruce King, ed. *West Indian Literature*, 2nd edition (Basingstoke: Macmillan, 1995), pp. 76-88 (Carter refs. 79-86).

Brown, Lloyd, *West Indian Poetry* (Revised edition) (Oxford: Heinemann, 1984). (Carter refs. 91-93).

Brown, Stewart, 'Unwrapping Wounds' in *Poetry Review*, Vol. 69, No. 2, 1979, pp. 47-50.

Brown, Stewart, 'All are Involved: The Poetry of Martin Carter' in *New Literature Review*, Canberra, Australia, No. 7, 1980, pp. 66-72.

Brown, Stewart, 'Poet in Opposition' in *Index on Censorship,* no. 5., 1980, pp. 32-36.

Brown, Stewart, 'Martin Carter: The Poet as Guerrilla' in *The New Voices*, (Trinidad) Vol. 9, Nos. 17-18, 1981, pp. 50-61.

Brown, Stewart, 'Of Dreams and Disillusion' in *The New Voices*, Trinidad, Vol. XI, No. 22, 1983, pp. 9-14.

Brown, Stewart, 'No Voice in the Emptiness: the poetry of Martin Carter' in *Planet: the Welsh Internationalist*, Aberystwyth, No. 129, June 1998 pp. 70-75.

Burnett, Paula, ed., 'Introduction' to *The Penguin Book of Caribbean Verse in English* (Harmondsworth, Middlesex: Penguin, 1986). (Carter refs. ivii/ixii-xiii and pp. 411-412)

Carr, W.I. 'The West Indian Novelist: Prelude and Context', *Caribbean Quarterly*, 2, no. 1 & 2, 1965, pp. 71-84.

Carr, Bill, 'Introduction' to *Poems of Affinity* (Georgetown: Release Publishers, 1980), pp. vii-xii.

Chamberlin, J. Edward, *Come Back to Me My Language: Poetry and the West Indies* (Urbana and Chicago: University of Illinois Press, 1993). Carter refs. p.3/ 23/95; a new edition published by Peepal Tree Press in 2019.

Collymore, Frank, 'Writing in the West Indies: A Survey', *The Tamarack Review,* No. 14, Winter 1960, pp. 114-121. (Carter ref. p.119)

creighton, al, "The poet is speaking': Martin Carter's politics of communication' in *West Indian Poetry*, eds. Jennifer Jackson and Jeanette B. Allis, (Proceedings of the Fifth Annual Conference on West Indian Literature, U.S. Virgin Islands, 1985), pp.130-142.

creighton, al, 'Martin Carter: Nothing to Declare' [obituary], *Sunday Stabroek,* Dec. 21st, 1997, p. 7a.

Dabydeen, David, 'Dreadtalk' in *Poetry Review*, Vol. 80. No. 4, Winter 1990/91, pp. 12-13.
Dawes, Neville, 'Preface' to the 2nd Edition of *Poems of Resistance* (Georgetown: University of Guiana, 1964).
Dawes, Neville, *Prolegomena to Caribbean Literature*, Monograph Series: no.1., Kingston, Institute of Jamaica, 1977. (Carter refs. p.18-20).
Gafoor, Ameena, 'The Love Songs of Martin Carter', in *The Sunday Stabroek*, June 8th, 1997, pp. 18/19.
Harris, Wilson, 'Poets – their place in modern society: a look at Seymour and Carter' in *Guyana Graphic, Independence Souvenir,* May 26, 1966, pp. 82-83.
Harris, Wilson, 'The Place of the Poet in Modern Society: A Glance at Two Guyanese Poets,' in *Explorations,* ed. Hena Maes-Jelinek (Aarhus, Denmark: Dangeroo Press, 1981), pp. 5-9.
James, Louis, 'The Necessity of Poetry' in *New World Quarterly, Guyana Independence Issue*, May, 1966, pp. 111-115.
James, Louis (ed.), 'The Second Voice: Aspects of West Indian Poetry' in the Introduction to *The Islands In Between: Essays on West Indian Literature* (Oxford: OUP, 1968), pp.23-35. (Carter refs. p.35).
James, Louis 'Caribbean Poetry in English – Some Problems,' *Savacou, 2*, Sept. 1970, pp. 78-86. (Carter refs. p.83).
James, Louis, *Caribbean Literature in English* (Harlow: Longman, 1999. (Carter refs. pp. 76-89)
Johnson, Linton Kwesi, 'Review of *Poems of Succession*', in *Race Today*, Nov/Dec 1977, p. 167.
King, Sydney, 'Foreword' to *Poems of Resistance from British Guiana* (London: Lawrence and Wishart, 1954).
Kwayana, Eusi, 'The Politics Of The Heart' in *Anales Del Caribe*, (Casa de las Americas, Cuba) No. 4/5, 1984-85, pp. 362-391.
Kwayana, Eusi, 'Tribute: Martin Wylde Carter, OR. 1927-97' [obituary] in *Guyana Review*, Jan-Feb, 1998, pp. 48/49.
Lowhar, Syl, 'Carter's *Resistance* and *Succession*', in *Caribbean Contact*, August 1977, p. 7.
Markham, E.A., 'Random Thoughts' the introduction to his anthology *Hinterland* (Newcastle: Bloodaxe Books, 1989), pp. 13-42 (Carter refs. pp. 24-25).
McDonald, Ian 'Foreword', *Martin Carter: Selected Poems*, revised edition (Georgetown: Red Thread Women's Press, 1997), pp. 21-26.
McDonald, Ian, 'Martin' [obituary] in *Sunday Stabroek*, Dec. 27th, 1997, p. 7.
McWatt Mark A., '"The Challenge of Space": being and consciousness in the poetry of Martin Carter', in *West Indian Poetry*, eds. Jennifer Jackson and Jeanette B. Allis (Proceedings of the Fifth annual Conference on West Indian Literature, U.S. Virgin Islands, 1985), pp. 143-152.
Morris, Mervyn, 'Martin Carter: more than an excellent poet', [obituary] in *The Sunday Observer* (Jamaica), Jan. 4th, 1998, p. 4.
O'Callaghan, Evelyn, 'Blood and Fire! Guyanese writers on Contemporary Guyana', paper presented to the 16th Annual Conference of West Indian Literature, Caribbean Writers Institute, Dept. of English, University of Miami, April 1997.
Paddington, Bruce, 'The Poems Man', in *Caribbean Beat*, no.13, Spring 1995, pp. 42-46.
Pearne, Judy, *Poetry in the Caribbean* (Sevenoaks: Hodder and Staunton, 1985). (Carter refs. pp. 29-31).
Persico, Alan, 'A note on Martin Carter's "Bent"' in *Kyk-over-al*, No. 37, December, 1987, pp. 59-65.

Pouchet-Paquet, Sandra, 'The Fifties' in Bruce King (ed), *West Indian Literature* (Basingstoke: Macmillan, 1979), pp. 63-77, (Carter refs. pp. 74-76).

Radzik, Vanda, 'One dream is enough: a tribute to Martin Carter' [obituary] in *Sunday Stabroek*, Dec. 21st, 1997, p. 16a.

Ramchand, Kenneth, 'The West Indies' in Bruce King, ed., *Literatures of the World in English* (London: Routledge, 1974), pp. 192-225. (Carter refs. p.199).

Ramchand, Kenneth, 'Parades Parades; Modern West Indian Poetry' in *The Sewanee Review*, Vol. 87, No.1, Winter 1979, pp. 96-118. (Carter refs.p.103-105).

Ramchand, Kenneth, 'The voice of one crying...' [obituary] in *Trinidad Guardian*, Dec. 17th, 1997, p. 9.

Robinson, Jeffrey 'The Guyaneseness of Guyanese writing', *Kyk-over-al*, No. 31, June, 1985, pp. 47-51.

Robinson, Jeffrey, 'The Root and the Stone: The Rhetoric of Martin Carter's *Poems of Resistance*', in *Journal of West Indian Literature*, vol.1. no.1, October 1986, pp. 1-12.

Rohlehr, F. G. 'West Indian Poetry: Some Problems of Assessment (Part Two)', *Bim*, No. 55 July-December 1972, pp. 134-144.

Rohlehr, Gordon, 'The Creative writer in the West Indies' in *Kaie*, No.11, August 1973, pp. 48-77.

Rohlehr, Gordon, *The Shape of that Hurt and other essays* (Port of Spain: Longman Trinidad, 1992); and Peepal Tree Press, Leeds, 2018.

Rohlehr, Gordon, 'Assassins of the Voice: Martin Carter's *Poems of Affinity*', in *The Shape of that Hurt and other essays*', ibid, pp. 129-149.

Rohlehr, Gordon, 'The Problem of the Problem of Form' in *The Shape of that Hurt and other essays*', ibid, pp. 1-65. (Carter refs. p.3-4).

Roopnarine, Rupert, *Web of October: Rereading Martin Carter* (Leeds: Peepal Tree Press, 1988).

Roopnaraine, Rupert, 'Martin Carter and Politics', *Sunday Stabroek*, Georgetown, 8 June 1997, p. 8.

Sander, Reinhard W., 'The Thirties and Forties' in Bruce King (ed), *West Indian Literature* (Basingstoke: Macmillan, 1979), pp. 45-62. (Carter refs. p. 59).

Salkey, Andrew, 'Introduction' to his anthology *Breaklight* (London: Hamish Hamilton, 1971), pp. xv-xix. (Carter refs. p. xviii).

Salkey, Andrew, *Georgetown Journal* (London: New Beacon Books, 1972). (Carter refs. pp. 344-350).

Salkey, Andrew, 'Introduction' to *Walter Rodney: Poetic Tributes* (London: Bogle L'Overture Publications, 1985), pp. i-viii. (Carter refs. p.ii-iv.).

Seymour, A. J., *Studies of Ten Guyanese Poems* (Georgetown: Ministry of Education, 1982). (Carter refs. 31-36, 45-50).

Seymour, A. J., 'The Biography of a Magazine', *Kyk-over-al*, Nos. 46/47, December 1995, pp. 14-22.

Singh, Paul, 'Poverty and liberation: Martin Carter's poetic struggles for a New Day' in *Release*, vol. 1, 1979, pp. 37-41.

Sparer, Joyce L., 'Attitudes towards 'Race' in Guyanese Literature' in *Caribbean Studies*, Vol. 8. No. 2. 1967, pp. 23-63. (Carter refs. pp. 54-59.)

Sparer, Joyce L., 'Carter: I am my poem' in 'Attitudes towards 'Race' in Guyanese Literature' published in May and June 1967 in the *Sunday Chronicle*, June 11th 1967, p. 4.

Stephanides, Stephanos, 'Language and Identity in the Poetry of Martin Carter', in *Kyk-over-al*, no. 39, December, 1988, pp. 76-81.

Swan, Michael, *British Guiana: the Land of Six Peoples* (London: HMSO, 1957).

(Carter refs. pp. 121-129).
Van Sertima, Ivan, 'Astride Two Visions' in *The Caribbean Artists Movement Newsletter*, Nos. 11 and 12, London, 1969/70.
Walmsley, Anne, *The Caribbean Artists Movement 1966-72* (London: New Beacon Books, 1992).
Westmaas, Nigel, 'Introduction' to 'A Martin Carter Prose Sampler', *Kyk-Over-Al*, No. 44, May 1993, pp. 27-29.

INTERVIEWS

Seymour, A.J., 'A Guyanese poet in Cardiff: Martin Carter reports in a radio interview' in *Kaie*, no.2, May, 1966, Independence Issue, p.18-21, 44.
Salkey, Andrew, *Georgetown Journal* (London: New Beacon Books, 1972), pp. 344-350.
Carr, Bill, 'In Contradiction: Bill Carr raps with Martin Carter' in *Release,* vol.1., 1978, pp. 5-23.
'An Interview with Guyanese poet, Martin Carter, who sees his environment as a "refined plantation"', in *Caribbean Contact*, Vol. 6, No. 10 (February, 1979), p. 9.
McAndrew, Wordsworth, 'You do not organise or want to control culture, but let it flower', in *Caribbean Contact*, February 1979, p. 3.
Skeete, Jean, 'On the reality of Independence', interview for *CARICOM Perspective*, No. 35, April - June, 1986, p. 8, 43. Reprinted in *Kyk-over-al*, no. 44, May 93, pp. 141-143.
Deodat, Rovin, 'Interview with Martin Carter', in *Kyk-Over-al*, Nos. 40, Dec. 1989, pp. 80-83.
Dance, Daryl Cumber, 'Conversation with Martin Carter and Denis Williams' in Dance's book of interviews with Caribbean writers, *New World Adams* (Leeds: Peepal Tree Press, 1992), pp. 46-64.
Treeves, Peter, 'Interview with Martin Carter' in E.A. Markham, ed. *Hinterland* (Newcastle: Bloodaxe, 1989), p.67-71. Reprinted in *Kyk-over-al*, No. 44, May 93, pp. 144-150.
Birbalsingh, Frank, 'Interview with Martin Carter', *Kyk-Over-al*, Nos. 46/47, Dec. 1995, pp. 218-234.

SUPPLEMENT TO THE BIBLIOGRAPHY 2020

Peepal Tree Press acknowledges the kind help of Gemma Robinson in assembling this supplement.

By Carter:

Poems by Martin Carter, edited Stewart Brown and Ian McDonald (London: MacMillan Caribbean, 2006).
University of Hunger: Collected Poems & Selected Prose, edited Gemma Robinson (Tarset: Bloodaxe Books Ltd., 2006).
"Every poem is incomplete" (selections from Carter's poetry notebooks, introduced by Rupert Roopnaraine), *Caribbean Review of Books*, November 2008.

Critical articles and reviews

Allen-Agostini, Lisa, 'Growing Breadfruit in Bed-Stu', *Trinidad and Tobago Guardian*, 23 August 2008.
Arnold, Josephine V., 'Guianese Identities'. In *A History of Literature in the Caribbean: English and Dutch-Speaking*, ed. Albert James Arnold, Julio Rodríguez-Luis, and J. Michael Dash (Amsterdam: John Benjamins, 2001), pp. 97-110.
Brown, Lloyd W., "Martin Wylde Carter", in Daryl Cumber Dance (ed.). *Fifty Caribbean Writers: A Bio-Bibliographical Sourcebook* (New York: Greenwood, 1986), pp. 108–114.
Brown, Stewart, "The Truth of Craft", *Caribbean Review of Books*, February 2006.
Bush, Ruth, 'Poems of Succession (1977)'. In *New Beacon Books – the Pioneering Years*, George Padmore Institute (2013), https://www.georgepadmoreinstitute.org/the-pioneering-years/gallery-of-publications/poems-succession-1977.
Capildeo, Vahni, 'The Day I Read This is the Dark Time My Love', *Poetry News*, Winter 2008-2009.
Capildeo, Vahni on Martin Carter's 'This Is the Dark Time My Love', What Sparks Poetry, *Poetry Daily,* https://poems.com/features/what-sparks-poetry/vahni-capildeo-on-martin-carters-this-is-the-dark-time-my-love/
Capildeo, Vahni, 'And did those feet…', review of *University of Hunger: Collected Poems and Selected Prose, by Martin Carter*, ed. Gemma Robinson, *Caribbean Review of Books*, November 2006.
Capildeo, Vahni, 'Letter from Trinidad', *PN Review 223,* Volume 41 Number 5, May-June 2018.
Capildeo, Vahni, 'Tongueless Whispering *TW: Sexual Violence*' (a reading of 'Listening to the Land'), *PN Review 240*, Volume 44 Number 4, March - April 2018.
Coates, Dave, 'You are Involved: Vahni Capildeo and Martin Carter', *Dave Poems*, 6 December 2019, https://davepoems.wordpress.com/2019/12/10/all-are-involved-vahni-capildeo-and-martin-carter/
creighton, al, '"The Mob at the Door": A "Biography" of Martin Carter'. *Guyana Under Siege,* December 2001. (Originally published in *Stabroek News*).
creighton, al, 'The Poets Companion', *Stabroek News*, 7 February 2010.
creighton, al, 'Martin Carter and his poems', *Stabroek News,* 24 June 2012.
D'Aguiar, Fred, 'Martin Carter', in *Talk Yuh Talk: Interviews with Anglophone Caribbean Poets*, ed. by Kwame Dawes (Charlottesville and London: University of Virginia Press, 2001), pp. 11-21.
D'Aguiar, Fred, 'A Theory of Caribbean Aesthetics', *Caliban*, 21 (2007), 91-99.
Dalleo, Raphael, 'Anticolonial Authority and the Postcolonial Occasion for Speaking: George Lamming and Martin Carter'. [Revised as 'Anticolonial Authority and the Postcolonial Occasion for Speaking', in *Caribbean Literature and the Public Sphere: from the Plantation to the Postcolonial* (Charlottesville: University of Virginia Press, 2011), pp. 152-74.
de Caires, Brendan, 'The ruins of a great dream', review of *University of Hunger*; *Stabroek News*, 24 September, 2006.
Evans, Lucy, '"Free to Come to Grief": The Problems of Formal Freedom in Mark McWatt's *Suspended Sentences*', *The Journal of Commonwealth Literature*, 44 (3), 2009, 33–49. https://doi.org/10.1177/0021989409342151 (includes discussion of political freedom and imprisonment in the context of Martin Carter's writing).
Florian, Sara, Contemporary West Indian Poetry: a "Creole" Aesthetics? PhD, University of Venice (2009) (Chapter 4: 'Martin Carter (1927-1997): The

Aesthetics of Social and Political Freedom in Post-Colonial Guyana').
Fomunyam, Kehdinga George, 'Contextualizing Postcolonial Niches in the Poetic Genre: A comparative Analysis of Mathew Takwi and Martin Carter', *Zoe International Journal of Social Transformation*, vol 2 (2018), 1-13.
Gafoor, Ameena, 'In Memory of Martin Carter', *Kaieteur News*, 14 December 2008.
Gyssels, Kathleen, 'The University of Hunger in the Guianas: Martin Carter and Leon Damas', in *Authority and Displacement in the English-Speaking World*, (Volume II: Exploring American Shores), ed. Florence Labaune-Demeule, Cambridge Scholars Publishing, 2015, pp. 117-142.
Hector, Tim, 'I believe we can fly', (obituary column written shortly after Carter's death). *The Outlet*, 19 December, 1997)
Holder, Calvin Cleophus, Victim and vehicle: the social, political and intellectual contexts of Martin Carter's poetry. PhD, Cave Hill, Barbados, University of the West Indies, 2006.
Hopkinson, Natalie, *A Mouth is Always Muzzled: Six Dissidents, Five Continents and the Art of Resistance* (New York: The New Press, 2018).
Johnson, Ruel, 'Phyllis Carter Recalls Life with 'the poems man', *Guyana Chronicle,* 27 October 2004.
Read more: Martin Carter Biography – Developed Early Passion for Poetry, Published First Poems of Protest, Found Fame with Prison Poetry – JRank Articles https://biography.jrank.org/pages/2449/Carter-Martin.html#ixzz6RnR5G5JD
Lindsay, Andrew O. ed., *Beacons of Excellence: The Edgar Mittelholzer Memorial Lectures Volume 1: 1967-1971* (includes Carter's *Man and Making – Victim and Vehicle* Lectures) (Georgetown: Caribbean Press, 2014). http://caribbeanpress.org/wp-content/uploads/2014/05/Edgar-Mittelholzer-Lectures-Volume-1.pdf
Low, Gail, 'At home? Discoursing on the Commonwealth at the 1965 Commonwealth Arts Festival', *The Journal of Commonwealth Literature*, 48(1), 2013, 97–111.
Laughlin, Nicholas, 'Everyday possessions', (review of *University of Hunger*), *Caribbean Beat,* July/August 2006).
Laughlin, Nicholas, 'Tomorrow and the world', (essay on reading Carter while watching the 2011 uprising in Egypt), *Caribbean Review of Books*, January 2011.
Laughlin, Nicholas, 'Proem by Martin Carter', *Poem as Friend Podcast Series,* https://www.thepoetryexchange.co.uk/proem-by-martin-carter. (May 2018).
McDonald, Ian, 'Tribute to Martin Carter', delivered at Moray House Trust Launch December 2011, https://www.youtube.com/watch?v=9LyRhUU6ud0.
Melville, Pauline, 'Guyanese Literature, Magic Realism and the South American Connection', *Wasafiri*, 28:3, 2013; 7-11. DOI: 10.1080/02690055.2013.802424
Morley, Jonathan, Review of *University of Hunger*, *Wasafiri* 23:1 (2008), pp. 74-76.
Osundare, Niyi, 'A Most Enduring Legacy', *Glendora Books Supplement*, Issue 6 2001 review of *All Are Involved.* http://digital.lib.msu.edu/projects/africanjournals/ and *Présence Africaine*, no. 161/162 (2000): 375-79.
Persaud, Petamber, https://guyanatimesgy.com/2020-it-is-a-good-time-to-reach-for-martin-carter/
Robinson, Gemma, 'Martin Wylde Carter', in *Censorship: A World Encyclopedia*, 4 vols, vol. 1, ed. by Derek Jones (London: Fitzroy Dearborn, 2001; Abingdon: Routledge, 2015), pp. 425-426.
Robinson, Gemma, '"If freedom writes no happier alphabet": Martin Carter and Poetic Silence', *Small Axe* 8(1):43-62, March 2004, pp. 43-62.
Robinson, Gemma, 'The Manuscripts of Martin Carter', (excerpt from a lecture delivered in Georgetown in 2004), *Stabroek News*, 3 December, 2004.

Robinson, Gemma, 'Redemptive Strategies in Wilson Harris's *Jonestown* and Martin Carter's *Poems of Affinity*', in *Bridges Across Chasms: Towards a Transcultural Future in Caribbean Literature*, ed. by Bénédicte Ledent (Amsterdam: Rodopi, 2004), pp. 55-63.

Robinson, Gemma, 'Vocabularies of Protest and Resistance: The Early Work of Wilson Harris and Martin Carter', *Journal of Caribbean Literatures*, Spring 2005, (1, 2 and 3): 37-46.

Robinson, Gemma, 'Chronology of Martin Carter', in *Martin Carter, The University of Hunger: Collected Poems and Selected Prose* (Tarset: Bloodaxe, 2006), pp. 11–13.

Robinson, Gemma, 'An Interview with Martin Carter', (recorded in Georgetown in 1995) and published in *Stabroek News*, 13 December, 2006.

Robinson, Gemma, 'Guyanese writers on the radio', *Arts Journal*, 2: 2, March 2006, pp. 41-62.

Robinson, Gemma, 'Introduction', in *Martin Carter, The University of Hunger: Collected Poems and Selected Prose* (Tarset: Bloodaxe, 2006), pp. 15–51.

Robinson, Gemma, '"From the plantation earth": Subjects of Slavery and the Work of Martin Carter', *Moving Worlds*, 7.2, 2007, pp. 17-30.

Robinson, Gemma, 'Writing and Remembrance' (essay on the relationship between Carter and editor David de Caires), *Stabroek News*, 21 December, 2008.

Robinson, Gemma, 'Poems of Mortality' (essay on Carter's never-completed late collection of poems), *Stabroek News*, 13 December, 2009.

Robinson, Gemma, 'Dream to Change the World' (essay on the global reach of Carter's work and its influence on writers and musicians), *Stabroek News*, 13 December 2011.

Robinson, Gemma, 'Martin Carter and the art of beginning', *Stabroek News*, 13 December 2019, https://www.stabroeknews.com/2019/12/13/features/martin-carter-and-the-art-of-beginning/.

Robinson, Gemma, 'Textual communities in Guyana: A "nearly go so" literary history', *The Journal of Commonwealth Literature*, 48(1), 2013, pp. 77–96. https://doi.org/10.1177/0021989412471137

Rohlehr, Gordon, 'Where is Here? What Jail is This? Who Are We? Part 1', *Tout Moun* 2.1 (2013), pp. 1-18, https://journals.sta.uwi.edu/toutmoun/papers/oct13/Tout_Moun_2_ROHLEHR_Where_Pt1.pdf.

Roopnaraine, Rupert, 'Every poem is incomplete', *Caribbean Review of Books*, November 2008.

Rupert Roopnaraine, 'This is a Good Time to Reach for Martin', *The Sky's Wild Noise: Selected Essays* (Leeds: Peepal Tree Press, 2012), pp 135-138.

Rupert Roopnaraine, 'Martin Carter and Politics', *The Sky's Wild Noise: Selected Essays* (Leeds: Peepal Tree Press, 2012), pp 139-148.

Clem Seecharan, 'The Shape of the Passion: the Historical Context of Martin Carter's Poetry of Protest 1951-1964', *Finding Myself: Essays on Race, Politics and Culture* (Leeds: Peepal Tree Press, 2015), pp 163-188.

Stone, Andrew, 'Inspiring poetry' (review of *University of Hunger*), *Socialist Review*, June 2006.

Trevis, Peter, 'Interview with Martin Carter (extract)'. In E. A. Markham (ed.). *Hinterland: Caribbean Poetry from the West Indies and Britain* (Newcastle-upon-Tyne: Bloodaxe, 1989), pp. 66–71.

Victor Jara Collective, *The Terror and the Time: Notes on Repressive Violence in Guyana* (Georgetown: Victor Jara Collective, 1979).

Winks, Christopher, *Symbolic Cities in Caribbean Literature* (New York: Palgrave, 2009, includes a discussion of 'The Great Dark').

Creative Responses

Capildeo, Vahni, *Active Silence* (a series of 'slow readings', including Carter's 'I Am No Soldier', 'Till I Collect' and 'Suite of Five Poems: No. 4', https://www.york.ac.uk/english/writing-at-york/active-silence/

Capildeo, Vahni, 'Astronomer of Freedom: Syntax Poems', in *Skin Can Hold* (Manchester: Carcanet, 2018).

Campbell, Christian, *The Martin Carter 70 Project* (2014-15) (Campbell reads seventy poems in seventy days, beginning 13 December 2014) https://soundcloud.com/christiancampbell-1/sets/the-martin-carter-70-project?fbclid=IwAR3e_d_OZBrnkyaLtNt2Z1yTSVhJ07zsHvqMUqAsYM43uZCKp_pinFNhPeE

Greaves, Stanley, *Horizons* (Leeds: Peepal Tree Press, 2002). Includes several poems of comradeship with Martin Carter.

Greaves, Stanley, *The Poems Man* (Leeds: Peepal Tree Press, 2009). Poems of close friendship, written over thirty years as an act of homage and dialogue with Martin Carter.

Kendall, Hannah, *The Great Dark* (2013), large music ensemble (7 mins), premiere at Queen Elizabeth Hall, London, UK, 10 June 2013.

Kendall, Hannah, 'Not Hands Like Mine' (2015), vocal work (5 mins 30). https://hannahkendall.co.uk/works. Premiere Juice Vocal Trio, Dora Stoutzker Hall, Cardiff, UK, 27 November 2015.

Kendall, Hannah, 'The Knife of Dawn' (2016), vocal work (15 mins). https://hannahkendall.co.uk/works.

Kendall, Hannah, *The Knife of Dawn* (2016), one-man chamber opera (60 mins), libretto by Tessa McWatt, premiere at the Roundhouse, London, UK, Thursday 6 October 2016. World premiere, *Hear and Now*, BBC Radio 3, Saturday 22 October 2016. https://hannahkendall.co.uk/the-knife-of-dawn

Kendall, Hannah, 'Verdala' (2018), large ensemble (5 mins). Commissioned by London Sinfonietta and 14-18 NOW in commemoration of World War 1. Inspired in part by 'O Human Guide'. Premiere at Roundhouse, London, UK as part of the BBC Proms, 21 July 2018.

Moray House Trust, 'Recital of Martin Carter Poems', by 'his friends, young Guyanese writers and students', December 2011, https://www.youtube.com/watch?v=jPBzE3gVuRY.

Moray House Trust, 'A tribute to Martin Carter in words and music', *Moray House Trust: "Culture Matters"*, 26 January 2017, https://www.morayhousetrust.com/events/a-tribute-to-martin-carter-in-words-and-music/.

Nichols, Grace, 'A Sacrament of Words (for Guyanese poet, Martin Carter)', *Passport to Here and There* (Hexam: Bloodaxe Books, 2020), p. 71.

Victor Jara Collective, *The Terror and the Time*, film (Guyana,1977; 70 mins) dir. Rupert Roopnaraine (includes Carter reading 'Cartman of Dayclean' and 'I Come from the Nigger Yard'), https://www.youtube.com/watch?v=dMMN2T3NaXw;https://www.youtube.com/watch?v=F9T-FgZTLtE (subtitled 2020).

NOTES ON CONTRIBUTORS

John Agard: Guyanese poet and performer, settled in the UK where he has had great success in recent years, including a period as Writer in Residence at the BBC. His collection *From the Devil's Pulpit* (Newcastle, Bloodaxe 1998) won the 1998 Guyana Prize for literature. Since the first edition of this book he has published a further six well-received collections of poetry and was awarded the Queen's medal for poetry in 2012.

Samuel O. Asein: Nigerian critic with a long standing interest in Caribbean literature. Professor in the English Department of the University of Ife, he has published many books and essays on aspects of modern African and Caribbean writing.

Edward Baugh: Jamaican poet and scholar, Emeritus Professor of English and retired Public Orator at the University of the West Indies, Jamaica. In 1998, The University of the West Indies Press published *Chancellor, I Present*, a collection of his addresses made as Public Orator at Honorary Degree ceremonies. He has published three collections of poems, *A Tale from the Rainforest* and *It was the Singing* (Sandberry Press, 1988 and 2000) and *Black Sand: New and Selected Poems* (Peepal Tree, 2013) and several works of criticism including *Derek Walcott: Memory as Vision: Another Life* (Longman, 1978) and *Frank Collymore: A Biography* (2009).

Frank Birbalsingh: Guyanese critic, based in Canada. Emeritus Professor at York University, Toronto. He has published several books on aspects of Caribbean literature, including *Passion and Exile: essays in Caribbean Literature*, (Hansib, London, 1988), *Frontiers of Caribbean Literature in English*, (New York, St. Martin's Press, 1996), *From Pillar to Post* (1998), *Guyana: History and Literature* (2016) and *West Indian History and Literature* (2017).

Kamau Brathwaite (1930-2020): one of the great poets of the Caribbean, also an important historian, cultural critic, editor and teacher. At the time of first publication of this book he was a professor at New York University but spending much time in Barbados. His then most recent and monumental work was *Barabajan Poems* (Savacou, 1994) and a selection of his essays on Caribbean literature, *Roots,* was published by the University of Michigan Press in 1993. Since the first publication of this book, he published a further dozen collections of poetry. In 2015 he was awarded the Robert Frost Medal. His death in 2020 brought forth an outpouring of grief and respect.

Stewart Brown: poet and critic, editor of several anthologies of Caribbean writing, including – with John Wickham – *The Oxford Book of Caribbean Short Stories*. He taught at the Centre of West African Studies at the University of Birmingham. Peepal Tree published his new and selected poems, *Elsewhere*, in 1999; and since the first edition of this book, he has published *Tourist,*

Traveller, Troublemaker: Essays on Poetry (2007) and edited *The Bowling was Superfine: West Indian Writing and West Indian Cricket* (2012), both with Peepal Tree. Since his retirement he has devoted himself to painting.

Jan Carew (1920-2012): Guyanese novelist, playwright, historian and poet. He was Emeritus Professor of African American studies at Northwestern University, where he taught for many years. He wrote many books in several fields, most recently *Rape of Paradise* (1994) and *Ghosts in Our Blood: with Malcolm X in Africa, England and the Caribbean* (1994). In 2015, Peepal Tree published *Episodes in my Life: The Autobiography of Jan Carew* and reissued *Black Midas* and *The Wild Coast* in the Caribbean Modern Classics series.

Bill Carr (d. 1992): British scholar and critic who taught for many years in the Caribbean, initially at the University of the West Indies in Jamaica and later as Head of English at the University of Guyana. He published many essays on aspects of Caribbean literature.

Merle Collins: Grenadian novelist, poet and scholar currently based in the USA. She co-edited the anthology of black British women's writing *Watchers & Seekers*. Her collections of poetry includes *Rotten Pomerack* (Virago, 1992) and *Lady in a Boat* (Peepal Tree, 2003). Her fiction includes *The Colour of Forgetting* (Virago, 1995), *Angel* (1987 and in a revised edition, Peepal Tree, 2011) and *The Ladies are Upstairs* (Peepal Tree, 2011)

al creighton: Jamaican poet, scholar and journalist, with a particular interest in Caribbean theatre. He has taught at the University of Guyana for many years and published many essays and articles on aspects of Caribbean literature in academic and popular journals. A selection of his poetry was included in the anthology *Caribbean New Voices* (Longman, 1997).

David Dabydeen: Guyanese scholar, poet and novelist. He is emeritus Professor of Literature at the University of Warwick, UK, where he was Director of the Centre for Caribbean Studies. He has published widely on Caribbean literature and cultural history and written six novels and three collections of poetry, including *Slave Song* (1984, Peepal Tree 2005); *Turner: New and Selected Poems* (Cape, 1994, Peepal Tree, 2002). Peepal Tree has reissued his earlier fiction, *The Intended*, *The Counting House* and *Disappearance*, and two new novels, *Our Lady of Demerara* (2008) and *Johnson's Dictionary* (2013)

Fred D'Aguiar: Guyanese poet, novelist and dramatist who moved to Britain in his teens, where he established a reputation as one of the most exciting writers of his generation. He is the author of six novels: *The Longest Memory*, *Dear Future*, *Feeding the Ghosts*, *Bloodlines*, *Bethany Bettany* and *Children of Paradise* and seven collections of poetry: *Mama Dot, Airy Hall, British Subjects,Bill of Rights*, *An English Sampler*, *Continental Shelf* and *The Rose of Toulouse*. He teaches at UCLA.

Kwame Dawes: Ghanaian-born, Jamaican-bred poet, musician, playwright and essayist, who teaches literature at the University of South Nebraska and edits the journal *Prairie Schooner*. He has published seventeen collections of poetry, most with Peepal Tree. Most recently he embarked on a poetic dialogue with the Australian poet, John Kinsella, which includes, to date, *Speak from Here to There*, *A New Beginning*, *Tangling with the Epic* and *In the Name of Our Families*. His major scholarly work is *Natural Mysticism* (Peepal Tree Press, 1999) a study of the reggae aesthetic. He is the author of three works of fiction. In 2019 he was awarded the Windham-Campbell Literature prize in poetry.

Neville Dawes (1926-1984): the Jamaica poet, novelist and literary scholar, (father of Kwame) who died tragically young in 1984. Author of *In Sepia*, a collection of poems, in 1958 and two novels, *The Last Enchantment* (1960) and *Interim* (1978). He taught for some years at the University of Ghana and was Director of the Institute of Jamaica in the 1970s. In 2012, Peepal Tree brought out a compendium of his short fiction, poetry, autobiographical and critical writing: *Fugue and Other Writings*.

David de Caires (1937-2008): a distinguished Guyanese journalist, founder and editor of the most independent of the Guyanese newspapers, *The Stabroek News*.

John Figueroa (1920-1999): One of the Caribbean's most outspoken men of letters until his death in 1999, the Jamaican poet, critic, educationalist, broadcaster and scholar, John Figueroa edited important anthologies of Caribbean literature, including *Caribbean Voices* (1971) and several collections of his own poems, including *The Chase: a collection of poems 1941-1989* (Peepal Tree Press, 1991). He taught at the University of the West Indies, the University of Jos in Nigeria and for the Open University in Britain. He was well known as a writer and commentator on cricket.

Michael Gilkes (1933-2020): Guyanese playwright, critic and poet, who taught for many years at the University of the West Indies in Barbados and then at the University of Guyana. He lived in St. Lucia for several years. He made films, directed theatre and published literary criticism and poetry. His play on Edgar Mittelholtzer won the Guyana Prize in 1996 and his book on Wilson Harris, *The Literate Imagination* (Warwick, Macmillan, 1989) was very highly regarded. Peepal Tree published his collection of poems *Joanstown and Other Poems* (2002) and reissued two plays, *Couvade and A Pleasant Career* in the classics series.

Stanley Greaves is a Guyanese painter and poet, who spent most of his working life in Guyana, settling in Barbados in the late 1980s, until recently leaving for the USA. His painting has attracted increasing critical attention following major contributions to the Biennale of Latin American and Caribbean Art in the Dominican Republic in 1992 and 1993. In 1999 his work was shown in the UK with that of Brother Everard Brown of Jamaica, in an exhibition titled *The Elders*. As a poet, three collections of Greaves's work has been published by Peepal Tree Press: *Horizons*, *The Poems Man* and *Haiku*. In 2005, Peepal Tree published a major study of Greaves's art by Rupert Roopnaraine: *The Primacy of the Eye: The Art of Stanley Greaves*.

Wilson Harris (1921-2018): Guyanese novelist, poet and essayist, long time resident of the UK until his death in 2018. One of the major figures in late twentieth century literature in English. He published more than a twenty-four novels, a collection of poems and several critical works. His last novel was *The Ghost of Memory*, (2006). Peepal Tree has reissued four of his novels in the Caribbean Classics series: *Heartland*, *The Eye of the Scarecrow*, *The Sleepers of Roraima & the Age of the Rainmakers* and *Ascent to Omai*. In 2014, Wilson Harris was knighted in the Queen's Birthday Honours.

Roy Heath (1926-2008): Guyanese author, who lived in the UK for many years. He published ten novels, including *The Murderer*, (Alison & Busby, 1989) which won the Guardian Fiction Prize, and most recently *The Ministry of Hope*, (London, Marion Boyers, 1997). He also published a much praised volume of autobiography, *Shadows Round the Moon* (1990).

Kendel Hippolyte: Saint Lucian poet and dramatist, very much committed to the cultural life of Saint Lucia. He worked for some time at the Folk Research Centre in Castries and taught at the Sir Arthur Lewis College. His poetry is included in most of the major regional anthologies and he has published four collections, most recently *Birthright*, Peepal Tree Press, 1997. Since the publication of this book, Kendel Hippolyte has published three further collections of poetry, *Night Vision*, *Fault Lines* and *Wordplanting*, all Peepal Tree Press. He has retired from teaching and plans a major project to recuperate the scattered publication of Caribbean drama.

Eric Huntley: Guyanese political and cultural activist and publisher. After being involved in the political turmoil in British Guiana in the early fifties, when he was interned as a subversive alongside Martin Carter, Eric Huntley settled in London. With his wife Jessica, who died in 2013, he was involved in running the publishing house Bogle L'Ouverture, which published the work of many distinguished Caribbean writers, and running the Walter Rodney Bookshop.

Janet Jagan (1920-2009): Elected President of Guyana in the elections which followed the death of her husband Cheddi Jagan in 1997. Born in America, Janet Jagan was involved in the political and cultural history of Guyana since the 1940s. She was a great supporter of the arts over the years and has published several volumes of fiction for children, including

When Grandpa Cheddi was a Boy, *Patricia the Baby Manatee* and *Anastasia the Anteater*, all published by Peepal Tree Press.

Louis James: British scholar with a long-standing commitment to Caribbean literature. After teaching for some years at the University of the West Indies in Jamaica, Louis James became Professor of Literature at the University of Kent at Canterbury. He was a member of the Caribbean Artists Movement in Britain in the 1960s. He edited *The Islands In Between*, a collection of critical essays on West Indian writing, in 1968, and recently published a study, *Caribbean Literature in English* (Longman, 1999). He is Emeritus Professor at the University of Kent.

Linton Kwesi Johnson: Jamaican born poet who came to Britain in his teens and became a major literary and cultural figure internationally. He has published several collections of poetry and many records and CDs of his work. His most substantial collection of poems as text is *Tings an Times*, (Bloodaxe, 1991) and his recent work on disc includes *LKJ a capella live*, (LKJ Records, 1995) which is an unaccompanied reading of a selection of his best known poems, and *More Time* (LKJ Records, 1998) which includes his setting of Martin Carter's 'Poems of Shape and Motion'. In 2002, *Mi Revalueshanary Fren': Selected Poems* was published as a Penguin Modern Classic.

Sydney King: See Eusi Kwayana, below.

Karen King-Aribisala: Guyanese writer and scholar, who has lived for many years in Nigeria, where she teaches at the University of Lagos. She has published critical essays, and three works of fiction: *Our Wife and Other Stories, Kicking Tongues* and *The Hangman's Game* (Peepal Tree, 2007).

Roi Kwabena (1956-2008): Trinidadian poet, historian and cultural activist, who for some time was a Senator in the Trinidad and Tobago parliament. He lived and travelled in Africa and performed his poetry internationally. He settled in Britain where he was Literature Officer for Coventry Libraries until his death in 2008. He published eleven collections of poetry, the last being, *In the Moment* (2006).

Eusi Kwayana: Guyanese political and cultural activist, as Sydney King he was interned alongside Martin Carter during the political upheavals of the early 1950s. He wrote the Foreword to the first edition of *Poems of Resistance.* For many years he has been one of the leaders of the Working People's Alliance, a tireless fighter against injustice, an essayist and newspaper columnist. Eusi Kwayana is respected in all quarters in Guyana as a political incorruptible. He currently lives in San Diego, California.

Barbara Lalla: Jamaican scholar who was Head of the Department of English at the University of the West Indies in Trinidad until her retirement as Professor Emeritus. Her study, *Defining Jamaican Fiction*, was published by the University of Alabama Press, in 1996. She has published three novels, *Arch of Fire*, *Cascade*, *Uncle Brother* and *Grounds for Tenure*.

George Lamming: Barbadian novelist and essayist. One of the great Caribbean writers, his novels of the 1950s and 60s chronicled the experience and concerns of a whole generation. His collection of essays, *The Pleasures of Exile* (1960) was perhaps the first expression of many of the issues that were to be formalised as 'post-colonial theory' many years later. His first novel, *In the Castle of My Skin* (1953) is probably still his best known, but his other novels are enjoying something of a critical revival. Peepal Tree republished his *Of Age and Innocence* and *Water with Berries* in the Caribbean Modern Classics series.

John La Rose (1927-2006): Trinidadian poet, publisher and cultural activist. Based in London since the 1950s, he founded New Beacon Books, which published the work of many West Indian writers, including Martin Carter's *Poems of Succession*. (1977). His own poetry was published in two collections, *Foundations* (1966) and *Eyelets of Truth within Me* (New Beacon Books, 1992).

Syl Lowhar (d. 2000): Trinidadian poet, journalist and political activist. He was one of those detained during the 1970 Black Power uprising. He was for many years associated with the New World group and later the Tapia group and he wrote regularly for the *Trinidad and Tobago Review*.

Ian McDonald: grew up in Trinidad but has lived in Guyana for almost sixty years. A poet, novelist, essayist and editor in his literary life, he was also a senior executive in the Guyana Sugar Corporation. His novel *The Hummingbird Tree*, (1969) was made into a BBC TV film. He edited the leading Guyanese literary journal, *Kyk-over-Al*, for more than a decade. His poetry is widely anthologised and he has published seven collections over the years, including *Essequibo* (Peterloo, 1992), and Between Silence and Silence (Peepal Tree, 2004) both of which won the Guyana Prize. His early work is collected in *Jaffo the Calypsonian* (Peepal Tree Press, 1994) and in 2018, Peepal Tree published the very substantial *New and Collected Poems*. In 1998 he was awarded an honorary Doctorate by the University of the West Indies for his contribution to West Indian literature.

Mark A. McWatt: Guyanese poet and scholar, Reader in West Indian Literature at the University of the West Indies, Cave Hill, Barbados. Mark McWatt has published three collections of poetry, *Interiors* (1989), *The Language of Eldorado* (Dangaroo, 1994 and Peepal Tree 2017) which won the Guyana Prize, and *The Journey to Le Repentir* (Peepal Tree, 2009). His collection of short stories: *Suspended Sentences: Fictions of Atonement* (2005) wonthe Commonwealth Writer's Prize for best first book. He has published many essays and articles on aspects of West Indian literature in academic and literary journals. He co-edited the anthology for Caribbean schools *A World of Poetry*, (Heinemann/CXC, 1995), and *The Caribbean Short Story: Critical Perspectives* (Peepal Tree, 2011).

Malik (Delano Abdul Malik De Coteau): Grenadian poet and cultural activist, associated with the black power struggles in Trinidad in the late 1960s. He was later a leading figure in development of a voice/ performance poetry movement in Trinidad. He currently lives and works in London. His most readily available collection is *Whirlwind*, (London, Panrun Collective, 1988).

E.A. Markham (1939-2008): Monserratian poet, critic, editor and novelist. He published many collections of poems, including *Human Rights: Selected Poems 1970-1982* (Anvil, 1984) and *Towards the End of the Century* (Anvil, 1989). His novel *Marking Time* was published by Peepal Tree in 1999. He was also a prolific and inventive writer of short stories, many collected in *Taking the Drawing Room Through the Customs* (Peepal Tree, 2002). He edited the *Penguin Book of Caribbean Short Stories* (1992) and the poetry anthology *Hinterland* (Bloodaxe, 1989). He was Professor of Creative Writing at Sheffield Hallam University. The publication of his memoir, *Against the Grain: A 1950s Memoir*, very sadly coincided with his sudden and much lamented death in Paris in 2008.

Marc Matthews: Guyanese poet and actor, long based in London. His first collection of poems, *Guyana, My Altar* won the 1987 Guyana Prize for poetry and a second collection, *A Season of Sometimes*, was published by Peepal Tree Press in 1992.

Pauline Melville: Guyanese author and actress, who lives in London. She has published two collections of stories, *Shapeshifter* (1990) and *The Migration of Ghosts* (Bloomsbury, 1998) and a highly acclaimed novel, *The Ventriloquist's Tale* (Bloomsbury, 1997) which won the Whitbread Prize for first novel and the 1998 Guyana Prize for Literature. Her most recent publication is a novel, *Eating Air* (2009).

Michael Mitchell : British scholar with a long interest in Caribbean writing. He currently teaches in Germany. He is the author of *Hidden Mutualities: Faustian Themes from Gnostic Origins to the Postcolonial* (2006).

Mervyn Morris: Jamaican poet, critic and editor, Emeritus Professor of West Indian Literature at the University of the West Indies, Jamaica. Editor of several important anthologies of Caribbean writing, including *Voiceprint* (Longman, 1989) and *The Faber Book of Caribbean Short Stories* (1990). He has published several collections of his own poems, including *Examination Centre* (New Beacon Books, 1995) and two collections of his literary essays *Is English We Speaking*, (1999) and *Making West Indian Literature* (2005).

His most recent publications are *Miss Lou: Louise Bennett and Jamaican Culture* (2014) and *Peelin Orange: Collected Poems* (2017). In 2014 he was appointed poet laureate in Jamaica.

Grace Nichols: Guyanese poet and novelist, working in Britain for many years where her work has won great acclaim. Her first book of poems *i is a long memoried woman* (Karnak House, 1983) won the Commonwealth Literature Prize. Other collections include, *Sunris* (1996), *I Have Crossed an Ocean* (2010), *Insomnia Poems* (2017) and *Passport to Here and There* (2020). Her novel, based on her remembered childhood in Guyana, *Whole of A Morning Sky* (Virago 1986) took its title from one of Martin Carter's poems.

Sasenarine Persaud: Guyanese poet, novelist and essayist, who lived in Canada for many years before recently relocating to Florida. He has published two novels, *Dear Death* and *The Ghost of Bellow's Man*, both published by Peepal Tree, and several collections of poems, including, *A Surf of Sparrows* (Toronto, Tsar, 1996). The title story of his recent collection of stories, *Canada Geese and Apple Chatney*, (Tsar, 1999) is included in *The Oxford Book of Caribbean Short Stories.* More recently he published the poetry collection, *Monsoon on the Fingers of God* (2018).

Alan Persico: Guyanese scholar and writer on Guyanese literature and on education, including *Toward the Improvement of School Management and Administration in Guyana*.

Vanda Radzik: founder member of the Red Thread Women's collective and longtime political and cultural activist. She was one of the editors of the revived *Kyk-over-Al* and remains a beacon of hope for a better Guyana.

Kenneth Ramchand: Trinidadian scholar and editor, author of – among many other publications – the first substantial study of the region's fiction, *The West Indian Novel and its Background* (Faber 1970, revised for the Heinemann edition in 1983.) He is Emeritus Professor of West Indian Literature at the University of the West Indies in Trinidad and is working on a collection of his essays, shortly to be published by Peepal Tree.

Gemma Robinson: British scholar whose work has focused on the writers of Guyana, she wrote a Doctoral thesis on the work of Martin Carter at Cambridge University and edited the now standard edition of his work, *University of Hunger: Collected Poems & Selected Prose* (2006). She teaches at the University of Sterling.

Jeffrey Robinson: Guyanese critic, based in Canada for many years, author of many essays on aspects of Caribbean writing.

Gordon Rohlehr: Guyanese scholar, Emeritus Professor of West Indian Literature at the University of the West Indies in Trinidad. A prolific critic whose many publications include a study of Kamau Brathwaite's *Arrivants*,

(1981), two volumes of essays on aspects of Caribbean writing, the poetry anthology *Voiceprint* and the major study of calypso *Calypso & Society in Pre-Independence Trinidad* (1990). Recently Gordon Rohlehr has published *Perfected Fables Now: A Bookman Signs Off on Seven Decades* (2019), and *Musings, Mazes, Muses, Margins* (2020), both Peepal Tree Press, which has also reissued his essay collections, *My Strangled City and Other Essays* and *The Shape of That Hurt*.

Rupert Roopnaraine: Guyanese poet, scholar, film maker and political activist, presently leader of the Working People's Alliance party in Guyana. As author he has written on aspects of Guyanese art and literature. His book *Web of October: Re-reading Martin Carter* (Peepal Tree Press, 1988) is a fascinating response to Carter's work, incorporating both poetry and critical analysis. His film *The Terror and the Time* explores the political context of Martin Carter's work. Since the publication of this volume, Rupert Roopnaraine has published a monograph, *The Primacy of the Eye: The Art of Stanley Greaves* (Peepal Tree 2005) and his *The Sky's Wild Noise: Selected Essays* (Peepal Tree, 2012) won the 2013 OCM Bocas non-fiction prize.

Andrew Salkey (1928-1995): Jamaican novelist, poet, anthologist and critic, one of that generation of West Indian writers who came to Britain in the 1950s to find publishers and an audience. He published many books across the whole range of Caribbean letters, including his *Georgetown Journal* (New Beacon, 1972) and most recently, the posthumous collection of his previously uncollected stories, *In the Border Country* (Bogle L'Ouverture, 1998).

Clem Seecharan: Guyanese historian and scholar, who taught on the Caribbean Studies programme at the University of North London and is now Professor Emeritus of that institution. He has published many books and essays on aspects of West Indian literature, including *India and the Shaping of the Indo-Guyanese Imagination*, Peepal Tree, 1993. Since the publication of this volume, Clem Seecharan has continued to publish widely on history and West Indian cricket. His most recent books include *Mother India's Shadow over El Dorado: Indo-Guyanese Politics and Identity 1890s-1930s* (2011) and *Finding Myself: Essays in Race, Politics and Culture* (Peepal Tree, 2015).

A.J. Seymour (1914-1989): Guyanese poet, editor and critic, one of the great men of Caribbean letters. Founder and editor of the literary journal *Kyk-over-al* and publisher of the Miniature Poets Series in the 1950s which included Carter's first collection *The Hill of Fire Glows Red*, in 1951. A prolific poet in his own right, his work is included in most of the region's anthologies, but his collections of poems – most of which were self published – were much harder to find until the publication of *Collected Poems 1937-1989*, edited by Ian McDonald, and published in 2000.

Janice Lo Shinebourne: Guyanese novelist, long based in London. She has published four novels, *Timepiece* (Peepal Tree, 1986) which won the Guyana Prize for first work of fiction in 1986, *The Last English Plantation* (Peepal Tree, 1988) *Chinese Women* (Peepal Tree, 2010) and *The Last Ship* (Peepal Tree, 2015). Her collection of short stories, *The Godmother and Other Stories* was published in 2004.

Stephanos Stephanides: Cypriot scholar who worked for some years at the University of Guyana. Currently teaching at the University of Cyprus in Nicosia. He published *Translating Kali's Feast: The Goddess in Indo-Caribbean Ritual and Action* (2000).

Ivan Van Sertima (1935-2009): Guyanese poet, anthropologist and scholar, based in the USA. He was the author of *They Came Before Columbus: The African Presence in Ancient America*, *African Presence in Early Asia* and *Egypt Revisited*. He is editor of the *Journal of African Civilisation*.

Derek Walcott (1930-2017): Saint Lucian poet, dramatist and essayist. He received many literary honours including the Queens Gold Medal for Poetry and, in 1992, the Nobel Prize for literature. His most recent publications include *The Bounty*, (Faber, 1997) and a collection of his essays *What the Twilight Says* (Faber, 1998). Since the first publication of this book, he published, T*iepolo's Hound* (2000), *The Prodigal* (2004), *White Egrets* (2010) and *Morning, Paramin* (2016, with Peter Doig).

Anne Walmsley: British scholar long associated with the Caribbean. As several contributors to this volume remark, her school anthology *The Suns's Eye* (Longman, 1968, revised 2nd edition 1989) changed the way whole generations of West Indian children related to the region's literature. Her study of *The Caribbean Artists Movement 1966-72* (New Beacon, 1992) is regarded as a model of the writing of cultural history. More recently she has worked on Caribbean visual arts, compiling *Guyana Dreaming: the Art of Aubrey Williams* (Dangaroo Press, 1990) and writing the Introduction to the catalogue of *The Elders* exhibition on the work of Stanley Greaves and Brother Everard Brown which toured in the UK. (South London Gallery, 1999). In 2010, she published, with Stanley Greaves, *Art in the Caribbean: An Introduction*. In 2009 she was awarded an honorary doctorate by UWI (Mona) and in 2018 she was presented with the Henry Swanzy Award for services to Caribbean letters by the NGC Bocas Litfest.

Nigel Westmaas: Guyanese scholar, member of the Working People's Alliance. He has done pioneering work on collecting Martin Carter's much dispersed prose articles and essays, a selection of which appeared in *Kyk-over-Al*, 44.

Denis Williams (1923-1998): Guyanese painter, novelist and scholar, author of two novels, major works of art history and much scholarly work on aspects of Guyanese Amerindian culture. He made his reputation as a painter in Britain in the early 1950s but after periods working in Africa returned to Guyana where he was director of the Walter Roth Museum of Anthropology in Georgetown for many years, until his death in 1998. Peepal Tree reissued his two novels, *Other Leopards* and *The Third Temptation* in the Caribbean Modern Classics series, and in 2012 Peepal Tree published *The Art of Denis Williams* by Evelyn A. Williams.

Milton Williams: Guyanese poet, part of the group which included Martin Carter and Wilson Harris, who has lived in Britain for many years, an experience reflected in his major collection of poems, *Years of Fighting Exile* (Peepal Tree Press, 1986).

INDEX

(Bold face denotes either the subject's essay contribution, or a significant discussion of a Martin Carter poem)